Globalization Effects on China's Influence on Taiwan Economy

Schriften zur Politischen Ökonomik
Evolutorische und ökologische Aspekte

Herausgegeben von
Udo Müller, Oliver Budzinski, Yücel Calbay, Jörg Jasper
und Torsten Sundmacher

Band 6

PETER LANG
Frankfurt am Main · Berlin · Bern · Bruxelles · New York · Oxford · Wien

Shin-Yuan Tsai

Globalization Effects on China's Influence on Taiwan Economy

PETER LANG
Europäischer Verlag der Wissenschaften

Bibliographic Information published by the Deutsche Nationalbibliothek
The Deutsche Nationalbibliothek lists this publication in the Deutsche Nationalbibliografie; detailed bibliographic data is available in the internet at <http://www.d-nb.de>.

Zugl.: Hannover, Univ., Diss., 2006

D 89
ISSN 1439-7528
ISBN-10: 3-631-55737-X
ISBN-13: 978-3-631-55737-2
US-ISBN 0-8204-8728-7

www.peterlang.de

Content

List of Figures 7

List of Tables 9

Acknowledgement 13

Abbreviation 15

1. Introduction 17

 1.1 Structure of Research 21

 1.2 Proposed Solutions 35

2. Globalization Turns China into a Challenge to Taiwan & the US 39

 2.1The Phenomena of Regionalism under Globalization 42

 2.2 The Emerging China 46

 2.3 The Integration of East Asia 54
  2.3.1 China's Influence in the Integration of East Asia 63
  2.3.2 The Economic Interdependence between Taiwan & East Asia 76

 2.4 The Outflow of Economic Resources from Taiwan to China 84
  2.4.1 China Effects On Taiwan's Economic Policy 86
  2.4.2 The Capital Flight 90
  2.4.3 The Mainland Operation of MNCs 96
  2.4.4 Brain Drain Effects of Taiwan 101
  2.4.5 Booming Trade across Taiwan Strait 108

 2.5 The China Policy of the US 112
  2.5.1 The Economic Interdependence between China and the US 116
  2.5.2 The US Domestic Politics and the US China Policy 120

3. Globalization Effects on the Relationships between Government & Corporation 125

 3.1 The Power Struggle between Government and Private Firm 129
  3.1.1 Taiwanese government's Paternalism toward Private Enterprises 130
  3.1.2 Taiwanese Firms & Governmental Restraints 132

 3.2 An Evolution in the Relationship among MNC, Host Country & Home Country 139

3.3 The Constraints on the Development of Taiwan Economy 142
3.3.1 The Barrier to the Implementation of Taiwan's Economic Policy 154
3.3.2 IT Industry of Taiwan in the Global Supply Chain 157
3.3.3 Chinese Cultural Effects on the Development of Taiwanese Enterprises 167
3.3.4 The Shortage of Resources for SMEs on R&D 174

3.4 The Growing Influence of China over Business Sector 188
3.4.1 The Chinese Deployment of MNCs in IT Industry 197
3.4.2 The Imbalance of Economic Clout between China & Taiwan 205

4. Cross-Strait Dilemma: Independence vs. Unification 211

4.1 One-China Principle 213
4.1.1 Historical Complex 214
4.1.2 Domestic Power Struggle 216
4.1.3 Domino Effect 222

4.2 Sino-Taiwan-US Relations: An Entangled Triangle 225

4.3 China vs. Taiwan in the International Arena 232

4.4 Taiwan's Domestic Politics 246
4.4.1 The Investments in Ethnicity 247
4.4.2 Pan-Blue vs. Pan-Green, a Bipolarizing Taiwan 254

4.5 War vs. Peace 263
4.5.1 The Failure of the US Cross-Strait Policy 265
4.5.2 Taiwan's Challenge to One-China Principle 271
4.5.3 The Deployment of the Game 276

5. Conclusion 279

Bibliography 285

List of Figures

2-1	Notification to GATT and WTO of Regional Integration Agreements	45
2-2	Intraregional Trade Share[a] of Selected Regions, 1962-94	54
2-3	Intraregional Trade Ratio[b] of Selected Regions, 1980-2003 (annual averages)	55
2-4	The Sources of Emerging East Asia's FDI Inflows, 1990-2002	62
2-5	The Vicious Circle of Taiwan's China Policy	100
3-1	The Amount of Taiwan's Outward Investment by Year	148
3-2	Taiwan's Exports in Selected Industries	149
3-3	The Approved Outward Investment of Traditional Industry	150
3-4	Outward Investments of Electronic & Electric Appliances Industry	151
3-5	The Position of Taiwan's PC Industry in Stan Shih's Smiling Curve	162
3-6	Mobile Phone Subscribers per 100 Inhabitants by Selected Nations (Data of 2002)	190
3-7	World Wide IC Market by Region (1999-2009)	194
3-8	New International (ISO and IEC), European, and National (German, I.E., DIN) Standards per Year (1986-99)	196
4-1	The Consequence of Taiwan's Choice on the Unification Issue	231
4-2	Unification vs. Independence Spectrum of Taiwan's Political Parties	255
4-3	The Political Positions of Major Actors on the Unification Issue	262

List of Tables

2-1 GNP per Capita of Selective Economies 47
2-2 The Largest Recipients of Inward FDI, 1975-80, 1990-96 and 1998-2003 (annual averages) 48
2-3 Top 20 Economies Ranked by Foreign Trade 49
2-4 Top 20 Economies Ranked by Total GDP, PPP GDP in 2003 50
2-5 Foreign Exchange Reserves of Selective Countries, Year End (Cumulative) 51
2-6 Economic Growth Rates of Selective Economies 52
2-7 The Intraregional Trade Shares and the Simple Intraregional Trade Concentration Ratio of Selected Region 60
2-8 2003 China's Approved FDI Outflows, by Region 63
2-9 East Asian Nations and Growing Regionalism 67
2-10 Taiwan's FDI to China and ASEAN 70
2-11 ASEAN Trade with China 71
2-12 China's Top 10 Trade Partners in 2004 75
2-13 Top Inward FDI Countries/Areas to China by Region (As of the end of 2004) 76
2-14 Taiwan's Export Value and Percentage to Total Export by Region 78
2-15 Taiwan's Import Volume and Percentage to Total Import by Region 79
2-16 Statistics on Approved Inward Foreign Investment by Region 80
2-17 Statistics on Approved Outward Foreign Investment by Area (China excluded) 81
2-18 Statistics on Approved Outward Foreign Investment by Area (China included) 82
2-19 The Number of Visitors between Taiwan and Mainland China 85
2-20 The Discrepancy between the Approved Amount of Taiwan and the Official Data of China 92
2-21 The Investments in China from Taiwan and Virgin Islands 94
2-22 The Top 10 Regions/Countries of Taiwan's Outbound Investments (As of the end of 2004) 95
2-23 The Motivations behind Outward FDI of Taiwanese Firms 98
2-24 Taiwan Investments in Mainland China 103
2-25 Statistics on Approved Indirect Mainland Investment by Industry 105
2-26 The Number of Business Operation Headquarters Established in Taiwan, as of July 2004 107
2-27 The Numbers of Chinese and Taiwanese Students Enrolled in US Universities 108

2-28 The Statistics of Trade with Chinese Areas* 110
2-29 The Foreign Trade Dependence of Selected Economies 111
2-30 Taiwan's Trade Balance 111
2-31 Top Trading Partners of the US (the Year of 2004) 117
2-32 US Trade with China, by Year 118
2-33 China's Total Imports and Exports by FIEs 119
3-1 Comparative Growth Experience 132
3-2 Top Ten Pure-Play Foundry Companies 134
3-3 Trade between Taiwan and Mainland China Recorded by Different Agencies 137
3-4 The Percentage of Taiwan's Trade with the US and Japan 144
3-5 Taiwan's Import Value of Technology by Nationality 145
3-6 Taiwan's TSE & OTC Listed Companies Investing in China (as of April 30, 2004) 153
3-7 The Statistics of Business Type of Selected Taiwanese IT Hardware 161
3-8 The Component Purchase Right of Taiwanese Notebook OEM Manufacturer 163
3-9 The Source of TFT-LCD Technology 164
3-10 The Deployment of Large-size TFT-LCD Manufacturers in Yangtze River Delta 165
3-11 The Ratio (%) of SMEs on Taiwan 171
3-12 The Workforce, Employees of Different Organizations 172
3-13 Sources of Borrowing by Private Firms: Large Firms vs. SMEs* 175
3-14 The Indicators of Taiwanese Bank Loans to SMEs 176
3-15 R&D Expenditure Accounting for Total Expenditure of High-Tech SMEs 178
3-16 R&D Staff of Total Employees 178
3-17 Technology Balance of Payments 179
3-18 Coverage Ratio of Technology Balance of Payments* 180
3-19 R&D Expenditures as a Percentage of GDP 181
3-20 R&D Expenditures by Sector of Performance, Selected Economies 183
3-21 Number of U.S. Patents (Excluding New Design) Granted and Rank by Nationality 184
3-22 R&D Expenditures of Taiwanese Private Enterprises by R&D Type 185
3-23 Comparison between Private R&D Expenditure and the Amount of Technology Import 186
3-24 The Statistics of China's Mobile Phone User and Fixed Lines, (Cumulative) 189
3-25 Asia/Pacific PC Unit Shipment Estimates by Country, 2002 191
3-26 Asia/Pacific (Exclude Japan) PC Vendor Unit Shipment 192
3-27 ROW IC Market by Country 194

3-28 The Investments of Foreign Investors (IT industry) in China 198
3-29 The Production Locations of Taiwanese IT Hardware Industry 199
3-30 The Production Locations of Taiwanese Monitor Manufacturers 201
3-31 The Production Locations of Taiwanese PC Manufacturers 202
3-32 The Profitability of the Chinese Operations of Taiwanese Firms 203
3-33 The Target Market of the Chinese Operations of Taiwanese Firms 204
3-34 Taiwan Investments in Mainland China before and after China Repudiated Pro-Independence Taiwanese Businessmen 205
4-1 Countries Recognizing the PRC between October 1, 1970 and September 31, 1971 235
4-2 The Result of Vote on China's Bid for UN Entry 1950-1971 237
4-3 Countries Recognizing the People's Republic of China from Oct. 24, 1971 to Nov. 13 1975 (listed chronologically) 239
4-4 The Number of Diplomatic Allies of the ROC 244
4-5 Composition of the KMT Central Committee, 1952-1993 248
4-6 Ethnic Composition of Top Positions (1987) 249
4-7 Policy-level Officials of "Taiwanese" Origins (1983) 249
4-8 Public Attitudes on the Unification issue by Party Preference 256
4-9 Public Perception on the Party Unification-Independence Position 257
4-10 The Self-Perception of Taiwanese People 258
4-11 Public Attitudes on the Unification Issue in Taiwan, by Trend 259
4-12 The Percentage of Votes in Legislative Yuan Election 261

Acknowledgement

First, I would like to express my deep gratitude to Prof. Dr. Udo Mueller. Without his offering me this precious opportunity to explore my potential in the academic program, this dissertation would not have been written. I also thank Prof. Dr. Lothar Huebl whose opinions offered me another angle to tackle the questions in my dissertation. Moreover, it was a pleasant experience to communicate with Prof. Huebl.

My special gratitude goes to PD. Dr. Joerg Jasper. As my advisor, Joerg is most responsible for guiding me through the process of completing the Ph.D. program and challenging my research to perfect my dissertation. Joerg has been a friend and mentor. He taught me not only how to proceed academic research but also how to survive in a foreign country.

I also have to thank the support of my family and friends. My friends collected information in Taiwan for me. I even once sent back a table with unfilled cells for my friend to fill in the data for me.

I thank them all.

Abbreviation

ASEAN:	Association of South East Asian Nations
ACCORD:	ASEAN-China Cooperative Operation in Response to Dangerous Drugs.
ACD:	Asian Cooperation Dialogue
AMBDC:	ASEAN-Mekong Basin Development Cooperation
APEC:	Asia-Pacific Economic Cooperation
ARF:	ASEAN Region Forum
ASEM:	Asia-Europe Meeting
CCIS:	China Credit Information Service, Ltd.
CCP:	Chinese Communist Party
CEPA:	Closer Economic Partnership Arrangement
CES:	Chinese Economic Sphere
CFB:	Chinese Family Business
CPPCC:	Chinese People's Political Consultative Conference
CPU:	Central Processing Unit
DIN:	the German Institute for Standardization
DPP:	Democratic Progressive Party
DRAM:	Dynamic Random Access Memory
DSC:	Digital Still Camera
DT:	Desktop PC
EALAF:	East Asia-Latin America Forum
EDAC:	Economic Development Advisory Conference
EU:	European Union
Fab:	Fabrication Plant
FAACEC:	Framework Agreement on ASEAN-China Economic Cooperation
FDI:	Foreign Direct Investment
FIE:	Foreign Invested Enterprise
FTA:	Free Trade Area
GATT:	General Agreement on Trade and Tariffs
GDP:	Gross Domestic Product
GMS:	Greater Mekong Sub-region
GNP:	Gross National Product
HD:	Hard Drive
IDEA:	Initiative for Development in East Asia
IEC:	International Electro-technical Commission
ISO:	International Organization for Standardization
IT:	Information Technology
KMT:	Kuomingtang (Nationalist Party)

MB:	Motherboard
MNC:	Multinational Corporation
MNE:	Multinational Enterprise
MRC:	Mekong River Commission
NAFTA:	North American Free Trade Agreement
NB:	Notebook Computer
NP:	New Party
OBM:	Original Brand Manufacturing
ODM:	Original Design Manufacturing
OEM:	Original Equipment Manufacturing
PC:	Personal Computer
PFP:	People First Party
PLA:	People's Liberation Army
PRC:	People's Republic of China (China)
RMB:	Ren Min Bi
ROC:	Republic of China (Taiwan)
RTA:	Regional Trade Agreement
R&D:	Research and Development
SME:	Small and Medium-Sized Enterprise
TAC:	Treaty of Amity and Cooperation
TAIP:	Taiwan Independence Party
TFT-LCD:	Thin Film Transistor-Liquid Crystal Display
TMD:	Theatre Missile Defense
TNC:	Transnational Corporation
TSU:	Taiwan Solidarity Union
UN:	United Nations
WMD:	Weapons of Mass Destruction
WTO:	World Trade Organization

1. Introduction

My hypothesis is as follows: Taiwan economy will face the consequence of being marginalized or completely ruined if Taiwan does not make any political compromise with China. Under the current trend of globalization[1], the future of Taiwan economy has grown out of the control of Taiwan, and at the same time, China has become the primary force to determine the future of Taiwan economy. In this dissertation, the question whether Taiwan can sustain its economic expansion without politically compromising with China will be answered. As Taiwanese businessmen have already made their choice, their westward deployment has made Taiwanese government's intention to maintain its economic autonomy impossible. Even though Taiwanese government can adopt an open policy to maintain the island's prosperity, the development of Taiwan economy will be susceptible to China's influence. It is out of the question that Taiwan can establish an autonomous economy in this globalization era. Therefore, a political compromise with China will be the best choice for Taiwanese government. Failing to do so, Taiwan may manage to maintain its economic expansion by incorporating more external talents and resources into Taiwan but will never be able to get rid of China's looming threat in both political and economical fronts.

Globalization has liberated corporations from the national boundary and enabled them to shop around in varied business operation environments. As most of the Taiwanese businessmen have already determined to explore the business opportunities of China market, it is the decision Taiwanese government has to make, whether or not it wants to extend its influence to China through politically compromising with China. In this globalized era, Taiwan economy is experiencing the Sinicization with Taiwanese characteristics. On one hand, China is Taiwan's largest FDI recipient and Taiwan's largest source of trade surplus. Moreover, thousands of Taiwanese expatriate bosses[2] and workers reside in China. On the other hand, Taiwanese government successfully blocks China's capital, goods and talents from entering Taiwan. This one-

---

[1] Though the term "globalization" in this article will primarily indicate the current phenomenon of "international economic integration" which interprets the booming intercourses of supranational economic activities, since the phraseology can be understood from the context of the article, I have no intention to differentiate the terminologies so specifically, and mostly "globalization" and "international economic integration" will be used interchangeably unless specified.

[2] As many Taiwanese small and medium enterprises are short of staff, it is impossible for them to dispatch their employees to explore the overseas possibilities. As a result, the owners have to expatriate themselves to watch over their businesses.

way economic integration will eventually erode Taiwan's economic foundation. Even though to open Taiwan for international resources including China's is the only way to revive Taiwan economy, Taiwan still has two options in its cross-Strait policy. First Taipei can continue its current political confrontation against China. This will eventually render the control of those Taiwanese firms which invest in China to Beijing because China has the immense market and abundant resources as its bargaining chips to coerce the compliance of them. Second Taipei can break the current cross-Strait deadlock by compromising politically. Taiwan will be able to manage those Taiwanese firms through Beijing's hand. The former will expose Taiwan economy to more political uncertainty and the latter will offer Taiwan a chance to determine the course of China's future.

The hypothesis is constructed upon the following assumptions:

My first assumption is under the trend of globalization the world is more regionalized than globalized. At current stage, the borderless world is not present and has no sign to be seen in the near future. As a result, for any single economic entity, the intraregional economic exchange will outweigh the interregional economic exchange. Those economies which are excluded from the regional integration will be gradually marginalized.[3]

The second assumption is that China is emerging as an economic power, and it will play an important role in the world economy, especially in Asian economy. Therefore, any economic sanction or a military action against China in this world of international economic interdependence will produce counterproductive effects upon Asian economy and even the world economy.

The third assumption is that since the economic activities of many private corporations have surpassed the habitual national boundary and ascended the supranational domain, the power of traditional governmental authorities based on the state line is corroded, and nation-states have to rely on international cooperation to contain the transnational business activities of the private enterprises.

The fourth assumption is that private enterprises are seeking for the maximization of their profits. Therefore, while private enterprises make business decisions, profit and cost are their only concern. Private enterprises will not be concerned about social responsibility, employee welfare, justice, nationalism, idealism or even governmental regulations, unless these issues will affect their return on equity (ROE). This assumption is going to play an important figure in this thesis because if private enterprises will take nationalism prior to their

[3] Here refers to those economic entities located within the three major economic regions: North America (NAFTA), Europe (EU), East Asia (ASEAN, Chinese Economic Sphere, Korea, and Japan).

profit-consideration, China will not be capable of coercing the compliance of those Taiwanese enterprises investing in China to undermine Taiwan economy.

The fifth assumption is that if Taiwan declares de jure independence, a cross-Strait war will ensue. If Taiwan can be free from the threat of a war with China, China will no longer play a destructive role in the future development of Taiwan economy, because the political normalization between China and Taiwan will liberate Taiwan from the fear of being annexed by China and cross-Strait economic relations will also be normalized. At that time, Taiwan can position itself in the "Chinese Economic Sphere (CES)[4]" and control its own enterprises through China's assistance.

The sixth assumption is that the US attitude is critical to the eruption of a cross-Strait war. If the US is willing to do "whatever it takes" to defend Taiwan without any precondition, Taiwan independence force will not hesitate to drag the US into a war against China because a cross-Strait war is the only way to Taiwan independence.

In this dissertation the possibility of China's failure in its economic development is deliberately ignored because section 2.2 provides evidences to prove that China maintains its rapid economic growth and has emerged as an economic power which influences the world economy. Although China faces severe challenges such as the implementation of floating Ren Min Bi (RMB) exchange rate, the widening gap between rich and poor, bad loans of Chinese banks and "the three farm-related issues (San Nong Wen Ti)[5]", the good sign is that China does not deny those problems and is willing to deal with them. Under the authoritarian political system, Chinese authority is better equipped than its democratic counterparts in controlling its domestic affairs. Moreover, the economic interdependence between Taiwan and China has placed the performance of Taiwan economy under China's influence. If China is caught in an economic crisis, first, Taiwan's over USD 38 billion[6] investments in China will be threatened and the production chain of Taiwanese enterprises will be shattered; second, Taiwan will no longer enjoy any trade surplus since China is the only

---

[4] CES is a concept which emphasizes the economic cooperation among the four major Chinese residing areas—Chinese mainland, Taiwan, Hong Kong and Macau. Although there are several different terminologies to describe the same concept such as "The Chinese International Community" and "The Chinese Economic Community", CES is chosen in this article for its simplicity. See Tian, 1998.

[5] Issues related to China's agriculture, countryside and farmers.

[6] Taiwan's amount of investments in China is USD 38.077 billion according to Taiwan's official record of July 2004, USD 38.382 billion according to China's official record of June 2004. Because of the complexity of cross-Straits politics, in order to bypass the restriction of Taiwan's authorities, many Taiwanese investors simply make investments through the third places without registering with Taiwan's authorities. See Kuo, 2003 for relating arguments.

resource of Taiwan's trade surplus; third, a chaotic China will reverse the current human flow and trigger a "refugee crisis"[7] in Taiwan which will destabilize Taiwan's social and economic order. Worst of all, if its economic crisis results in a political turmoil, Chinese government may try to divert its domestic public grievances by targeting at Taiwan, a renegade province in China's eyes. Thus, a collapsed China indicates an immediate threat to Taiwan's economic, social and political stability. On the contrary, an emerging China represents a challenge as well as an opportunity to Taiwan's future on both economic and political fronts.

---

[7] A one-million-refugee problem will impose a heavy burden on Taiwan's society and economy. Although there is no official statistics about the number of Taiwanese living in China, according to unofficial reports, it is nearly one million Taiwanese permanently residing in China. See *Freeman Report, Volume 1, Issue 2,* CSIS, and *Taiwanese Flood Home for Key Poll,* BBC News, March 16, 2004.

1.1 Structure of Research

The whole Section 2 intends to verify my first and second assumptions. First, by illustrating the trend of regional integration, China's macroeconomic performance, and cross-Strait economic interchanges, it proves Taiwan has been confined in a regionalized Asia with China, an emerging economic power and a potential regional hegemon that happens to be Taiwan's political archrival for over five decades. Moreover, in terms of economy, Taiwan can be better described as Sinicized than regionalized or globalized. Taiwan and China have already developed an inseparable economic relation. Second, it reveals the fact that the US, Taiwan's sole patron in the world, is caught in a dilemma of dealing with China. By pointing out that international economic interdependence has interwoven both countries into economic interdependence, even though the US is worried about China's emergence, their indispensable relations remind not only China but also the US that cooperation is better than confrontation.

The whole Section 3 is established to substantiate the third and fourth assumptions. Globalization has granted flexibility to private actors to evade national regulations by exporting their business operations overseas, but transnational cooperation between their host countries and home countries can prevent them from breaking away from national regulations. As corporations are profit-driven organizations, the development of their home countries will be the least concern to them as long as they can make a profit outside the domain of their home countries by exporting their major business operations. Even though both cross-Strait governments still hold grudges against each other, China has become the foremost destination of Taiwanese investment. Without official contact with Chinese government, Taiwanese government has difficulty in extending its supervision to the mainland operations of Taiwanese companies. As a result, for Taiwanese companies, when their mainland operations are crucial to maximizing their profit, Taiwanese government and people will be marginalized in their decision-making.

The whole Section 4 is set to prove the trueness of the fifth and six assumptions. By reiterating its One-China Principle and implementing the Anti-Secession Law, China demonstrates its will to regain Taiwan, either peacefully or forcefully. It is the consensus of Taiwanese people that without the military involvement of the US Taiwan will not survive over the military attack from China. The US attitude will influence Taiwan's domestic politics. As a result, the cross-Strait peace is hinged on Taiwan independence movement; at the same time, Taiwan independence movement depends on the US attitude.

Section 2 introduces the effect of globalization has obsoleted the traditional intercourses between Taiwan and China. As globalization brings various challenges and opportunities to different countries, China's emergence as an economic power in a regionalized Asia is the most vexatious challenge that Taiwan has ever confronted. Even though Taiwanese government remains in fear of being engulfed or dwarfed by its political archenemy, China, without the blessings from Taiwanese government, Taiwanese private enterprises pour their capital into China regardless. Moreover, the post-Cold War atmosphere makes the US difficult to implement a containment strategy against China. As the US is Taiwan's sole patron, its China policy will directly influence cross-Strait relations.

Section 2.1 deals with the reality of globalization. As the emergence of regionalism in Western Europe and North America has created trade blocs in the world trade system, although scholars still argue about whether trade blocs act as a stepping stone or a hindrance to a liberal trading system, the formation of trade blocs has already posed potential threat to Taiwan economy. As a regionalized trade system is discriminative, an outsider will be marginalized after the trade bloc is formed. However, Taiwan's limited scale and meager political influence prevent Taiwan from catching the trend of regionalism. With China's political interference, Taiwan is absent from most of the major regional fora.

Section 2.2 provides macroeconomic data to prove that China has become a large economy which is capable of influencing the performance of the world economy. Having the largest population in the world, China is equipped with the advantage of aggregate economic strength. China ranks as the world's second largest economy in terms of purchasing power parity (PPP) GDP, second only to the US, but it is the largest in Asia. Similarly, China is the world's seventh largest economy in terms of nominal GDP but nonetheless Asia's second largest. China is also the world's forth largest economy in terms of foreign trade. Moreover, it is the world's largest FDI recipient and owns the world's second largest foreign reserve. As a result, China is a prospective candidate to be a regional hegemonic power.

Section 2.3 intends to verify that East Asia is experiencing the trend of regional economic integration in terms of trade and investment. In East Asia, the dispersion of production initiated by Japanese transnational corporations has contributed to the creation of regional production networks which facilitate the regional economic integration through the intra-industry trade and investment. China's emergence will be capable of restructuring East Asian economy.

Moreover, China plays as a catalyst to commence the Asian regionalization. After China decides to forge a China-ASEAN Free Trade Area (CAFTA), other Asian powers such as Japan, Korea and India feel the urge to participate into the competition for forming the Free Trade Area with ASEAN. Aside from the economic cooperation, in order to assuage the fear of its neighbors, China poses its theory of peaceful rising and actively engages with its neighbors, even its arch-rivals—Japan and India. Although the relations between China and its neighbors are full of challenges, the economic interdependence has bound them together. While the historical complex between China and Japan hinders both sides from further engagement, they remain to be each other's major trade partner.

In contrast to China's vigorous participation in the activities of regional economic integration in East Asia, Taiwan is flung into the trend of regionalization but facing the threat of being marginalized. Statistics prove that Taiwan has developed an even more intimate tie in terms of both trade and investment with its neighbors, especially with China than ever. However, the political disagreements between Taiwan and China rules out the possibility of Taiwan's signing any bilateral economic treaties with its neighbors and Taiwan is excluded by most of the regional organizations.

Section 2.4 provides evidences to verify Taiwan's losing economic edge to China as Taiwan has unilaterally exported its capital, talents and goods to China and prohibited China from exporting any of its resources to Taiwan. The one-way flow of goods earns Taiwan billions of trade surpluses against China, but the one-way flow of capital and talents has undermined Taiwan's economic foundation. Worst of all, Taiwan also loses the investment of multinational enterprises to China in lack of "three links"[8] between two sides across the Strait. So far, Taiwanese government has not been able to adopt any effective policy to reverse this one-way flow, even though it imposes restrictions on the westward investment of Taiwanese enterprises and the westbound migration of human capital. On the contrary, Taiwan has been effective in prohibiting the inflow of Chinese capital and talents.

In order to halt the China fever of Taiwanese investors, Taiwanese government once promoted "no haste, be patient" policy to restrain the mainland-bound investment projects but only turned their investments underground. As a result, the official statistics relating to China-bound investments from Taiwan are twisted and the investment transparency and accountability are compromised. As Taiwanese government has to offer grace periods from time to time to those Taiwanese businessmen who invest in China without governmental approval to make retroactive registration, its authority is inevitably jeopardized. Moreover, even with its rigid China policy, the official statistics indicates that the China-bound investments of Taiwanese enterprises account for 56.51% of Taiwan's total outward investments as of the end of 2004. If the capital channeled through a third place to China is included, the percentage will go even higher.

The stern China policy of Taiwanese government will eventually backfire on Taiwan economy. As its conservative China policy induces the incon-

[8] "Three links" indicate direct transport, trade and postal links.

venience of multinational enterprises (MNEs) and forces them to move their business operations away from Taiwan, they not only withdraw themselves from Taiwan but also bring along their Taiwanese contract manufacturers to mainland China. When Taiwanese manufacturers relocate their production to China, they also take their suppliers, employees, the employees of their suppliers and their expatriate workers' purchasing power to China. As a result, their relocation is at the expense of low-skilled Taiwanese workers and will cause woe to Taiwan economy.

The one-way economic integration between two sides across the Strait is reflected not only on the investment front but also in terms of trade. As a small island-economy, Taiwan has relatively higher foreign trade dependence than those larger economies like the US, Japan, South Korea, Germany. Foreign trade plays an important role in Taiwan's economic development. China has become Taiwan's major export destination and the exports to China account for over 30% of Taiwan's total exports. Although Taiwan successfully blocks goods made in China from entering Taiwan, it can not prevent China from becoming its major trade partner. China is Taiwan's major source of trade surplus. Taiwan earned over USD 28 billion from China in 2004.

Section 2.5 pointed out that the US China policy plays an important role in cross-Strait relations. The war on terrorism consolidates the once-fragile Sino-US relations. Although the US has viewed China as a potential strategic competitor, under the threat of terrorism, the US determines to temporarily shelve the arguments of "China threat". Moreover, the economic interdependence between China and the US complicates the US stance toward China. According to China's official statistics, the US is the second largest FDI provider to China. China is the third largest trade partner of the US and also the second largest holder of US Treasury securities. Although China enjoys over USD 100 billion trade surplus against the US, because the foreign investing enterprises contribute to almost half of China's trade surplus, any trade war between the US and China will hurt not only Chinese manufacturers but also foreign-funded firms in China. In this globalized world, cooperation will be more beneficial to both China and the US than confrontation. However, in fear of the growing economic power will transform China into a military power threatening the US hegemonic status, the US has been suspicious to China's emergence, yet the US has not figured out a strategy which can successfully contain China's development without jeopardizing itself.

The US feels insecure because China is big and unpredictable. However, the US has not devised any effective strategy to deal with China. The US domestic politics has hindered its capability to develop a complete strategy in dealing with the big and unpredictable China. The infighting between Blue Team and Red Team obscures the purpose of the US China policy. The Blue

Team is doing its best to depict China as the heir of the "evil empire" and proposes a strategy of containment to confine China's development; the Red Team focuses on the economic interests and suggests a strategy of engagement to bring China into the world system. Aside from these two extremist strategies, some scholars advocate "congagement"—a hybrid strategy of containment and engagement. However, none of these strategies produces and will produce any satisfactory result to the US. The US is trapped in a dilemma: the US containment will not be effective and risk-free in strangling China's expansion under the trend of the international economic integration; the US engagement may enhance China's military capacity and eventually jeopardize its interest; the US "congagement" will not increase China's predictability and the US is still encumbered by the fear of a future China threat.

Section 3 illustrates that the economic activities have surpassed the habitual national boundary and ascended the supranational domain in the process of globalization. The contemporary business practices bestow novel eschewals to private actors against traditional governmental mechanism. Even though the world has not reached the realm as a borderless one, the transnational activities of private actors have restructured the function of national government. While private corporations are striving for the enlargement of their worldwide market share to survive in the globalization, public administrations are experiencing severe hardships at steering their domestic economy through the transnational activities of the private actors who are no longer contented with domestic-bound business opportunities. Although governments still have the right to propose, implement and supervise its domestic regulations, they are incapable of dealing with the overseas activities of their enterprises without the cooperation of their foreign counterparts.

Section 3.1 points out that market is only a part of the social system. A sound moral system and an effective governmental mechanism are indispensable to a smoothly functioning market. The behaviors of the corporations have to be confined by ethic or regulations. Without regulations, the market participants will have no rule to follow and the market system will eventually collapse. Thus, regulations are important to the existence of a market. Whichever institution has right to design, implement and monitor regulation will have power to negotiate with and even to coerce its governor and counterparts. Thus, the behaviors of institution and the formation of regulation hinge on each other, and economic activities are embedded in the institution-regulation link.

Anarchy is harmful to business. Governments are required to safeguard the proper operation of business. However, as globalization has liberated transnational corporations (TNCs) from national boundary, TNCs are able to shop around for the best business environment. Moreover, globalization also bestows extra bargaining power on some corporations because the development of the exchange system enables them to enforce their own regulations on their employees, suppliers, and demanders. As a result, private actors are influential in determining national economy.

Government intervention has positive effect on economic expansion in some occasions and Taiwanese government used to be competent at controlling both the public and private sectors to create Taiwan's "economic miracle". However, globalization liberates the vigor of private sector and empowers private actors to condition the national economic environment. As a result, although Taiwanese government sets up multiple restrictions to avoid the capital and technological flow to China from semiconductor industry to infrastructure industry, Taiwanese businessmen evade the governmental regulations and swarm to China anyway. Moreover, as most Taiwanese businessmen who invest in China have obtained dual nationality, the strict law enforcement of Taiwanese government will only force them to side with China.

Section 3.2 indicates that globalization has restructured the power balance between multinational enterprises (MNEs) and nation-states. The geographic proximity, cultural affinity and a common language magnetize Taiwanese enterprises into China despite governmental restrictions. As China serves as the major host country of Taiwan's foreign direct investments (FDI), no matter Taiwanese government likes it or not, without China's cooperation, Taiwanese government can not oversee the mainland operations of Taiwanese companies. As a result, Taiwanese government is trapped in a dilemma. If Taiwan eases the restrictions regarding mainland-bound investments, in order to garner profits from China market, Taiwanese companies will bend over to China's demand. If Taiwan imposes severe restrictions on the westbound investments, it is difficult for Taiwanese firms to compete with their foreign counterparts as they can access China's abundant resources even with the assistance of their governments; as a result, Taiwanese government will throttle the viability of Taiwanese companies because they will wither in Taiwan; otherwise they will seek a way to bypass the restrictions of Taiwanese government and exclude Taiwan from their global deployment.

Section 3.3 will offer the explanation about the indispensableness of the China-bound deployment for Taiwanese companies. Taiwanese corporations were accustomed to a business pattern: they imported raw materials, key components, machineries and technologies from primarily Japan and the US, poured in Taiwan's manpower and resources to produce and then exported the finished goods to mainly the US. Thus, when the rising labor, land and infrastructure costs forced Taiwanese manufacturers to diversify their business activities, although some strive hard to increase their value-added activities, most of them chose to migrate to countries where labor, land and resources were cheaper. Among those countries, China attracted almost one half of total

Taiwan's outward investments from 1991 to now. Many Taiwanese firms renovate their business model by adding China into their business operation. They manufacture their goods in China and export the goods from China.

In contrast to the enthusiasm of Taiwanese enterprises in China, Taiwanese government discarded its ambition to construct Taiwan as an "Asia-Pacific Regional Operations Center" in order to extricate from the economic dependence on China. Taiwanese government determined to develop technological industry as the foundation for the future development of Taiwan economy. However, Taiwan's technological strength is not solid enough to make Taiwan indispensable in the global supply chain. Taiwan's technology is established on paying for ready-to-use technology and making follow-up research; therefore, Taiwan contains the capacity of transferring the buying technology into a profit generator, and devotes generous resources on applied science and technology, but its lack of efficacy on basic science is fatal to its technological autonomy.

Moreover, due to the influence of Chinese culture and Taiwan's domestic politics, Small and Medium-Sized Enterprises (SMEs) become the backbone of Taiwan economy. SMEs have the features of flexibility and adroitness, but are short of resources. As research and development (R&D) is time consuming, costly and "brain-power" intensive with uncertain return, for Taiwan's resource-limited SMEs, they would rather disburse the technology transfer fee for the ready-to-use technology than distribute resources on open-ended R&D with an unknown result. The booming SMEs contribute to Taiwan's vigorous economy and to the loss of Taiwan's technological autonomy.

Aside from the scale of Taiwanese businesses, the original equipment manufacturing (OEM) model of operating business has constituted the other structural weakness of Taiwan's industry. Although Taiwanese companies have succeeded in using the OEM model to make themselves indispensable in the global supply chain, the indispensability of Taiwanese companies does not guarantee that Taiwan will be needed. Because of the OEM model, Taiwanese companies are good at establishing flexible production lines and reducing production costs but neither advantage of Taiwanese companies assists them to play a linchpin role in the supply chain. In the upstream, they face the constraints from the suppliers of key components and their technology transferors[9];

[9] Taiwanese companies have to pay technology transfer fee and royalties. Moreover, because they do not have the autonomy of technology, when their technology transferors decide to withdraw from the market, they have no other choice but to withdraw from the market correspondingly. Steve Appleton, the Chairman of the Board, CEO, and President of Micron, the world's second largest DRAM manufacturer, said that the famous Taiwanese DRAM manufacturer—Winbond Electronics Corporation was forced out of the market because its technology transferor, Toshiba, decided to withdraw from the DRAM market. That was the consequence for those DRAM manufacturers without autonomous technology. See

in the downstream, they are conditioned by their OEM customers who even own the power to dictate the location of production. Moreover, as the assembly has become the lowest value added segment in the product value chain, the profit of Taiwanese OEM manufacturers have been squeezed. Therefore, China's cheap land, labor and resources become the lifesaver of Taiwanese enterprises. As the westward investment of Taiwanese enterprises becomes a crucial factor in their survival; they have no other choice but to dismiss the political concern of Taiwanese government.

Section 3.4 points out that China is no longer a backward country unable to accommodate Western-style commerce. China is mastering the capitalist quintessence and demanding a reasonable portion of the world influence on both political and economic fronts by its economic scale. Being China's sole legitimate governing apparatus, Chinese government can determine market winners by establishing its domestic regulations and standards. The large scale of China market and its quick expansion make China an indispensable investment location for those companies which encounter the growth bottleneck in the developed countries.

China's magnetism attracts not only Taiwanese companies but also world well-known MNEs. More and more private corporations are drawn to China. China is a continuously expanding market, whichever company is interested in participating China market has to conform to China's demand. More and more Taiwanese companies are seeking for local supply for the raw materials, semi-manufactured products and even machineries in China. Moreover, in order to gain access to China market and to reduce the tax burden, the downstream assembly manufacturers are demanding their Taiwanese upstream suppliers also move their production line to China. When the investment in China is a sine qua non in the global deployment of Taiwanese enterprises, Chinese government will play a vital role in the success of their Chinese business operation. As a result, Taiwan will be marginalized if the emerging China properly exerts its influence on private enterprises.

Politically, Taiwan can insist on its political ideology[10] to refuse direct communication with China. Economically, without any direct contact and dia-

---

"Micron Predicted the Decline of Taiwan DRAM (Mei Kuang Chang Shuai Tai Wan DRAM)," May 15, 2004, *China Times*, (in Chinese).

[10] In two-Chiang's (Chiang Kai-shek and Chiang Ching-kuo) era, Taiwan insisted on the policy of "Gentlemen won't coexist with thieves (Han Ze Bu Liang Li, meaning Kuomintang wouldn't stand together with the Communists)" policy against China, thus Taiwan did not have any official communication, contact and dialogue with China. In Lee's and Chen's reign (Lee Teng-hui, Chen Shui-bian), Taiwan worried about being dwarfed by China and expected China to negotiate with Taiwan on a nation-to-nation basis on which China would never agree.

logue between two governments across Taiwan Strait, Taiwanese government is rendering its influence on Taiwanese enterprises to Chinese government. In the absence of cross-Strait investment protection agreements, and with no official representative stationed in China, Taiwanese businessmen have to rely on their personal relationships and China's governmental apparatus to ensure the smooth operation of their businesses in China. As a result, Taiwanese government is placing Taiwanese businessmen under China's control, and this phenomenon will eventually jeopardize Taiwan economy.

Section 4 illustrates that Taiwan independence issue is an ideological conflict between China and Taiwan's pro-independence activists and the essence of an ideological conflict is a zero-sum game in which the winner takes all. China represents the unification force which insists on Taiwan's unification with the motherland; on the contrary, Democratic Progressive Party (DPP), Taiwan's ruling party has a "Taiwan Independence Clause" on its party platform, which intends to separate Taiwan from China not only de facto but also de jure. Because there is no elbowroom between independence and unification for Chinese Communist Party (CCP) and DPP to maneuver, as a result, unless DPP forsakes its Taiwan independence ideology, it is impossible for Chinese government to engage in a cross-Strait dialogue with Taiwanese government as long as DPP controls the governmental apparatus.

Section 4.1 points out that China holds adamantly on the One-China Principle but Taiwan is deviating from it. President Chen Shui-bian even declared that if China does not shelve One-China Principle and the "one country, two systems" formula, the door to cooperation between China and Taiwan will not open. Because of the historical complex, China's domestic power struggle and the fear of domino effect, Chinese leaders will never denounce One-China Principle.

The existence of leased areas reminded Chinese their humiliation in the late Qing Dynasty. After China regained Hong Kong and Macao, Taiwan becomes the last missing piece in the completion of China's territorial integrity and glorious past. Although Taiwan is no longer Japanese colony, its colonial past and "renegade province" present represents the unfinished mission for Chinese leaders. In view of the fact that Taiwan's separation from the motherland is the result of the civil war between CCP and KMT, being on the winner's side, Chinese leaders bear the historical mission of preserving the completeness of national territory. For Chinese leaders, Taiwan's return to China will end the one-century long historical humiliation and signify the personal glory of those who unify the nation. However, if Taiwan permanently drifts away from China, those Chinese leaders who fail to retain the integrity of national territory will be labeled as "historical sinners".

The fierce domestic power struggle forces all Chinese leaders to take a tough stance on Taiwan issue. In the political power struggle, all ambitious politicians are waiting for their rivals to commit mistakes. To tolerate Taiwan's separation will be a fatal mistake to Chinese politicians because Taiwan issue is sensitive and emotional. Moreover, the geographical proximity across the Strait makes Taiwan a security concern to Chinese leaders. As any leader who ignores the national security will be vulnerable in the political rivalry, no Chinese leader will provide this cause to his opponents to attack him. Since Taiwan's return to China is the vox populi of 1.3 billion Chinese, any Chinese leader who dares to renounce the recuperation of Taiwan is no other than committing political suicide. Thus, it is unrealistic for Taiwan to fancy that Chinese leaders will disagree with one another when dealing with Taiwan issue. One-China Principle is China's bottom line beyond which the political responsibility will be too heavy for any Chinese leader to take.

Since Taiwan is stealthily drifting away from the One-China Principle, China is the only linchpin force which prevents the one-China domino from falling. Once China renounces the One-China Principle, Taiwan will not hesitate to push down the domino by lobbying the world to follow China's suite. If China does not want the One-China Principle, no country in the world has the obligation to maintain it for Chinese. Thus China realizes that once it drops its guard on the One-China Principle, it will start to lose control. Aside from the external domino effect, China is in fear of the internalization of the domino effect. China is afraid that Taiwan's separation might trigger a chain reaction from the separation movements of Tibet and Xingjian and eventually lead to China's collapse.

The coexistence of independence and unification is the balance of terror among China, Taiwan and the US. As China intends to move the cross-Strait relations towards the unification and Taiwan struggles for independence, the US becomes the sole power which forces both sides across the Strait to compromise under the current status quo—the de facto separation and de jure unification.

Section 4.2 illustrates the predicament of the trilateral relations among China Taiwan, and the US and the potential confrontation behind the disequilibrium between the status and the scale. China is looking forward to Taiwan's unification, but without a peaceful resolution, Taiwan issue may cause the US military involvement. At the same time, Taiwan is pursuing de jure independence, but can never extricate itself from China. The US wants to maneuver Taiwan as a pawn to contain China but is in fear of being dragged into a premature war against China.

When the social position is in rank disequilibrium, aggression might be aroused to adjust the misplaced status. China, a large state which is emerging from its past backwardness is seeking a new position in a preset world order; Taiwan, a small state which accumulates enough wealth is seeking for self-identification. In pursuing the goal of becoming a great nation, Taiwan's unification is China's final trophy; without it, China will never achieve its greatness. In search for self-identification, without formal independence, Taiwan will not be able to claim itself as a nation. Since their goals cannot be satisfied at the same time, sooner or later one side must yield. However, Taiwan independence means a war against China; with or without the US military involvement, after a cross-Strait war, Taiwan economy will be devastated.

Section 4.3 points out that China and Taiwan used to conduct diplomatic competition on the One-China Principle. Countries can not establish diplomatic ties with Taiwan and China at the same time and only one side across the Strait can be recognized as the representative of all Chinese. Although Taiwan intends to switch to the policy of dual-recognition, China insists on its One-China Principle and up to now obstructs any possibility of dual-recognition. Ever since China successfully capitalized on its Third World Policy and replaced Taiwan as the officially recognized Chinese government in United Nation (UN), Taiwan has encountered difficulties in maintaining its diplomatic allies. In order to offset the diplomatic isolation, Taiwan switched its diplomatic strategy to cultivate economic, cultural, and educational ties with most of the countries. After Taiwan suffered defeat upon defeat in its competition with China for global recognition, Taiwan's "economic miracle" rescued Taiwan from its diplomatic cul-de-sac. Through "pragmatic diplomacy", Taiwan effectively acquired some formal ties with countries in need of financial support. The diplomatic war between both sides across the Strait will wage on until the One-China Principle is resolved.

Section 4.4 points out that Taiwan's domestic political power struggle has hindered any slim chance of rapprochement between China and Taiwan. In Taiwan's domestic politics, in order to win an election, Taiwanese politicians bipolarize Taiwan's society into pro-unification vs. pro-independence. Pro-independence politicians dominate the discourse of Taiwan identity and smear their political rivals by labeling them as "the fellow-travelers of the Chinese Communist Party" or "the fifth column of China" to woo the votes away from the pro-unification camp; at the same time, pro-unification politicians accuse their counterparts of dragging Taiwan into a cross-Strait war to coerce voters not to vote for the candidates of pro-independence camp.[11]

[11] The pro-unification camp is addressing itself as pro-status quo, but the pro-independence camp labels its opponent as pro-unification. In order not to complicate the article further, I will simply put pro-unification to differentiate it from pro-independence.

Because the tragic incident began on February 28, 1947[12] triggering confrontations between Taiwan's early and newly immigrants[13] and the political power disparity originating from the misallocated power of Taiwan's former ruling party Kuomintang[14] (KMT) offer "Taiwanese" politicians an excuse to accuse the KMT government as a foreign regime, Taiwan's society becomes a fertile land for Taiwanese politicians to cultivate ethnicity. As KMT was established on Chinese mainland and its former leaders were mainlanders, while it first reigned over Taiwan, it allocated more political power to mainlanders than "Taiwanese". As mainlanders had controlled power disproportional to its number, when the electorate system was introduced, ethnicity offered leverage to "Taiwanese" politicians to defeat their mainlander competitors, the quondam vested interest.

Aside from the investment in ethnicity, to gain the political momentum in an electorate system, Taiwanese politicians involve cross-Strait relations into Taiwan's domestic power struggle and are divided into two camps: pro-unification (Pan-Blue) vs. pro-independence (Pan-Green). China, an "enemy state" in the mindset of pro-independence extremists, is easily depicted as a vicious neighboring state which has the ambition to annex Taiwan. To maximize their political benefit, pro-independence politicians develop an argument that China is an enemy, whoever holds the dream of unifying with China is a traitor to Taiwan; thus, pro-independence becomes the political righteousness in Taiwan, whoever questions this logic will be labeled as "not loving Taiwan". Moreover, by bipolarizing Taiwan's society, eliminating the possibility of pro-status-quo, slashing at the enemy state and resembling their opponents as the fellow traveler of the enemy state, the pro-independence politicians successfully enlarge their social base. On the contrary, the pro-unification politicians who do not renovate their theorem but repeat the old argument that Taiwan independence will set off a cross-Strait war lose their edge over their pro-independence counterparts.

Because of the fierce inter- and intra-camp competition, the camp activists successfully dominate the center stage of both political camps in Taiwan. All Taiwanese politicians have to comply with the principium of their belonging political camp to maintain their political power. As a result, Taiwan's politics is trapped in a vicious circle of devastating polarization. Moreover, as the pro-independence social base is on the wax and the pro-unification one is on the wane, the Pan-Blue camp have to adhere to the argument of pro-status-quo and modify the concept of the pro-unification to enlarge its social base. Al-

[12] It is generally addressed as "228 Incident".
[13] The early immigrants are called "Taiwanese", the newly ones mainlanders.
[14] Kuomintang is also known as Chinese Nationalist Party.

though China still holds its long lasting One-China Principle, the political in-fightings in Taiwan have driven Taiwan further away from One-China Principle. As long as the structure of Taiwan's bipolarized society is not decomposed, the differences between China's unification proposal and Taiwan's independence mindset will be difficult to mitigate.

Section 4.5 discusses that even though China does not want to appeal to force in resolving Taiwan issue, the escalating of Taiwan's provocative actions will eventually educe China's counteractions. In consideration of China's increasing comprehensive national power, Taiwanese independence leaders advocate to construct a new nation on Taiwan in 2008, in which year China will host Olympic Games. They intend to take the Olympic Games as a hostage and shelter themselves behind the peaceful purpose of the Olympics to seek for Taiwan independence. Aside from the protection of Olympics, they also believe in the US military involvement in a cross-Strait war. President George W. Bush issued a "blank check" which the US claimed back later but Bush administration offered momentum to Taiwan independence movement and unconsciously rewrote the US cross-Strait policy of "strategic ambiguity" by promoting greater "moral clarity" concerning Taiwan security. Furthermore, President Chen's successful "transit diplomacy" sponsored by the Bush administration and American weaponry dealers aggrandized not only Chen's personal reputation but also the sentiment for Taiwan independence as Chen has been a pro-independence advocate.

Although Bush administration at last realized the threat behind Taiwan independence movement and adopted some subtle diplomatic measures to deter Taiwan from further drifting towards independence, however the US subtlety could be intentionally twisted or unconsciously misinterpreted by Taiwanese officials to lessen the effect which the US intended to convey to Taiwanese people. As a result, even though President Bush openly opposed the intention of Taiwan's leader to unilaterally alter the currents status quo, 52% of Taiwanese people still believed that once the cross-Strait war erupted, the US would come to Taiwan's rescue. Taiwanese vox populi reflected the mindset of Taiwanese people. They were misled by Taiwanese politicians. Furthermore, President Chen's personal feature is a threat to cross-Strait stability because he tends to gain progresses in conflicts. As the US plays a pivot in cross-Strait stability, it must convey a convincing message to not only China but also Taiwan that the US will contain whoever escalates first to make its pivotal deterrence effective.

For the US, with its military supremacy it should be a relatively easy task to win each battle against China, but China supported by its size will be a nation difficult to conquer. The US might have to withdraw itself from Chinese mainland with empty hands as what it won in the Vietnam War. Moreover,

China's massive population will cause moral dilemma on American troops. A massive killing is against humanity, in China's doctrine of fighting a "people's war", American soldiers will encounter difficulties in distinguishing Chinese soldiers from civilians. China might not be equipped with the most advanced weaponry, but it is the world's most populous country. Its bountiful human resources has been the most effective weapon of deterrence which has successfully deterred the attack of the Soviet Union in Sino-Soviet border dispute and the US ground troops from entering North Vietnam in the Vietnam War. Even China's "people's war" does not guarantee a victory for Chinese People's Liberation Army (PLA) but certainly will impede the movement of its enemy to an easy victory.

Sec 4.6 discusses the strategic alternatives between two sides across Taiwan Strait. China prefers unification, tolerates the status quo, but will never accept Taiwan independence. On the other hand, Taiwan's current ruling party seeks for independence, compromises at status quo but refuses unification. The US represents a variable which conditions both China and Taiwan from serving their own ends to disarray the regional stability in this cross-Strait scenario. The US had maintained its neural ground by adopting a policy of "strategic ambiguity", and refrained China and Taiwan from deviating from the status quo. However, as President Bush assumed the office, his tilt towards Taiwan triggered the sentiment for a de jure independent Taiwan. Although President Bush has shifted his stance back to the neutral ground by publicly rebuking Taiwanese leader Chen Shui-bian, one of the Taiwan independence leaders, Taiwan independence movement has generated momentum and it will take more effort to prevent Taiwan independence activists from escalating. Moreover, in order to capitalize on the fragile cross-Strait relationship, the pro-independence ruling party claimed it would "create a new Constitution in 2006 and implement it by 2008". The declaration was tantamount to setting up a "Taiwan independence timetable" in Chinese mindset. In order to counter the "Taiwan independence timetable", China implemented Anti-Secession Law regardless the US displeasure. This time, the US took a cautious stance on this issue and was reluctant to condemn China in public. The US finally realizes that the consequence will be dire if the US cannot effectively prevent both sides from further escalations.

1.2 Proposed Solutions

In Taiwan, there are two distinct opinions relating to what Taiwan should do to deal with the challenges of globalization. One suggests that Taiwan should shelve the political dispute with China and economically integrate with China to explore the enlarging China market;[15] on the contrary, the other argues that Taiwan is already economically over dependent on China—Taiwan's enemy and Taiwan should integrate its economy with the global market, not China market.[16] The former falsely assumes that Taiwan can harvest economic benefits in the CES without paying the political price. As China is the major actor in the CES, the cross-Strait economic integration will render China more power in containing Taiwanese private businesses and eventually China will be able to dominate the development of Taiwan economy.[17] The latter is based on another false assumption that the world has become borderless so Taiwan can focus on the world market to dilute China's influence. However, the reality is the globalization tends to favor regionalism over multilateralism. As a result, Taiwan is confined by its geographic location. Moreover, even in a globalized world, based on the calculation of national interests, no country would offend China for Taiwan; otherwise Taiwan will not be confined in the spell of One-China Principle and maintains formal diplomatic ties with usually less than thirty countries while there are at least 191[18] countries in this world. I suggest that Taiwan should trade its political ideology of Taiwan independence with China for a role in constructing China's economic, social and political system and in the deployment of Taiwanese businesses. By embedding in the CES Taiwan will suffer less for the political uncertainty and have a better chance to ensure its economic prosperity.

Because Taiwan's democratization is further materialized in the process of globalization, more and more Taiwanese people are seeking for self-asser-

---

[15] Those who support this argument are opposition political leaders and Taiwanese entrepreneurs.

[16] Those who support this idea are ruling party leaders and pro-Taiwan independence scholars.

[17] The economic development of Hong Kong will stand out as the best example. While the Closer Economic Partnership Arrangement (CEPA) between Hong Kong and China revitalizing Hong Kong economy, China also extends its political influence in Hong Kong. From the 2004 economic assessment for Hong Kong, mainland visitors accounted for more than half of the total visitors to Hong Kong, and the retail sales surged by 9.1% in terms of volume because of the booming tourism. See Asian Development Outlook 2005, Hong Kong, China, Asian Development Bank.

[18] That is the number of UN members. If Taiwan and Vatican City are included, there will be 193 countries in the world.
http://geography.about.com/cs/countries/a/numbercountries.htm

tion. The Taiwan identity which is created more by domestic political power struggle than by cultural or social identification triggers the identification alienation between China and Taiwan and will make the road to unification in distress. If this situation continues, the cross-Strait relations will be trapped into a vicious circle: the Taiwan identity hinders the process of unification; the hindered unification will rouse China's dissatisfaction; the hospitality caused by China's discontent will further strengthen the Taiwan identity. As a result, the stronger Taiwanese people embrace the Taiwan identity, the less chance for two sides across the Strait to reach peaceful coexistence. Chinese government has faced the dilemma of dealing with the growing Taiwan identify, and realized that its rigid attitude toward Taiwan will be counterproductive to the future unification. Since China will not budge on its political stance, unless China intends to use force to solve the Taiwan issue, to serve its ends of peaceful unification with Taiwan, China will take an ameliorative position on cross-Strait economic exchanges. However, the economic integration without political engagement will render China more influence on Taiwanese business-men investing in China and eventually endanger the development of Taiwan economy. The Taiwan identity becomes stumbling block not only to the cross-Strait peace but also the development of Taiwan economy.

On the contrary, as long as Taiwan can shelve the ideology of seeking for Taiwan independence, China and Taiwan can engage on a political dialogue and devise a viable framework to ensure the peace between two sides across Strait. As the trend of globalization is irreversible, the closely intertwined economic interdependence between Taiwan and China will ease the tension across the Strait, and offers both sides more time to deal with internal problems. As long as the domestic politics does not interfere into the process of economic integration, China and Taiwan can reach a win-win situation through explicit economic cooperation and tacit political collaboration. Nonetheless, if the domestic politics hinders economic integration, we may have to construct another framework to revive Taiwan's war-raged economy. In order to ensure this catastrophe will not occur, the cross-Strait pivot, the US, should assist or even enforce the performance of cross-Strait dialogue.

If the purpose of the US policy is to make China manageable to the US government such as to create a small and vulnerable China, to subjugate China as its client state or to cultivate a pro-US regime in China, this grandiose purpose will be difficult to achieve by any US policy. Chinese nationalism will prevent China from kowtowing to the US under any circumstance. Moreover, unless the US is willing to conduct a full-scale military confrontation against China to dismantle it, as China emphasizes on the integrity of its territory, it will be difficult to expect China to adopt a self-dismantling policy by renouncing its One-China Principle. However, if the US is willing to accept a large and predictable China, the purpose is manageable without aggression.

When the US considers the options for its China policy, it focuses on what can best serve its own national interests instead of what can serve the best interests of both US and China. It is outrageous to argue that what betters China will certainly worsens the US. Unless China and the US compete in a zero-sum game in which the object has the feature of indivisibility, the cooperation and the mutual-benefit are accomplishable. However, the US focuses overly on its position of the world's super power and is in fear of losing it to the newly emerging power. As a result, the US is anxious to use Taiwan as a pawn to contain China and not as a peaceful platform to communicate with China to increase the transparency of China's decision-making processes and to transform China into a law-abiding country which respects human right and even embraces democracy.

Taiwan is what China wants, and China is willing to risk a war against the US to prevent Taiwan from independence. A war between two nuclear-armed nations is an unimaginable disaster. It will be a war of no winner, for not only China, Taiwan and the US but all China's surrounding neighbors will be victimized. Therefore, Taiwan independence should not be a viable option for Taiwan and the US. The US has its nominal one China policy which the US pledges that it acknowledges that both Taiwan and Chinese mainland belong to one China but in reality the US adopts the Taiwan Relations Act to perform a "one China, one Taiwan" policy. Up to now, the US leaders have never considered the possibility of the peaceful unification between China and Taiwan.[19] The US China-Taiwan policy oscillates between maintaining cross-Strait status quo and indulging Taiwan independence. Not until China threatens a war against Taiwan does the US realize the sensitivity of Taiwan independence to China. As a cross-Strait war will jeopardize not only China's and Taiwan's economic interests but also the US' and East Asia's, it will be destructive for the US to hold Taiwan as a voluntary hostage to destabilize the cross-Strait region if China misbehaves. The US has a more constructive option to improve not only the US national interests but also China's as well as Taiwan's.

The US should conduct "Trojan-horse engagement" with China by offering a present which it cannot refuse. Since Taiwan's return to the motherland signifies not only the end of the historical humiliation but also the personal glory of Chinese leaders, no matter how difficult the process of unification will be, Chinese leaders will be willing to accept it. The US should assist or even coerce Taiwan to perform a constructive dialogue with China. Through the interaction between China and Taiwan, Taiwan can demand its participation in

[19] Tucker, 2002

constructing the structure of China's social mechanism, economic arrangement, legal framework and even political system to transform China into a society of fairness and openness. As China is going to dominate the central government after the unification, the unification based on China's "one country two system" formula will not offer a trustworthy guarantee to Taiwan's welfare. However, as long as Taiwan can participate in building the framework of China's domestic system, "one country one system" will serve the best interest of Taiwan.

In this strategy of "Trojan-horse engagement", the US will be better off by planting a seed of hope in China's soil to transparentize China's decision-making processes and the US can expect a large but predictable China, which is definitely more cooperative. China will also be better off. As the political uncertainty regarding Taiwan independence disappears, China can divert its resources to resolve its domestic problems and to focus on the economic development with the help from Taiwan. The interests of Taiwanese people will also be covered. Stable cross-Strait relations will reunify Taiwan's bipolarized society, and most important of all, through the cooperation of Chinese government, Taiwan can regain its control over Taiwanese corporations which operate on Chinese mainland. By positioning itself in the deployment of Taiwanese businessmen, Taiwan economy will no longer suffer from the threat of being marginalized. With China's assistance, Taiwan will not be an absentee in Asian regional economic integration. Taiwan independence force will be the only loser in this strategy. Taiwan independence force should exist and will exist during the process of unification, as it is the most important bargaining chip for Taiwan to coerce China's cooperation. Like nuclear weapon, Taiwan independence force is required but should be locked in the storage.

The strongest counterargument against my proposal is that if China is an obstinate rogue state which resists any change, the strategy of "Trojan-horse engagement" is doomed to fail. However, China has been changed. The living standard of its people has been improved. It no longer exports the revolutionist ideology to its neighboring states, and it no longer devotes on massive political movements. Even though China still remains as an authoritarian regime, the mass political suppression has disappeared. The system of mandatory retirement is in place, and no political figure can dominate the party and government position until his death. The power transition poses less threat to the social stability in China. Since China is capable of reshaping itself, it only needs more time and some guidelines to accomplish its transformation. In the use of Taiwan independence, Taiwan can participate in China's transformation or hinder the process of transformation. How Taiwan capitalizes on its Taiwan independence ideology will determine the future development of its economy.

2. Globalization Turns China into a Challenge to Taiwan & the US

There still exist disagreements on the dimensions of the term "globalization" should be applied to. Most analysts refer globalization to the phenomena of expanding trade internationally, liberalizing investment globally, dispersing production worldwide, introducing new technology and disseminating democracy, but others insist on the inclusion of other contemporary developments such as the spread of environmental pollution, drugs smuggling, illegal cross-border immigration, the adoption of English as the lingua franca, the diffusion of American culture, the erosion of state sovereignty and even the phenomenon of the worldwide protest against globalization.[20]

As globalization can be applied to such a wide range, each nation encounters different challenges and opportunities from the phenomena of globalization, and therefore, there is no identical solution for all nation-states. To put it in a simple way, each state faces its own challenges and opportunities of globalization, and it must provide its own measures to maximize the benefits and to minimize the threats from globalization. For Americans, the internationalization of their national language and culture does not post any threat to their economic development and social stability but enhances their worldwide position, and as a major foreign direct investment recipient, the US also benefits from the deregulation of international finance, yet the evacuation of domestic manufacturing jobs, the illegal immigrants and the drugs smuggling post threats to social stability of the US.

In specifying the aspect of global economic development, Rodrik would rather use the term "international economic integration" than "globalization". He argues globalization is a term interpreted differently by different analysts, and moreover, globalization usually evokes specific value judgments in people's mind.[21] Beck suggests that the essence and nature of globalization, globalism and globality should be clearly differentiated. Globalism implies the ideology of the advent of a dominant world market which replaces the position of politics. Globality indicates that all people have been living in a world society; not a single state or group can entirely isolate itself from interacting with others. Globalization mainly points out the processes of penetrating and eroding nation-states' sovereign by transnational actors.[22]

Keohane and Nye conjecture that globalization refers to the increase of globalism vis-à-vis the concept of deglobalization which means the decline of

[20] Schaeffer, 2003
[21] Rodrik, 2000
[22] Beck, 2000, 9-11

globalism. Globalism denotes that the world is constructed into interdependent networks spanning across geographies. The phenomena such as the deregulation of financial control and international trade, the exchanges of ideas and information, the smuggling of human beings and goods, the deterioration of environmental pollution and the dispersion of contagious diseases structure the multiple linkages of the global networks.[23]

For Taiwanese, the trend of globalization highlights another transient stage of the cross-Taiwan-Strait relations and bestows China supreme power to determine the future of Taiwan economy. The contemporary history points out that the cross-Strait relations have undergone many different phases such as mutual exclusion[24], military confrontation[25], and cold war[26]. In this globalization era, the cross-Strait relations enter a phase of economic integration but political alienation. On one hand, Taiwan is drawn by China's abundant resources—cheap labor, low-cost land and large market; but on the other hand, Taiwan's democratic movement and domestic political power struggle make Taiwan politically alienate China. This phenomenon of economic interdependence accompanying political disintegration traps Taiwan in a dilemma—Taiwan economically depends on an "enemy nation"[27]. These complicated cross-Strait relations become critical to not only Taiwan's political system, but also the future of Taiwan economy. In other words, the future of Taiwan will be hinged on Taiwan's interaction with China, and globalization is the cause and catalyst which propel the transformation of the cross-Strait relations.

Ever since China abandoned its autarkic, anti-market economic policies, the economic intercourses between Taiwan and China have increased dramatically. The major factors which influence the contacts between two sides across Taiwan Strait can be illustrated as follows: externally, the trend of regional cooperation, the effectiveness of the supranational institutions and the economic stagnation in the developed countries facilitate the economic integration between Taiwan and China; internally, Taiwan's private actors which seek for business opportunities in China also contribute to the cross-Strait economic

---

23 Keohane and Nye, 2000, 104-105

24 Taiwan was ceded to Japan in 1895.

25 After Taiwan was returned to China by Japan, the civil war between Chinese Communist Party (CCP) and Kuomintang (KMT) again separated Taiwan from Chinese mainland.

26 Ever since the rapprochement between Chin and the US, the military confrontation across Taiwan Strait phased out but the formal communication between China and Taiwan was still suspended. Taiwan put strict restrictions on Taiwanese citizens to visit mainland China until 1987 Taiwanese citizens were allowed to visit their relatives in mainland.

27 President Chen Shui-bian openly describes China as an "enemy nation". See "How Far Chen Shui-bian's Taiwan-Independent-Train Plans to Go," Chinatimes Evening News, Nov. 11, 2004 and "Tests for History and Geography, Bian: China is Another Nation, Not Our Nation," Epochtimes, Nov. 8, 2004

integration, but the political divergence between Taiwan and China interferes the process of the integration.[28] Therefore, although the international economic integration ignites the process of economic convergence between Taiwan and China, Taiwan is bewildered in the vices and virtues of the economic integration with China because China offers Taiwanese enterprises bountiful human resources, land, natural resources and a huge market, yet at the same time China is seen as a threat to Taiwan's security. As a result, although China maintains its belief in the eventual unification with Taiwan, through the process of democratization, Taiwan independence movement has garnered enough momentum to unsettle China's One-China Principle. Anti-China becomes an effective way for Taiwanese politicians to garner votes, and the peaceful coexistence of Taiwan and China will become more difficult to manage. Section 4.4 will offer proof to demonstrate that Taiwan's domestic politics is tilting towards Taiwan independence which will provoke a violent reaction from China.

China's rise on the tide of globalization not only challenges the future development of Taiwan but also places the US into a dilemma regarding its China policy. As the sole patron of Taiwan, the US capitalizes on the cross-Strait hardship to manipulate Taiwan as its pawn to contain China's expansion. At the same time, the international economic interdependence bewilders the US about its containment strategy towards China as the US will never be able to harm China and at the same time remains intact. China acting as "an economic power and a political enigma"[29] challenges the US China policy. On the one hand, the US wants to maintain the de facto separateness between two sides across the Strait because it is afraid that China's emerging economic power will translate into military power which will eventually enable China to undermine the US dominance in Asia Pacific region or even in the world. Thus, it needs Taiwan as an ally to contain China and as an arsenal to stockpile the US weapons at Taiwan's own expense. On the other hand, the US does not want to create a self-fulfilling prophecy by deeming China as an enemy. Moreover, on the international political arena, China can play as a valuable help or a competent hindrance to the US, and the US action will certainly incite China's counteraction.

---

[28] Jiang, 2003

[29] The term is borrowed from "China: Economic Power, Political Enigma", Kurlantzick, 2002.

2.1 The Phenomena of Regionalism under Globalization

In conventional theoretical literature, regionalism is analyzed at an approach of reciprocity-base. In reality, as the dominant motive for smaller countries to join a trading bloc is to gain future access to the large market, smaller countries with less negotiating power usually have to pay the premium in negotiating free trade agreements with larger ones. As a result, regionalism offers larger countries more leverage not only to extract a price from the concessions of smaller countries, but also to enhance their power in bloc-wide negotiations.[30]

As Gibb mentions the formation of regional trading blocs is GATT-consistent, for the Article XXIV of the Agreement allows contracting parties to establish free trade areas and customs unions. Although the GATT held a principle of non-discrimination, it did not rule out the preferential trade arrangements between states.[31] Regionalism may not violate the guidelines of the GATT, but it may hinder the further integration of world economy. Levy takes an angle on the benefits of the domestic interest groups to signify that bilateral free trade agreements can undermine the political support for further multilateral trade liberalization. The disproportional gain of the key agents from the regionalism will motivate them to block multilateral free trade.[32]

In 1980s, the emergence of regionalism in Western Europe and North America influences the structure of the world trade system, and also sparks fierce debate about the role which the regionalism plays in the process of multilateral trading system. Preeg optimistically states trading blocs will act as the stepping stone towards a more liberal trading system[33]; on the contrary, Krugman argues that the formation of trading blocs will hinder the progress of the multilateral trading system. He also concludes that there should be either numerous trading blocs which are so small that no one will deviate from the principle of free trade or only one trading bloc which contains all nations. He conjectures that only these two extreme opposite scenarios will enhance the world welfare most. Under other situations, each trading bloc has the incentive to raise external trade barriers to improve its terms of trade, and should three trading blocs exist, the world welfare will be hindered most.[34] Thurow echoes Krugman's omen by asserting the existence of three major trading blocs centered on the US, Europe and Japan, and he furthermore announces the death of GATT.[35] Bhagwati is also concerned about the expansion of regionalism may

---

[30] Perroni and Whalley, 2000
[31] Gibb, 1994
[32] Levy, 1997
[33] Preeg, 1989
[34] Krugman, 1994
[35] Thurow, 1992

impede the process of the global free trade and the booming bilateralism may erode the base of multilateralism.[36]

To explore the importance of economic geography in economic development, Krugman looks into the approaches regarding the location in which economic activities take place. He argues that the geographical aspects of development are guided by a tug of war between centripetal and centrifugal forces. Centripetal forces such as market size effect, thick labor markets and pure external economies draw the economic activities to certain regions; on the contrary, centrifugal forces such as immobile factors, lend rents and pure external diseconomies disperse them away.[37] Furthermore, Fujita, Krugman and Venables single out the importance of transportation cost in the development of spatial economy. As distance to their suppliers and customers will affect the transaction cost, while other conditions being the same, the producers have the propensity to locate close to their suppliers and customers.[38]

As distance plays a vital role in the location of manufacturers, entrepreneurs may want to reach out the world, but most of them have to start regionally. Regardless the regionalism is only a transient phase to an indiscriminate multilateral trading system or to an imperial tri-polar trading "fortress"; the current trend of regionalization has already posed potential threat to Taiwan economy. Baldwin introduces the domino theory of regionalism which emphasizes the magnetism of regionalization. He argues that the liberalization of the internal trade within a trading bloc will hamper the profits of nonmembers' firms. This disadvantage will entice those governments which previously feel indifferent to membership to join the bloc. As the trading bloc enlarges, the cost to nonmembers will also increase in view of the fact that their firms now face a cost disadvantage in a larger market. The larger the trading bloc becomes, the more pressure the nonmembers will feel.[39] Because of the political disputes with China, Taiwan is excluded in the process of regional economic integration. As of January 4, 2005, 162 Regional Trade Agreements are reported to WTO, and Taiwan participates in none of them.

Whether the formation of regionalization is a step stone toward globalization or a stone on the road to impede the progress of globalization, so far the fierce debate among scholars does not reach any assertive conclusion. Even so, most of the scholars are pessimistic about the ultimate accomplishment of multilateral trading system through regionalism. Although WTO plays a role as the supranational governing institution to supervise the global trade, as it allows nation-states under its supervision to form alliance, the trading blocs will

[36] Bhagwati, 1990, 1991
[37] Krugman, 1998 and 1999
[38] Fujita, Krugman and Venables, 1999
[39] Baldwin, 1993

act as the trade feudalists eroding the function of the WTO, and worst of all small countries will be driven to seek for alliance to sustain the trend of trade blocs.

In the world trading system, though Taiwan has vigorously participated in world trade activity, however, Taiwan's embedded structural weaknesses make it difficult to act as an initiator to promote global trading regulations but as a follower. Regarding the development of Taiwan economy, there are two structural weaknesses. The most significant weakness is Taiwan's scale of populace, land and resources; with scant nature resources and 23 million people crowded on small islands[40], the expansion of Taiwan is limited. The other is the constraint of Taiwan's political power; with only around 25 countries which have formal diplomatic ties with Taiwan[41], Taiwan does not and will not gain assistance from the international community to dominate the international trade regulations.

Ever since Taiwan shifted its import substitution to export-led expansion in 1960s, the international trade has been an important momentum to stimulate the expansion of Taiwan economy. As Dessus, Shea, and Shi observe that in scale, Taiwanese domestic market alone accounts for only a small portion of the world market. A small increase in the world demand will function as a proportionally gigantic demand for a "small country" like Taiwan.[42] Thus if the trend of globalization is multilateralism-oriented, when Taiwan and China compete in the worldwide market, Taiwan has a better chance to avert China's direct influence under this international framework. After all, in a globalized world China's land area is less that one tenth of the world's land area, and China's population is one fifth of the world's; however, in a regionalized world, China accommodates one fifth of Asian land area and one third of Asian population. In a borderless world, China's influence will be diluted by the grand scale of the world, but when the world is regionalized, China's neighbors including Taiwan will be placed under China's influence because of China's scale. China not only plays a significant role in propelling the integration of East Asia but also acts as an economic magnetism which pulls capital, talents and technologies from Taiwan. When the trend of regionalism surpasses multilateralism, Taiwan will be confined in the Asia-Pacific region and will have to directly confront its political arch-rival—China.

---

[40] The total area of Taiwan is close to 36,000 sq. km, much less than 1‰ of the area of the whole world. According to the statistics from UN, the world area was one hundred thirty three million and eight hundred seventy thousand sq. km in 1996.

[41] The number may vary from time to time, but it seldom reaches 30 because of the fierce competition from China.

[42] Dessus, Shea and Shi 1995, P.55

Figure 2-1 Notification to GATT and WTO of Regional Integration Agreements

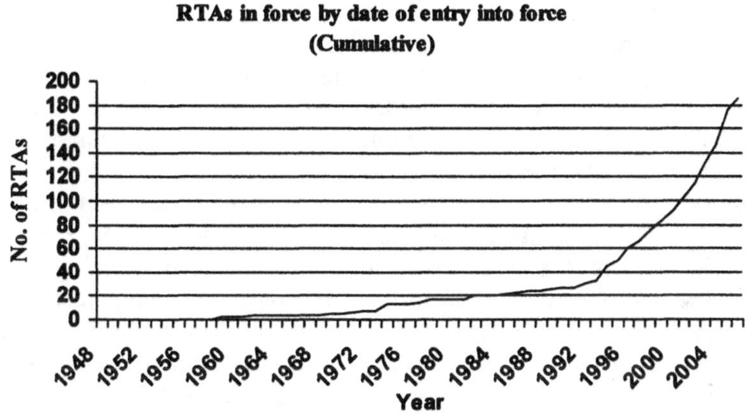

Source: WTO Secretariat

Although so far there is no conclusion about whether the current regionalism is the harbinger of multilateral system or not, however, it is an undisputable fact that the current world economic integration has been more regionalized. From the empirical data, during the last decade, the international community is eager in pursuing regional integration. Figure 2-1 illustrates the surge in the number of regional agreements notified to the General Agreement on Trade and Tariffs (GATT) and the World Trade Organization (WTO) during the 1990s. As of 22 November 2005, there are total 186 notifications from 1948, and 159 out of the 186 agreements enter into force after 1990. Fujita, Krugman and Venables point out as increasing returns and transportation costs make distance an indispensable factor in firms' locational decisions, the flow-on effects will determine the spatial structure of economic activities and create agglomeration.[43] As geographic structure in economic development has its constraint of distance, the outreach of firms' economic activities will be limited. Especially when worldwide consensus is much more difficult to reach than regional one in the real world practice, regionalism will persevere until the integrated regions feel the pressure to further integrate.

[43] Fujita, Krugman and Venables, 1999

2.2 The Emerging China

As long as China maintains its pace of expansion, it is highly possible that China will emerge as a "comprehensive power" which implies China can possess economic and military strength at the same time. Furthermore, because China's rise coincides with the trend of globalization, the trajectory of China's development is embedded into the interdependent world. Therefore, China's active cooperation with other members in the world community becomes critical to maintain stable world order.[44]

China's "open door" policy accompanying with the phenomena of international economic integration such as expanding international trade, disseminating manufacturing processes, diffusing technologies, and liberalizing financial markets has significantly altered China's economy. The compound effect strengthens China's outlook for long-term economic growth and also enhances China's position in the international arena. Although in terms of per capita income, most of China's 1.3 billion people still struggle on the brink of poverty, nevertheless the economic indicators illustrate that China has reached the top rank as an aggregate economy.

The populous base is China's source of economic expansion, and also poses as a difficult development task for China. From Table 2-1, the statistics of GNP per capita shows that the general living standard of Chinese criticizes is still far lagging behind the standard of developed countries and that of newly industrializing economies. In 1986, China's GNP per capita is US$ 277, which was far less than US$ 18,542 of the US, US$ 3,897 of the ROC[45], US$ 16,542 of Japan, US$ 14,552 of the Germany, US$ 13,348 of France, US$ 6,570 of Singapore, and US$ 2,612 of South Korea. Although China's GNP per capita for the first time broke the barrier of US$ 1,000 to reach US$ 1,090 in 2003, it still poses a great gap to Taiwan's US$ 12,725, not to mention the GNP per capital of the developed countries. However, with almost reaching 1.3 billion people as its potential market and cheap labor, China steadily and continually attracts the influx of FDI and its economy expands at a high speed.

[44] Funabashi, Oksenberg, and Weiss, 1994
[45] ROC, Republic of China, the official title of Taiwan

Table 2-1 GNP per Capita of Selective Economies

Unit: USD

Year	ROC	The US	Japan	Germany	France	Singapore	South Korea	PRC
1986	3,897	18,542	16,542	14,552	13,348	6,570	2,612	277
1987	5,192	19,517	19,963	18,134	16,143	7,404	3,249	297
1988	6,223	20,827	24,143	19,415	17,461	8,900	4,302	364
1989	7,455	22,174	24,062	19,080	17,430	10,275	5,200	402
1990	7,918	23,217	24,617	18,961	21,441	12,110	5,891	342
1991	8,769	23,733	28,040	22,136	21,422	13,773	6,817	353
1992	10,274	24,818	30,492	25,076	23,441	15,427	7,193	415
1993	10,757	25,796	34,884	24,103	22,206	17,601	7,822	510
1994	11,613	27,138	38,298	25,690	23,391	20,640	9,015	455
1995	12,488	28,124	42,106	30,104	26,878	23,806	11,471	581
1996	13,073	29,447	37,279	29,097	26,798	25,122	12,244	671
1997	13,449	30,985	34,155	25,767	23,991	25,156	11,237	730
1998	12,268	32,360	31,099	26,216	24,858	20,886	7,477	729
1999	13,114	33,989	35,164	25,677	24,629	20,850	9,549	791
2000	13,985	35,664	37,416	22,757	21,770	23,052	10,888	856
2001	12,621	35,466	32,741	22,550	21,847	20,816	10,180	924
2002	12,588	36,366	31,192	24,093	23,487	21,162	11,479	989
2003	12,730	37,839	33,665	30,667	30,970	21,825	12,628	1,090
2004	14,032	40,150	37,265	33,310	34,112	24,559	14,108	1,300*

Note: * GDP per Capita & the data of PRC in 2004 is calculated by author according to China's *2005 Government Work Report*.
Data from 1986-2003 come from "Taiwan Annual Report (Taiwan Nian Jian)"
Data of 2004 come from the website of Taiwan's Ministry of Economic Affairs
Source: Taiwan Annual Report & Ministry of Economic Affairs, ROC

From Table 2-2, the statistics indicates that during the period of 1975-1980, China remains as a lackluster investment target for FDI, and Brazil poses as the number one FDI recipient among developing countries and its average amount of received FDI is US$ 1.84 billion accounting for 24.4 % of the total FDI flowing into developing countries. However, from 1990 to 1996, China's average inward FDI reaches US$ 22.42 billion accounting for 30% of total FDI flowing into the developing countries and enables China to rank as the number one FDI recipient among the developing country and as the second largest FDI recipient of the world, second only to the average inward FDI of the US. The US attracts an average of US$ 44.76 billion during this period of time. At the same time, the former champion, Brazil drops to the sixth largest FDI recipient among the developing countries and receives an average of US$ 3.22 billion. Moreover, China's average inward FDI in the period of 1998-2003 doubles the average amount in the period of 1990-1996 to US$ 46.6 billion and China remains as the largest FDI recipient in the developing economies. According to the report of OECD Observer[46], since 1996, China has outperformed other developing countries on attracting FDI, but still lags behind several OECD member countries till 2002. In 2002, China surpasses other developing countries as well as developed countries and becomes the world's largest FDI recipient for the first time.

Table 2-2 The Largest Recipients of Inward FDI, 1975-80, 1990-96 and 1998-2003 (annual averages)

Developed Economies								
Economy	75-80 ($m)	%[a]	Economy	90-96 ($m)	%[a]	Economy	98-03 ($m)	%[a]
USA	7,894.0	32.0	USA	44,757.1	29.2	USA	170,653	26.7
UK	5,795.4	21.1	UK	19,613.4	12.8	Belgium[b]	73,953	11.6
France	2,127.3	8.6	France	19,080.1	12.4	UK	62,663	9.8
Netherlands	1,276.6	5.2	Belgium[b]	10,012.1	6.5	Germany	58,161	9.1
Australia	1,271.4	5.2	Spain	8,579.3	5.6	France	44,524	7.0
Belgium[b]	1,203.1	4.9	Netherlands	7,770.9	5.1	Netherlands	39,866	6.2
Germany	1,052.6	4.3	Canada	6,185.3	4.0	Canada	28,240	4.4
Spain	970.5	3.9	Australia	6,118.9	4.0	Sweden	21,809	3.4
Top 8	20,992	85.2	Top 8	122,117.1	79.6	Top 8	543,212	78.1
All	24,642	100	All	153,380.9	100	All	639,975	100
Developing Economies								
Economy	75-80 ($m)	%[d]	Economy	90-96 ($m)	%[d]	Economy	98-03 ($m)	%[d]
Brazil	1,835.8	24.4	China	22,424.7	30.0	China	46,604	22.8
Mexico	1,023.5	13.5	Singapore	7,081.7	9.5	Hong Kong	24,717	12.1
Malaysia	524.3	7.0	Mexico	5,622.1	7.5	Brazil	23,234	11.4
Singapore	502.0	6.7	Malaysia	4,289.0	5.7	Mexico	15,738	7.7
Egypt	376.1	5.0	Argentina	3,690.3	4.9	Singapore	12,192	6.0
Iran	315.5	4.2	Brazil	3,222.7	4.3	Argentina	7,521	3.7
Indonesia	289.9	3.8	Indonesia	2,842.6	3.8	ROK	5,587	2.7
Hong Kong	241.1	3.2	Thailand	2,179.9	2.9	Chili	4,553	2.2
Top 8	5,108.2	67.8	Top 8	51,353.0	68.7	Top 8	140,146	68.5
All	7,339.1	100	All	74,777.6	100	All	204,627	100

Notes: [a] Of all developed country investment.
[b] And Luxembourg.
[c] The tax haven was excluded from the rankings.
[d] Of all developing country investment.

Source: Dunning (2000), Table 2-2 & updated according to *World Investment Report 2004*

[46] OECD Observer No. 237, May 2003

Table 2-3 Top 20 Economies Ranked by Foreign Trade

Unit: Billion USD

Rank	2001		2002		2003		2004	
	Nation	Volume	Nation	Volume	Nation	Volume	Nation	Volume
1	The U.S	1,910.0	The U.S	1,896.3	The U.S	2,029.2	The U.S	2,344.3
2	Germany	1,057.5	Germany	1,105.0	Germany	1,353.3	Germany	1,629.2
3	Japan	752.8	Japan	753.9	Japan	855.1	**China**	**1,154.6**
4	France	599.2	France	623.5	**China**	**851.0**	Japan	1,020.4
5	The U.K.	588.3	**China**	**620.8**	France	734.8	France	914.2
6	**China**	**509.7**	The U.K.	611.8	The UK	685.1	The UK	810.3
7	Canada	481.6	Italy	500.8	Italy	585.9	Italy	700.2
8	Italy	480.4	Canada	474.4	Canada	511.8	Nether-lands	677.5
9	Nether-lands	411.0	Nether-lands	416.1	Nether-lands	492.0	Canada	596.3
10	Hong Kong	391.0	B & L*	414.0	B & L*	489.9	Belgium	592.0
11	B & L*	369.1	Hong Kong	407.7	Hong Kong	455.7	Hong Kong	538.4
12	Mexico	326.8	Mexico	329.4	S. Korea	372.6	S. Korea	478.3
13	S. Korea	291.5	S. Korea	314.6	Spain	364.6	Spain	427.9
14	Spain	268.8	Spain	287.1	Mexico	335.9	Mexico	395.5
15	Singa-pore	237.8	R.O.C.	243.1	Singa-pore	272.1	R.O.C.	350.9
16	R.O.C.	230.1	Singa-pore	241.6	R.O.C.	271.4	Singa-pore	343.5
17	Malaysia	161.9	Malaysia	173.1	Switzer-land	189.2	Russia	279.8
18	Switzer-land	155.2	Switzer-land	163.1	Sweden	183.9	Malaysia	231.8
19	Russia	141.8	Russia	152.9	Malaysia	181.3	Switzer-land	230.1
20	Sweden	139.3	Sweden	148.0	Russia	178.5	Sweden	221.9

Note: * B & L indicate Belgium & Luxemburg. The data of 2004 shows only Belgium's in WTO.

Source: *Import & Export Statistics Monthly*, Ministry of Finance, Executive Yuan, R.O.C., and WTO.

Table 2-3 indicated that China had stabilized itself among the top ten leading trading countries. The ranking of China's foreign trade is 32nd in 1978, and 11th in 1998[47]. In 1999, for the fist time, with the total foreign trade volume of US$ 360.9 billion, China advances itself into the top ten leading economies. In 2000, China surpasses Hong Kong to be the world's eighth largest trading

[47] Information was gotten from Embassy of the People's Republic of China in the Kingdom of Norway.
http://www.chinese-embassy.no/eng/13595.html

economy with the total volume of US$ 455.4 billion. In 2001, pushing down Canada and Italy, China improves its position further to the world's number six leading trading economy with the total trade volume of US$ 509.7 billion. In 2002, its trade volume reaches US 6,208 billion which surpasses that of UK and China becomes the world's fifth largest trading country. In 2003, with the total trade value of USD 851 billion, China replaces France as the world's fourth largest trading country. In 2004, China for the first time becomes one of the world's top three trading economies. China replaces Japan as the world's third largest trading economy with USD 1154.6 billion. Being a developing country, China has demonstrated its economic vigor to catch up the developed countries.

Table 2-4 Top 20 Economies Ranked by Total GDP, PPP GDP in 2003

Unit: Billion USD

Type	Total GDP		PPP GDP	
Ranking	Nation	Amount	Nation	Amount
1	The US	10,881.61	The US	10,871.10
2	Japan	4,326.44	**China**	**6,435.84**[a]
3	Germany	2,400.66	Japan	3,582.52
4	The U.K.	1,794.86	India	3,096.24[b]
5	France	1,747.97[c]	Germany	2,279.13
6	Italy	1,465.90	France	1,632.12
7	**China**	**1,409.85**	The U.K.	1,606.85
8	Spain	836.10	Italy	1,559.32
9	Canada	834.39	Brazil	1,371.66
10	Mexico	626.08	Russia	1,318.83
11	South Korea	605.33	Canada	963.55
12	India	598.97	Mexico	934.55
13	Australia	518.38	Spain	915.07
14	Netherlands	511.56	South Korea	858.03
15	Brazil	492.34	Indonesia	721.58
16	Russia	433.49	Australia	579.66
17	Switzerland	309.47	Turkey	477.26
18	Belgium	302.22	Netherlands	476.91
19	Sweden	300.80	South Africa	475.22[b]
20	Austria	251.46	Iran	474.38

Note: [a]. Estimate is based on a bilateral comparison between China and the United States (Ruoen and Kai, 1995).

[b]. Estimate is based on regression; other PPP figures are extrapolated from the latest International Comparison Programme benchmark estimates.

[c]. Data include the French overseas departments of French Guiana, Guadeloupe, Martinique, and Réunion.

The data of 2004 has not been released on the website of World Bank.

Source: World Bank

From Table 2-4, in 2003, with the total GDP of US$ 1,409.85 billion, China is listed as the world's seventh largest economy, lagging behind the US, Japan, Germany, the UK, France and Italy. The US is the largest economy of the world with the total GDP of US$ 10881.46 billion. However, China is the second largest economy in terms of GDP in Asia, second only to Japan, whose total GDP was US$ 4,326.44 billion. If China's GDP is calculated on a base of purchasing power parity (PPP) exchange rate, in 2003 Chinese GDP is estimated at US$ 6,435.84 billion, second only to the US, which has a total GDP on PPP of US $ 10,871.10 billion. However, when compared with other Asian economies, China is the largest economy in terms of GDP on PPP. Japan has $3,582.52 billion and India has US$3.096.24 billion, ranking second and third respectively in Asia.

Table 2-5 Foreign Exchange Reserves of Selective Countries, Year End (Cumulative)

Unit: Billion USD

Year	ROC	The US	Japan	Germany	France	The UK	South Korea	PRC
1991	82.41	45.90	61.80	57.50	28.30	38.70	13.30	42.70
1992	82.31	40.00	61.90	85.90	24.40	34.10	16.60	19.40
1993	83.57	41.50	88.70	72.70	20.00	34.60	19.70	21.20
1994	92.45	41.20	115.10	72.20	23.50	38.50	25.00	51.60
1995	90.31	49.10	172.40	77.80	23.10	39.20	31.90	73.60
1996	88.04	38.30	207.30	75.80	23.10	37.10	33.20	105.00
1997	83.50	30.80	207.90	69.90	27.10	28.90	19.70	139.90
1998	90.30	36.00	203.20	64.10	38.80	27.40	52.00	145.00
1999	106.20	32.20	277.70	52.70	33.90	30.10	73.70	154.70
2000	106.70	31.20	347.20	49.70	32.10	39.30	95.90	165.60
2001	122.20	29.00	387.70	43.60	26.40	31.90	102.50	212.20
2002	161.70	33.80	451.50	42.50	22.00	32.80	120.80	286.40
2003	206.60	39.72	652.80	41.10	23.10	35.10	154.50	403.30
2004	241.74	42.72	824.26	39.90	29.08	39.48	198.18	609.93

Source: Directorate General of Budget Accounting and Statistics, Executive Yuan, R.O.C.

The corroboration of China's aggregate economic power can also be provided from its increasing foreign exchange reserves. Table 1.5 indicates that China's foreign exchange reserves has been stably accumulated from US$ 19.4 billion in the year end of 1992 to US$ 609.93 billion in the year end of 2004. In the year end of 1992 ROC has US$ 82.31 billion in its foreign exchange reserves, America US$ 40 billion, Japan US$ 61.9 billion, Germany 85.9 billion, France US$ 24.4 billion, the UK US$ 34.1 billion, South Korea US$ 16.6 billion. Among them, only the amount of foreign exchange reserves of the South Korea is less than China's. However, China's fast economic expansion helps it accumulate foreign exchange reserves quicker than most of the industrialized nations and the newly developing economies. China becomes the holder of the world's second largest foreign exchange reserves, only next to Japan, which accumulates US$ 824.26 billion in the year end of 2004.

Table 2-6 Economic Growth Rates of Selective Economies

Unit: annual rate, %

Year	ROC	The US	Japan	Germany*	France	The UK	Italy	South Korea	Hong Kong	PRC
1986	11.6	3.4	2.9	2.3	2.3	4.0	2.8	11.6	11.9	8.8
1987	12.7	3.4	3.8	1.4	2.1	4.6	3.1	11.1	13.4	11.6
1988	7.8	4.1	6.8	3.6	4.3	5.0	3.9	10.6	8.0	11.3
1989	8.2	3.5	5.3	3.7	3.8	2.2	2.9	6.7	2.7	4.1
1990	5.4	1.9	5.2	5.8	2.7	0.8	2.2	9.2	4.0	3.8
1991	7.6	-0.2	3.4	...	1.2	-1.4	1.1	9.4	5.7	9.2
1992	7.5	3.3	1.0	2.2	1.9	0.2	4.3	5.9	6.5	14.2
1993	7.0	2.7	0.2	-0.8	-1.0	2.3	-0.9	6.1	6.3	13.5
1994	7.1	4.0	1.1	2.7	2.1	4.4	2.2	8.5	5.6	12.6
1995	6.4	2.5	2.0	1.9	2.4	2.9	2.9	9.2	3.9	10.5
1996	6.1	3.7	3.4	1.0	1.1	2.8	1.1	7.0	4.2	9.6
1997	6.4	4.5	1.8	1.8	2.4	3.3	2.0	4.7	5.1	8.8
1998	4.3	4.2	-1.0	2.0	3.6	3.1	1.7	-6.9	-5.5	7.8
1999	5.3	4.5	-0.1	2.0	3.3	2.9	1.7	9.5	4.0	7.1
2000	5.8	3.7	2.4	3.2	4.1	3.9	3.2	8.5	10.0	8.0
2001	-2.2	0.8	0.2	1.2	2.1	2.3	1.7	3.8	0.6	7.5
2002	3.9	1.6	-0.3	0.1	1.2	1.8	0.4	7.0	1.8	8.3
2003	3.3	2.7	1.4	-0.2	0.8	2.2	0.4	3.1	3.1	9.5
2004	5.7	4.2	2.7	1.6	2.3	3.1	1.0	4.6	8.2	9.5
AVG	6.3	3.1	2.2	2.0	2.2	2.7	2.0	6.8	5.2	9.2

Note: 1 * Before 1990, the data indicate only Western Germany.
2 AVG: Average
3 The data of ROC, Japan, Germany, South Korea, Singapore, Hong Kong and China have not been adjusted for seasonal variation.

Source: Directorate General of Budget Accounting and Statistics, Executive Yuan, R.O.C.

Aside from these aggregate economic indicators, up to recently, China also keeps a stable pace on its economic growth. China has enjoyed the high single digit growth in the 1990s and the early part of the 21st century, and China's economic expansion seems sustainable. Even though the abrupt downturn of the world economy in 2001 slows down the expansion of the world economy, with gross world product (GWP) increasing by 1.3 percent, China is intact by the worldwide economic slowdown. According to Table 2-6, in 2001, Taiwan suffers a 2.2% economic contraction comparing with previous year's 5.8% economic expansion; the US suffers a setback from previous year's 3.7% increase to 0.8% increase; the economic growth rates of South Korea and Hong

Kong also suffer a serious setback from 8.5% to 3.8% and from 10% to 0.6% respectively; nonetheless China still maintains its robust economic growth rate at 7.5%. In 2002, the world economy experiences a slow recovery and the GWP increases by less than 2 percent. Regardless of the gloomy outlook of world economy, China maintains its fast economic growth rate at 8.3% in 2002. In 2003 and 2004, its economic growth rates are as high as 9.5%. In 2004, Chinese government even has to implement macroeconomic adjustment to manage its overheated economy.

2.3 The Integration of East Asia

Asia lags behind its North American and West European counterparts in its pace to regional economic integration. However, the intraregional economic integration in Asia, especially in East Asia has gradually gathered its momentum. The intraregional economic integration in East Asia starts from the production relocation of Japanese transnational corporations after the Plaza Accord in mid-1980s, and later the depreciation of dollar drive firms from Asian NIEs (Taiwan, Hong Kong, South Korea and Singapore) to look for cheaper labor and land in Southeast Asian nations and China. Consequently, the dispersion of production within East Asian economies boosts intra-industry trade and investment and creates regional production networks.[48]

Figure 2-2 Intraregional Trade Share[a] of Selected Regions, 1962-94

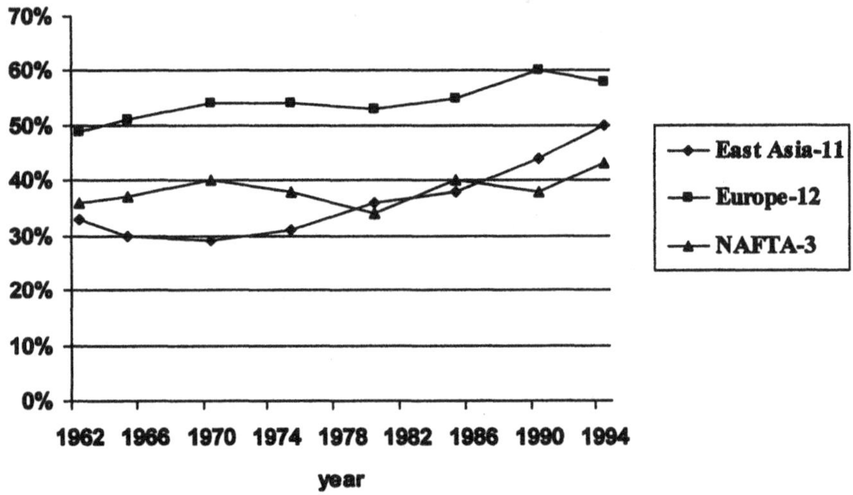

Note: [a] The intraregional trade share (also called intrabloc trade share): intraregional trade as a share of total regional trade.
East Asia-11: the six ASEAN countries (Brunei, Indonesia, Malaysia, Philippines, Singapore and Thailand) plus China, Hong Kong, Korea, Taiwan and Japan.
Europe-12: Belgium-Luxembourg, Denmark, France, Germany, Greece, Ireland, Italy, Netherlands, Portugal, Spain and United Kingdom.
NAFTA-3: the United States, Canada and Mexico.
For the trend of the East Asian trade share after 1994, please see Figure 2-3.
Source: Frankel, 1997, Table 2.1

[48] Kawai and Motonishi, 2004

Figure 2-3 Intraregional Trade Ratio[b] of Selected Regions, 1980-2003

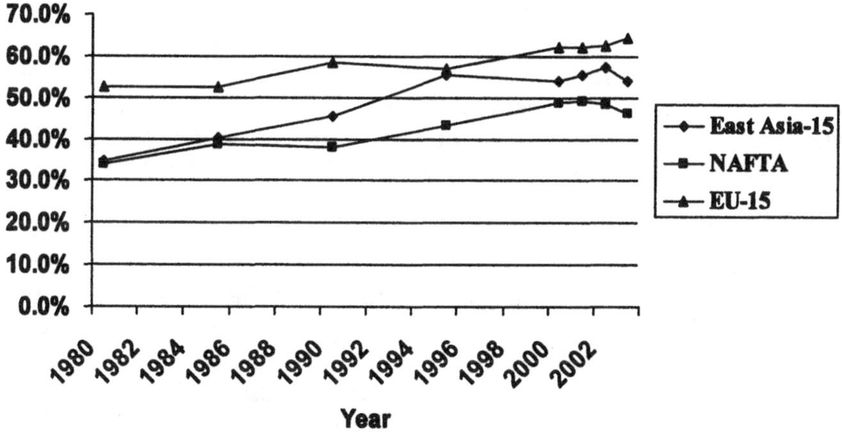

Note: [b] the intra-regional trade ratio: $\dfrac{X_{i,i}}{\left(\dfrac{X_{i,w}+X_{w,i}}{2}\right)}$

$X_{i,i}$ = exports of region i to region i

$X_{i,w}$ = total exports of region i to the world

$X_{w,i}$ = total exports of the world to region i

East Asia-15: Taiwan, Korea, Hong Kong, China and Japan plus the ten ASEAN countries (Brunei, Cambodia, Indonesia, Laos, Malaysia, Myanmar, the Philippines, Singapore, Thailand and Vietnam).
EU-15: Austria, Belgium-Luxembourg, Denmark, Finland, France, Germany, Greece, Ireland, Italy, Netherlands, Portugal, Spain, Sweden, and UK.
Source: Kawai and Motonishi, 2004

Figure 2-2 illustrates that the intraregional trade share of East Asian countries (East Asia-11, EA-11) increases from 1962's 33 percent to 1994's 50 percent. It indicates a 17 percent gain within 32 years. Although in the period of 1962-70, the intraregional trade share of EA-11 has suffered a minor downturn from 33 percent to 29 percent, it later gathers its momentum to go upward.

It rises to 31 percent in 1975, 36 percent in 1980, 38 percent in 1985, 44 percent in 1990, and 50 percent in 1994. At the same period of time, European Union (EU-12) and NAFTA (NAFTA-3) remain relatively stable in their intraregional trade shares. In 1962, the intraregional trade share of EU-12 is 49 percent and rises to 58 percent in 1994, which poses a 9 percent gain in the period of 32 years. In the same period of time, the intraregional trade share of NAFTA-3 rises from 36 percent to 43 percent, a 7 percent gain. As a result, although EA-11 may not be the most integrated region in terms of intraregional trade, it has outpaced its counterparts on the velocity of regional trade integration.

Not only Frankel's data illustrates the trend of integration in terms of regional trade in East Asia, but also Kawai and Motonishi's research confirms it.[49] Figure 2-3 shows the intraregional trade ratio of East Asia-15 rises all the way from 34.7% in 1980 to reach the peak of 57.3% in 2002 and declines slightly back to 54%. During the same period of time, although upward trend of the intraregional trade ratio of EU-15 suffers a minor setback in 1985, the ratio almost follows an upward line from 1980's 52.4% to 2003's 64.4%. The intraregional trade ratio of NAFTA rises from 1980's 33.8% to reach its peak of 49% in 2001 and starts to slide down. In 2002, it slides to 48.3%; in 2003, it slides further to 46%. Both Figures 2-2 and 2-3 demonstrate that the intraregional trade ratio of East Asia has surpassed that of NAFT but is still lower than that of EU-15.

Although some economists adopts the simple trade concentration ratio or trade intensity ratio to verify the geographic concentration of trade and to conclude that the intraregional concentration of the East Asia trade in fact declines from 1960s to 1990s,[50] their conclusion is completely contradict to the result of the intraregional trade share. However as the method of the intraregional trade concentration ratio easily draws biased and inaccurate results, therefore this method is entirely discarded in this article. The following provides the base for the abolition of the simple trade concentration ratio.

---

[49] Kawai and Motonishi, 2004
[50] Frankel 1997

$T_{r,r}$ indicates intraregional trade amount of region r.
$T_{r,w}$ indicates the total trade amount of region r.
$T_{w,w}$ indicates the total world trade amount.
$T_{o,r}$ indicates the trade amount of region r with partners outside of the region.
$T_{o,w}$ indicates the total world trade outside of region r.
$I_{r,r}$ indicates the trade intensity ratio of region r.
$S_{r,r}$ indicates the intraregional trade share of region r.

Trade intensity ratio is defined as:

$$I_{r,r} = \frac{\dfrac{T_{r,r}}{T_{r,w}}}{\dfrac{T_{r,w}}{T_{w,w}}}$$ [51]

Therefore,

$$I_{r,r} = \frac{T_{r,r}}{T_{r,w}}\frac{T_{w,w}}{T_{r,w}} = \frac{T_{r,r}}{T_{r,w}}\frac{(T_{r,w}+T_{o,w})}{T_{r,w}} = \frac{T_{r,r}}{T_{r,w}}\left(\frac{T_{r,w}}{T_{r,w}}+\frac{T_{o,w}}{T_{r,w}}\right) = \frac{T_{r,r}}{T_{r,w}}\left(\frac{T_{o,w}}{T_{r,w}}+1\right)$$

$$= S_{r,r}\left(\frac{T_{o,w}}{T_{r,w}}+1\right)$$

As a result, $I_{r,r}$ is influenced not only by the regional trade ($T_{r,r}$ and $T_{o,r}$) but also by the trade totally irrelevant to the regional trade ($T_{o,w}$). Consequently, the increase of trade outside of the region r ($T_{o,w}$) will increase the intraregional concentration trade ratios of region r.

Take a quasi real life example: during the Cold War era, the communist camp led by Soviet Union can be viewed as an independent and secluded economy which trades within itself. Thus, $S_{r,r}$ is equal to one for the communist region. However, the increased trade between the US and Canada which is to-

[51] This equation is rewritten from Clarete, Edmonds and Wallack (2002).

tally irrelevant to the communist camp will at the same time increase the intraregional concentration trade ratios of the communist camp. Even though the communist camp entirely depends on its intraregional trade, its intraregional concentration trade ratios will fluctuate according to the trade amount of the free camp.

$T_{c,r}$ indicates intraregional trade amount of communist camp.
$T_{c,w}$ indicates the total trade amount of communist camp.
$T_{w,w}$ indicates the total world trade amount.
$T_{o,r}$ indicates the trade amount of communist camp with partners outside of the region.
$T_{o,w}$ indicates the total world trade outside of communist camp.
$I_{c,r}$ indicates the trade intensity ratio of communist camp.

$$I_{c,r}=\frac{T_{c,r}}{T_{c,w}}\left(\frac{T_{o,w}}{T_{c,w}}+1\right)=\frac{T_{o,w}}{T_{c,w}}+1$$

In this case, as the assumption that communist camp trades only within their bloc, $T_{c,r}=T_{c,w}$ is concluded. As 1 is a constant, $I_{c,r}$ will fluctuate according to the change of $T_{o,w}$ and $T_{c,w}$. The increase of $T_{o,w}$ will increase the value of $I_{c,r}$; simultaneously, the increase of $T_{c,w}$ will decrease the value of $I_{c,r}$. Thus, the intraregional concentration trade ratio of the communist camp will increase when the intrabloc trade of the communist camp decreases or the free camp increases its intrabloc trade, and this phenomenon is entirely contradict to the logical conjecture that the increasing intrabloc trade will augment the intraregional concentration trade ratio.

Table 2-7 provided further evidences to question the credibility of the simple intraregional trade concentration ratios. First of all, when the intraregional trade shares of EA-11 ($S_{ea,r}$) increase, the simple intraregional trade concentration ratios of EA-11 ($I_{ea,r}$) simultaneously decrease. From 1962 to 1994, $S_{ea,r}$ increases from 0.33 to 0.50 but $I_{ea,r}$ decreases from 3.93 to 2.09.

From the equation: $I_{ea,r}=S_{ea,r}\left(\frac{T_{oea,w}}{T_{ea,w}}+1\right)$, the only reason that $I_{ea,r}$ does not increase proportionally to $S_{ea,r}$ is that the increase of $T_{ea,w}$ outpaces the increase of $T_{oea,w}$. This result implies that when regional trade of EA-11 expands at a much faster rate than the total world trade outside EA-11, the simple intraregional trade concentration ratios decrease. The consequence is that the simple intraregional trade concentration ratios can be enlarged by the expansion of trade irrelevant to the region or by the contraction of the regional trade. To rephrase the conclusion in a more lively way, that is even when the regional trade of EA-11 remains stable, the increased trade between the US and the European Union will also increase the simple intraregional trade concentration ratio of EA-11.

Moreover, in 1975, the intraregional trade share of EU-12 ($S_{eu,r}$) is 0.54, the intraregional trade share of Andean-4 ($S_{a,r}$) 0.04 and the intraregional trade share of Mecosur-5 ($S_{m,r}$) 0.07; the simple intraregional trade concentration ratio of EU-12 ($I_{eu,r}$) is 1.41, the simple intraregional trade concentration ratio of Andean-4 ($I_{a,r}$) 2.63 and the simple intraregional trade concentration ratio of Mecosur-5 ($I_{m,r}$) 3.82. As a result, a contradict phenomenon emerges. Even though the EU-12's intraregional trade accounts for more than half of its total trade, Andean-4's accounts for only 4 percent of its total trade and Mecosur-5's contributes only 7 percent of its total trade, both Andean-4 and Mecosur-5 have higher simple intraregional trade concentration ratios than EU-12 does. The year of 1975 is not the only year which reflects the contradictory consequence between the intraregional trade share and the intraregional trade concentration ratio. Through 1970s to 1990s, almost all interregional comparison provides the same result that the higher intraregional trade shares accompanying the lower concentration ratios. When the intraregional trade concentration ratio can not be interpreted into the density of intraregional trade, as concentration is defined as the act or process of bringing or directing toward a common center or objective in Merriam-Webster Dictionary, the question of what intraregional trade concentration ratio is directing toward would be raised.

Table 2-7 The Intraregional Trade Shares and the Simple Intraregional Trade Concentration Ratio of Selected Region

Region	Ratio	1962	1965	1970	1975	1980	1985	1990	1994
EA-11	$S_{ea,r}$	0.33	0.30	0.29	0.31	0.36	0.38	0.44	0.50
	$I_{ea,r}$	3.93	3.51	2.86	2.74	2.53	2.24	2.22	2.09
EU-12	$S_{eu,r}$	0.49	0.51	0.54	0.54	0.53	0.55	0.60	0.58
	$I_{eu,r}$	1.18	1.23	1.31	1.41	1.47	1.58	1.51	1.63
Andean- 5	$S_{a,r}$	0.01	0.02	0.02	0.04	0.05	0.05	0.05	0.10
	$I_{a,r}$	0.29	0.69	1.57	2.63	3.37	4.41	8.06	12.63
Mecosur-4	$S_{m,r}$	0.06	0.11	0.10	0.07	0.11	0.07	0.11	0.19
	$I_{m,r}$	2.45	6.42	5.57	3.82	6.14	4.84	9.07	12.84

Note: $S_{r,r}$ represents intraregional trade shares; $I_{m,r}$ represents simple intraregional trade concentration ratios.

The first $_r$ is replaced by the $_{ea}$, $_{eu}$, $_a$, and $_m$ to represent EA-11, EU-12, Andean-5 and Mecosur-4 respectively.

Andean-5 includes Bolivia, Colombia, Ecuador, Peru, and Venezuela.

Mecosur-4 includes Argentina, Brazil, Paraguay and Uruguay.

Source: Frankel, 1997, Table 2.1 and Table 2.2

Therefore, to tackle the problem of geographic trade concentration by adopting the simple intraregional trade concentration ratio is only an econometric illusion. Even though the intraregional trade concentration ratios have been revised, corrected or improved[52], as they derive the results from a variable totally independent from the regional trade, their conclusion will not be applicable to verify the level of how concentrated the intraregional trade will be. Therefore, the decline of East Asia-11's simple intraregional trade concentration ratios do not imply that East Asia-11 concentrates less on its intraregional trade and can not be interpreted as its intraregional economic integration has worsened in terms of trade.

[52] Frankel, 1997

Aside from the integration of intraregional trade, the flow of regional investment caused especially by the shift of production from higher to lower cost location also suggests that East Asia is experiencing the process of regional economic integration. As more and more transnational corporations join the trend of exploring the creation of regional production networks, the process of knitting East Asian economies into more widespread production networks enhances the intraregional FDI flow. According to the data of UNCTAD, FDI within East Asian economies accounted for 49% of flows into this region in 2001-2002, up from 38% in 1999-2000.[53] Figure 2-4 indicates that from 1990 to 2002, the FDI inflows of emerging East Asia mostly come from East Asia. The FDI from Asian NIEs accounts for 33.29% of emerging East Asia's FDI inflows and FDI from Japan accounted for 11.27%. As a result, the FDI from Taiwan, South Korea, Hong Kong Singapore, and Japan accounts for almost 50% (44.56%) of emerging East Asia's FDI inflows.

Moreover, UNCTAD points out that China is not only the most attractive destination for FDI but also one of the top five most expected investing countries worldwide.[54] The emerging China as a source of FDI will reshape Asian economic integration. The FDI flow within East Asia has been molded as a one way flow: Asian NIEs receive direct investment from the developed countries such as the US and Japan and then NIEs provide foreign direct investment to newly emerging ASEAN countries[55] and China.[56] However, as the rapid expansion of China's economy, the one-way-flow East Asian intra-regional investment will experience a structural transformation. As China transforms itself from a FDI recipient to a potential FDI source, the one way FDI flow from NIEs to China may be transformed to a reciprocal base, and Hong Kong now ranks as China's top one FDI recipient. Moreover, China has become the largest foreign investor in some Southeast Asian economics such as Cambodia and by investing into gas and oil industries China has placed large capital on Indonesia's energy sector.[57] As China has dedicated itself on working closely with its neighbors, East Asia will not be ruled out in China's international deployment.

---

[53] UNCTAD, World Investment Report 2004

[54] UNCTAD, E-Brief: "China, an Emerging Outward Investor".

[55] Such as Philippine, Malaysia, Indonesia, Thailand, Vietnam and so on

[56] Isogai and Shibanuma, 2000 and Kawai and Motonishi, 2004

[57] "Emergence of China in the Asia-Pacific: Economic and Security Consequences for the U.S.," by Christopher R. Hill, Assistant Secretary for East Asian and Pacific Affairs, Testimony before the Senate Foreign Relations Committee, Subcommittee on East Asian and Pacific Affairs, June 7, 2005

Figure 2-4 The Sources of Emerging East Asia's FDI Inflows, 1990-2002

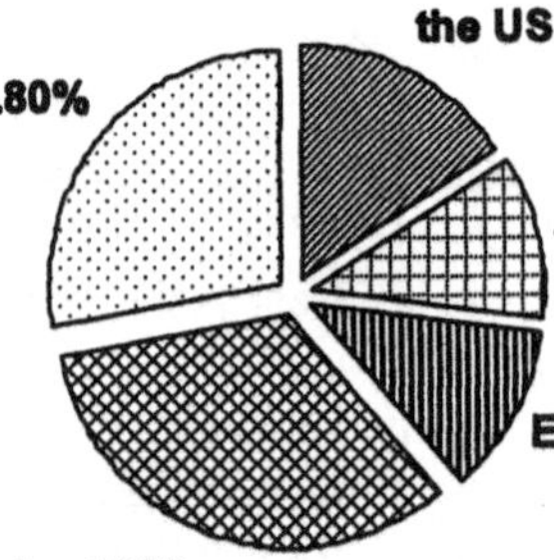

Note: Emerging East Asia: ASEAN, Asian NIEs, and China
Source: Kawai and Motonishi, 2004, calculated

From Table 2-8, Asia receives most of Chinese outward FDI, USD 26.56 billion in total during the year of 2003. China allocates 79.95% of its outward FDI to Asia, 13.91% to Latin America, 1.66% to North America, 1.6% to Europe, 1.47% to Africa, and 1.42% to Oceania. The deployment of China's outward FDI is centered on its neighboring countries. They will be the major beneficiaries from China's economic expansion. In fact China's outflow FDI highly concentrates on Hong Kong and Macao, its Special Administrative Regions. From 1979 to 2002, the FDI outflow to Hong Kong and Macao accounted for 45.6% of China's total outward FDI. During the same period of time, Thailand ranks as the number five FDI recipient from China, Cambodia as number 11, and Vietnam as number 15.[58]

With China's increasing economic power and its willingness to embed itself in an integrated East Asian community, China will play an active and pivotal role in the regionalization of East Asian. Aside from seeking for an ASEAN-China FTA, China also signs a Joint Declaration on the Promotion of Tripartite Cooperation among the People's Republic of China, Japan and the

[58] UNCTAD, World Investment Report 2004, Annex table A.I.12.

Republic of Korea.[59] Due to the historical and cultural differences, aside from a small progress in economic cooperation, East Asian political and security co-operation is dramatically lagging behind EU and NAFTA. However, as China is advancing its economic cooperation with ASEAN, the spillover will promote the political integration and jolt the other regional powers such as Japan and South Korea to join the integration.

Table 2-8 2003 China's Approved FDI Outflows, by Region

Unit: Million USD

Rank	Region	Cumulative Investment Value	Ratio
1	Asia	26,560	79.95%
2	Latin America	4,620	13.91%
3	North America	550	1.66%
4	Europe	530	1.60%
5	Africa	490	1.47%
6	Oceania	472	1.42%
	Total	33,222	100.00%

Note: The statistics includes only non-financial businesses.
Source: Ministry of Commerce of China, 2003 Annual Statistic Gazette of China's Outward FDI (2003 Nien Du Zhong Guo Dui Wai Tou Zi Tong Ji Gong Bao).

China's fast growing consumption market has triggered the hope of its neighbors to expand their economies on China's consumption power. Bearing the thoughts of "a rising tide lifts all boats", Asian nations are eager to join the China's rise.[60] As China's quick economic expansion opens a door for China's peaceful ascending, the effect will soon spill over to the political front, and bring more pressure on its neighbors to further cooperate with it. As China functions as the biggest domino in forming the Asian trade bloc, sooner or later, China will gather enough momentum to draw its neighbors together; at that time, whether Taiwan will be further marginalized on both political and economic fronts will be determined on the cross-Strait political relationships, not on Taiwan's political will.

2.3.1 China's Influence in the Integration of East Asia

Although Association of Southeast Asian Nations (ASEAN), which is established in 1967, is the first organization in East Asia aimed at regional economic cooperation and development, because almost all of the ASEAN members

[59] Chinese Premier Wen Jiabao even initiated to establish a "Tripartite Committee" of China, Japan and South Korea and to study the possibility of a China-Japan-South Korea Free Trade Area.

[60] "China Makes New Friends in the Developing World," by Smith and Prakash, Jan 12, 2004 *Bloomberg News*.

aside from Singapore are positioned in the same phase of economic development, they basically compete with each other for the international trade and FDI rather than coordinate themselves into an economic bloc. However, China's willingness to make a concession to the ASEAN nations commences the process of Asian regional integration. China and ASEAN signed Framework Agreement on ASEAN-China Economic Cooperation (FAACEC), under which both parties agreed to implement an "early harvest program". China would offer early benefits to the ASEAN nations by unilateral tariff reduction. The signed agreement is an overture to eventually accomplish a Free Trade Area (FTA).[61]

Although the ASEAN-China FTA will not be completed until 2010, should the benefit of the ASEAN-China be significant, Japan and South Korea, the other two members in ASEAN+3[62] will be prompted to accelerate their progress in FTA negotiation with ASEAN.[63] Moreover, India also feels the pressure of engaging with ASEAN for a FTA.[64] After all, the ASEAN-China FTA will contain 1.7 billion consumers with a GDP combination of USD 2 trillion and a total trade of USD 1.23 trillion. Although the ASEAN-China FTA is relatively small in comparison to EU and NAFTA, it triggers a "domino effect" on its neighboring countries such as Japan and South Korea.

With its increasing economic strength and subtle diplomatic approach, China has successfully transformed its image from "an intimidating trading competitor, a diplomatic bully and a potential military threat" to "a responsible regional power and an essential engine of Asian economic growth."[65] China's geopolitical location symbolizes the inevitability of its presence in the whole Asian region and results in the intertwined interests and interdependent influence between China and its neighbors.[66] As the process of regional integration moves forward, China will regain its past influence in the region; at the same

---

61 "ASEAN, China Launch First Stage of Free-trade Plan" http://www.globalpinoy.com/old-news/business/2003/oct/07/07busi1.htm

62 ASEAN+3 indicate ASEAN with China, Japan and South Korea.

63 Ever since China concluded its FTA deal with ASEAN, Japan has been anxious to catch up with China's speed. Japanese Prime Minister Koizumi invited ASEAN leaders to Tokyo to pave the way for Japan's economic cooperation with ASEAN, and Japan signed a Framework for Comprehensive Economic Partnership with ASEAN in 2003 to balance China's influence in South East Asia. See Pang (2004), Lee, Kuan Yew, (2004) and "Solidifying East Asian Cooperation," in *Korean Herald*, Apr. 30, 2004.

64 The China-ASEAN FTA in process is the catalyst to prompt India to engage ASEAN for a FTA. See "Asean-India Strategic Engagement: Singapore-India Synergy" Ali, Mushahid and Manjeet S. Pardesi, IDSS Commentaries (Institute of Defence and Strategic Studies).

65 "China's Improving Image Challenges U.S. in Asia," by Pan, Washington Post, Nov. 15, 2003 P. A01.

66 Godwin, 2004

time, Taiwan will be marginalized if it does not seek an effective way to manage its relations with China.

From Table 2-9, China has actively engaged in the intraregional activities, and through the participation into the intraregional dialogues, China will be able to exert the influence parallel to its scale in Asia. China joins the ASEAN+1[67], ASEAN+3[68], and IDEA[69] to promote the East Asian economic cooperation, the ACD[70] to implement Asian cooperation on all aspects, the ARF[71] to conduct security dialogue for the security cooperation of Asia Pacific region, the ACCORD[72] to fight against illicit drugs with ASEAN partners, and initiates Boao Forum for Asia to encourage regional economic integration to accomplish the objective of Asian sustainable development. Aside from joining the intraregional forums, China also devotes itself in sub-regional cooperation by participating in GMS[73], AMBDC[74], Quadrilateral and MRC[75]. Moreover, China is also vigorous in joining the interregional mechanism such as APEC[76], ASEM[77] and EALAF[78] to strengthen the cross-regional cooperation.

In contrast to China's omnipresence in all regional forums, Taiwan is excluded by all but APEC because of China's increasing political power in Asian region. China is the only country centered by Russia, Northeast Asia, Southeast Asia, South Asia and central Asia. China's pivotal geographic position makes it an indispensable core of Asian development. Not only the intraregional forums but also the sub-regional dialogues require China's participation. As countries along the Mekong River intend to explore the wealth of the river, without China's cooperation, all their efforts will be futile because China locates on the upstream of the river, and once China recklessly pollutes the river, all the countries along the shore will suffer. Moreover, China's huge size determines China's capability in sabotaging Asian development through the export of its internal instability as well as in buoying Asian economy through the spill-over effect of its economic expansion. China's stable progress becomes the linchpin to Asian development. Moreover, China's economic presence in Asia carries real potential to spill over into international political and diplo-

67 ASEAN+1 mean ASEAN with China, South Korea or Japan.
68 ASEAN+3 indicate ASEAN, China, South Korea and Japan.
69 IDEA is Initiative for Development in East Asia.
70 ACD is Asia Cooperation Dialogue.
71 ARF is ASEAN Regional Forum.
72 ACCORD is ASEAN-China Cooperative Operation in Response to Dangerous Drugs.
73 GMS is Greater Mekong Sub-region.
74 AMBDC is ASEAN-Mekong Basin Development Cooperation.
75 MRC is Mekong River Commission, and China is invited as an observer.
76 APEC is Asia-Pacific Economic Cooperation.
77 ASEM is Asia-Europe Meeting.
78 EALAF is East Asia-Latin America Forum.

matic fields. In order to consolidate the Sino-ASEAN economic relationships, ASEAN leaders respond to China's purposiveness by unprecedentedly issuing a chairman's statement to reaffirm their commitment to the one China policy at the eighth China-ASEAN summit held on 29 November 2004.[79]

Not only ASEAN nations but also Japan and South Korea are under the pressure of siding with China on the Taiwan issue. China has superseded the US as Japan's and South Korea's largest trading partner. From a geopolitical and geostrategic perspective, Japan may not embrace the thought of the Sino-Taiwan unification, but Japanese government has never publicly defied one-China policy. As South Korea relies on China to stabilize the troubled relationships with its North counterpart, it has no reason to challenge China's stance on Taiwan issue. As a result, from Japan, South Korea, to East Asian nations like Indonesia, Philippine, Thailand, Singapore, this belt-shaped regional integration will encircle Taiwan's economic development. In order to seek for Taiwan independence, Taiwanese leaders[80] have been implicitly expecting the US exert its influence in Asia and develop a containment strategy by coordinating Japan, South Korea, Taiwan and ASEAN nations to cripple China's development. Conversely, the US vacillates in adopting a containment strategy against China, and the flourishing regional economy of East Asia led by China complicates any US attempt to forge an East Asian frontline coalition against China.

By emphasizing the importance of resolving disputes with its neighbors through the framework of international institutions, and taking unilateral trade concessions to members of ASEAN,[81] China has assuaged the fear of its neighbors about "China threat". According to a poll, about 76 percent of residents in Bangkok named China as Thailand's closest friend. In contrast, fewer than 8 percent choose Japan; only 9 percent pick the US.[82] Thailand is not the only country which has been susceptible to China's "charm offensive", Indonesia, Malaysia and Philippine also feel China's growing soft power and are eager to improve the bilateral ties with China by frequent exchanges of high-level visits.

---

[79] Official Website of ASEAN

[80] The former President and current President of Taiwan are pro-Taiwan-independence extremists.

[81] "China: Global Citizen or Growing Menace?" *The Daily Yomiuri*, Tokyo: May 16, 2004, P. 1

[82] "China's Improving Image Challenges U.S. in Asia," by Philip P. Pan, *Washington Post Foreign Service*, Nov. 15, 2003, P. A01

Table 2-9 East Asian Nations and Growing Regionalism

Forums	ASEAN 10	ASEAN 7	China	Japan	South Korea	DPRK & Mongolia	Hong Kong	Taiwan	Mekong Countries
ASEAN+1	y	n	y	y	y				
ASEAN+3	y	n	y	y	y				
APEC		y	y	y	y		y	y	
ASEM		y	y	y	y				
GMS			y						y[1]
ARF	y	n	y	y	y	y			
EALAF	y	n	y	y	y				
IDEA	y	n	y	y	y				
ACD	y[2]	n	y	y	y				
AMBDC	y	n	y	Invited	Invited				
ACCORD	y	n	y						
Quadrilateral			y						y[3]
MRC			Observer						y[4]
Boao Forum	y	n	y	y	y				

Note:

ASEAN 10 means all the 10 Member Countries of the Association.

ASEAN 7 means the older 7 Member Countries, except Cambodia, Laos and Myanmar.

n means not applicable.

y[1] The Mekong countries in the ADB-organized Greater Mekong Sub-region (GMS) Economic Cooperation Conference are Cambodia, Laos, Myanmar, Thailand and Viet Nam. Cambodia will host the first GMS Summit in Phnom Penh on 3 November 2002 to commemorate the 10th anniversary of the GMS. The President of the ADB and the Chinese Premier have been invited to attend.

EALAF is East Asia-Latin America Forum. ASEAN, China, Japan and the RoK have teamed up to engage 17 countries in Latin America in economic cooperation consultations.

IDEA is Japan's Initiative for Development in East Asia. Japan convened the Ministerial Conference on IDEA in Tokyo on 12 August 2002.

y[2] in **ACD** is Thailand's initiative on Asia Cooperation Dialogue. Myanmar did not attend the inaugural meeting in Cha-am, Thailand, last June because of border tensions with Thailand. Thailand will host the second ACD in Chiang Rai next year

ACCORD is ASEAN-China Cooperative Operations in Response to Dangerous Drugs.

AMBDC is ASEAN's initiative on ASEAN-Mekong Basin Development Cooperation. The AMBDC's best known flagship project is the Singapore-Kumning Rail Link (SKRL). Japan and the RoK have been invited to join the AMBDC as its core members; but both of them have declined the invitation, saying that they need more time to study the AMBDC's activities.

y[3] in **Quadrilateral** are Laos, Myanmar, Thailand and China. The Quadrilateral are promoting, among others, river transport on and tourism along the Mekong River.

MRC is the Mekong River Commission based in Phnom Penh.

y[4] are Cambodia, Laos, Thailand and Viet Nam; China and Myanmar are Observers in the MRC. Both China and Myanmar are seriously considering joining the MRC.

*The **Boao Forum for Asia** was initiated by China. Though it saw active participation of several government leaders, the BFA is considered as a Track II forum.*

Source:

ASEAN Secretariat

China and most of the ASEAN members (aside from Singapore) are positioned in their developing phases. While China acting as a newly Industrializing economy which attracts most of the FDI pouring into Asian region, ASEAN nations will inevitably suffer from the FDI diverting effect. From Table 2-10, while Taiwan's FDI flowing to China surges from USD 174.16 million in 1991 to USD 6,940.66 million in 2004, the money pouring into ASEAN relatively decreases from USD 3,512.37 million of 1991 to USD 1,780.36 million of 2004. In 1991, when choosing between China and ASEAN, Taiwanese businessmen invest almost 95 percent of their fund into ASEAN, but in 2004, the percentage of Taiwan's FDI to ASEAN against Taiwan's FDI to ASEAN and China drops to 20.41%. While Taiwan's FDI to China follows an upward trajectory, the FDI to ASEAN moves in the opposite direction. Thus, China may have been the cause of diverting FDI away from its neighbors, but it is difficult to conclude that the diversion effect will definitely harm the economy of its neighbors because of the effect of "a rising tide".

China has successfully persuaded its neighbors that the spillover effect of its booming economy will bring the prosperity to the whole region. The short-term economic hardship at the commencing phase of China's ascendance may be inevitable, but by building bilateral ties, promoting institutions for regional cooperation, and taking a much more active and responsible role in multilateral organizations, Chinese government assures its trading partners and rivals that China is willing to cooperate with them, to abide by the international norm and to share China's economic development.[83] Moreover, China's high-speed economic growth will transform China from a one-way FDI-recipient to a potential source of capital supplier to benefit its neighbors.[84]

---

[83] "China: Global Citizen or Growing Menace?" *The Daily Yomiuri*, Tokyo: May 16, 2004, P. 1

[84] "On order from the government, Chinese investment in Asia is growing, too, by more than 20 percent annually and by more than 40 percent in some countries. In some cases, Chinese companies are buying assets from U.S. and European investors who are pulling out. The biggest investments have been in minerals, oil and other raw materials needed to fuel the Chinese economy." By Philip P. Pan, "China's Improving Image Challenges U.S. in Asia," Washington Post Nov. 15, 2003.

Singapore's Ministry of Trade and Industry also expected China's booming economy will spill over to the rest of Asian region by claiming, "As China develops, and as the coastal regions of China become more expensive, the outflow of Chinese FDI will also grow." http://www.mti.gov.sg/public/FTA/frm_FTA_Default.asp?sid=180&cid=1904

Table 2-10 Taiwan's FDI to China and ASEAN

Unit: Million USD

Year	FDI Amount to ASEAN (1)	FDI Amount to China (2)	Total (3)	(1)/(3) %	(2)/(3) %
1991	3,512.37	174.16	3,686.53	95.28	4.72
1992	2,007.40	246.99	2,254.39	89.04	10.96
1993	1,170.28	1,140.37	2,310.65	50.65	49.35
1994	4,975.42	962.21	5,937.63	83.79	16.21
1995	4,231.86	1,092.71	5,324.57	79.48	20.52
1996	4,430.03	1,229.24	5,659.27	78.28	21.72
1997	4,842.35	1,614.54	6,456.89	75.00	25.00
1998	1,420.84	1,519.21	2,940.05	48.33	51.67
1999	2,000.22	1,252.74	3,252.96	61.49	38.51
2000	1,347.31	2,607.14	3,954.45	34.07	65.93
2001	1,418.49	2,784.15	4,202.64	33.75	66.25
2002	692.68	3,858.76	4,551.44	15.22	84.78
2003	1,011.25	4,594.99	5,606.235	18.04	81.96
2004	1,780.36	6,940.66	8,721.023	20.41	79.59

Note:

(1) ASEAN here includes only Thailand, Singapore, Malaysia, Indonesia, Philippine, Vietnam, and Cambodia.

(2) The retroactive registered figures are excluded. Thus, Taiwan's investments into China are underestimated.

Source:

- Investment Commission, Ministry of Economic Affairs
- Industrial Development & Investment Center, Ministry of Economic Affairs

Aside from being a potential FDI supplier, the expansion of China's domestic market has granted its neighboring countries generous trade surplus and created an economically interdependent environment for Asian region. Table 2-11 indicates that in 1993 China suffered a minor USD 0.19 billion trade deficit against ASEAN nations, but during the period of 1994 to 1998 China enjoyed trade surplus against them. However, since 1999, China's improving economic well being has benefited ASEAN nations in terms of trade. In 1999, ASEAN nations enjoy a trade surplus of USD 7.06 billion against China, and in 2001, the surplus raises to USD 7.72 billion. In 2002, ASEAN nations suffer USD 3.66 billion trade deficit, and the deficit shrinks to 1.23 billion. Moreover, from 1993 to 2003, the Sino-ASEAN trade amount increases over five folds from USD 8.87 billion to USD 55.31 billion. The bilateral trade basically follows an upward trajectory even though suffers minor setbacks in 1998 and 2001. However, as the data of 1999 to 2001 includes Hong Kong, the special administrative region of China, the trade amount of those years may reflect the real economic power of China than that of remaining years.

Table 2-11 ASEAN Trade with China

Unit: Billion USD

Year	Export	Import	Total	Trade Difference
1993	4.53	4.34	8.87	0.19
1994	5.30	5.76	11.06	-0.46
1995	6.20	7.13	13.33	-0.93
1996	7.47	9.22	16.69	-1.74
1997	9.17	13.48	22.65	-4.31
1998	9.20	11.21	20.41	-2.01
1999	26.47	19.41	45.88	7.06
2000	35.03	26.48	61.52	8.55
2001	31.55	23.83	55.39	7.72
2002	19.55	23.21	42.76	-3.66
2003	27.04	28.27	55.31	-1.23

Note: 1.Here ASEAN including only Brunei Darussalam, Cambodia, Indonesia, Malaysia, Myanmar, Philippines, Singapore, and Thailand.

2. China including Hong Kong in 1999 – 2001.

Source: ASEAN Secretariat.

China's economic performance has strengthened Beijing's regional and international roles. In Asian financial crisis happening in 1997, China effectively sustains its currency against depreciation. China's effort to stabilize the financial market reestablishes China's image as a responsible regional power. Furthermore, China wins over the trust and respect from its financial-crisis-badgered neighboring countries by offering economic aid to them.[85] Aside from the economic front, China has also actively sought for cooperation on the diplomatic front. By emphasizing on marinating stability as stability can help China focus on economic growth and domestic problem, China's arguments about its peaceful ascendance demonstrate high credibility to its neighboring countries. Since China becomes the locomotive of the regional expansion, China's economic growth also has spillover effects on political and diplomatic aspects. Especially China has shifted from "not meddling in others' affairs, minding one's own business and developing oneself (Shao Guan Shi, Kan Hao Men, Fa Zhan Hao Zi Ji)"[86] to actively participating into the regional disputes.

[85] "It (China) actively participated in the IMF-organized aid projects for some Asian countries. In the wake of the financial crisis in 1997, the Chinese Government provided Thailand and other Asian countries with over 4 billion US dollars in aid, within the framework of IMF or through bilateral channels. It offered Indonesia and other countries export credit and emergency medicine given gratis."
http://www.fmprc.gov.cn/eng/ziliao/3602/3604/t18037.htm

[86] "After the disruption of Soviet Union, China developed a 24-word strategic guidance: calmly observing, placidly dealing with, stabilizing foundation, avoiding spotlight, never

Moreover, instead of appealing to might, China takes a lead to look for diplomatic solutions in the regional disputes, even in the international affairs. China takes a leading role in hosting the six-party negotiations to resolve the standoff over North Korea's nuclear crisis. China supports a political solution instead of a military action in dealing with Iraq issue. Although it fails to stop the US military action against Iraq, China apparently stands by the side of France, Germany and Russia in Security Council and wants to tackle the Iraq crisis peacefully.

Ever since ASEAN invited the heads of state from China, South Korea and Japan to take part in a summit meeting held on the occasion of the 30th anniversary of the founding of ASEAN in December 1997, the annually-held ASEAN+3 summit meeting has offered China a chance to consolidate its relations with ASEAN nations. Because this forum excludes the participation of the US, with the geographical proximity, China stands a good chance to balance the US influence in this region. For Southeast Asian nations realize that none of them can stand against China alone, therefore they have insisted on dealing with regional disputes with China under the multilateral framework, but in the past, China preferred bilateral negotiations. However, to cultivate its relations with ASEAN nations, Beijing is willing to place itself under the multilateral framework of ASEAN+1[87] or ASEAN+3. In Nov. 4, 2002, China and ASEAN signed Declaration on the Conduct of Parties in the South China Sea, in which the governments of ASEAN and China reaffirm they will fortify their friendship and cooperation to promote mutual trust.[88]

By signing Declaration on the Conduct of Parties in the South China Sea, China caves in to ASEAN's demand for a multilateral framework. By doing so, China wins the ticket to advance into Southeast Asia and replaces the image of "China threat" with that of "a benign China with opportunities (for business adventures)" in the perception of its neighbors. As a result, the strengthening bonds between China and ASEAN nations will inevitably threaten Taiwan's already-marginalized international status. China has played an active role in promoting regional integration. On the contrary, Taiwan seldom has a stage to play as a member in the regional community.

---

taking a lead and acting on something (Leng Jing Guan Cha, Chen Zhuo Yin Fu, Tao Guang Yang Hui, Jue Bu Dang Tou, You Suo Zuo Wei)."
See "Meddle not Other's Affairs; Watch Over One's Door; Avoid Spotlight, " *Xin Dao Daily*, Sep 20, 1999

[87] Although ASEAN+1 can imply indicate ASEAN with China, South Korea or Japan, here it indicates with China.

[88] See "Declaration on the Conduct of Parties in The South China Sea," in the website of ASEAN Secretariat.

Table 2-12 China's Top 10 Trade Partners in 2004

Unit: USD Billion

Period & Items / Region	Ranking	Trade Volume	Percentage (%)
Japan	3	167.89	17.51
Hong Kong	4	112.68	11.75
ASEAN	5	105.88	11.04
South Korea	6	90.07	9.39
Taiwan	7	78.32	8.17
East Asian Sub-Sum	-	**554.84**	**57.86**
US	2	169.63	17.69
Canada	10	15.52	1.62
North American Sub-Sum	-	185.15	19.31
EU	1	177.29	18.49
Russia	8	21.23	2.21
Australia	9	20.39	2.13
Others Sub-Sum	-	139.5	22.83

Source: Ministry of Commerce, the People's Republic China

Japan is China's third largest trade partner and China is Japan's largest trade partner. Moreover, Japan acts as China's third largest investor. The strengthening Sino-Japanese economic ties have cultivated a strong interdependence between China and Japan. China is a developing country with the potential to become the world's largest market; Japan is the world's second largest economy in terms of GDP with abundant capital and technologies. Japan can provide capital and knowledge for China's economic development, and at the same time, China can supply cheap human resources and massive market to rehabilitate Japan's sluggish economic performance. Thus, although China and Japan may disagree with each other in terms of politics, the economic symbiosis between China and Japan will make these two countries indispensable to each other.

Table 2-13 Top Inward FDI Countries/Areas to China by Region
(As of the end of 2004)

Unit: USD million

Country/Area	Rank**	Contractual Value	Share %	Realized Value	Share %
Total	-	109,660.9	100.00	56,210.1	100.00
Hong Kong	1	46,465.2	42.37	24,157.4	42.98
Japan	**3**	6,665.0	6.08	4,684.6	8.33
Taiwan	4	7,933.5	7.23	3,960.5	7.05
South Korea	6	5,056.4	4.61	2,593.5	4.61
Singapore	7	4,799.1	4.38	2,553.9	4.54
Macau	13	1,396.9	1.27	573.6	1.02
Sub-Total	-	**72,316.1**	**65.95**	**38,523.5**	**68.53**
United States	2	9,860.9	8.99	4,802.9	8.54
Virgin Islands*	5	8,140.8	7.42	3,689.5	6.56
Cayman Islands*	11	1,442.0	1.31	671.2	1.19
Canada	14	1,418.9	1.29	453.5	0.81
Sub-Total	-	**14,548.8**	**13.27**	**9,617.1**	**17.11**
United Kingdom	8	2,212.6	2.02	1,223.1	2.18
Germany	9	1,799.5	1.64	990.9	1.76
France	10	914.5	0.83	680.4	1.21
Netherlands	12	1,091.8	1.00	587.4	1.05
Sub-total	-	**5,012.1**	**4.57**	**3,481.8**	**6.19**
Others	-	**10,464.0**	**9.54**	**4,587.7**	**8.16**

Note: * Taiwan had maintained its position as China's second largest investor until 1996. After that, Taiwan's nominal investment to China declined, but at the same time, these famous tax havens such as Virgin Islands and Cayman Islands started to emerge as China's major investors. See Kuo, 2003.

** Ranked by Realized Value.

Source: Ministry of Commerce of P.R.C., modified by the author

2.3.2 The Economic Interdependence between Taiwan & East Asia

Therefore, due to the phenomenon of nominal globalization but regionalization in essence, Taiwan economy has already been involved in the trend of regionalism, and as China acts as the primary advocate of East Asian integration, this trend of regionalization will eventually suffocate Taiwan's economic growth if the current economic integration and political disintegration with China remain unchanged.

China has transformed itself into an amicable neighbor and sought for cooperation instead of confrontation with its neighbors. By concluding an agreement on the creation of a CAFTA, China plays an active role in cementing the East Asian regional integration. In contrast to the previous forecast that

China's prosperity would be at the expense of its neighbors, Asia is flourishing with China's growth.[95]

Rasul mentioned that the dynamic politico-economic processes as regional integration are driven by two human motivations: association and dissociation. As human beings survive better in group than individually, mankind are driven to seek for association; on the other hand, as self-interest acts as an indispensable element for the individual motivation, individuals are often enticed to deviate from the group guidelines for personal interests.[96] After all, in the processes of integration, group members can enhance individual interests though unity especially when confronting outsiders, but they have to accommodate themselves with other group members and to endure the inconvenience of group regulation to maintain esprit de corps. The urge to associate and to dissociate facilitates and impedes the process of regional integration.

As "domino theory" indicates the larger the region becomes, the stronger the magnetism will be. Therefore, though the future of multilateral trading system is still hinged on the power struggle of those major players like the US, European Union, Japan, and even China, the pattern of Taiwan's trade has been woven into the processes of East Asian economic integration. From Table 2-14, Taiwan's export value with the Asian area has increased from 1981's USD 6.56 billion which account for 29.01% of Taiwan's total exports to 2004's USD 107.96 billion which account for 62.04% of Taiwan's total exports. At the same time, Taiwan's export amount to its former major export market—North America has increased from USD 8.73 billion in 1981 to USD 29.76 billion in 2004, but the percentage of Taiwan's exports from North America has declined from 38.61% to 17.10%. Taiwan's exports to Europe remain at a relatively stable status. Taiwan's exports to Europe have increased from 1981's USD 2.89 billion to 2004's USD 23.3 billion, but from 1981 to 2004, the ratios of Taiwan's exports to Europe accounting for total export fluctuate between the lowest 9.75% to the highest 18.38%. Table 2-14 clearly illustrates that Asia has become Taiwan's most important export region; on the contrary, the importance of America as Taiwan's export market is decreasing.

Aside from the export, Asian area is also Taiwan's most important import source. From Table 2-15, the import value from Asian area increases from USD 7.97 billion in 1981 to USD 97.72 billion in 2004 and it represents an over tenfold increase. The percentage of Taiwan's imports from Asian region was 37.60%, and it followed an almost perfectly upward trajectory to reach its peak of 58.24% in 2003 and slid slightly back to 58.20% in 2004. Although

---

[95] "*China's Stature Growing in Asia; The nation's economic power is fueling trade, prosperity and a new sense of shared destiny*" Los Angeles Times, December 28, 2003, P. A1.
[96] Rasul, 2002

Taiwan's imports from North America also increase from USD 5.03 billion to USD 22.83 billion from 1981 to 2004, the percentage of Taiwan's imports from North America on the other hand decreased from 23.74% to 13.60%. During the same period of time, the percentage of Taiwan's imports from Europe increases at first from 1981's 9.35% to reach its peak at 1986's 19.68%, suffers a minor setback to 1997's 18.88% but regains its upward momentum to 1998's 19.67%, and goes down almost all the way to 2004's 12.69%. Therefore, in terms of trade, Taiwan has been heavily rely on its Asian partners and gradually integrated into the Asian region.

Table 2-14 Taiwan's Export Value and Percentage to Total Export by Region

Unit: USD Billion

Year	**Asia**	**%**	Europe	%	North America	%	Others	%
1981	6.56	29.01	2.89	12.77	8.73	38.61	4.43	19.60
1982	6.07	27.36	2.59	11.65	9.27	41.74	4.27	19.25
1983	6.48	25.80	2.76	10.99	12.06	48.01	3.82	15.20
1984	7.63	25.07	3.06	10.06	15.78	51.83	3.97	13.05
1985	8.36	27.20	3.00	9.75	15.72	51.16	3.65	11.89
1986	10.34	25.94	4.77	11.98	20.29	50.89	4.46	11.20
1987	15.14	28.21	7.89	14.70	25.25	47.03	5.40	10.06
1988	19.91	32.82	9.89	16.30	25.05	41.29	5.82	9.59
1989	23.40	35.29	10.95	16.52	25.80	38.91	6.15	9.28
1990	25.69	38.22	12.23	18.20	23.30	34.67	5.98	8.90
1991	31.15	40.89	14.00	18.38	23.95	31.43	7.08	9.29
1992	34.80	42.72	13.93	17.10	25.22	30.95	7.52	9.23
1993	39.07	45.92	12.90	15.16	25.13	29.53	7.99	9.39
1994	45.94	49.38	12.93	13.89	25.80	27.72	8.38	9.01
1995	58.67	52.54	15.73	14.08	27.84	24.93	9.43	8.44
1996	60.75	52.40	16.94	14.61	28.27	24.38	9.98	8.61
1997	61.54	50.41	18.42	15.08	31.15	25.52	10.97	8.99
1998	50.15	45.35	19.64	17.76	30.95	27.99	9.85	8.90
1999	59.21	48.70	20.32	16.71	32.65	26.85	9.41	7.74
2000	76.67	51.69	23.71	15.99	36.70	24.74	11.24	7.58
2001	64.50	52.50	19.81	16.12	29.22	23.78	9.34	7.60
2002	74.29	56.88	18.55	14.21	28.30	21.67	9.46	7.24
2003	85.63	59.39	20.45	14.19	27.41	19.01	10.68	7.41
2004	107.96	62.04	23.43	13.47	29.76	17.10	12.86	7.39

Source: Directorate-General of Budget, Accounting & Statistics (DGBAS) Executive Yuan, Taiwan, R.O.C. Calculated by Author

Table 2-15 Taiwan's Import Volume and Percentage to Total Import by Region

Unit: USD Billion

Year	Asia	%	Europe	%	North America	%	Others	%
1981	7.97	37.60	1.98	9.35	5.03	23.74	6.21	29.30
1982	6.48	34.31	2.11	11.16	4.88	25.83	5.42	28.69
1983	7.43	36.64	2.27	11.19	5.01	24.69	5.58	27.49
1984	8.75	39.83	2.38	10.84	5.44	24.78	5.39	24.55
1985	7.74	38.52	2.45	12.21	5.12	25.45	4.79	23.82
1986	10.77	44.53	3.24	13.38	5.92	24.47	4.26	17.61
1987	15.73	44.96	5.28	15.09	8.30	23.72	5.68	16.22
1988	20.93	42.14	8.01	16.12	13.96	28.11	6.78	13.64
1989	23.27	44.51	8.38	16.04	13.00	24.87	7.62	14.58
1990	23.85	43.59	9.59	17.52	13.45	24.58	7.83	14.31
1991	28.94	46.04	9.97	15.87	15.15	24.11	8.79	13.99
1992	33.60	46.66	12.47	17.32	16.95	23.54	8.99	12.48
1993	36.25	47.04	13.56	17.60	17.84	23.15	9.41	12.21
1994	40.93	47.95	15.95	18.69	19.29	22.61	9.18	10.75
1995	51.20	49.45	18.70	18.06	22.37	21.60	11.28	10.89
1996	48.87	47.74	20.14	19.68	21.33	20.84	12.03	11.75
1997	55.02	48.08	21.60	18.88	24.82	21.69	12.99	11.35
1998	52.90	50.55	20.59	19.67	20.84	19.91	10.34	9.88
1999	60.60	54.75	17.58	15.89	20.82	18.81	11.69	10.56
2000	78.48	56.05	19.01	13.58	26.40	18.86	16.11	11.51
2001	58.65	54.69	14.99	13.98	19.23	17.93	14.38	13.41
2002	64.08	56.94	14.64	13.01	19.04	16.92	14.77	13.13
2003	74.11	58.24	16.24	12.76	17.90	14.07	19.00	14.93
2004	97.72	58.20	21.30	12.69	22.83	13.60	26.05	15.51

Source: Directorate-General of Budget, Accounting & Statistics (DGBAS) Executive Yuan, Taiwan, R.O.C. Calculated by Author

Aside from the trade, the inward and outward Foreign Direct Investment (FDI) also suggests that Taiwan has gradually shifted its economic focus to Asian region. According to the statistics of the Taiwan Investment Commission, the Asian area and the American area have been the major FDI contributors and recipients of Taiwan. From Table 2-16, although the percentage of Taiwan's approved inward FDI from the Asian area and from the American area fluctuates fiercely. The former ranges from as high as 66.16 percent in 1983 and as low as 22.11 percent in 1981, the latter from 69.14 percent in 1981 to 27.18 percent in 1989. Although Table 2-16 does not illustrate any special pattern for Taiwan's inward FDI, the approved foreign investment from the Asian area and the American area constantly accounted for over 80% of its FDI. The phenomenon that the most of the FDI flows into Taiwan from Asia and

America coincides with the fact that Taiwan maintains a special relationship with the US and with Japan.[97]

Table 2-16 Statistics on Approved Inward Foreign Investment by Region

Unit: USD million

Year	Asia	%	America	%	Others	%
1981	78.77	22.11	246.33	69.14	31.20	8.76
1982	179.65	56.09	93.42	29.17	47.22	14.74
1983	248.35	66.16	103.90	27.68	23.14	6.16
1984	162.69	31.35	261.30	50.35	94.98	18.30
1985	164.01	24.82	347.52	52.60	149.17	22.58
1986	321.56	45.57	195.63	27.73	188.39	26.70
1987	493.40	40.34	508.71	41.59	220.96	18.07
1988	564.29	53.18	341.25	32.16	155.62	14.66
1989	894.14	39.90	609.08	27.18	737.80	32.92
1990	1,080.28	51.90	693.98	33.34	307.39	14.77
1991	704.67	45.20	671.72	43.09	182.56	11.71
1992	635.27	55.28	328.65	28.60	185.32	16.13
1993	489.88	44.94	355.85	32.65	244.24	22.41
1994	804.08	52.76	421.65	27.67	298.20	19.57
1995	747.69	27.12	1,633.11	59.24	375.99	13.64
1996	1,013.35	44.24	1,047.43	45.73	229.61	10.02
1997	1,486.89	38.33	1,278.71	32.96	1,113.57	28.71
1998	1,070.82	30.13	2,011.70	56.60	471.53	13.27
1999	1,012.49	24.70	2,497.01	60.92	589.53	14.38
2000	2,367.45	31.33	3,903.44	51.65	1,286.47	17.02
2001	1,357.85	26.72	2,468.72	48.58	1,254.74	24.69
2002	987.30	30.60	1,516.61	47.00	722.87	22.40
2003	1,083.35	30.42	1,676.28	47.08	801.11	22.50
2004	1,480.32	37.58	1,303.73	33.10	1,155.00	29.32

Source: Investment Commission, Ministry of Economic Affairs, ROC, calculated by Author

Aside from the trade, the inward and outward Foreign Direct Investment (FDI) also suggests that Taiwan has gradually shifted its economic focus to Asian region. According to the statistics of the Taiwan Investment Commission, the Asian area and the American area have been the major FDI contributors and recipients of Taiwan. From Table 2-16, although the percentage of Taiwan's approved inward FDI from the Asian area and from the American area fluctuates fiercely. The former ranges from as high as 66.16 percent in 1983 and as low as 22.11 percent in 1981, the latter from 69.14 percent in 1981 to 27.18 percent in 1989. Although Table 2-16 does not illustrate any special

[97] Taiwan was Japan's colony before World War II and the client state of the US during the Cold War.

pattern for Taiwan's inward FDI, the approved foreign investment from the Asian area and the American area constantly accounted for over 80% of its FDI. The phenomenon that the most of the FDI flows into Taiwan from Asia and America coincides with the fact that Taiwan maintains a special relationship with the US and with Japan.[98]

Table 2-17 Statistics on Approved Outward Foreign Investment by Area (China excluded)

Unit: USD million

Year	Asia	%	America	%	Others	%
1981	6.74	62.60	1.80	16.68	2.23	20.73
1982	9.13	78.51	2.50	21.49	0.00	0.00
1983	6.56	62.11	2.86	27.06	1.14	10.83
1984	6.55	16.68	32.18	81.96	0.53	1.36
1985	4.21	10.18	35.83	86.68	1.30	3.14
1986	8.41	14.78	46.74	82.12	1.76	3.09
1987	21.30	20.73	80.25	78.10	1.20	1.17
1988	69.30	31.68	130.34	59.59	19.10	8.73
1989	296.37	31.83	624.43	67.07	10.18	1.09
1990	602.91	38.84	838.71	54.03	110.59	7.12
1991	929.82	56.15	658.96	39.79	67.25	4.06
1992	369.93	41.69	449.10	50.62	68.23	7.69
1993	663.51	39.95	740.11	44.56	257.31	15.49
1994	559.47	34.60	988.34	61.13	68.96	4.27
1995	467.74	34.47	787.11	58.01	102.03	7.52
1996	661.72	30.56	1,442.95	66.64	60.73	2.80
1997	818.74	28.29	1,915.95	66.21	159.14	5.50
1998	580.82	17.62	2,637.02	80.00	78.46	2.38
1999	836.38	25.59	2,267.71	69.37	164.93	5.05
2000	851.07	16.76	3,946.02	77.72	279.98	5.51
2001	814.98	18.56	3,460.90	78.81	115.77	2.64
2002	528.05	15.67	2,475.58	73.46	366.42	10.87
2003	1,063.20	26.79	2,731.27	68.82	174.11	4.39
2004	1,274.90	37.70	1,881.38	55.63	225.74	6.67

Source: Investment Commission, Ministry of Economic Affairs, ROC, calculated by Author

However, the most noticeable phenomenon is the outflow investments illustrated in the Table 2-17 and Table 2-18. Table 2-17 offers an illusion that Taiwan allocates most of its investments in American countries, yet in fact Asian region is the primary investment target for Taiwanese businessmen. This distortion mainly comes from the fact that China has been excluded in this offi-

[98] Taiwan was Japan's colony before World War II and the client state of the US during the Cold War.

cial statistics while Taiwan deals with its investments to China in a separate section. After the official statistics of Taiwan's investments in China is added, the Table 2-18 indicates the value of outward investments into Asian countries surge to account for almost over half of Taiwan's total outward investments.

Table 2-18 Statistics on Approved Outward Foreign Investment by Area (China included)

Unit: USD million

Year	Asia	%	America	%	Others	%
1991	1,103.98	60.32	658.96	36.01	67.25	3.67
1992	616.92	54.39	449.10	39.59	68.23	6.02
1993*	3,831.93	79.35	740.11	15.33	257.31	5.33
1994	1,521.68	59.00	988.34	38.32	68.96	2.67
1995	1,560.45	63.70	787.11	32.13	102.03	4.17
1996	1,890.96	55.70	1,442.95	42.51	60.73	1.79
1997*	5,153.05	71.29	1,915.95	26.51	159.14	2.20
1998*	2,615.44	49.06	2,637.02	49.47	78.46	1.47
1999	2,089.16	46.20	2,267.71	50.15	164.93	3.65
2000	3,458.21	45.00	3,946.02	51.35	279.98	3.64
2001	3,599.13	50.16	3,460.90	48.23	115.77	1.61
2002*	7,251.11	71.84	2,475.58	24.53	366.42	3.63
2003*	8,761.99	75.10	2,731.27	23.41	174.11	1.49
2004	8,215.56	79.59	1,881.38	18.23	225.74	2.19

Note: There is no official record relating to the investment in China before 1991.
* includes the amount of the registration of previously unregistered China-bound investments.

Source: Investment Commission, Ministry of Economic Affairs, ROC, Calculated by Author

From Table 2-17, Taiwan investment in Asia is USD 1,274.9 million accounting for only 37.7 percent of total investment in 2004. At the same year, when the investment in China is included, the amount surges to USD 8,215.56 million which accounts for around 79.59 percent of total Taiwanese outward investments (Table 2-18); the percentage of Taiwan's investments in American changes from 55.63 percent (Table 2-17) to 18.23 percent (Table 2-18). Table 2-17 suggests that Taiwan's outward investments concentrate on America when China is excluded. The percentage of Taiwan's investment in America increases from 16.68 percent in 1981 to 55.63 percent in 2004. At the same period of time, the percentage of Taiwan's investment in Asia decreased from 62.6 percent to 37.7 percent. However, when China is included, table 2-18 illustrates that Asia attracts more Taiwan's investment than America from 1990 to 2004 except for 1998, 1999 and 2000. However, as Taiwanese investors incline to invest in China through the third place, Taiwan's investments to Asia can only be underestimated. This phenomenon indicates that Taiwan's investment in China have diluted its ability or intention to invest in other regions. In terms of both trade and investment, Taiwan has entered a process of integration with its neighbors, especially its gigantic neighbor—China. Moreover, the statistics confirms that the integration has been strengthening without a sign of receding.

2.4 The Outflow of Economic Resources from Taiwan to China

After the US severs its formal diplomatic tie with Taiwan and shifts its recognition to China in 1979, China alters its long time militant attitude toward Taiwan, and appeals to the peaceful reunification. The three-decade long mutual confrontation finally yields to peaceful reconciliation. China proposes for a two-side negotiation between KMT and CCP, to lift bans on transportation direct mail, trade, visitation, tourism, academic, cultural and athletic exchanges, but the KMT government refuses any official contact with China. Though Taiwanese government rejects China's proposal, China's "peace offensive" had cracked the door slightly open for the non-official communication.

In fact, ever since Chinese authority adopted an "open door" policy, Taiwan has been striving to establish an effective mechanism to minimize the exchanges between two sides across Taiwan Strait. Though Taiwanese government has performed relatively well on stifling the inflow of capital, people and technologies from China, it fails to control Taiwanese businessmen from investing into mainland and Taiwanese talents from working in China. Taiwan has been worried about the "hollowing out" of Taiwan's resources because whenever Taiwanese firms relocate their production overseas they transfer not only the capital but also the talents and technologies away from Taiwan.

Table 2-19 illustrates that Taiwan is more capable at preventing mainland Chinese from visiting Taiwan but fails to stop the one-way flow of Taiwan's visitors to China and Taiwan's official statistics have been seriously distorted because of the cross-Strait political grudge. Although the visitors from Chinese mainland increase from 388 people in 1988 to 139,344 people in 2004, when China's total population is considered, only a minor portion of mainland Chinese are allowed to visit Taiwan. In 2002, Taiwan set a record high to allow 153,923 mainland Chinese to visit Taiwan, but it stood less than 0.011840% of total China's population. In 2000, Chinese outbound travelers totaled 10.47 million,[99] but Taiwanese government allowed only 117,125 Chinese to visit Taiwan. Taiwan accommodated less than 1.12% of China's total outbound travelers.

Moreover, in Taiwan's official statistics, the number of Taiwanese visiting China ranges between 1992's 6,965 to 2002's 648,545, but according to China's record, the number of Taiwanese visitors increases almost all the way from 1988's 437,700 to 2004's 3,685,250, but it suffers a setback to 2,730,860 in 2003 because of the outbreak of SARS (severe acute respiratory syndrome). Table 2-19 also illustrates that the huge discrepancy between Taiwan's official data and China's regarding the number of Taiwanese visitors can reach as

[99] The number comes from the official website of China Tourism.

many as over 3 million persons (in 2002 and 2004). This inconsistency verifies not only the difficulty for Taiwanese government to control the overseas activities of its citizens, but also the fact that China demonstrates its magnetism to attract Taiwanese on their way to pilgrimage.

Table 2-19 The Number of Visitors between Taiwan and Mainland China

Unit: Persons

Year	Visitors from China to Taiwan[a] (1)	(1)/Population of China (%)	Taiwanese Visitors to China[a] (2)	Taiwanese Visitors to China[b] (3)	(3)/Population of Taiwan (%)
1988	381	0.000029	236,839	437,700	1.90
1989	4,838	0.000372	195,235	541,000	2.35
1990	7,520	0.000578	60,001	948,000	4.12
1991	11,074	0.000852	14,346	946,632	4.12
1992	13,134	0.001010	6,965	1,317,770	5.73
1993	18,343	0.001411	420,948	1,526,969	6.64
1994	23,562	0.001812	433,660	1,390,215	6.04
1995	42,634	0.003280	273,388	1,532,309	6.66
1996	58,010	0.004462	97,294	1,733,897	7.54
1997	72,346	0.005565	83,420	2,117,576	9.21
1998	90,626	0.006971	134,805	2,174,602	9.45
1999	106,699	0.008208	272,082	2,584,648	11.24
2000	117,125	0.009010	511,809	3,108,650	13.52
2001	133,655	0.010281	548,764	3,441,960	14.97
2002	153,923	0.011840	648,545	3,660,570	15.92
2003	139,672	0.010744	269,361	2,730,860	11.87
2004	139,344	0.010718	75,848	3,685,250	16.24

Note: [a] indicates Taiwan's official statistics. Since Taiwanese may not report their visits to Mainland China, figure in (2) is to be underestimated.
[b] indicates China's official statistics. Before May 2000, the statistics were offered by China Travel Service in Hong Kong in the Monthly data of "The Number of Taiwan People Applied for Mainland China Traveling Visa ", which are replaced by "Number of Taiwan Tourists to Mainland China" which is from "China Monthly Statistics" published by The China Statistical Information and Consulting (Beijing) Co. Ltd. since May, 2001.

Source: 1. China Monthly Statistics and China Travel Yearbook
2. Bureau of Entry and Exit, NPA, MOI, ROC.

The noticeable imbalance of the personnel exchanges between Taiwan and China further proves that Taiwanese government has been more effective in restricting the mainland Chinese from visiting Taiwan than in preventing its citizens from visiting Chinese mainland. The one-way exchanges will sooner or later drain Taiwan's resources and put economic pressure on Taiwanese government. Therefore, in order to reverse the current one-way exchanges, Taiwanese government has expresses its willingness to grant the permission to mainland Chinese to visit Taiwan, because at current moment, Taiwan allows only overseas Chinese citizens to visit Taiwan by organized tour groups.[100]

The economic integration between Taiwan and China is reflected not only on the one-way personnel exchanges, but also on the aspects of trade and investment. As the globalization proceeds, the government's ability to control the overseas activities of private organizations has been weakened by the advancement of technology, the deregulation of capital flow, the expansion of trade, and the dispersion of production. The globalization liberates the economic activities of Taiwanese enterprises, but instead of pursuing a global deployment, most of them are looking for business opportunities in China. After all, Taiwan can relatively be more effective in controlling the inflow of China's capital, technology, goods as well as talents. Without China's cooperation, it is very difficult for Taiwanese government to extend its domestic regulations to its private actors' mainland-bound activities.

2.4.1 China Effects On Taiwan's Economic Policy

Since 1949, there has been no official contact between Taiwan and China. Though after China launches its economic reform and adopts an "open door" policy in 1979, China has tried to reach out olive branch to Taiwan, Taiwan responds with a "three no's" policy which indicates no contacts, no negotiations, and no compromise.[101] Not until 1985 does Taiwan announce the "Non-interference Principle of Indirect Exports to the Mainland", which formally lifts the ban on the communication of the private channel. Taiwan for the first time legitimizes the indirect trade between Taiwan and China.[102]

In 1991, Taiwanese government eases the ban on indirect investments on the mainland, and divides indirect Taiwanese investments in the mainland into three categories: the first category of investments is strictly forbidden; the second category is required the approval of government on a case-by-case basis; the third category belongs to the permitted list.[103] Although Taiwan does not lift the ban on investment in China until 1991, in fact, Crane observes that in the early 1980s Taiwanese businessmen have already established small-scale enterprises in China's Special Economic Zone regardless of the governmental restriction. By 1987 roughly US$ 100 million have flowed into China from

[100] "Mainland Chinese to Visit Taiwan, It Is Under the Control of the Opposite Side," Jun 22, 2004, *Economic Daily*, (in Chinese).

[101] "Taiwan China Relations," Taipei Representative Office in the United Kingdom, http://france.roc-taiwan.org.uk/taiwan/5-gp/brief/info04_5.html

[102] Tung, 2004

[103] Leng, 1998

Taiwan.[104] Long before the permission of Taiwanese government, Taiwanese entrepreneurs have been venturing in Mainland China, and the legitimization of Taiwanese investments on the mainland is merely a retroactive rectification by Taiwanese government. The mainland policy of Taiwanese government has a difficulty to catch up with the actions of Taiwanese businesses and Taiwanese businessmen can effectively evade the management of Taiwanese government. This phenomenon makes cross-Strait statistics seriously biased.

As the door of investment has been cracked open, the economic intercourses between Taiwan and China surge. According to the estimation of Mainland Affairs Council, the total trade volume between China and Taiwan is US$ 8.62 billion in 1991. The trade amount is US$ 23.79 billion in 1996, and it is almost tripled in 6 years. The investments from Taiwanese businesses to mainland China also experience a boom. The investment amount approved by Taiwanese government is US$ 174.16 million in 1991, and it expands to US$ 1,229.24 million in 1996. It grows more than six times in six years. The thriving economic contacts alarms Taiwanese government, which is afraid that the deeper economic integration with China will endanger Taiwan's sovereignty.

In view of China's magnetism towards Taiwan's businesses, in order to avoid economic dependence on mainland, in 1996 Taiwanese government tightens its mainland policy by announcing the "no haste, be patient" policy toward mainland-bound investment projects. President Lee emphasizes that Taiwan should guard against "haste", be "patient" and move with "sureness and foresight," and Taiwanese government claims that the "no haste, be patient" policy is aimed at protecting the interests of Taiwanese citizens.[105] On the perspective of Taiwanese government, since China refuses to forswear the use of military force against Taiwan and Taiwanese government is unable to safeguard the benefits and security of its businessmen in China, for the consideration of its national security, it must ponder on the economic relations across Taiwan Straits and control the pace of the cross-Strait development. The "no haste, be patient" policy is promulgated to regulate only the economic activities, and is designed to control the investment in China, but not the trade with China. Under the "no haste, be patient" restrictions, no investment relating to the advanced high-tech industry and infrastructure projects is allowed, and Taiwanese government places a US$ 50 million cap on each project.[106]

After examining Lee's "no haste, be patient" policy, Kuo concludes that although the establishment of the "no haste, be patient" policy is aimed at pre-

[104] Crane 1993, P. 710

[105] "Strait Talk from Mainland Affairs Council Chairman Chang King-yuh", http://www.sinorama.com.tw/en/1998/199801/701114e2.html

[106] Mainland Affair Council (1998) "Da Lu Zheng Ce Yu Liang An Guan Xi Da Ke Wen," (in Chinese) http://www.mac.gov.tw/big5/rpir/880508.htm

venting Taiwanese firms from over-focusing on the mainland and at safeguarding Taiwan from the menace of China, however, the market mechanism overwhelms the political deliberations in the investment strategic planning of Taiwanese businessmen. The goal of the "no haste, be patient" policy is to prevent industries from hollowing out and slowing down the deployment of Taiwanese businesses in China, but it may cause boomerang effect as Taiwanese businessmen simply channel their capital through the third place to China and keep all the earnings from China-bound investments away from the reach of Taiwanese government.[107] As a result, Taiwan's official statistics record a huge discrepancy against China's. Moreover, whenever Taiwanese government provides a grace period to its businessmen to make retroactive registration for the investments which they have bypassed the national regulation to invest in China, it discovers that billions of US dollars have been poured into China without its pre-acknowledgement.[108]

After Taiwan's first-ever "rotation of ruling parties" in 2000, the newly elected president soon faces the challenge of economic downturn which Taiwan has not experienced for over three decades. In 2001, Taiwan suffers an economic contraction of 2.18 percent, down from previous year's 5.8 percent expansion, and the jobless rate surges to 4.57 percent from previous year's 2.99 percent. The lackluster performance of Taiwan economy highlights China's booming economy, as in 2001 China enjoys an economic growth rate of 7.5 percent. Taiwan's economic contraction in 2001 makes Taiwanese companies even more desperate than ever to expand in China.

In 2001, the five-year old "no haste, be patient" policy is formally abolished and replaced by the "active opening, effective management" policy. In order to revive the domestic economy, Taiwanese government organizes the Economic Development Advisory Conference (EDAC) to acquire opinions from 120 influential advisors. In the EDAC meetings, they urge Taiwanese government to abandon the "no haste, be patient" policy, and to relax the limits on Taiwanese investments in the mainland. The new investment screening mechanism re-classifies the prospective investment projects from former three into two categories ("forbidden" and "general"), and the US$ 50 million investment ceiling is also eliminated. Moreover, it will allow Taiwanese businessmen to make direct investments in China without having to go through a third place. The tax regulations are also adjusted, and Taiwanese firms are allowed to report and deduct the amount of taxes which they have paid in China. On the aspect of "effective management", in order to prevent the misuse

[107] Kuo, (2003)
[108] Section 2.4.2 will have further discussion.

of the domestic financial resources[109], the government intends to establish a transparent and institutionalized capital management mechanism to monitor the capital flows of Taiwanese firms.

The EDAC suggests the government do more than just abandon the "no haste, be patient" policy and adopt a policy to promote "three links" between Taiwan and China, but the implementation of "three links" is still under the power struggle between Taiwanese government and Taiwanese enterprises, because though the business sectors favor the implementation of "three links", Taiwanese government insists that the "three links" must be negotiated on the government-to-government basis. On the other hand, Chinese government at first insists the negotiations of "three links" must be conduct on the One-China Principle but later China realizes that it can base on the principle of separating economic interaction from political issues to treat "three links" as an economic issue and suggests "three links" be negotiated through private organizations.[110] China's concession does not bring a fruitful result to the implementation of the "three links". However, Taiwan's domestic politics complicates the "three links" issue. After the presidential election in 2004, as pro-independence activist, Chen Shui-bian is reelected, China decides to impose a precondition for the negotiation of "three links". The Chen administration has to agree with the One-China Principle to discuss "three links" with China. As One-China Principle reappears on the negotiation table, unless Chen is willing to forsake his pro-independence stance, any possible cross-Strait negotiation will be suspended. Thus, the stalemate will persist and Taiwan economy will suffer.

Formosa Group chairman Yung-ching Wang has been an aggressive "three links" advocate.[111] He said Taiwanese are the one who need "three links" to commute between two sides across the Strait. The implementation of "three links" will benefit Taiwan.[112] Due to the lackluster future of "three links" under the Chen administration, Evergreen Group chairman Yung-fa Chang who once endorsed Chen Shui-bian's candidacy in the 2000 presidential election now openly criticized Chen by accusing him of neglecting shipping

---

[109] Taiwanese government has been concerned about when Taiwanese businessmen invest in China, they will "inject money into China and leave the debt in Taiwan". Further information can be referred from the commentaries of the National Policy Foundation (NPF): "Zhai Liu Tai Wan, Dong Yao Guo Ben" by Tang Zheng-Yi and "Qian Jin Da Lu, Zhai Liu Tai Wan Ping Xi" by Chen Jin Long. (in Chinese)

[110] For the Taiwanese government response, the following website offers a more detailed explanation. http://www.mac.gov.tw/english/english/macnews/enews/enews900824.htm
For the whole process of power struggle, Ezra N. H Chen (2003) offers a more complete description.

[111] For Yung-ching Wang's persistent stance on "three links", please see "Three Links' Debate," E Taiwan News, May 24, 2002.

[112] Quote from Mao (2003, P. 88).

policy and even switched his support to Chen's opponent in the 2004 presidential election.[113] Evergreen Group once was categorized as a "pro-Bian"[114] enterprise by Taiwan Affairs Office of State Council, but now positions itself as a "China enterprise" after Chen administration thwarts the process of implementing "three links".[115]

Since globalization has altered the rule of games, private organizations can effectively flee from the surveillance of the government. Enterprises are no longer the silent victims of government policies. For Taiwan's mainland economic policy, three-links can be treated as the first step to normalize cross-Strait relations. However, no economic exchange can replace the function of political interactions. Without political exchanges between Taiwan and China, it is difficult for Taiwanese government to extend its jurisdiction into China's field. As "time and tide wait for no man", even though Taiwanese government is still pondering on the possibility of the One-China Principle (or how to turn down the One-China Principle), the impending "three links" has disturbed the business operation of MNEs and forced them to rearrange their business operation.[116] As a result, the number of Western business executives in Taipei is decreasing. In contrast to Taipei's loss of foreign executives, Shanghai enjoys a boom in the number of both the members of American Chamber of Commerce (AmCham) and European executives.[117]

2.4.2 The Capital Flight

By regulating and deregulating policies, states play a significant role in the contemporary liberalization of global financial order. So far, on the national level or even the supranational level, states still play the solely legitimate role in the creation of regulations. However, Pauly argues that although states still withhold the ultimate right to defy markets, as the expansion of supranational

---

[113] For Yung-fa Chang criticized Chen, please see "Evergreen Chairman Says Shipping Industry Ignored," *Taipei Times*, Nov 06, 2003, Page 3.
For Yung-fa Chang switched his support, please see "Evergreen Tycoon Switches Support from Chen to Lien," *Taipei Times*, Mar 20, 2004, Page 5.
For Yung-fa Chang' criticism stemmed from the frustration of cross-Strait stalemate, please see "Evergreen Tycoon Motivated by Self Interest, Critics Say," *Taipei Times*, Nov 07, 2003, Page 3.

[114] "Pro-Bian" implies supporting Taiwan independence.

[115] Refer from Mao (2003, P. 88)

[116] Phillips Semiconductors plans to relocate its marketing center for Asia Pacific in Taipei to Shanghai. It alters the reporting line of its business operation. The affiliate in Taipei will be subordinated to Great China marketing center in Shanghai, "Don't Want to Wait for Three Links, the Headquarter of Philips Semiconductors Shifted to Mainland," Aug 2, 2005, Economic Daily, (in Chinese)

[117] See "Fewer Western Executives Working in Taiwan," Taiwan Headlines, Nov. 13, 2001.

capital flow is the result of international financial liberalization, any single state which takes unilateral actions to immobilize the international capital movements will jeopardize its financial liquidation and foreign investments.[118] Cohen further points out the vulnerability of government mechanism in a globalized world. Private organizations which have constructed a vast network outside of public authorities are capable of operating their businesses on their own terms in spite of the governmental legal system.[119]

Actually, this is exactly the difficulty that Taiwan's China policy encounters. Ever since President Lee brought up "no haste, be patient" investment policy toward China in 1996, in contrast to worldwide "China fever", Taiwanese government basically had chosen a road which less people, especially businessmen, traveled. Taiwanese government implemented the "no haste, be patient" policy to restrain the westward investment and "go south" policy to diversify the risk of over-dependence on China. By imposing rigid restrictions on China-bound investments in specific industries like infrastructures, high-tech and capital-intensive industries, Taiwanese government intended to slow down the capital outflow to China and to maintain the competitive edge over China; by imposing an investment ceiling of USD 50 million on individual investment in China, it wanted to restrain the investment of large corporations. Though Taiwanese government has tried to put on a control mechanism to prevent massive capital flight to China, after decades of capital liberation, the capital control mechanism does not function as well as the government expected. Therefore, the "no hast, be patient" policy existed in name only before President Lee's successor officially terminated it, because Taiwanese businessmen simply bypass governmental regulations when investing in China.

As Taiwan and China have been ideological foes and China has been deemed as a hostile state by Taiwan, to alleviate the economic influence from the hostile state, Taiwanese government has brought up policies to constrain the investments to China. However, whenever the government offered a grace period for the unauthorized investments on mainland to make a retroactive registration, it will uncover millions of dollars investing in China without its rectification. It has become a common practice for Taiwanese government, once in a while it will have to allow those investors who jump the gun to make retroactive registration, and otherwise it will be embarrassed by the fact that its regulations can not be performed.

---

[118] Pauly, 1995

[119] Cohen, 2000

Table 2-20 The Discrepancy between the Approved Amount of Taiwan and the Official Data of China

Unit: US$ million

Year	Amount Approved by ROC (1)	Realized Amount, Official Data of PRC (2)	Discrepancy (2)-(1)
1991	174.16	844.00*	669.84
1992	246.99	1,050.00	803.01
1993	1,140.37	3,139.00	1,998.63
	2,028.05*		(2,028.05)
1994	962.21	3,391.00	2,428.79
1995	1,092.71	3,162.00	2,069.29
1996	1,229.24	3,475.00	2,245.76
1997	1,614.54	3,289.00	1,674.46
	2,719.77*		(2,719.77)
1998	1,519.21	2,915.00	1,395.79
	515.41*		(515.41)
1999	1,252.74	2,598.70	1,345.92
2000	2,607.14	2,296.28	(310.86)
2001	2,784.15	2,979.94	195.79
2002	3,858.76	3,970.64	111.88
	2,864.30*		(2,864.30)
2003	4,594.99	3,377.24	(1,217.75)
	3,103.80*		(3,103.80)
2004	6,940.66	3,117.49	(3,823.17)
Total	41,249.20	39,605.29	(1,643.95)

Note:
*: Including data before 1991.
*: The retroactively registered unauthorized investments in China.
Source: Investment Commission, Ministry of Economic Affairs of ROC and Ministry of Foreign Trade and Economic Cooperation, PRC

Table 2-20 shows that in 1993, the retroactive investment amount is USD 2.03 billion; in 1997-1998, it surges to USD 3.24 billion; in 2002-2003, it mounts to USD 5.97 billion.[120] Moreover, according to the official data of Taiwanese government, the total retroactive registered amount reaches USD 11.23 billion; and the total amount of regulation-abiding investments is USD 30.02 billion. Therefore, almost over one forth of the investments from Taiwanese firms to China bypass the governmental supervision, and this phenomenon indicates Taiwanese government fails to control the outflow of Taiwanese capital.

[120] The government allowed unauthorized China-bound investments of Taiwanese firms to register retroactively in 1993, 1997 and 2002, but because of the delay in processing the applications, some retroactive registering investments were listed in the official statistics in the following year.

Furthermore, Table 2-20 further illustrates the discrepancy between Taiwan's and China's official data. In 1992, the amount form Taiwan's official statistics is USD 803.01 million less than that from China's; in 1993 the amount registered with Taiwanese government is USD 1,998.63 million less than the amount registered with Chinese government; in 1994, the discrepancy expands to USD 2,428.79 million; in 1995, the discrepancy decreases a little to USD 2,069.29 million; in 1996, the discrepancy enlarges to USD 2,245.76; in 1997, the discrepancy shrinks to USD 1,674.46 million; in 1998, the discrepancy shrinks further to USD 1,395.79 million; in 1999, the discrepancy is USD 1,345.92 million. However, in 2000, the trend is interrupted and the registered amount with Taiwanese government is USD 310.86 million over the amount of Chinese statistics. Although in 2001 and 2002, China still registers more Taiwanese investments than Taiwan, the discrepancy is narrowed down to less than USD 200 million. In 2003 and 2004, Taiwan registers USD 1,217.75 million and USD 3,823.17 million respectively over China's official data.

According to Kuo's research, he argues that because Taiwanese enterprises don't want to provoke Taiwanese government, which implemented "no haste, be patient" policy to cool down the heat of Taiwanese investments towards China, therefore, many Taiwan enterprises invested into China through tax havens like Virgin Islands. Thus, he concludes that the real Taiwanese investments in China have to add up the investments from Virgin Islands[121]. From Table 2-21, when Taiwanese government brings up the "no haste, be patient" policy in 1996, although the amount of the realized investments from Taiwan to China remains relatively stable during this policy-tightening period; it slides from 1996's USD 3,475 million to 1997's USD 3,289 million and from 1992 to 1996 the contracted amount always surpasses the realized amount. In 1997, it is the first time ever that the realized amount surpasses the contracted amount. The contracted amount of investments from Taiwan takes a sudden dive from 1996's USD 5,141 million to 1997's USD 2,814 million but at the same time the contracted amount of investment from Virgin Islands surged from 1996's USD 3,121 million to 1997's USD 5,156 million. Moreover, in this policy-tightening period, the realized amount investing from Virgin Islands tripled from 1996's USD 538 million to 1997's USD 1,717 million. 1996 stands out as a turning point for the China-bound investments from Virgin Islands. Ever since then, the China-bound investments from Virgin Islands get a boost. In 1998, it surges to USD 4,031 million; in 1999, it decreases to USD 2,659 million, and then it follows an upward trajectory from 2000's USD 3,833 million, 2001's USD 5,042 million to 2002's USD 6,117 million, but it

[121] Kuo, 2003

suffers a minor setback in 2003 to USD 5,777 million and gathers its momentum to hike to the historical high of USD 6,730 million.

Table 2-21 The Investments in China from Taiwan and Virgin Islands

Unit: US$ million

Year	The Investment Amount from Taiwan		The investments from Virgin Islands	
	Contracted Amount	Realized Amount	Contracted Amount	Realized Amount
1992	5,543.00	1,050.00	43.00	4.00
1993	9,965.00	3,139.00	299.00	14.00
1994	5,395.00	3,391.00	836.00	128.00
1995	5,777.00	3,162.00	1,321.00	304.00
1996	5,141.00	3,475.00	3,121.00	538.00
1997	2,814.00	3,289.00	5,156.00	1,717.00
1998	2,982.00	2,915.00	6,136.00	4,031.00
1999	3,374.44	2,598.70	3,488.00	2,659.00
2000	4,041.89	2,296.28	7,522.00	3,833.00
2001	6,914.19	2,979.94	8,771.00	5,042.00
2002	6,740.84	3,970.64	12,650.00	6,117.00
2003	8,557.87	3,377.24	12,664.16	5,776.96
2004	9,305.94	3,117.49	19,395.65	6,730.30
Total	76,552.17	38,761.29	81,402.81	36,894.26

Source: Kuo (2003, P.106), Invest in China[122], calculated by the author.

As many Taiwanese businessmen like to channel their investments through the third place, like Virgin Islands, Cayman Islands,[123] Hong Kong,[124] or even the US[125], it is difficult to calculate the exact amount of Taiwanese in-

[122] http://www.fdi.gov.cn/main/index.htm

[123] Lee-in Chen Chiu, a Research Fellow at the Chung Hua Institution for Economic Research, claimed, according to China's official data, Taiwan had maintained its position as China's second largest FDI injector until 1996. Ever since, Taiwan's investment into China has declined. At the same time, the famous tax havens like Virgin Islands and Cayman Islands began to emerge as China's major investors. See Kuo, 2003, P. 105 Footnote 216.

[124] According to the report of Asia Times, it stated "Although putting an exact number on Taiwanese investment in China is notoriously difficult because of the common practice of channeling funds through Hong Kong and overseas tax havens such as the British Virgin Islands..." Therefore, aside from tax havens, Hong Kong also represents a channel for Taiwanese capital to flow in China.
http://www.atimes.com/atimes/China/DH27Ad03.html

[125] The author personally knows some Taiwanese businessmen who invest through the US. As Taiwanese government permits dual citizenship, they can be Taiwanese citizens and Americans at the same time. Richard Chang is the most noticeable case. He is the founder of SMIC (the world's fourth largest pure-play foundry company). He claimed himself as an

vestments in China. Moreover, because Taiwanese government takes a hostile stance against China and deems investments in China as "capitalizing the communist bandits (Zi Fei)", therefore, Taiwanese businessmen sacrifice the investment transparency and accountability to perplex Taiwanese government and to cause the inaccuracy of official statistics of China-bound investments.

Table 2-22 indicates that as of the end of 2004 China has been the most favorable investment target for Taiwanese enterprises and attracted USD 41.24 billion which accounts for 56.51 percent of total Taiwanese outward investments. Moreover, the British territories serve as the second largest Taiwanese outbound investment destination and have attracted USD 14.46 billion. The US and Hong Kong rank as the third and fourth largest FDI recipients from Taiwan, and receive USD 7.57 billion and USD 2.23 billion respectively. As the British territories are the tax havens such as Virgin Islands and Cayman Islands, via which Taiwanese businessmen incline to invest in China. Aside from those tax havens, Hong Kong is another preferred location for Taiwanese businessmen to channel their mainland investments. Therefore, the factual amount of Taiwanese investments in China should be far more than 56.61 percent of total Taiwanese outbound investments.

Table 2-22 The Top 10 Regions/Countries of Taiwan's Outbound Investments (As of the end of 2004)

Unit: US$ million

Rank	Region/Country	Amount	Percentage
1	China	41,249.20	56.51
2	British Territories	14,456.43	19.80
3	the US	7,567.25	10.37
4	Hong Kong	2,226.38	3.05
5	Singapore	1,821.47	2.50
6	Malaysia	1,549.23	2.12
7	Thailand	1,114.78	1.53
8	Panama	1,045.77	1.43
9	Vietnam	1,041.72	1.43
10	Japan	908.03	1.24
-	Others	6,955.23	9.53
-	Total	72,994.84	100.00

Source: Investment Commission of ROC, calculated by the author

The flourishing westbound investments prove not only Taiwanese government's inability to execute its China policy, but also the flexibility of Taiwan's enterprises to evade the regulations of Taiwanese government. As a re-

American to defy the law-enforcement of Taiwanese government, which fined him NTD 5 million for his investment in China and demanded he withdraw such investment.

sult, those enterprises which are more capable of bypassing domestic regulations to pursue self-interests will be a paradigm for their followers, and sooner or later, the regulations of Taiwanese government will impose no mandatory on Taiwanese companies. In fact, without China's cooperation, Taiwanese government has few bargaining chips to bring Taiwanese businessmen's mainland investments into its regulatory system. There are too many channels, legal or illegal, to assist the investments of Taiwanese corporations. Whether Taiwanese government likes it or not, investments towards China have become Taiwanese corporations' most important strategy in their global deployment.

The capital flight to China may not be totally attributed to the failure of the economic policy of Taiwanese government, but is also the results of globalization and an emerging China. The multinational enterprises (MNEs) have already created a modern business model, in which, MNEs set up manufacturing bases on countries which offer cheap labor, land and resources, and sell those goods to countries which can pay higher prices. Usually, the former indicate the economic lagging states; the later economic-developed nations. However, China has surpassed the role of a backward state providing cheap labor and vast resources for manufacturing bases, and poses as one of the world's largest consumption markets. As China's magnetism has drawn thousands of Taiwanese companies into mainland China, although Taiwan authority has tried to curb this trend, the trend is irresistible and irreversible.

2.4.3 The Mainland Operation of MNCs

As Taiwan is located in the adjacent zone of Asian continent and Pacific Ocean and in the center of the first island chain[126], the natural inheritance makes Taiwan serve as a gateway to Chinese mainland. Even though the geographic location bestows Taiwan a chance to operate as an intermediary agent between China and foreign investors, the impediment of lacking proper communication between two sides across the Strait has threatened the development of Taiwan economy. Instead of serving as an asset to MNEs which want to make business in China, Taiwan becomes a liability to their mainland operations. The staffs employed on China can not visit Taiwan and the inconvenience of cross-Strait transportation consumes time and money. All these problems without a possible solution in foreseeable future will discount Taipei's geographic advantage. Moreover, time is not on Taipei's side. Regarding the mainland deployment, the MNEs will not wait for Taiwanese government to uplift its restrictions.

---

[126] From the geographic perspective, China's territorial waters are contained within the first island chain which from north to south includes the Kurile Islands, Japan, the Ryukyu Islands, Taiwan, the Philippines, and Indonesia (Borneo to Natuna Besar). See The People's Liberation Army and China in Transition, Chapter 7, The PLA Navy and "Active Defense" by Bernard D. Cole

They will only turn their back on Taiwan and leave to look for a convenient place to explore their business opportunities.

Even under the framework of WTO, yet the "three links" is still hanging. Without "three links", Taiwanese government has imposed extra operation costs on corporations which require mainland operations. Moreover, the relocation to Chinese mainland for some Taiwanese enterprises is a requirement for survival, not a luxury for expansion. Table 2-23 illustrates the motivations behind the outward investments of Taiwanese companies. When Taiwanese companies are dealing with the issue of outward investments, their primary concerns are the market potential and cheap labor of the host country as well as the deterioration of domestic environment.

Furthermore, the request from their customers is also important to their decisions when they consider their international deployment. As a result, complying with the foreign customers' request and following the deployment of their domestic buyers rank number 4 and 5 respectively on the priority list of the motivations behind their outward investments. As the figure in 1996, 1998 and 2002 denotes the percentage of interviewees choosing the item which is equal to the number of interviewees choosing the item divided by the number of total interviewees, in 2002, one out of the three Taiwanese firms investing outwards is under the request of their foreign buyers. In 1996, 24.47% of Taiwanese firms is requested by their foreign buyers to invest outwards, in 1998, the percentage climbs up to 30.22%, in 2002, the percentage reaches 33.36%. Moreover, in 2002, one out of the four Taiwanese firms investing outwards is under the influence of their Taiwanese buyers. In 1996, the percentage is 19.82 percent; in 1998, it increases to 21.91 percent; in 2002, 27.19 percent of Taiwanese firms feel the urge to follow their Taiwanese buyers to invest outwards.

American Chamber of Commerce in Taipei warns that Taiwan has to implement direct transportation links with China to avoid being marginalized in its 2004 Taiwan White Paper.[127] European Chamber of Commerce Taipei (ECCT) criticizes that Taiwan's ban on goods made in China violates the WTO commitments of Taiwan.[128] Moreover, ECCT warns Taiwanese government not to force foreign investors to take sides between Taiwan and China, because if they have to choose, China will be their choice.[129]

---

[127] "Taiwan Risks Becoming Irrelevant: AmCham" by Rickards, Jane, *China Post*, June 2, 2004

[128] "ECCT Urges Faster Liberalization", By Chung, Amber, *Taipei Times*, April 13, 2005

[129] "ECCT: Don't Force Foreign Investors to Take Sides" China Times, April 13, 2005 (in Chinese)

Table 2-23 The Motivations behind Outward FDI of Taiwanese Firms

Unit: %; (): Ranking

Year / Motivation	1996*	1998*	1999**	2000**	2002*
Market Potential of Host Country	49.62 (2)	50.47 (2)	67.6 (2)	68.9 (2)	63.55 (1)
Cheap Labor of Host Country	63.72 (1)	65.19 (1)	74.2 (1)	80 (1)	62.76 (2)
Deteriorating Domestic Business Environment	33.46 (3)	36.71 (3)	50.5 (3)	65.5 (3)	36.08 (3)
Request of Foreign Buyers	24.47 (4)	30.22 (4)	40.6 (5)	47.4 (4)	33.36 (4)
Following Taiwanese Buyers	19.82 (5)	21.91 (5)	-11.1 (9)	-2.8 (9)	27.19 (5)
Land Accessibility	15.24 (6)	17.09 (7)	31.3 (6)	40.6 (5)	19.03 (6)
Supply of Raw Material	12.73 (8)	17.09 (7)	28.7 (7)	25.4 (7)	15.3 (7)
Effective Use of Company's Capital and Technology	13.11 (7)	18.12 (6)	41.1 (4)	34.9 (6)	12.63 (8)
Governmental Remuneration of Host Country	-	-	15.1 (8)	13.5 (8)	10.74 (9)
Technological Accessibility	-	-	-13.7 (10)	-18.2 (10)	5.02 (10)

Note: * The percentage of interviewees choosing the item = the number of interviewees choosing the item/the number of total interviewees

** The importance index = the ratio of very important + the ratio of important – the ratio of unimportant – the ratio of no idea

Source: Report of Manufacturers Outward Investments Survey (Zhi Zao Ye Dui Wai Tou Zi Shi Kuang Diao Cha Bao Gao), Department of Statistics, Ministry of Economic Affairs, ROC.

In fact, Kinpo-Compal Group chairman Rock Hsu admits for notebook manufacturers, the relocation of their production line to mainland China is not based on the consideration of cost-efficiency but is resulted from the request of their foreign buyers.[130] Therefore, when the foreign buyers can no longer tolerate the inconvenience caused by political factor, they not only withdraw themselves from Taiwan, but also carry their suppliers with them. The IT heavyweights, Dell and Sony contribute directly to the westbound investments of Taiwanese notebook manufacturers by "coercively compelling their Taiwanese

[130] Mao, 2003, P. 94-95.

contract manufacturers to stride over the other side of the Taiwan Straits[131]" and "demanding their contract partners to ship all notebook PCs from mainland".[132] As a result, whichever Taiwanese companies refuse to move westward will suffer the loss of the order to their competitors which are willing to comply with the demand of their customers. The global deployment of MNEs has enforced the redistribution of the manufacturing bases on Taiwanese companies and will cause a far-reaching impact to Taiwan economy.

The phenomenon that once a company moves to China, it brings along its suppliers, its own employees, its suppliers' employees, and their expatriate workers' purchasing power will send out an alarming signal to Taiwan economy. With the exodus of Taiwanese high-skilled workers to China, Taiwan also exports their purchasing power to mainland. The outflow of high-skilled workers will not only reduce the present domestic income, but also risk at losing a higher-than-average spending power because highly skilled individuals usually enjoy a higher-than-average income. Therefore, the outflow of talents is not only a question of brain drain but also a problem of losing the power of consumption.[133]

Therefore, the conservative China policy of Taiwanese government has trapped Taiwan economy into a serious vicious circle which is depicted in Figure 2-5. Taiwanese government is afraid the economic interdependence with China will endanger the national security, thus Taiwan adopts a conservative policy in dealing with cross-Strait relations. However, the rigid China policy induces the inconvenience of MNEs and forces them to move their business operations away from Taiwan. While MNEs withdraw their business operations from Taiwan to China, they also bring along their Taiwanese contract manufacturers to mainland China. When Taiwanese manufacturers redistribute their manufacturing bases to China, their action is at the expense of low-skilled workers and will cause woe to Taiwan economy. The deteriorating of Taiwan economy will only intrigue the worrisome of Taiwanese government, which may again tighten the control over business activities of Taiwanese firms on

---

[131] See internet news, "Taiwanese Notebook Contract Manufacturers Shipping over Half of Their Products from China Base," (in Chinese)
http://news.taiwannet.com.tw/newsdata/showdetail1.php?ID=5418

[132] See internet news, "The Percentage of Notebook PCs Shipping from Mainland Will Exceed Fifty Percent," April 15, 2002 (in Chinese)
http://www.uniwill.com.tw/C-news_detail.asp?no=77

[133] Chiu Chien-ming, a finance executive at a technology firm, said "Eighty percent of the expatriates in my company are from Taiwan." Quoted from "Taiwan Suffers Brain Drain as Talent Goes to China" by Alice Hung, *Reuters News*, Aug. 12, 2003.

Chinese mainland, and the tightening China policy will further cause the inconvenience of MNEs.[134]

Figure 2-5 The Vicious Circle of Taiwan's China Policy

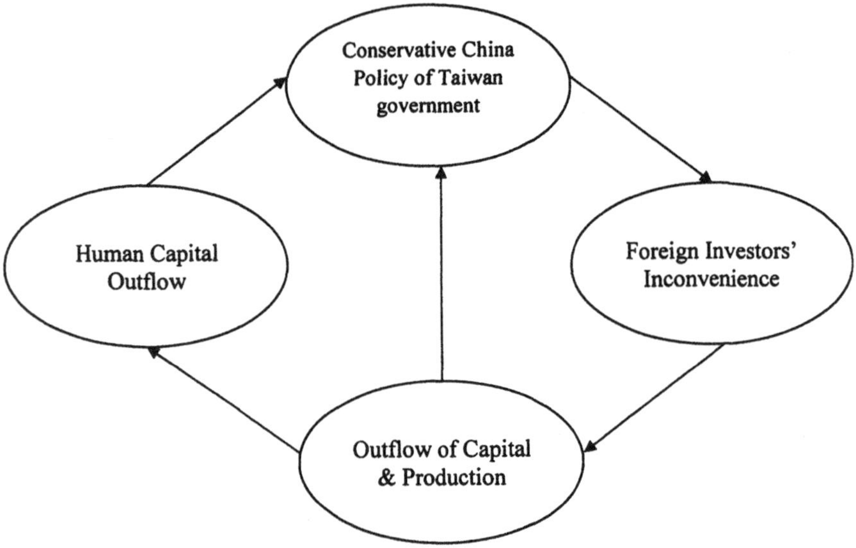

Complied by the author

As Taiwanese manufacturers dispatch high-skill workers to China, the brain-drain effect has aroused the serious concern of Taiwanese government, which has promulgated regulation to restrain the high-tech professionals from working in Chinese mainland.[135] Therefore, the worry of losing edge over China entraps Taiwanese government into the consideration of tightening its control over business community instead of loosening up. In a world of globalization, a home country government can exert little influence on those private corporations that are highly dependent on the international market to obtain their capital, labor, raw material and technology and to consume their production,.[136] Since most of the export-oriented Taiwanese firms have embedded in the global supply chain, if Taiwanese government cannot recognize that

[134] "Hello Shanghai: A Place to Call Home" by David Murphy, *Far Eastern Economic Review*, July 5, 2001
[135] See "NSC to Regulate High-tech Labor Across the Strait", *Taipei Times*, Apr 18, 2002,Page 1
[136] Leng, 1998, P. 494-495

Taiwanese firms have to live on the international market to thrive and globalization inevitably invites foreign influence into domestic business community, its unilateral containment policy on the economic exchanges between Taiwan and China will impede the development of Taiwan economy and eventually risk to drive Taiwanese firms away from Taiwan. Some Taiwanese firms have claimed that it is Taiwan's booming capital market which keeps them in Taiwan. Once Taiwan's capital market turns sluggish or China constructs its capital market soundly, they will consider moving away from Taiwan.[137]

2.4.4 Brain Drain Effects of Taiwan

While the trend of globalization contributes to China's economic ascendance, it also facilitates the interdependence of cross-Strait economic relations. During this irreversible process of economic integration, Taiwan has played as a high-skill manpower supplier to China. While relocating their production sites to China, Taiwanese manufacturers also bring along their managerial and technical talents. Even though it is difficult to estimate how serious the brain drain effect on Taiwan, from the transition of Taiwan investment to China, Taiwan's human capital outflow has two noticeable features: first the outflow was spontaneous but now is more systematic and organized; second the outflow talents were from traditional industries but now are from high-tech industries. Moreover, aside from the inestimable China-bound human capital flow from Taiwan, Taiwan's China policy induces another sequela to Taiwan economy: Taiwan is inhibiting itself from tapping China's large human resource. China is abundant with not only low-cost labor but also high-skill human resources.

Table 2-24 shows that in the early 1990s, the average amount of Taiwan investments in mainland China approved by Taiwanese government is less than USD one million. In 1991, the average amount is USD 0.73 million; in 1992, it increases to USD 0.94 million; in 1993, it is USD 0.9 million. Moreover, the average amount of retroactive registration is also less than USD 1 million. In 1993, the average amount of those previously unregistered investments is USD 0.25 million; in 1997, it is USD 0.34 million; in 1998, it is USD 0.8 million; in 2003, it is USD 0.73 million; in 2004, it is USD 0.38 million. Not until 1994 does the average amount of Taiwanese investments reach USD 1 million. In 1994, it is USD 1.03 million; in 1995, it doubles to USD 2.23 million. In 1996, it reaches the peak to USD 3.21 million. From then on, it fluctuates between USD 2.22 million and USD 3.1 million.

From the distinct difference between the average amounts in different time periods, it will be reasonable to assume that the investments in the early

[137] The conclusion is drawn from the interview with Lan-Yin Chou, Assistant Vice President, Barits International Securities Co., Ltd.

stage and the retroactive registered investments are mostly contributed by small and medium enterprises (SMEs). Most of the Taiwanese large corporations join the heat of the China-bound investments after 1994. This phenomenon indicates that Taiwanese SMEs are adroit and adventurous in exploring new business opportunities and bypassing governmental regulations.

As most of Taiwanese SMEs are family own businesses, aside from the bosses, the major business partners are their multi-function wives who have to take care of both the company and the family and play multiple roles as financial, personnel, managerial, purchasing, and even production managers to lower down managerial costs.[138] Therefore, they usually start their businesses in China by themselves or with their family members only, and gradually they will uproot the whole family from Taiwan to stay in China permanently.[139] Unlike SMEs, large corporations have more resources to dispense; as a result, they can allocate more expatriate workers to tend their investments in China. Thus, the outflow of Taiwanese talents shifts from the spontaneous human resources allocation of SMEs to the organized and systematic style of large firms. This transition indicates more and more professional talents are dispatched to explore China as more and more large firms invest in China.

However, regardless their identities, the expatriate bosses who are the owners of the SMEs or the professional talents who are assigned to work in China, once they migrate westwards, they inevitably take away their consumption power from Taiwan. This one-way outflow of talents will sooner or later affect Taiwan economy. Since there are no official statistics or reliable figures about the number of Taiwanese in China, the non-official statistics may provide evidence to how serious Taiwan's brain drain effect will be. The unofficial statistics claims that there are 250,000[140] or 300,000[141] Taiwanese in Shanghai, and almost a million Taiwanese in Chinese mainland.[142]

---

[138] Wu and Huang, 2003, P. 4

[139] "Taiwan businesswoman Doris Lu has spent most of the past eight years in southern China managing her family's speaker manufacturing factory… Lu will soon close the family's remaining business in Taiwan and move permanently to Guangdong—with her husband, two children, in-laws and sister-in-law…" By Alice Hung, Reuters News, Aug. 12, 2003.

Another example is Chinese food giant Tinghsin International Group, which was founded by four brothers of the Wei Family from Taiwan. Tinghsin is currently the market leader in instant food and beverage industry in China.

[140] According to the unofficial estimation from MGR Search & Selection, there are 250,000 Taiwanese in Shanghai area, and among them, 15,000 are looking for jobs.
http://www.mgr.com.tw/news/getNews.asp?NewsID=87

[141] See Leng (2002, P. 233)

[142] See Heard in Asia: China's Success Is a Problem for Taiwan's Material Makers, by Philip Segal, *Asian Wall Street Journal*, New York, N.Y.: Aug 15, 2001, P. M.1

Table 2-24 Taiwan Investments in Mainland China

Unit: USD Million

Period	Cases	Amount	Average Amount
1991	237	174.16	0.73
1992	264	246.99	0.94
1993	1,262	1,140.37	0.90
	(8,067)	(2,028.05)	(0.25)
1994	934	962.21	1.03
1995	490	1,092.71	2.23
1996	383	1,229.24	3.21
1997	728	1,614.54	2.22
	(7,997)	(2,719.77)	(0.34)
1998	641	1,519.21	2.37
	(643)	(515.41)	(0.80)
1999	488	1,252.78	2.57
2000	840	2,607.14	3.10
2001	1,186	2,784.15	2.35
2002	1,490	3,858.76	2.59
	(3950.00)	(2864.30)	(0.73)
2003	1,837	4,594.99	2.50
	(8,268)	(3,103.80)	(0.38)
2004	2,004	6,940.66	3.46
Total	33,155	41,249.23	1.24

Note: 1. ( ) represents the cases or amount for registration of previously unregistered investments.
2.*includes data before 1991.
3. The figures are not added up to the total due to rounding up.
Source: Investment Commission, Ministry of Economic Affairs, ROC.

Table 2-25, Taiwan's investments towards China have shifted from the traditional industry which is more labor-intensive to the high-tech industry which is more capital- and technology-intensive. In 1991 the percentage of China-bound investments from traditional industry is 32.95%; in 1992, it increases to 39.93%; in 1993, it decreases to 29.48%. At the same time, the percentages of investments from high-tech industry increases from 25.34% to 29.17%. In 1994, although the percentage of investments from high-tech sector slides to 28.63%, it for the first time exceeds the percentage of investments from traditional industry. Since then, Taiwanese high-tech companies have invested more than their traditional counterparts. The percentages of investments from traditional industry have decreased from the peak of 39.93 percent in 1992 to the dip of 5.83 percent in 2000. Although the investments from tradition sector pick up their vitality after 2000, they never really regain the former vigor during the early 1990s. In contrast to the lackluster performance of industry sector, the investments from high-tech industry surge from 25.34% in 1991 to 63.80% in 2000. Although the ratio of the investments from high-tech industry has declined to 44.30 percent in 2003, but it regains its ground and stands on 54.39% in 2004. Because the workers in high-tech industry enjoy a relatively higher salary than their counterparts in traditional industry, the outflow of high-tech workers will be an even more serious threat to the consumption market of Taiwan.

In fact, expatriate bosses and workers of Taiwanese firms are not the only source of outflow talents, as some of Taiwanese workers have been recruited or dispatched by foreign-owned companies or even Chinese companies. So far, the one-way human capital flow from Taiwan to China shows no sign of reversal. Moreover, once those Taiwanese expatriate workers land on Chinese mainland, most of them will not think of going back to Taiwan even though they have been replaced by local Chinese.[143]

The surging outflow of Taiwanese investments to China causes Taiwanese workers' concern of losing their jobs to the other side of Taiwan Strait. As a result, many Taiwanese are willing to position themselves in China's job market earlier. Ten years ago, Taiwanese expatriate workers get double-pay of their Taiwanese salary for the work in China; five years ago, the pay to expatriate Taiwanese workers drops to 1.3-1.5 times of their salary in Taiwan; now some of Taiwanese employees are willing to accept a salary lower than what they can get in Taiwan to gain working experience in China.[144]

The relocation of production sites causes a lapse in job opportunities and exodus talents. The lack of sufficient high-skilled workers will further hamper the possibility of Taiwanese firms to construct their division of labor across Taiwan Strait. After Taiwanese firms export their production sites to China, Taiwanese government expects they will maintain their R&D and operation centers in Taiwan. However, Taiwanese firms are not satisfied with R&D centers only in Taiwan but have a propensity to also establish R&D centers in China. By establishing R&D centers in China, they can tap China's huge talent pool and access to China's large domestic market.[145]

---

[143] "Most of the Taiwanese expatriate workers will not go back to Taiwan. They will not be able to find a job in Taiwan," said A Fa Chen, Vice President of Ya Hsin Electronic Co. in Dong Guan. By Li-Juang Lan, "Mainland, an Opportunity for Taiwanese? Or a Nightmare?" in *Cheers*, July 2002. (in Chinese)

[144] "Replace Taiwanese Managers within One Year" by Yi-Zhi Jang, in *Globalview Magazine,* April 2003. (in Chinese)

[145] Leng, 2002, P. 248.

Table 2-25 Statistics on Approved Indirect Mainland Investment by Industry

Unit: USD 1,000

Year	Traditional Industry		High-Tech Industry		Services Industry		Others	
	Amount	%	Amount	%	Amount	%	Amount	%
1991	57,382	32.95	44,138	25.34	200	0.11	72,438	41.59
1992	98,634	39.93	64,011	25.92	7,441	3.01	76,906	31.14
1993	934,022	29.48	924,362	29.17	301,932	9.53	1,008,095	31.82
1994	264,286	27.47	275,517	28.63	93,894	9.76	328,512	34.14
1995	256,749	23.50	379,731	34.75	185,675	16.99	270,558	24.76
1996	296,843	12.99	482,759	21.12	206,922	9.05	1,298,987	56.84
1997	1,003,877	23.16	1,456,209	33.60	504,930	11.65	1,369,297	31.59
1998	373,035	18.33	985,184	48.42	260,604	12.81	415,798	20.44
1999	154,577	12.34	628,935	50.20	108,993	8.70	360,275	28.76
2000	151,927	5.83	1,663,336	63.80	248,961	9.55	542,918	20.82
2001	286,136	10.28	1,554,574	55.84	286,102	10.28	657,335	23.61
2002	734,698	10.93	3,502,941	52.10	751,757	11.18	1,733,662	25.79
2003	1,186,827	15.42	3,410,810	44.30	1,102,927	14.33	1,998,220	25.96
2004	549,056	7.91	3,775,072	54.39	808,629	11.65	1,807,906	26.05

Note:

1. Traditional Industry: 1) Agriculture & Forestry, 2) Fishery & Animal Husbandry Industry, 3) Mining, 4) Food & Beverage Processing, 5) Textile, 6) Garment & Footwear, 7) Leather & Fur Products, 8) Lumber & Bamboo Products, 9) Paper Products & Printing.
2. High-Tech Industry: 1) Machinery Equipment, 2) Electronic & Electric Appliances, 3) Transport Equipment, 4) Precision Instruments
3. Services Industry: 1) Whole Sale & Retail, 2) Trade, 3) Restaurant, 4) Transportation, 5) Storage, 6) Banking & Insurance, 7) Services
4. Others: 1) Chemicals, 2) Rubber Products, 3) Plastic Products, 4) Non-Metallic Minerals, 5) Basic Metals & Metal products, 6) Construction Instruments, 7) Others

Source: Investment Commission, Ministry of Economic Affairs, ROC, calculated by Author

Although so far, Taiwanese firms still maintain parallel R&D centers in Taiwan, and in order to gain tax reduction[146], they even respond to the demand of Taiwan's government to locate their operation headquarters in Taiwan.[147] From Table 2-26, on the surface, the "Operation Headquarters Development Plan[148]" seems fruitful that it has attracted up to 197 enterprises to set up their

---

[146] According to Article 70-1 of the Statute for Upgrading Industries, business income tax on income derived from providing management services or R&D services to overseas affiliates is exempted, so are business income taxes on income derived from royalty payments payable by offshore affiliates and on income derived from capital gains and dividends payable by offshore affiliates.
http://www.moeaidb.gov.tw/idy/english/measure2.htm

[147] Ibid.

[148] Ibid. "Operation Headquarters Development Plan" is developed by Industrial Development Bureau, Ministry of Economic Affairs.

operation headquarters in Taiwan as of July 2003, and over 50% of them are from electronic information industry, the high-tech sector. However, those enterprises do not expand their operation in Taiwan, but gather all their island-wide affiliates into one operation center to enjoy the tax benefit. On the other hand, the number of those which establish operation headquarters in Taiwan is less than 1% of total Taiwanese companies investing in China. According to a field survey of *Fortune China Monthly*, the number of Taiwanese firms investing in China has reached 68,115 as of the end of 2003,[149] and this outnumbers the official statistics of Taiwan and that of China. Taiwanese government registered 24,160 cases of Taiwanese investments, Chinese authority 50,838. Since the official statistics regarding cross-Strait exchanges has the tendency to be underestimated by both Taiwan and China because some Taiwanese firms will disguise themselves as foreign investors through the third country, 68,115 should be a more reliable estimation than both official statistics from Taiwan and China. Thus, in contrast to the booming China-bound investments, the effect of "Operation Headquarters Development Plan" seems limited.

At current stage, most of Taiwanese enterprises expand their operations in China, but maintain their operations in Taiwan at previous level[150]. In order to transform Taiwan into a "High Added Value Industrial Base", Industrial Development Bureau commences the Operation Headquarters Development Plan, which intends to "integrate the industrial resources available in the Asian Pacific Region"[151]. However, as the current domestic politics impedes the normal business and human capital exchanges across Taiwan Strait, Taiwanese government has to determine first whether China is included or excluded in its defined "Asian Pacific Region" because Chinese talents are emerging as one of the world's most human resources.

Taiwanese "overseas returnees" have been the major contributor to the success of Taiwan information technology industry, but now less and less Taiwanese study abroad. From Table 2-27, while Chinese students studying in the US increase from 45,126 in 1992/1993 academic year to 64,757 in 2002-2003 academic year and the increase of Chinese students poses a 43.5 percent increase in the 11-year period, on the contrary, Taiwanese students decrease from 37,432 to 28,017 at the same period of time, a 25.15 percent decrease in the number of Taiwanese students enrolled in US universities. Although the terrorist attack on September 11, 2001 has influenced the number of Chinese students who enroll in the US, Taiwanese students are still outnumbered by Chi-

---

149 Fortune China Monthly, Vol. 124, June 2004. (Tou Zi Zhong Guo, in Chinese)

150 The conclusion is drawn from the interview with Lan-Yin Chou, Assistant Vice President of Barits International Securities Co., Ltd.

151 This information is disclosed in the website of Industrial Development Bureau, Ministry of Economic Affairs. http://www.moeaidb.gov.tw/portal/english/measure2.jsp

nese students. In 2003, the number of Chinese students who enroll in the US is 61765; that of Taiwanese students is 26,178. In 2004, there are 62,523 Chinese students and 25,914 Taiwanese students in the US. In contrast to the upward trajectory of Chinese students studying in the US, Taiwanese students are no longer enthusiastic in pursuing a higher education in the US. Less and less Taiwanese students studying in the US implies the insufficient human resources supply in the future. To Taiwan's dismay, according the Zeng's observation, the post-graduation performance of Chinese students is far superior to that of Taiwanese students, as Taiwanese students seldom serve a high-level executive position in the US companies but Chinese students fill in the positions as chief scientists, vice presidents of R&D, vice presidents of engineer and so on in the newly founded enterprises of Silicon Valley.[152]

Table 2-26 The Number of Business Operation Headquarters Established in Taiwan, as of July 2004

Field of Industries of the 197 Enterprises Having Established their Operation Headquarters in Taiwan						
Manufacturing Industries 177			Service Industries 18			
Metal Machinery	Electronic Information	Consumer Goods and Chemicals	Technical Service	Wholesale and Retail	Financial Insurance	Transportation Warehousing
35	103	40	6	5	4	4

Source: Collected by the Industrial Development Bureau, Ministry of Economic Affairs.

In concern with the brain drain effect, Taiwan faces two challenges. First, the endless outflow of Taiwanese talents to China so far seems irreversible. Although Taiwanese government has promulgated regulations to restrain high-tech professionals from obtaining a job in China, however from the factory operating professionals to high-tech talents,[153] Taiwanese government wields little influence on the natural flow of human capital. Second, Taiwanese government does not construct an environment which is attractive to worldwide talents. Although Taiwan has gradually lifted the ban on the inflow of Chinese high-tech talents, the skeptical attitudes of the government and the general pub-

[152] In 1998, 20% cadres of the newly founded enterprises in Silicon Valley were Chinese students. Zeng, 2001, P. 216.

[153] According to the introduction of Te-Min Chang, vice president of Semiconductor Manufacturing International Corporation (SMIC), among the total 2,400 employees of SMIC, there are 450 Taiwanese. SMIC is a semiconductor foundry manufacturer in China. Taiwanese government intended to ban Taiwanese talents in semiconductor fabrication and manufacturing from obtaining employment in China.
http://tw.people.com.cn/BIG5/14813/14877/951432.html

lic will prevent mainland Chinese talents from integrating into the local Taiwanese environment and diminish their willingness to work in Taiwan.[154]

Table 2-27 The Numbers of Chinese and Taiwanese Students Enrolled in US Universities

Unit: Number

Place of Origin / Academic Year	China	% Change	Taiwan	% Change
1992/93	45,126	-	37,432	-
1993/94	44,381	-1.65	37,581	0.40
1994/95	39,403	-11.22	36,407	-3.12
1995/96	42,503	7.87	30,487	-16.26
1996/97	39,613	-6.80	32,702	7.27
1997/98	46,958	18.54	30,855	-5.65
1998/99	51,001	8.61	31,043	0.61
1999/00	54,466	6.79	29,234	-5.83
2000/01	59,939	10.05	28,566	-2.29
2001/02	63,211	5.46	28,930	1.27
2002/03	64,757	2.45	28,017	-3.16
2003/04	61,765	-4.84	26,178	-7.02
2004/05	62,523	1.21	25,914	-1.02

Source: Institute of International Education, Open Doors

Since the development of Taiwan economy, especially in the IT sector, depends on the "overseas returnees",[155] with the trend of the increasing number of Chinese students vis-à-vis the decreasing number of Taiwanese students in the US, if Taiwan expects to maintain its edge in IT industry, mainland Chinese talents will constitute an important talent pool for the development of Taiwan economy.

2.4.5 Booming Trade across Taiwan Strait

Aside from the westbound flow of capital, talents and foreign investors, the globalization also facilitates the surge of the cross-Strait trade. Table 2-28 indicates that the amount of Taiwan's exports to Chinese areas increases from 1981's USD 1,897 million to 200's USD 64,136.52 million; it was an over 30-

---

[154] Leng, 2002, P. 248.

[155] "After suffering a severe brain drain for 30 years, Taiwan is being fortified by expatriates returning home from the US. Many are setting up high-technology companies. The talent pool is deep: By some estimates, 50,000 Taiwanese engineers and scientists live in the US, and 20% of Silicon Valley semiconductor engineers are Chinese." See "Brain Drain in Reverse (Taiwanese Leaving US and Returning to Taiwan)" by Andrew Tanzer, *Forbes*, April 17, 1989.

fold increase. At the same time, the amount of Taiwan's imports from Chinese areas increases from 1981's USD 309 million to 2004's USD 18,804.09 million; it represented a 60-fold increase. The percentage of Taiwan's exports to Chinese areas against Taiwan's total exports has increased from 1981's 8.39 percent to 2004's 36.86 percent. During the same period of time, the percentage of Taiwan's imports from Chinese areas against Taiwan's total imports increases from 1.46 percent to 11.2 percent. Although due to the effective inflow-control of Taiwanese government, the percentage of Taiwan's imports from Chinese areas against total Taiwan's imports is relatively low to that of Taiwan's exports to Chinese areas against Taiwan's total exports, the uptrend of Taiwan's trade with China is irreversible. China has surpassed the US becomes Taiwan's largest export market. Taiwan's exports to China has bee on an upward trajectory. As Taiwanese businessmen aggressively deploy their businesses in China market, the expansion of Taiwan's exports to China will be able to sustain for a long time. At the same time, the growth of imports from China area has been relatively slow but steady according to the statistics of Table 2-28.

As a small-island economy, Taiwan is short of natural resources and highly relies on the international trade to facilitate its economic expansion. From Table 2-29, Taiwan economy is getting more vulnerable towards the fluctuation of the foreign trade; in 2001, Taiwan's foreign trade dependence was 80.71%; in 2002, it increased to 84.26%; in 2003, it reaches 91.84%; in 2004, it increases to 107.96%. Taiwan's four-year average foreign trade dependence is 91.19%, which is lower than Hong Kong's 296.3% and Singapore's 272.9% but higher than USA's 18.35%, Japan's 19.34%, German's 56.59% and South Korea's 62.41%. From the previous comparison, the smaller the economic entity is, the more susceptible its economic development is toward the international trade.

Table 2-28 The Statistics of Trade with Chinese Areas*

Unit: USD million

Year	Imports from Chinese areas	Exports to Chinese areas	Imports from Chinese areas/ Total Imports	Exports to Chinese areas/ Total Exports
1981	309.35	1,897.33	1.46%	8.39%
1982	307.44	1,566.48	1.63%	7.05%
1983	299.01	1,644.89	1.47%	6.55%
1984	370.51	2,090.61	1.69%	6.86%
1985	319.78	2,546.98	1.59%	8.29%
1986	378.89	2,933.75	1.57%	7.36%
1987	754.42	4,146.01	2.16%	7.72%
1988	1,923.94	5,619.53	3.87%	9.26%
1989	2,208.41	7,106.33	4.23%	10.72%
1990	1,452.74	8,654.47	2.66%	12.88%
1991	2,246.89	12,521.73	3.57%	16.44%
1992	2,541.20	15,500.90	3.53%	19.03%
1993	2,763.03	18,566.89	3.59%	21.82%
1994	3,414.33	21,528.69	4.00%	23.14%
1995	4,962.05	26,670.39	4.79%	23.89%
1996	4,792.60	27,647.68	4.68%	23.85%
1997	5,949.58	29,625.77	5.20%	24.27%
1998	6,104.33	25,973.26	5.83%	23.49%
1999	6,667.19	28,821.87	6.02%	23.70%
2000	8,457.83	35,867.80	6.04%	24.18%
2001	7,796.79	31,983.24	7.27%	26.03%
2002	9,716.32	41,067.66	8.63%	31.45%
2003	12,714.26	50,058.78	9.99%	34.72%
2004	18,804.09	64,136.52	11.20%	36.86%

Note: * Chinese Areas indicate Hong Kong, Macao & Chinese Mainland. Although Hong Kong and Macao do not belong to China until 1997 and 1999 respectively, the inclusion of Hong Kong and Macao is more consistent in explaining the transition between Taiwan and these Chinese areas.

Source: Directorate-General of Budget, Accounting & Statistics (DGBAS) Executive Yuan, Taiwan, R.O.C.

Table 2-30 illustrates that since 1993 China has been the major source of Taiwan's trade surplus. In 1992, without China market, Taiwan still enjoyed a trade surplus up to USD 887 million; however, in 1993, if the trade surplus with China is deducted, Taiwan's trade deficit is USD 3, 682 million. Although in 1998, Taiwan's trade surplus against China slides to USD 14,270 million from previous year's USD 16,603 million, basically, Taiwan's trade surplus against China is on an upward trajectory. With the ambitious China-bound deployment of Taiwanese enterprises, Taiwan will retain its strategic position in exploiting China market until the process of "hollowing out" is complete. In 2004, Taiwan's trade deficit against the world excluding China even sets a record high up to USD 22,157 million; simultaneously, Taiwan's trade surplus against China also peaks at USD 28,282 million to help Taiwan maintain its positive trade balance.

Table 2-29 The Foreign Trade Dependence of Selected Economies

Unit: %

Economy \ Year	2001	2002	2003	2004	Average
Taiwan	80.71	84.26	91.84	107.96	91.19
USA	18.39	17.66	17.95	19.42	18.35
Japan	17.76	18.63	19.53	21.44	19.34
German	56.42	55.18	55.59	59.15	56.59
France*	52.97	50.39	47.97	34.17	46.38
UK*	42.32	40.23	38.44	37.97	39.74
South Korea*	60.48	57.52	61.29	70.34	62.41
HK*	276.80	279.55	299.14	329.71	296.30
Singapore	234.83	249.08	287.66	320.06	272.90
China	44.08	49.44	60.42	-	51.31

Note: * Total trade divided by GDP.

Source: Department of Statistics, Ministry of Economic Affairs, ROC, calculated by the author.

Table 2-30 Taiwan's Trade Balance

Unit: USD million

Year	Trade Surplus against China	Trade Balance without China	Total Trade Balance
1992	8,577.80	885.70	9,463.50
1993	11,712.30	-3,682.00	8,030.30
1994	12,794.29	-5,094.69	7,699.60
1995	14,806.89	-6,698.09	8,108.80
1996	16,088.45	-2,516.35	13,572.10
1997	16,602.69	-8,946.69	7,656.00
1998	14,269.59	-8,352.59	5,917.00
1999	16,694.99	-5,793.89	10,901.10
2000	19,920.74	-11,610.84	8,309.90
2001	18,159.39	-2,530.49	15,628.90
2002	21,517.26	-3,450.56	18,066.70
2003	24,397.20	-7,466.20	16,931.00
2004	28,281.71	-22,157.31	6,124.40

Source: Department of Statistics, Ministry of Economic Affairs, ROC

2.5 The China Policy of the US

The US is Taiwan's patron state. Taiwan has survived and thrived under the US shelter. While making a speech in the Ketagalan Institute[156], Chiou I-jen, the chairman of the National Security Council, claims Taiwan has to kowtow to the US.[157] He argues Taiwan has to face the reality that Taiwan needs the US to resolve the cross-Strait issue, because no matter how China strengthens its national power, China has to act according to the US likings and dislikes.[158] Thus, regardless of the willingness of the US to get involved in the cross-Strait dispute, Taiwan's ruling party resolves to drag it in. Moreover, the US has the Taiwan Relation Act as an excuse or a proper cause to interfere into the cross-Strait affair. As the world's sole super power, if the US cannot separate Taiwan from China, the chance for Taiwan to win independence is slim. Therefore, the China policy of the US plays an important role in shaping the structure of cross-Strait relations.

Moreover, the Sino-US relations have evolved on the basis of resistance to a common threat rather than on the basis of mutual understanding. Therefore, when the external threat disappears, the Sino-US friendship also evaporates. The Soviet Union had been the major cause for the existence of Sino-US alliance. After the collapse of the Soviet Union, the disappearance of the common threat has put the Sino-US relations on a roller-coaster journey. The lack of mutual trust forces both sides to take a conservative and precautionary attitude during their engagement. The US suspects the future development of China, and is worried about China might turn into another "evil empire" which will threat the US interests; on the other hand, Chinese leaders are concerned about the true intention of the US behind the engagement which is only a tactic of American plots to subvert Chinese communist regime and to accomplish its goal of "peaceful evolution" in China. After all, China may not be the worst among the "rogue states" in the US mind, but definitely ranks the largest among its kind.

After Tiananmen massacre, the US can no longer trust that its engagement with China will lead to a renovated China and begin to suspect that China

---

[156] The Ketagalan Institute was founded by President Chen Shui-bian in March 2003 to propagate and glorify his political ideology.

[157] The direct translation of Chiou's phrase should be "can we not embrace the US thigh? (Wuo Meng Bu Bao Mei Kuo De Da Tui Xing Ma?)" Embracing someone's thigh is more like bootlicking.

[158] The direct translation of Chiou's words will be "watch the US facial expression (Kan Lian Se)." Referred from "The Record For the Well-known Remarks and Conducts of the Bian Administration, (Bian Zheng Fu Min Yen Jia Xing Lu)" NPF Commentary, National Policy Foundation, Nov 20, 2003

will accept human right and democracy as international value in this globalized world. Moreover, as China emerges as an economic power and a potential military one, economic benefits and political challenges presented by China trouble American politicians and scholars, and the opinions split on the China policy of the US within the US polity pester the enhancement of Sino-US relations and further hinder the effectiveness of Washington's China policy.

As the globalization has deepened the economic interdependence among states through international trade and cross-border investment, if the US considers tailoring its China policy based on its national interests, it will realizes that it is not in America's best interest to be permanently at odds with the growing economic power and the world's third largest nuclear power arsenal. However the economic interdependence and the political uncertainty between China and the US make the US confused about its China policy. As a result, the US does not have an affirmative China policy and its China policy is more spontaneous than well-planned.

Since the US China policy highly depends on circumstantial events, its former effort is easily beset by its later performance, and any single incident will upset the fragile Sino-US relations. When depicting the Sino-US relations during the 1970s and 1980s, Harding points out that it is the common threat from the Soviet Union pushes China and the US together. As a result, when Soviet Union is preoccupied with its internal affairs and poses less threat to both countries, the ad hoc alliance begins to crumble.[159] However, while the Soviet "evil empire" reemerges to the surface as the most minacious common enemy, China and the US will put away their minor frictions and revitalize their collaboration.

The massacre on Tiananmen Square in June 1989 disillusioned both parties and the dissolved enemy—Soviet Union further impaired their fragile relations.[160] Although the US feels no obligation to engage with China any longer, it soon discovers that China, as a permanent member in UN Security Council, and world's third largest nuclear power and most populous country, can disturb the US political agenda as much as it can assist the US political ambition. The effectiveness of economic boycott induced by Tiananmen incident is quickly diluted by another urgent agenda, the Iraqi invasion of Kuwait. The first Persian Gulf War makes the US realize it needs China to obtain an endorsement on launching a war against Iraq from UN Security Council. Therefore, in hope to obtain the full support of a military action against Iraq from Beijing, Washington lifts the ban to allow Qian Qichen, a senior Chinese official, to

[159] Harding, 1992, P. 9-10
[160] Tucker, 1991

have a meeting with American president in spite of the Tiananmen Square incident but secures only an abstention from China.[161]

After the Cold War, although the strategic alliance against the Soviet Union with China becomes an obsolete past to the US, China's strong presence in the international community forces the US to take into account this emerging country in its diplomatic policy, and China's economic strength even ruptures the US sanctions caused by the Tiananmen massacre. Because the navigation systems for a certain kind of commercial jets are banned by the US because they can be converted into military, it requires the special waiver from the president to lift the restriction to sell four commercial jets to China. To complete the deal, the US scales back its sanction against China by proclaiming that the US does not ban on the development work which has been agreed before the implementation of the sanction. Thus the US allows Chinese officials to get back to the USD 550 million Peace Pearl project and the project is aimed to improve Chinese fighter planes.[162]

Considering the economic benefits, the US has to adopt a more lenient approach toward China. Moreover, China's ability to proliferate mass destructive weapons enhances its strategic importance to the US. Even though the Tiananmen massacre casts a cloud over the Sino-US relationship, to solve the problem of China's proliferation of missiles and other weaponry in the Middle East, Baker[163], though reluctant, has to visit China personally. During this visit, China refuses Baker to deliver the letter from Bush to Deng Xiaoping, and Baker's trip to China secures only China's verbal commitment to curb the proliferation of weapons of mass destruction (WMD).[164]

When Tiananmen massacre takes place, the Western countries have tried to contain China, but fail. At that time (1989), China's foreign trade is USD 111.68 billion but has reached USD 1,154.6 billion in 2004; its inward FDI is USD 3.39 billion but has reached USD 60.63 billion in 2004; at the end of 1989, China accumulates USD 18 million of foreign exchange reserves but its foreign exchange reserves have reached USD 609.93 million. When China acts as one of the world fast-growing economies, any containment scheme without a proper cause will only hurt the one who intends to contain China. As a result, China has no reason to be afraid of the US containment because in the globalized world, the Cold-War doctrine will not perform as effective as it did. If the US can not recognize the reality, it will encounter more difficulty in dealing with China.

---

[161] Mann, 1999, P.248

[162] Ibid, 218-219

[163] James Baker is the former Secretary of State.

[164] Ibid. P. 250-252

The current US China policy can be better described as engagement-flawed or containment-failed. The US expects to engage China through the economic, cultural, and social exchanges to integrate China into the world system and to pin China in the world regulation. However, on the perspective of Chinese, China pays its share to induce all sorts of exchanges with foreign powers and nothing is a windfall fortune bestowed on China from Western world. China wins its reward by adopting an "open door" policy—opens the large domestic market and provides cheap labor—to initiate the economic exchanges and so on. China does not feel obliged to appreciate the American engagement and the US should not expect any special favor from China because the exchanges between China and the US are based on the mutual interests and not on China's interests alone.[165] Especially when China assumes the intention behind the US engagement policy is "to influence the domestic evolution of Chinese society in a more liberal and open direction[166]", for China, this encouragement of "peaceful evolution" is the American plots to subvert Chinese communist regime, and China will never accept it.[167] When China consider the US policy being on the surface benign but containing vicious intentions inside, it is illogical to expect a growing power like China to acquiescently agree on the set-international-norm which has been set by other powers, especially the US.

Although the uncertainty over China's future geopolitical intentions clouds the US China policy, Wang thinks the Sino-US relations should be able to develop stably. He argues for over thirty years, China and the US have not been the major foes for each other, and both parties maintain the bottom-line of the most sensitive issue—Taiwan issue unchanged. Moreover, the superpower status of the US and the rising international status of China highlight the importance of Sino-US relations. Although the domestic politics influences the Sino-US relations, the full-scale economic and social engagement between China and the US will offer China opportunities to influence the US society.[168]

In the post-Cold War era, the US appears as the de facto world dominating power. However, in the anarchic structure of the international political system, the emergence of a unipolar world dominated by the US may be acknowledged but not welcomed. Thus, if the US intends to contain China, it will en-

---

[165] "Why shouldn't America engage China? We are a great power," one of the China's leading America specialists said, when interviewed about the US China policy debate. Shambaugh, 1996, P. 208

[166] Ibid, P. 184

[167] Tucker, 1991

[168] Wang Ji Si is the director of the Institute of North American Studies at the Chinese Academy of Social Sciences. Quoted from "The steadiness and vicissitude of Sino-US relations" in United Daily News, Jan. 27, 2003.

counter the difficulty of persuading the international community to believe China has to be contained, especially when China has emerged as an Asian economic locomotive. Moreover, Russia may not believe China represent a more serious threat than the US does. Aside from Russia, the other major powers such as France, Germany and Japan also have their own considerations. If the US unilaterally imposes any economic sanctions on China, it is no less than to yield the enormous China market to European and Japanese firms.[169] Therefore, if the US intends to manage its relationship with China, the US should put pressure on Taiwan to start a cross-Strait dialogue with China and manage China's political agenda through Taiwan's hand, because China loathes the interference of foreign powers in its domestic affairs and according to China's One China Principle, Taiwan is a part of China.

2.5.1 The Economic Interdependence between China and the US

Aside from China's ability to unsettle the world order, China's emerge as a "world's factory" also enhance its strategic position in the US thinking. In the post-Cold War era, economic and trade ties construct an important cornerstone for the Sino-US relationship. From Table 2-31, in 2004, China imports USD 34.7 billion from the US and exports USD 196.7 billion to the US; the total amount of bilateral trade is USD 231.4 billion. China has been the third largest trade partner of the US and the Sino-US trade accounts for 10.1 percent of the US total trade. In terms of bilateral trade with the US, China lags only behind Canada and Mexico—the other two major participants of the North America Free Trade Agreement (NAFTA). At the same time, the total trade between Taiwan and the US is USD 56.3 billion and Taiwan ranks as the eighth largest trade partner of the US.

---

[169] "SEMI (Semiconductor Equipment and Materials International) is pushing the US government to make it easier for U.S. tool exports into China, which is now the hottest market for semiconductor equipment. The group favors the changes to help level the playing field between U.S. vendors and their foreign rivals. Chip-equipment makers from Europe, Japan, and elsewhere are perceived to have an unfair advantage in China, because they have less stringent export laws in their respective nations, according to SEMI representatives." Referred from http://www.my-esm.com/business/showArticle.jhtml?articleID=18201865

Table 2-31 Top Trading Partners of the US (The Year of 2004)

Unit: USD billion

Country	Exports	Imports	Total Trade	Rank	Percent of Total Trade
Canada	190.2	255.9	446.1	1	19.5%
Mexico	110.8	155.8	266.6	2	11.6%
China	**34.7**	**196.7**	**231.4**	**3**	**10.1%**
Japan	54.4	129.6	184.0	4	8.0%
Germany	31.4	77.2	108.6	5	4.7%
United Kingdom	36.0	46.4	82.4	6	3.6%
Korea, South	26.3	46.2	72.5	7	3.2%
Taiwan	**21.7**	**34.6**	**56.3**	**8**	**2.5%**
France	21.2	31.8	53.1	9	2.3%
Malaysia	10.9	28.2	39.1	10	1.7%
Italy	10.7	28.1	38.8	11	1.7%
Netherlands	24.3	12.6	36.9	12	1.6%
Ireland	13.9	21.2	35.0	13	1.6%
Brazil	2.4	2.6	5	14	1.5%
Singapore	19.6	15.3	34.9	15	1.5%

Note: Data are goods only, on a Census Basis.
Source: Foreign Trade Division, U.S. Census Bureau

Table 2-32 indicates a fast growing trade between China and the US and the bilateral trade is on an upward trajectory without setback. Their trade value increased from USD 7.72 billion in 1985 all the way up to 2004's 231.42 billion, and which indicates a nearly 29 times increase in less than 20 years. During the same period of time, Chinese imports increased from USD 3.86 billion to 196.7 billion, an approximately 40 times increase; Chinese exports increase from USD 3.86 billion to USD 34.72 billion, a roughly 8 times increase. The fast-growing Chinese exports enlarged the US trade deficit against China from USD 6 million to USD 161.98 billion. Thus, the growing trade between China and the US facilitates the interdependence of both parties and impedes the US unilateral action in implementing trade sanctions against China. Even though the US trade deficit against China has risen sharply, China's high stake in trade with the US does not put China in a relatively vulnerable bargaining position. Mann points out igniting a trade war is not a dollar for dollar calculation; it is the test of the political will. The US government must be well prepared to weather through the pressure from the US business community when threats any trade retaliation against China, because it will face not only those Americans exporting to China, but also those importing from China.[170]

[170] Mann, 1999, 276

Table 2-32 US Trade with China, by Year

Unit: USD Million

Year	Exports	Imports	Total	Balance
1985	3,855.7	3,861.7	7,717.4	-6.0
1986	3,106.3	4,771.0	7,877.3	-1,664.7
1987	3,497.3	6,293.6	9,790.9	-2,796.3
1988	5,021.6	8,510.9	13,532.5	-3,489.3
1989	5,755.4	11,989.7	17,745.1	-6,234.3
1990	4,806.4	15,237.4	20,043.8	-10,431.0
1991	6,278.2	18,969.2	25,247.4	-12,691.0
1992	7,418.5	25,727.5	33,146.0	-18,309.0
1993	8,762.9	31,539.9	40,302.8	-22,777.0
1994	9,281.7	38,786.8	48,068.5	-29,505.1
1995	11,753.7	45,543.2	57,296.9	-33,789.5
1996	11,992.6	51,512.8	63,505.4	-39,520.2
1997	12,862.2	62,557.7	75,419.9	-49,695.5
1998	14,241.2	71,168.6	85,409.8	-56,927.4
1999	13,111.1	81,788.2	94,899.3	-68,677.1
2000	16,185.2	100,018.2	116,203.4	-83,833.0
2001	19,182.3	102,278.4	121,460.7	-83,096.1
2002	22,127.7	125,192.6	147,320.3	-103,064.9
2003	28,418.5	152,379.1	180,797.6	-123,960.6
2004	34,721.0	196,699.0	231,420.0	-161,978.0

Source: U.S. Census Bureau, Foreign Trade Division

In fact, once a trade war starts between China and the US, Chinese manufacturers will not be the only victims. Thousands of foreign owned enterprises (FIEs) will also be involved in the fight of giants and suffer, as more than 50 percent of China's exports are contributed by FIEs and that is to say most of China's trade surplus comes from those FIEs. Table 2-33 illustrates in terms of volume and ratios, the FIEs have gradually played an important role in the international trade of China. In late 1980s, the trade volume of FIEs is less than USD 15 billion and that of Chinese enterprises ranges from USD 70 billion to USD 100 billion, but in late 1990s, the trade volume of FIEs is almost tantamount to that of Chinese firms. In 2001, the export amount of FIEs for the first time supersede that of Chinese firms; in 2002, the export amount of FIEs accounts for 52.2% of China's total exports; in 2003, the percentage of the exports from FIEs against total China's trade surges to 54.83%; in 2004, the percentage rises again to 57.06%. The imports of the FIEs account for less than 15% of China's total trade in the late 1980s, and the percentage of the imports from the FIEs almost ascends all the way to 2004's 57.81%. AS many FIEs primarily take advantage of China's cheap labor and vast land, many of them import components, machinery and raw materials, and after production processing, they will re-export the final products.[171] This explains the phenomenon of the nearly simultaneous growth in the exports and imports of the FIEs.

Table 2-33 China's Total Imports and Exports by FIEs

Unit: USD billion

Year	Imports & Exports			Imports			Exports		
	National	FIEs	%	National	FIEs	%	National	FIEs	%
1986	73.85	2.99	4.04	42.90	2.40	5.60	30.94	0.58	1.88
1987	82.65	4.58	5.55	43.22	3.37	7.81	39.44	1.21	3.07
1988	102.78	8.34	8.12	55.27	5.88	10.64	47.52	2.46	5.18
1989	111.68	13.71	12.28	59.14	8.80	14.87	52.54	4.91	9.35
1990	115.44	20.12	17.43	53.35	12.30	23.06	62.09	7.81	12.58
1991	135.70	28.96	21.34	63.79	16.91	26.51	71.91	12.05	16.75
1992	165.53	43.75	26.43	80.59	26.39	32.74	84.94	17.36	20.44
1993	195.70	67.07	34.27	103.96	41.83	40.24	91.74	25.24	27.51
1994	236.62	87.65	37.04	115.62	52.93	45.78	121.01	34.71	28.69
1995	280.85	109.82	39.10	132.08	62.94	47.66	148.77	46.88	31.51
1996	289.90	137.11	47.29	138.84	75.60	54.45	151.07	61.51	40.71
1997	325.06	152.62	46.95	142.36	77.72	54.59	182.70	74.90	41.00
1998	323.92	157.68	48.68	140.17	76.72	54.73	183.76	80.96	44.06
1999	360.65	174.51	48.39	165.72	85.88	51.83	194.93	88.63	45.47
2000	474.31	236.71	49.91	225.10	117.27	52.10	249.21	119.44	47.93
2001	509.77	259.10	50.83	243.61	125.86	51.67	266.16	133.24	50.06
2002	620.79	330.22	53.19	295.22	160.29	54.29	325.57	169.94	52.20
2003	851.21	472.26	55.48	412.84	231.91	56.18	438.37	240.34	54.83
2004	1,154.79	663.16	57.43	561.42	324.56	57.81	593.37	338.61	57.06

Source: Ministry of Commerce, P.R.C.

Aside from a close trade relationship, according the statistics of China's Ministry of Commerce, the US, lagging behind Hong Kong, serves as the second largest FDI provider to China.[172] The US investors have contracted USD 9.86 billion accounting for 8.99 percent of total contracted FDI to China and already invested USD 4.8 billion into China as of the end of 2004. Moreover, according the statistics released by the US Department of Treasury, China's holdings of US treasury securities totaled USD 223.5 billion at the end of March, 2005 and China, second to Japan, is the second largest foreign holder of US treasury securities. The intertwined economic relationships between China and the US complicate the US strategic choice against China. As a result,

[171] It mentions the trade increase between China and Taiwan can be contributed to Taiwan's investments to Chinese mainland. Taiwan businessmen' investments in China cause the effect of trade increase because China functions as the industrial base of manufacture. Bureau of Foreign Trade's Newsletter, April 19, 2004

[172] See Table 2-13.

if the US intends to contain China, the US government will not only face the challenges from its domestic importers and exporters but also the difficulty of its budget deficit and those who invest in China. Both China and the US are bound together in a system of economic cooperation; whichever defects from the system will suffer an economic loss.

2.5.2 The US Domestic Politics and the US China Policy

The US China policy has been torn between different opinions regarding the future China. Will China turn into a future threat to the international security? Will the rise of China threaten the world hegemonic position of the US? The unpredictability about China's future turns the "China issue" into a fierce debate among American policy makers and scholars. The US is enticed to China's huge potential market, but at the same time repulsed by China's dismal human rights record. The ambiguous sentiment toward China can be reflected on American foreign policy toward China.[173]

Khalilzad points out that the China Policy of the US is torn between the competing perspectives of engagement and containment and argues China is on its way to a great power, but so far, no one is certain about where China is heading with its rise, and that is the most troublesome part for those who deal with the "China issue". China can play the role as a benign neighbor and an economic locomotive to stabilize the Asia Pacific region. On the contrary, China also has the capacity to seek regional dominance and take an aggressive role to confront the existing powers, especially the US.[174] As a result, because no American can predict the future of China, the US is lost in the fierce debate and can only make ad hoc responses to China's action.

Goldstein argues that economic strength serves as the last podium to bolster the stage for China's rise. Now, dealing with Chin's rise becomes the most difficult task for most policy makers in the twenty-first century. China is equipped with three of the least requirements for lifting itself into the world-class great power club—vast land, rich resources, and a large population. Furthermore, Chinese Communist Party (CCP) retains the territorial integrity of Chinese mainland and wards off foreign encroachment. After replacing Taiwan as the sole representative of the Chinese state in major international organization, China breaks through the international isolation and regains its international prestige. The development of strategic weaponry such as nuclear warheads and ballistic missiles protects China from the nuclear extortion of foreign hegemony.[175]

[173] Tien and Nathan (2001)
[174] Khalilzad (1999a)
[175] Goldstein, 1997-1998

To avoid a self-fulfilling prophecy, the US has been cautious in uttering the term "containment" to describe the US China policy as Nye argues at least there is 50 percent of chance that China will not become an enemy; there is no need for the US to adopt a policy of containment against China to increase the probability of "China threat" to 100 percent.[176] Thus, on the surface, the US emphasizes its policy toward China is engagement, not containment, but a string of U.S. policy decisions and statements push forward the impression of "containment" in the mind of many China specialists and senior Chinese officials. Tucker, a specialist in U.S.-China relations at Georgetown University says that it is obvious that the Chinese will think the US has a plot to keep a weak and divided China. [177]

Since no one is certain which road China will head on—a benign power which embeds itself in the world system and abides by the norm or a vicious one that possesses the ambition to expand its territory and unsettle the peace of Asia-Pacific and the whole world, it leaves a plenty large room for policy makers, Chinese specialists and foreign relation experts to dwell on what the world (mainly the US) should react to cope with the rising China. Cable and Ferdinand take a positive view about the emerging China and say that from the historical perspective, China's prosperity should be viewed as a positive sign. Thus, aside from incorporating China into the world system, they also suggest the Western powers should learn to accept a "richer and economically strong China" for further implications because there may come several economic giants: India, Brazil, probably Russia in time.[178]

Shambaugh argues that containment of China is a badly flawed policy option, but that a policy of "engagement" will not be fully reciprocated by Beijing. Although China will be reluctantly to respond positively to the policy of "engagement", this remains the best option available to the international community.[179] However, the truth is the US has never adopted an engagement policy towards China. When asked about whether he thinks the US adopts a friendly "engagement" policy or a more adversarial "containment" policy toward China, Jiang Ze-ming, the former chairman of China responds by "Sometimes I hear containment, [sometimes] engagement. Sometimes I hear containment mixed with engagement. Later I find out that this is called American democracy." [180]

---

[176] Quoted in Jim Mann, "US Starting to View China as a Potential Enemy," *Los Angeles Times,* April 16, 1995, P. 1

[177] "US Sees Engagement in Current Policy, China Feels Containment," *Washington Post,* July 9, 1995, p. A-23.

[178] Cable and Ferdinand, 1994

[179] Shambaugh, 1996

[180] "Storm Warnings," *Newsweek*, October 23, 1995, P. 40

Roy favors the idea that a rising China with xenophobia will turn China into the greatest threat to East Asia since the Pacific War.[181] Moreover, the conflicts between China and the US are expected. He argues that the accommodation of the US concerns serves only as a temporary measure to Chinese, and once the US continuously infringes on vital Chinese interest, China will no longer accommodate the US.[182] Indeed, while vital national interest is violated, not a single sovereign state will be willing to accommodate another state, even which is the only super power in the world, especially under the situation that the state whose national interest is violated is well equipped to protect its own interest.

Krauthammer advocates containment against China by allying with China's former enemies—Vietnam, Russia and India and by revitalizing US-Japan alliance which was dampened by trade friction. Moreover, he suggested the US should abase China's international prestige by fighting human-rights against China in the public arena. The most important, the US should support Chinese dissidents to undermine the CCP regime.[183] Rachman claims a low-key but outright containment policy against China.[184] Mosher recommended that US should adopt a "containment" policy which would impose a position of military inferiority on China to depress China's influence over its neighbors and to make sure China will hesitate to take a direct military confrontation against the US.[185]

Aside from containment and engagement, Khalilzad proposed a "congagement" strategy which contains a flexible position toward China. When China cooperates with the international society and democratizes, the US will accommodate China to encourage China's positive cooperative behavior. If China becomes hostile, the US will pursue a containment policy to punish China's misbehavior.[186]

Containment—a residue of cold war strategic thinking is difficult to yield expected result in this globalization era. Moreover, China emphasizes on its peaceful rising which obstructs any excuse from the US to organize an international coalition against China and China is too big to contain by the unilateral effort of the US. Neither does engagement produce any fruitful result to the US. The Tiananmen massacre and the Falun Gong crackdown witness that China is capable of resisting any outside force which intends to interfere in its domestic affairs. When the US intends to impose the US universal value, such

---

181 Roy, 1994, P. 168
182 Ibid.
183 "Why We Must Contain China," *Time*, July 31, 1995 P. 72.
184 Rachman, 1996
185 Mosher, 2000
186 Khalilzad, 1999a

as democracy and human right, on China by engagement, the US will not get what it expects. Therefore, the US considers that China is too unpredictable to engage. Nor can "congagement" assist the US get expected result from China. China joins the US-led coalition against terrorism and at the same time refuses to renounce the use of the military force against Taiwan independence even with the US military presence in a cross-Strait war. In fact, none of the above mentioned strategies will yield satisfactory result to the US. Since the "best-ever Sino-US relations" are constructed on a "common threat" instead of a "common belief", when the threat disappears, the relations between China and the US will be back on the up-and-down cycle. As a result, as long as the substance of Sino-US relations remains unchanged, China will maintain its figure as a big and unpredictable regime which troubles the US policy-makers because China is too big to be coerced compliance from, too unpredictable to be ignored, and too confusing to be understood.

The US will never be able to manage its China policy on the thinking of engagement, containment or congagement because their intertwined relationships make the US difficult to take a tough stance against China without hurting itself and the engagement without mutual trust will be easily offset by unpredictable incidents. Moreover, the US officials have a tendency to adopt a double standard at evaluating its own intentions and China's. When the US military expenditure is as much as the rests of the world's, it is to safeguard the US security and maintain the world order; on the other hand, China spend less than one seventh of the US military expenditure and the US is worried about China's ambition to dominate the world. If the US officials keep seeing through the biased prism to evaluate Sino-U.S. relations, the US will never be able to provide an effective policy to maximize its own benefits.

When we examine the fact that China is too large to be contained and China does not appreciate the interference of foreign powers, it is easy to conclude that China will act according to its own agenda except for the interference from Taiwan as any suggestion made from Taiwan is included in the domestic affairs of China. The US should abandon the cold war mentality of capitalizing on Taiwan to contain China but use Taiwan as a source to help China renovate its domestic economic, social and even political system. As China insists that Taiwan is also a part of China and embraces the hope of unifying with Taiwan, with the assistance of Taiwan independence movement, China must have already realized China has to pay the price for unifying with Taiwan. The US should not expect China will be willing to dismantle itself and become the vassal of the US but Taiwan can help China construct a transparent system to make China more predictable.

3. Globalization Effects on the Relationships between Government & Corporation

Though there has been fierce debate about whether the trend of globalization would devastate the sovereignty of states, up to now, the conclusion is still inconclusive. Through the process of liberating capital market, relocating manufacturing base, advancing new technology, and increasing international trade, the members of corporate bourgeoisie have gained their right in playing a role in the international community. The transnational corporations can negotiate their access to resources and markets in the peripheral areas of the world without the assistance of their home states. In their pursuit of global comparative advantage, they conduct their business under an ideology which separates the political sphere from the economic. In the corporate hegemonic world, the imperialist power of home countries is marginalized.[187]

Lawrence questions the governmental mechanism has the capability to regulate markets effectively. He argues the discrepancy between the world economic and political structures has been gradually enlarged and the exclusive authority of national sovereignty has been challenged by the increasing interdependence of cross-border economic activities. The nature of internationalization has effectively eroded the traditional authority of government. Therefore, the influence of nation-state has been diminished to a degree of irrelevancy by the global strategies of transnational corporations.[188] Provided with certain phenomena of globalization, Ohmae has audaciously claimed "the end of nation state". He argues the temptation to revive the concept of traditional nation state is a pure illusion. With the ending of the Cold War, although the existence of political borders is still fiercely debated, in the economic front, the essence of borderless world has gradually penetrated into the daily reality of citizens and consumers.[189]

As a result, liberals hail the erosion of nation-state sovereignty and support the self-regulating market. They argue that multinational corporations (MNCs) play a role of transferring prosperity from the industrialized core states to the developing peripheral ones. The MNCs contribute to the global economy by enhancing the international economic exchanges, obscuring the national boundaries and facilitating the efficiency. Because their operations surpass national border, the national tariff and exchange control will not be able to confine their activities. Thus, the local governments will be forced to

[187] Ankie, 1997, P 58-59
[188] Lawrence, 1996
[189] Ohmae, 1995

face their own irrational restraints on the business. Moreover, MNCs can fully use the world resources efficiently. They can mobilize the worldwide resource to where the resource is needed most. Aside from freer capital movement, they also facilitate the transfer of technology, the dissemination of managerial skill, and the dispersion of talents to backward countries.[190]

Unlike liberals' optimism about the coming borderless and corporation-dominated world, Dicken argues that in order to take advantage of national differences, transnational corporations (TNCs) have the tendency to carefully scrutinize the comparative advantage of each regulatory regime, thus the state regulatory policies still preserve a powerful leverage on the operations of TNCs, especial the regulations concerning international trade, industrial policies and foreign investment. Consequently, each party attempts to capture the greatest gain through the dynamic negotiation. Since the TNCs no longer confine themselves on the national level operations, the regional economic integration in Europe and North America and the GATT negotiation reflect the need of a regulatory system on a broader international level.[191]

Arndt says that private actors can influence state activities which intend to condition the economic activities of private actors. He elaborates further on this concept by stating that firms can manipulate the decisions of states by means of lobbyism and also can evade, at least partially, the regulations of states by means of being multinational or transnational. With their ability to take measures such as intra-firm pricing, intra-firm credit and credit creation in all currencies of their host countries, it is therefore difficult to regulate multinational firms by national monetary policy.[192]

Woods points out that the technological renovation and governmental deregulation have enabled corporations to establish transnational networks in production, trade and finance. As the nature of internationalization has rewritten the rules for the business operations of TNCs, not a single state can effectively regulate TNCs on its own. The phenomena of the international economic integration require states to cooperate at levels above the national mechanism to effectuate their regulations on TNCs. He further argues that strong states have not only influenced the nature and pace of globalization but also controlled their own integration into the world economy. As strong states retain more bargaining power, the process of globalization may alter but definitely not erode the sovereignty of strong states. In contrast, weak states face the risk of being further weakened by globalization. At the same time, however, globalization reshapes the world system. New kind of governance such as regional

[190] McKinlay and Little, 1988, P. 96-111

[191] Dicken, 1992

[192] Ibid.

institutions is installed into the system and new actors such as non-governmental organizations and transnational regulators are also added into the system. These developments will open up new opportunities as well as challenges to both strong and weak states in the system.[193]

Therefore, the structural transform of contemporary commerce has also transformed, if not erode, the clout of states on commercial behaviors of corporations. Any single state holds no complete capability to contain the behaviors of MNCs. The regulation of any single state can be easily bypassed by means of transnational activities. Only through the transnational cooperation, the national regulation can be effected internationally. Regionalism is not a superficial phenomenon, but a structural transform of governance which states have to adopt to deal with the trend of globalization because the TNCs are no longer dwelling within the traditional framework of national states. TNCs are capable of pursuing their interests and leaving the social responsibility to nations which they leave behind. They can access the best possible infrastructure and pursue the various subsidies, and at the same time minimize their tax burden and evade the social responsibility for the unemployed.[194]

As the trend of globalization continues, states have no other choice but to cooperate through the construction of supranational institutions and the agreements between governments to contain the transnational commercial behaviors of firms. Does politics have capitulated to the market force? The answer is no. It takes only the transnational design of governmental mechanism to control and supervise the international activities of corporations. The age of globalization "brings not the end of politics but a new beginning."[195]

Therefore, in this globalization era, a national government must prove itself capable of cooperating with others or of coercing others' cooperation to bring the international activities of private corporations back to national norm and regulations; otherwise, it will face the challenge of being left behind and marginalized. Taiwanese government has also suffered from the influence of the transnational activities of firms. In this globalization era, when Taiwanese corporations determine to devote most of their energy on exploring business opportunities in China and Taiwanese government cannot restrain their China-bound activities, Taiwan faces the threat of being insignificant in their transnational deployment unless Taiwan can acquire the cooperation from Chinese government. The globalization era offers Taiwan a chance to reposition itself in the world community, and the key to a prosperous future will rely on whether Taiwan can manage the transnational activities of local enterprises or

---

[193] Woods, 2000, P. 2-4

[194] Beck, 2000, P. 7

[195] Ibid, P. 129

even the behaviors of multinational corporations to ensure when those private enterprises work out their transnational deployment, Taiwan will not be excluded from their plans. As China emerges as the world's factory and a promising consumption market, Taiwanese government will have difficulty in reaching its goal: Taiwan wants to woo economic benefits from China but to distance itself from China's economic influence.

3.1 The Power Struggle between Government and Private Firm

Polanyi repeatedly emphasizes in his masterpiece The Great Transformation that the economic system is embedded in the social system and a so-called self-regulating market will cause a disastrous effect on mankind. He further argued the economic order is merely a part of social function.[196] Thus, a market economy can never be independent from a market society. To allow the market mechanism to act as the only dominant factor in determining the fate of human beings and their environments, human beings would at last exhaust the nature resources and destroy the environment.[197]

Polanyi was not the only one who suggested that the economic system has to be imbedded into social norm to function properly. Adam Smith also suggested the same concept. According to Evensky's analysis, Adam Smith constructed his liberal market thoughts on the ethical foundation because he recognized that mankind's adherence to the rules of justice is the indispensable requirement for any society to exist and the actuality of ethic is the prerequisite for the coordination of markets to function smoothly.[198]

In fact, though Adam Smith brought up the concept of "an invisible hand" to support the utility of free market, he did not forsake the necessity of governmental involvement in the market mechanism. He called on government action for the rectification of market failure[199] as well as for specific policy purposes. He demanded government involvement in the provision of public goods. He wanted governmental institutions to be responsible for the society rather than some special commercial interests. Adam Smith recognized the limitations of governmental institutions on economic matters, but he insisted that even though government is limited but needed because natural justice is not enough.[200]

Therefore, the smooth operation of an economic system can not depend solely on a self-regulating market mechanism which is generated as if by "an invisible hand", but more or less on a regulation-creating and -imposing mechanism which may be derived form moral standards or government actions. Regulation indicates intervention in certain activities and does not limit itself

[196] According to Polanyi's (1974, P. 68) definition, "a market economy is an economic system controlled, regulated, and directed by markets alone; order in the production and distribution of goods is entrusted to this self-regulating mechanism. An economy of this kind derives from the expectation that human beings behave in such a way as to achieve maximum money gains."

[197] Polanyi 1974, P. 68-73

[198] Jerry Evensky, 1993, 396-397

[199] Market failures are defined as the inability of a market economy to reach certain desirable outcomes in resource use. Datta-Chaudhuri, 1990, P.25

[200] Farmer, 1997, 252

on explicit legal control but extends itself to some official, semi-official or even non-official organizational control by government. In general, regulation usually stems from two grounds: 1. market failure, and 2. paternalistic nature. As market failure impedes the process of economic operation, people expect government to take action to justify the market failure. However, some forms of the regulation are enforced to safeguard individuals or private organizations from the foreseeable future turbulence[201] by governments[202].

However, only when private actors comply with the regulations of governments, governments hold the power to justify the market failure or to fulfill their paternalistic nature. Otherwise, if governments fail to enforce their regulations on private actors, their regulation-imposing mechanism will be sabotaged and they will face the threat of being marginalized in the activities of private actors. As a result, private actors can either demand the concession from governments or discard their peripheral operations to disconnect themselves from the governments which hinder their core activities of profit generation.

3.1.1 Taiwanese government's Paternalism toward Private Enterprises

Whether government intervention can effectively remedy the market failure is still debatable, so far there is no such a thing as perfect human mechanism to govern and to regulate. However empirical evidence suggests that government interventions do not necessarily impede market mechanism from achieving the goal of market expansion. As Rodrik points out during the 1950s Taiwan and South Korea has initiated their traditional import-substitution policies by the means of a multiple exchange rate system, trade protection and repressed financial markets. Later, due to the change of international environment, both parties shifts their import-substitution policies to export-oriented policies accompanying with higher interest rates, duty-free for the imported raw-material for exporters, the abolishment of the multiple exchange rate system and the appreciation of the local currencies.[203]

Rodrik attributes Taiwan's "economic miracle" to government's proper intervention into not only the public fields but even the private economic sec-

---

[201] When Taiwanese government adopted "no haste, be patience" policy to restrict the investment of Taiwanese enterprises into mainland China, it claimed that because of political obstruction, there was no official agreement to protect Taiwanese investments in mainland, thus Taiwanese investments in mainland were exposed under unpredictable political risk. In order to protect Taiwanese enterprises, Taiwan authority therefore enforce the regulation to cap Taiwanese investments and required Taiwanese enterprises to get approval from Ministry of Finance before they invested westwards.

[202] Uche, 2001, P. 1-2

[203] Rodrik, 1994, P. 1

tors.[204] Taiwanese government controlled the monetary policy by fixing the foreign exchange rate, directing the capital, controlling the inflation, and encouraging savings to certain investments which the government preferred. In Taiwan, investment subsidies take different forms. Real lending rates are generally positive and credit subsidies are much less important. However, public enterprises do get credit at more favorable terms, and they also serve to socialize investment risk. The most important direct subsidies in Taiwan come in the form of tax incentives.

Aside from providing incentives to channel investments into certain areas emphasized by the government, the government also took initial steps to inject capitals into industries such as steel, semiconductors and plastics and then gradually privatized the public-run businesses.[205] Basically, Taiwanese government played a directly hands-on role to supervise, guide and organize private entrepreneurs in investments.

It should not be exaggerate to say that the "economic miracles" of Taiwan and South Korea are the fruit of government-led economy. Table 3-1 indicates that both the economies of Taiwan and South Korea outperform their counterparts' even under the situation that both parties do not possess any significant economic bases during the initial stage. In 1960, the GDP per capita of Taiwan and of South Korea are USD 1,359 and USD 883 respectively but the GDP per capita of Mexico and of Argentina are USD 2,798 and USD 3,294. Taiwan and South Korea do not possess a stronger base than their counterparts; however, the GDP per capita of Taiwan and South Korea grow at an average annul rate of 6.17 percent and 6.82 percent respectively, which far surpass Brazil's 3.58 percent, Mexico's 2.35 percent, Argentina's 0.63 percent, Senegal's 0.16 percent, Ghana's -0.54 percent and Mozambique's -2.29 percent.

However, globalization restrains Taiwanese government's capability to control not only private economic sectors but also the public fields. The globalization has liberated the foreign exchange rate of New Taiwan Dollar (NT) from the hand of Taiwan's Central Bank of China, which can no longer adopt a NT-dollar peg policy to stabilize Taiwan's financial market. Instead, it has to throw in real capital to obstruct the speculation of opportunists or to adopt a less effective method—moral persuasion[206] to bring the exchange rate into

---

[204] Ibid.

[205] China Steel Corp, Taiwan Semiconductor Manufacturing Company Ltd. and United Microelectronics Corp stand out as the most prominent cases for Taiwanese government capital venture.

[206] Whenever they sense human-factor behind the fluctuation of foreign exchange rate, the officers of Taiwan's central bank will invite those who take in charge of the business of NT/USD exchange in foreign banks to "drink coffee" and demand them stop speculating on the exchange rate of NT/USD. See *Abrupt Appreciation, NTD Will Challenge 32 NT/USD*

control. Moreover, Taiwanese government loses its grip not only in public economic field but especially in private economic sector, and the following Section will prove Taiwanese government can no longer take effective measures in containing the behaviors of private corporations.

Table 3-1 Comparative Growth Experience

Country	Per capita GDP, 1960 (1985 dollars)	Per capita GDP, 1989 (1985 dollars)	Per capita GDP growth, 1960-89 (%)
Taiwan	**1,359**	**8,207**	**6.17**
South Korea	**883**	**6,206**	**6.82**
Ghana	873	815	-0.54
Senegal	1,017	1,082	0.16
Mozambique	1,128	756	-2.29
Brazil	1,745	4,138	3.58
Mexico	2,798	5,163	2.36
Argentina	3,294	3,608	0.63

Source: Rodrik, 1994

3.1.2 Taiwanese Firms & Governmental Restraints

The "no haste; be patient" policy died long before its official death. An old Chinese saying, "the superiors have policies; the subordinates have counter-plots (Shang You Zheng Ce, Xia You Dui Ce)," can best describe the spirit of Taiwanese corporations. As Taiwanese businessmen are adroit at circumventing the official restraints without provoking the government, the unpopular policies of the government usually die before their official death. Taiwanese enterprises often act ahead of the government regulations, and the government is eventually forced to tolerate their misbehaviors and even to tailor the regulations to accommodate the requirements of private actors.

To counter the trend of cross-Strait economic integration, Taiwanese authority promulgates restraining regulations and tries to impose them on the private actors, but fails. Taiwanese businessmen form a unique business-venture to evade governmental restraints. For Taiwanese businessmen, it is profitable to venture into the unregulated field or even the illegal sphere as long as they will not be caught; moreover, even though their illegal operations bear the risk of being caught by the government, as long as they can exert enough pres-

Next Week, China Times Nov. 27, 2004; *Cover Story: 1:34 Comes Again, President of Central Bank Tracing the Prime Criminals for NT Depreciation.* Win-Win Weekly, Vol. 78, 1998

sures on the government, it is a common practice that the government will yield and legalize those illegal operations[207].

As a result, even though Taiwanese government has set strict regulations on China-bound investments of Taiwanese firms, it has to offer grace periods from time to time to those Taiwanese companies which violate the regulation in their westward investments to make retroactive registration. Ever since Taiwanese government officially lifts the ban on China-bound investments in 1991, it has offered three chances to Taiwanese companies to retroactively register their unauthorized investments in China, in 1993, 1997 and 2002 respectively. As of the end of 2004, according to the statistics of Taiwanese government, over one fourth of Taiwanese investments in China are registered retroactively during the grace periods. The amount of retroactive registration is USD 11,231.33 million and the amount of legal investments is USD 30,017.87 million.[208]

Table 3-2 illustrates that the market share of Taiwanese companies is over 70% in contract chip-making. In 2002, TSMC enjoyed a 54.29 % of total market share, UMC 25.12%; in 2003, TSMC's market share slid to 51.68%, UMC's to 24.18%. At the same time, SMIC, a Chinese company which is founded by a Taiwanese, expanded its market share from 0.58% to 3.23%. As foundry chip-making is one of few Taiwanese leading industries in which Taiwan control the technology and production, Taiwanese government has been reluctant to lift the ban for private actors to invest in China's contract chip-making industry. However, as China market is indispensable to their global deployment, Taiwanese contract chip manufacturers adopt different strategies to invest in China.

Seeing that Taiwan is hesitant to permit chipmakers to set up wafer fabrication plants in China, Robert Tsao, the chairman of UMC (the world's second largest pure-play foundry company), claims that as long as UMC guarantees those who are interested in establishing wafer fabrication plants in China that UMC will buy off the plants after Taiwan authority relaxes the

---

[207] TVBS (Television Company) reported, Ministry of the Interior was going to legalize those illegally-operated hot-spring hotels which were build on hillsides. "Yu Cheng-hsien Plays Push-hand; the Illegal Hot-spring Operation Is Expected to Be Legalized," Oct 29, 2003 http://www.tvbs.com.tw/news/news_list.asp?no=eveno20031029125916
Libertytimes reported, last year (2002) Ministry of Economic Affairs proposed methods of guidance to legalize those illegal factories. This year (2003) legislature wanted to amend the law to legalize those illegal factories. The officials of Construction and Planning Agency thought this might endanger the environment. However, because local governments were short-staffed, they had difficulty to execute the law.
http://www.libertytimes.com.tw/2003/new/mar/17/today-e5.htm

[208] See Table 2-20. More details can be seen in section 2.4.2.

investment restriction, there is no need for UMC to directly invest in China. This strategy is legal on all fronts and even the government knows about it can do nothing to constrain it. As a result, UMC manages a secret alliance with He Jian Technology which operates chip foundry in China.[209]

Table 3-2 Top Ten Pure-Play Foundry Companies

Unit: USD million

Rank 2003	Company	Headquarter	Sales 2002	Share of Total 2002	Sales 2003	Share of Total 2003
1	TSMC	Taiwan	4,655	54.29%	5,855	51.68%
2	UMC[1]	Taiwan	2,154	25.12%	2,740	24.18%
3	Chartered	Singapore	485	5.66%	728	6.43%
4	SMIC	China	50	0.58%	366	3.23%
5	Dongbu/Anam	S. Korea	260	3.03%	330	2.91%
6	Jazz	US	160	1.87%	185	1.63%
7	HHNEC	China	150	1.75%	170	1.50%
8	SSMC[2]	Singapore	85	0.99%	155	1.37%
9	X-Fab	Europe	100	1.17%	127	1.12%
10	Silterra	Malaysia	60	0.70%	82	0.72%
	Others	-	416	4.85%	592	5.23%

Note: [1] Include UMC Japan sales.
[2] Partially Owned by TSMC.
TSMC: Taiwan Semiconductor Manufacturing Company
UMC: United Microelectronics
SMIC: Semiconductor Manufacturing International Corp
HHNEC: Hua Hong NEC
SSMC: Systems on Silicon Manufacturing Co

Source: IC insights, company report, modified.

In contrast to UMC's law-shunning strategic deployment, TSMC dedicates itself in lobbying Taiwanese government and wrestles out official permission in investing China on exception condition.[210] On the other hand, Richard Chang, who takes no consideration of the investment restrictions of Taiwanese government, establishes SMIC in China. His founding fund comes from the selling of his fledgling chip company, Worldwide Semiconductor Manufactur-

[209] Although Taiwanese government cannot punish UMC by the investment regulations but it manages to criminate Robert Tsao with "breach of trust". "Investors and Government Losing Patience with UMC," by Lisa Want, April 4, 2005, Taipei Times

[210] TSMC chairman Morris Chang was a China skeptic and claimed China was not ready to compete in the advanced integrated circuit industry. In 2001, he changed his attitude and declared the future of IC industry was in China. He then teamed up with other business tycoons like Wang Yung-ching and Stan Shih to pressure the government for lifting investment restrictions in Economic Development Advisory Conference.

ing Corp, which was based on Taiwan and acquired by TSMC. Although recently Richard Chang is fined by Taiwanese government and demanded to withdraw his investments in China, as he is also an American citizen and has moved all his family to China, it will be difficult for Taiwanese government to enforce the penalty.[211] Even though Taiwanese government determines to pursue Richard Chang, as long as he does not set a foot on Taiwan, whatever the efforts it makes will be in vain. As a result, the law-enforcement of Taiwanese government successfully drives Taiwanese businessmen away.

The Journalist[212] had a special report relating to the schemes of how Taiwan enterprises bypass the governmental regulations to accomplish their ends, investing in China. It reported the first common tactic was to apply for the official permission with a nominal production purpose to conceal the real production. The second scheme is investing through overseas companies. There is no need for Taiwanese companies to provide capital, talents and technologies. Taiwanese companies can ask overseas companies to invest in China, and after the government relaxes the regulations, they will buy back the ownership. The third strategy which Taiwanese enterprises adopt to avoid governmental restriction is to invest in mainland China through a dummy account owned by a foreigner.

Although it is very difficult to estimate how much Taiwanese capital has been channeled to Chinese mainland through foreign dummy accounts as the legitimacy of this strategy is debatable, Taiwanese government has trapped itself in an awkward situation in which it is incapable of demanding Taiwanese businessmen to follow its regulations. Among all the investments through dummy accounts, Wang Yung-ching's power plant venture at Zhangzhou in China's Fujian Province has been the most conspicuous case because almost every Taiwanese knows the coexistence of two facts: Taiwanese government bans Taiwanese investors from capitalizing China's infrastructure and Wang Yung-ching is the investor of the Zhangzhou power plant.[213] Moreover, although Taiwan prohibits its businessmen from investing in semiconductor

---

[211] "SMIC Founder Gets Legal Advice," Taipei Times, Apr 2, 2005.

[212] See the Journalist Vol. 788. The Journalist is a weekly magazine issued on Taiwan (in Chinese). http://www.new7.com.tw/weekly/old/788/788-062.html

[213] Wang Yung-ching is the chairman of Formosa Plastics Group (FPG), which is the largest private conglomerate in Taiwan. Taiwanese government bans China-bound investments in strategic sectors like semiconductors, petrochemicals, infrastructure projects. Due to the pressure from private businesses, Taiwanese government had partially lifted the ban on semiconductor investment in China to conditionally allow companies to build plants for the less-sophisticated 8-inches wafers, but power generating facilities are still in the banned list. However, Wang raised capital on overseas market and used a dummy account for the investment of the thermal power plant to bypass the governmental supervision.

packaging and testing manufacture of China, Wang's daughter (Cher Wang) invests personal capital to found Global Advanced Packaging Technology Limited, which is exactly a provider for semiconductor packaging and testing services.

To the dismay of Taiwanese government, it can only restrain those companies which are law-abiding; for those law-shunning companies, it lacks an efficient and effective measure to manage them. First, without the cooperation of China, Taiwan authority has difficulty to gather sufficient evidence to convict those companies which violate the investment regulation. Second, many corporations register their companies in tax-haven like Cayman Islands, British Virgin Islands, and Netherlands Antilles, establish some paper subsidiaries and then invest in China though their overseas subsidiaries. Taiwanese government surely has difficulty to extend its jurisdiction overseas. Third, especially some small and medium enterprises transfer their money overseas and then invest in China from some proxy accounts which are owned by foreigners.

Moreover, even the trade figures disclose the ineffectiveness of Taiwanese government in controlling the mainland-bound activities of the Taiwanese firms. Table 3-3 illustrates the difference between the statistics of Taiwan Customs and that of China Customs can be as large as over USD 20 billion. Even the estimation from Mainland Affair Council (MAC) indicates serious discrepancy with China's official data, up to USD 16.68 billion in the data of 2004. In 1992, according to the statistics of Taiwan Customs, Taiwan exports USD 1.1 million and imports USD 747.1 million; however, the statistics of China Customs indicates that Taiwan exports USD 5,881 million and imports USD 698 million; the difference between two official statistics reaches USD 5.83 billion. As time passes, the discrepancy enlarges accordingly. In 1993, the difference between the statistics of China Customs and that of Taiwan Customs increases to USD 13.36 billion; in 2004, it expands to USD 27.6 billion. Even though MAC realizes the unreliability of the statistics of Taiwan Customs and tries remedial measures to adjust the statistics, its estimation still is in discordance with the statistics of China customs. In 1991, MAC estimates that the total trade between Taiwan and China is USD 8.62 billion, but China Customs records USD 4.23 billion. In 2004, MAC estimates USD 61.64 billion in cross-Strait trade, but China Customs posts a figure of USD 78.32 billion.

Table 3-3 Trade between Taiwan and Mainland China Recorded by Different Agencies

Unit: USD million

	Hong Kong Customs			Taiwan Customs			China Customs			Estimation of MAC, ROC		
Period	Exports	Imports	Total	Exports	Imports	Total	Exports	Imports	Total	Exports	Imports	Total
1991	4,667.2	1,126.0	5,793.1	-	597.5	597.5	3,639.0	594.8	4,233.9	7,493.5	1,125.9	8,619.4
1992	6,287.9	1,119.0	7,406.9	1.1	747.1	748.2	5,881.0	698.0	6,579.0	10,547.6	1,119.0	11,666.6
1993	7,585.4	1,103.6	8,689.0	16.2	1.015.5	1,031.7	12,933.1	1,461.8	14,394.9	13,993.1	1,103.6	15,096.7
1994	8,517.2	1,292.3	9,809.5	131.6	1,858.7	1,990.3	14,084.8	2,242.2	16,327.0	16,022.5	1,858.7	17,881.2
1995	9,882.8	1,574.2	11,457.0	376.6	3,091.4	3,468.0	14,783.9	3,098.1	17,882.0	19,433.8	3,091.4	22,525.2
1996	9,717.6	1,582.4	11,300.0	623.4	3,059.8	3,682.7	16,182.2	2,802.7	18,984.9	20,727.3	3,059.8	23,787.1
1997	9,715.1	1,743.8	11,458.9	626.5	3,915.4	4,543.2	16,441.7	3,396.5	19,838.2	22,455.2	3,915.4	26,370.6
1998	8,364.1	1,654.9	10,019.0	834.7	4,110.5	4,945.2	16,629.6	3,869.6	20,499.2	19,840.9	4,110.5	23,951.4
1999	8,174.9	1,628.1	9,803.0	2,536.9	4,522.2	7,061.7	19,537.5	3,951.7	23,489.2	21,312.5	4,522.2	25,834.7
2000	9,593.1	1,980.5	11,573.7	4,217.5	6,223.3	10,440.8	25,467.1	4,994.9	30,492.1	25,009.9	6,223.3	31,233.1
2001	8,811.5	1,693.3	10,504.8	4,745.4	5,902.2	10,647.8	27,339.4	5,000.2	32,350.0	21,945.7	5,902.2	27,847.9
2002	10,311.8	1,708.1	12,019.8	9,945.0	7,947.7	17,892.8	38,063.1	6,585.9	44,649.0	29,465.0	7,947.7	37,412.8
2003	11,789.4	2,161.1	13,950.4	21,417.3	10,960.5	32,377.8	49,362.3	9,004.7	58,367.0	35,357.7	10,962.0	46,319.7
2004	14,761.9	2,485.4	17,247.3	34,046.7	16,681.6	50,728.4	64,778.6	13,545.2	78,323.8	44,960.4	16,678.7	61,639.1

Note: Exports indicates amount of exportation from Taiwan to Mainland China, and Imports indicates the amount of importation from Mainland China to Taiwan.
Source: CROSS-STRAIT ECONOMIC STATISTICS MONTHLY, NO.148

The confusedness of the official data between Taiwan and China fortifies the concept of the old Chinese saying "The superiors have policies; the subordinates have counterplots." However, it also offers Taiwanese government a solution to resolve this hardship. Since China serves as the host country of Taiwanese firms, as long as Taiwanese government wins the support from Chinese authority, Taiwanese government should be able to keep track on its private actors. Moreover, because China has endeavored to pursue peaceful unification with Taiwan, Taiwan can extract better economic deals from China than the rest of the world can.

3.2 An Evolution in the Relationship among MNC, Host Country & Home Country

According to the definition of Dunning, "a multinational or transnational enterprise is an enterprise that engages in foreign direct investment (FDI) and owns or controls value-adding activities in more than one country."[214] Since multinational or transnational corporations conduct supranational activities, therefore, they incline to carefully examine the national differences in regulatory systems and wedge their way through national boundaries in pursuit of their global comparative advantage.

As a result, the relationship between MNCs and host countries is formed in a dynamic structure instead of a static structure. It varies according to the relative bargaining power between them; the ownership structure of an MNC affiliate, the location of the economic activities and the technology transferred to the host countries are all negotiable. Their bargaining position will be determined by their opportunity costs, and the one which possesses more indispensable resources than its counterpart will have its coign of vantage in the bargaining process.[215] Dunning also points out home countries may be able to exert some influence on the timing and scale of outbound activities of MNCs but have little power to control outward direct investment.[216] As a result, in view of the global strategies of MNCs, the ability of any single state to restrain the behaviors of MNCs is enfeebled by their transnational activities, and neither the home country nor the host country has the ability to unilaterally constrain the activities of MNCs.

As globalization initiates the process of production dispersion, the overseas affiliates are getting important in the economic activities of MNCs. Consequently, the law and regulations of host countries will exert more influence on the daily operations of MNCs than the policies of home countries. Moreover, the globalized competition provides bargaining power to private corporations and forces states to accommodate them in hope that MNCs will operate within the territory of the sate and national firms will maintain their roots in the home state.[217] Thus, following the process of internationalization, MNCs gradually win more bargain power over states, because MNCs can maneuver the regulatory divergence and the incoherent attitude between countries to their advantages, but through the cooperation of countries, countries can effectively constrain the behaviors of MNCs. Even though MNCs have the capability to operate transnationally, they still need a base, a real location to station their staff

---

[214] Dunning, 1992, P. 3
[215] Ibid, P. 169, 324
[216] Ibid. P. 554
[217] Leng, 1998, P. 495

and to storage their goods and materials. Even though MNCs can conduct businesses through virtual world like internet, their personnel will be confined within national boundary with limited travel freedom and their products will also be restrained by national trade regulations. Thus, Taiwanese government can control the mainland-bound activities of Taiwanese firms only through the cooperation with Chinese authority. After all, China serves as the host country of most of Taiwan outward investments.

Taiwanese government has tried to curb the China-bound activities of Taiwanese firms on the ground of national security. However, as the interests between them are not compatible and the restraints have already sacrificed the gains of the firms, the conflicts between public and private sectors will sooner or later emerge.[218] With their limited resources, when considering outbound economic activities, Taiwanese SMEs does not have many Choices aside from China. China shares the same language, culture and geographic location with Taiwan and is a large market attracting foreign investors. As the large China market can enhance Taiwan's attractiveness, as far as economic development is concerned, China is an asset, not a liability to Taiwan.[219]

As the jurisdiction of Taiwanese government cannot reach China's territory and Taiwan does not reach any official agreement with China regarding the protection of the investments from Taiwanese enterprises, it is Chinese government which unilaterally determines how their investments will be protected. Moreover, according to a survey conducted by the Chinese National Federation of Industries, 44.5 percent of Taiwanese investors in China made a profit in 2003; the percentage of profit-making Taiwanese companies rose to 52.9 percent in 2004; the percentage was expected to increase to 69.6 percent in 2005. In addition, the survey showed that 26.7 percent of Taiwanese investors in China operated at a loss in 2003; the percentage increased to 30.4 percent in 2004, but was expected to drop to 10.4 percent in 2005.[220] Since the operation in China gradually becomes the major profit-generator for most of the China-bound Taiwanese businessmen and Taiwanese government plays no role in their commercial activities in China but only as a hindrance in their China-bound investments, unless Taiwanese government can obtain the coop-

---

218 During 2000 presidential election, shipping tycoon Chang Yung-fa, chairman of the Evergreen Group endorsed Chen Shui-bian in the hope for implementing "three links". However, Chang was disappointed by President Chen's refusal to conduct "three links". Chang turned to support Chen's opponent, Lien Chan on 2004 presidential election.

219 See "Little Taiwan", the Economist, November 7, 1998, U.S. Edition, Survey; P. S16.

220 See Table 3-32

eration from China, its influence over Taiwanese enterprises will gradually diminish during the process of their pursuing profits.[221]

[221] Hours before Taiwan's ruling party held a mass rally against China's new anti-secession law, Hsu Wen-lung, a pro-independence businessman, denounced his pro-independence stance by issuing an open letter expressing support for China's one China principle and anti-secession law. Some of the ruling party members expressed their sympathy to Hsu as he was under the pressure of Chinese government; others expressed their dissatisfaction against Hsu as he betrayed his belief. However, no one in Taiwan could persuade him to retract his pro-unification rhetoric. Hsu is the founder of Chi Mei Group, which includes the world's largest ABS/SAN manufacturer (Chi Mei Corporation) and the world's forth largest TFT-LCD manufacturer (Chi Mei Optoelectronics Corporation). ABS is a copolymer of Acrylonitrile, Butadiene, and Styrene. SAN is the abbreviation of Styrene-acrylonitrile.

3.3 The Constraints on the Development of Taiwan Economy

The political concern of Taiwanese government towards the "hostile" China becomes the major constraint on Taiwan economic development. In consideration of the changing international environment, Taiwanese enterprises flexibly relocate their production base to preserve the likelihood of survival or to obtain the opportunity of expansion, and their economical activities nonetheless reshape Taiwan's economic structure. Taiwanese firms were used to a trade pattern in which they imported key components, machinery and technology from Japan and the US, and after processing, they exported finished products mainly to the US. However, as New Taiwan dollar (NT) appreciated sharply in 1980s, Taiwanese manufacturers decided to move their production lines overseas. Because China shares the same language and culture with Taiwan, with its cheap labor and vast resources, China becomes the top choice of Taiwanese companies in moving their production bases overseas. As a result, China is transformed to become Taiwan's largest export destination. The international deployment of Taiwanese firms may contradict to the interests of Taiwanese government as the government is inclined to focus on political power struggle with China, but no matter Taiwanese government like it or not, whatever Taiwanese companies do has already reshaped the development of Taiwan economy. As Taiwanese firms have drawn both sides across-Strait together by economic force but Taiwanese government is resisting the cross-Strait economic interdependence by promoting political disintegration,[222] Taiwanese government set itself in the dilemma of an economic-integrated but political-alienated cross-Strait relationship.

According to Taiwan's trade data, Taiwan has a tendency of concentrating most of trade on its major trade partners. Table 3-4 illustrates during the late 1970s, the trade with Japan and the US constantly accounts for over 50 percent of Taiwan's total trade, and this phenomenon continues through 1980s till early 1990s. In 1976, the imports from Japan account for 32.26% of Taiwan's total imports, and Taiwan's imports from the US account for 23.66% of Taiwan's total imports; as a result, the imports from both countries account for 55.92% of Taiwan's total imports. In the same year, Taiwan export 13.4% of

[222] In order to cool down the China fever commenced by opposition leaders' trips to China, President Chen Shui-bian openly discouraged the ruling party lawmakers from visiting China by claiming that between two sides across the Strait, "there is no need to communicate (Mei You She Me Hao Jie Chu De)" and "there is no need to understand (Mei You She Me Hao Liao Jie De)" as five ruling party lawmakers intend to attend an economics forum in China. "Pan-Green Lawmakers' Plan to Visit China Come to An Abrupt Halt by Bian's Objection (Lu Yin Li Wei Ji Hua Fan Wen Da Lu, Bian Qiang Sheng Jia Ran Zhi)", China Times, July 8, 2005

its total exports to Japan and 37.21% to the US; Taiwan's exports to both Japan and the US account for 50.62% of Taiwan's total exports. In 1977, the percentage of Taiwan's imports from Japan and the US declines slightly to 54.13%, but the percentage of exports to both Japan and the US increases to 50.81%. In 1978, the percentage of Taiwan's imports from both nations increases slightly to 54.9%, and the percentage of Taiwan's exports to them increases to 51.87%. In 1979, Taiwan imports 53.8% of its total imports from Japan and the US, and the exports to both nations drop to 49.06% of its total exports.

In the early 1980s, although the percentages of Taiwan's trade with Japan and the US do not record as high as the percentages in the late 1970s, they maintain at a range of 45 % to 55%. In the mid 1980s, the percentages of Taiwan's trade with them rise to the range of 50% to 60%. However, in the late 1980s, Taiwan's trade with both nations starts to slide down. In 1987, Taiwan's imports from both countries account for 55.71% of its total imports; its exports from them account for 57.14% of its total exports; however, in 1988, although the percentage of Taiwan's imports from Japan and the US increases slightly to 56.03%, the percentage of Taiwan's exports to them decreases 4% to 53.14%. In 1989, the percentage of Taiwan's imports from Japan and the US accounting for Taiwan's total imports decreases to 53.64% and the percentage of Taiwan's exports to them also decreases to 49.92%.

Since 1990, the percentages of Taiwan's trade with Japan and the US almost follow a gentle downward trajectory in terms of both import and export. In 1990, the percentage of Taiwan's imports from both countries decreases from previous year's 53.64% to 52.29%; the percentage of Taiwan's exports to them declines from 1989's 49.92% to 44.76%. In 1991, Taiwan imports 52.45% of its total imports from Japan and the US, and exports 41.36% of its total exports to them. In 1992 and 1993, the percentages of Taiwan's imports from Japan and the US decrease to 52.13%, 51.79% respectively, and the percentages of its exports to them also drop to 39.85% and 38.27% respectively. In 1994, the percentage of Taiwan's imports from both countries decreases to 50.18%, in 1995 to 49.29%, and in 1996 46.37%. The percentages of Taiwan's imports from Japan and the US linger between 44.6% and 45.67% from 1997 to 2000, but drop again to 41.1% in 2001, 40.32% in 2002 and 38.87% in 2003. In 2004, the percentage of Taiwan's import from both countries remains at previous year's 38.87%. The percentage of its exports to them decreases to 37.14% in 1994, 35.43% in 1995, 34.95% in 1996 and 33.78% in 1997. From 1998 to 2000, the percentages of its exports to Japan and the US range between 34.66% and 35.2%, and resume the downward path to drop to 32.89% in 2001, to 29.67% in 2002, to 26.25% in 2003 and 23.75% in 2004.

Table 3-4 The Percentage of Taiwan's Trade with the US and Japan

Year	% of Import from Japan (1)	% of Export to Japan (2)	% of Import from US (3)	% of Export to US (4)	(1)+(3)	(2)+(4)
1976	32.26%	13.40%	23.66%	37.21%	55.92%	50.62%
1977	31.05%	11.97%	23.07%	38.85%	54.13%	50.81%
1978	33.36%	12.38%	21.55%	39.49%	54.90%	51.87%
1979	30.90%	13.96%	22.90%	35.10%	53.80%	49.06%
1980	27.13%	10.97%	23.68%	34.12%	50.81%	45.10%
1981	27.97%	10.96%	22.48%	36.10%	50.45%	47.06%
1982	25.31%	10.73%	24.16%	39.45%	49.47%	50.18%
1983	27.54%	9.86%	22.90%	45.11%	50.44%	54.97%
1984	29.34%	10.46%	22.96%	48.82%	52.30%	59.28%
1985	27.60%	11.26%	23.61%	48.08%	51.21%	59.35%
1986	34.14%	11.44%	22.47%	47.70%	56.60%	59.14%
1987	33.85%	13.01%	21.86%	44.12%	55.71%	57.14%
1988	29.85%	14.46%	26.18%	38.68%	56.03%	53.14%
1989	30.67%	13.67%	22.97%	36.25%	53.64%	49.92%
1990	29.24%	12.40%	23.05%	32.35%	52.29%	44.76%
1991	30.00%	12.06%	22.45%	29.30%	52.45%	41.36%
1992	30.23%	10.92%	21.90%	28.93%	52.13%	39.85%
1993	30.09%	10.55%	21.70%	27.72%	51.79%	38.27%
1994	29.04%	10.98%	21.14%	26.15%	50.18%	37.14%
1995	29.23%	11.78%	20.06%	23.65%	49.29%	35.43%
1996	26.86%	11.78%	19.51%	23.17%	46.37%	34.95%
1997	25.36%	9.58%	20.30%	24.21%	45.67%	33.78%
1998	25.80%	8.43%	18.80%	26.57%	44.60%	35.00%
1999	27.64%	9.79%	17.79%	25.41%	45.43%	35.20%
2000	27.54%	11.19%	17.95%	23.47%	45.49%	34.66%
2001	24.10%	10.38%	17.00%	22.51%	41.10%	32.89%
2002	24.24%	9.18%	16.08%	20.49%	40.32%	29.67%
2003	25.65%	8.26%	13.22%	17.99%	38.87%	26.25%
2004	25.99%	7.59%	12.89%	16.16%	38.87%	23.75%

Source: Directorate-General of Budget, Accounting & Statistics (DGBAS), Executive Yuan, Taiwan, R.O.C., calculated by the author.

Moreover, the Table 3-4 also demonstrates one phenomenon that as a trading partner, Japan imports less from Taiwan but exports more to Taiwan. Taiwan's imports from Japan account for 24.1% to 34.14% of Taiwan's total imports during 1976 to 2004, but in the same period of time, Taiwan's exports to Japan have never exceeded 14.46% of its total exports. On the other hand, the US serves as Taiwan's major export market from 1970s to early 1990s. During 1976 to 1982, the percentages of Taiwan's exports to the US ranged from 34.12% to 39.49%. In 1983, Taiwan's exports to the US accounted for 45.11% of Taiwan's total exports. In 1984, the percentage of Taiwan's exports to the US peaked at 48.82%, and then it almost slid all the way down to 2004's 16.16% except for 1997 and 1998. Although in terms of imports, the US is still an important partner to Taiwan, nevertheless Japan is the primary source of Taiwan's imports.

Table 3-5 further points out that Japan and the US are the major source of Taiwan's technology. In 1992, Taiwan imports NTD 5.04 billion of technology from the US and NTD 3.44 billion from Japan. In the same year, the value of technology imports from the US and Japan accounts for 61.77% of Taiwan's total import value of technology. In 1993, Taiwan imports NTD 3.91 billion which account for 28.58% of Taiwan's total import value of technology from the US and NTD 5.4 billion which account for 39.44% of Taiwan's total import value of technology from Japan. In 1994, the import value of technology from Japan and the US accounts for 76.29% of Taiwan's total import value of technology. In 1995, the percentage of import value of technology from Japan and the US decreases to 72.35%. In 1997, it decreases further to 67.32%, and in 1998, it decreases again to 62.79%, but in 1999, it surges to 78.33% and in 2000, it decreases to 68.8%, but in 2002, it increases to 71.48%. From 1992 to 2002, the ratios of the import value of technology from Japan and the US range from 62.79% to 78.33%.

Table 3-5 Taiwan's Import Value of Technology by Nationality

Unit: Million N.T.

Year	The US		Japan		Germany		Others	
	Amount	Ratio	Amount	Ratio	Amount	Ratio	Amount	Ratio
1992	5,038	36.69%	3,445	25.08%	563	4.10%	4,687	34.13%
1993	3,912	28.58%	5,398	39.44%	659	4.81%	3,717	27.16%
1994	5,075	34.97%	5,996	41.32%	489	3.37%	2,953	20.34%
1995	3,746	20.54%	9,450	51.81%	420	2.30%	4,625	25.35%
1997	14,639	45.16%	7,185	22.16%	6,391	19.71%	4,202	12.96%
1998	9,623	24.91%	14,634	37.88%	7,427	19.23%	6,943	17.98%
1999	12,858	33.24%	17,441	45.09%	1,589	4.11%	6,795	17.57%
2000	13,717	33.68%	14,304	35.12%	5,446	13.37%	7,260	17.83%
2002	16,404	36.25%	15,938	35.23%	2,243	4.96%	10,661	23.56%
T/A	85,011	32.67%	93,792	37.02%	25,227	8.44%	51,842	21.88%

Note: T: Total Amount A: Average Ratio,
The related data of 2003 has not released yet.
The related data of 1996 and 2001 is not available.

Source: Indicators of Science and Technologies, Republic of China, 2003 and 2004, Calculated by the Author

Taiwan's trade pattern is created by Taiwan's historical and political background. Because Taiwan is Japan's colony from 1895 to 1945, many older-generation Taiwanese are educated under the Japanese system and some of them even study in Japan. Since they can speak fluent Japanese and are accustomed to Japanese norm, Taiwanese businessmen have an edge over their counterparts in other Eastern Asian countries when they make business with Japanese. Moreover, due to the Cold War effect, the US inclines to subordinate the potential economic conflicts to the needs of political and security cooperation from its allies. As a result, the US capitalizes on Taiwan to be a bulwark and an unsinkable aircraft carrier against communist expansion; in exchange for Taiwan's adamant support in this war on communism, the US provides economic aid to Taiwan. More than that, after Taiwan shifts its import substitution policy to export oriented expansion,[223] the US tolerant attitude enables Taiwan to enjoy the US huge market without the obligation to reciprocally open its domestic market to the US products. The USAID program provides a stable economic environment that establishes the further development of Taiwan economy, and the US tolerance of unequal trade assists Taiwan's economic take-off. Under such a unique background, Taiwan has developed a successful model of conducting business—Taiwan companies import raw materials, key components, technology-know-how and machinery equipment from Japan and the US (more from Japan than from the US, Table 3-20), and then after processing and assembling, exported the finished goods to the US market.

As the international climate evolves, Taiwan's old pattern of trade faces a serious challenge. The rapprochement between the US and China offers the US a chance to reexamine its open door policy towards its Asian allies. After the détente between the US and China, the US pursues a tough trade policy against its allies, among which Japan is the first one to take the heat. In 1985, France, Germany, Japan, the United Kingdom, and the United States reach the consensus to devalue the dollar under the Plaza Accord.[224] Ever since then, Japanese Yen has appreciated dramatically against US dollar. Later, the heat spreads to Taiwan and South Korea. The US pressures its allies for a more open trade policy, and forces them to appreciate their currencies to solve the problem of their trade surplus against the US.

As a result, the appreciation of NT dollar brings in bubble prosperity for Taiwan. The surge of land price, the rocket-hiking stock price, and the rise of the wage stimulate a new wave of overseas investment. At that time, for Taiwanese manufacturers, there are two paths paved before them: on the first path, they can put their resources and energy into R&D to control technological development and key components or into marketing and logistics to promote brand names and channels; on the second path, they can invest overseas to seek for cheaper labor and land to continue their accustomed model of doing busi-

---

[223] See "History of Economic Development in Taiwan" for more details relating to Taiwan's policy transformations. http://english.tier.org.tw/05publish/president/14.htm

[224] See "Announcement the Ministers of Finance and Central Bank Governors of France, Germany, Japan, the United Kingdom, and the United States (Plaza Accord)" for further details. http://www.g8.utoronto.ca/finance/fm850922.htm

ness. Most of the Taiwan's traditional industries do not choose the former path but move their production lines to Southeast Asia and China.

Figure 3-1 indicates that Taiwan's outward investment takes off at late 1980s. From 1975 to 1985, the amount of Taiwan's outward investment has never exceeded USD 41.33 million. In 1986, it surges to USD 56.91 million and in 1987 it almost doubles to USD 102.75 million. In 1988, the amount of Taiwan's outward investment doubles again from 1987's USD 102.75 million to USD 218.74 million. From then on, Taiwan's outward investments maintain an approximately upward movement till the peak of 2000. In 2000, the amount of Taiwan's outward investment reaches USD 5.08 billion, and the next year, it declines slightly to USD 4.39 billion. The amount of Taiwan's outward investment decreases again to USD 3.37 billion in 2002 but gathers its moment to increase to USD 3.97 billion in 2003. In 2004, it declines to USD 3.38 billion. The takeoff of Taiwan's outward investment coincides with the appreciation of New Taiwan Dollar (NTD). Before the US pressures Taiwan to appreciate its currency, Taiwan adopts a dollar-pegging policy and fixes its exchange rate at about NT 40 dollars for one US dollar. In 1983, the exchange rate of NTD against USD is 40.06, and appreciates slightly to 39.62 in 1984, and depreciates a little to 39.87 in 1985. However, in 1986, the foreign exchange rate of NTD starts to feel the pressure of appreciation and appreciates to 37.85. In 1987, the foreign exchange rate of NTD climbs up to 31.87 NTD/USD from previous year's 37.85 NTD/USD, which indicates a 15.8 percent of yearly appreciation and also registers a historical record of NTD appreciation.

The comparison of Table 3-4 and Table 2-28 illustrates that while Taiwanese enterprises relocate their production lines to China, Chinese areas (including China mainland, Hong Kong, and Macau) gradually surpass the US as Taiwan's major export market. The percentage of Taiwan's export to the US declines from the peak of 1984's 48.82% to the bottom of 2004's 16.16%; on the contrary, the percentage of Taiwan's export to Chinese areas increases from 1981's 8.39% to 2004's 36.86%. This phenomenon does not imply that the US market is no longer important to Taiwan's economic prosperity, but suggests the transformation of Taiwan's business pattern. Though many Taiwan industries still rely heavily on the import of key components, machinery and manufacturing technology from Japan, by conducting a triangle trade, they have already shipped their products to the US market through their Chinese affiliates instead. Therefore, those Taiwanese manufacturers who shift their production lines to China have contributed heavily to this trade shift.

Figure 3-1 The Amount of Taiwan's Outward Investment by Year

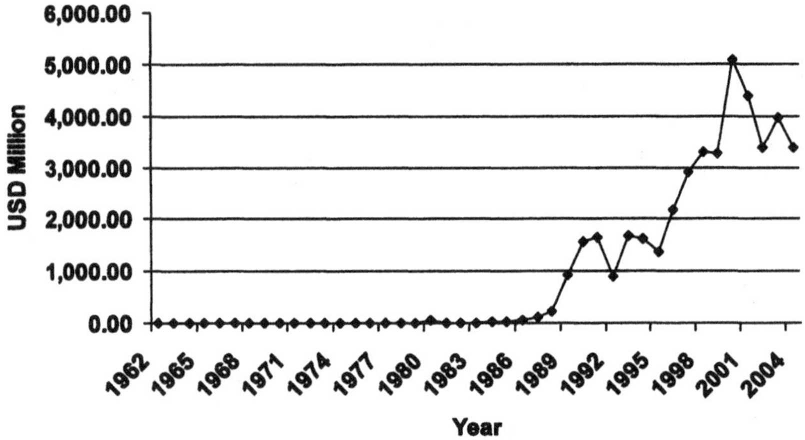

Note: FDI towards China is excluded.
Source: Investment Commission, Ministry of Economic Affairs

The early successful pattern of Taiwan's economic development has become an unpredictable variable for the future development of Taiwan. Ever since the KMT government shifted its import substitution policy to export-led expansion, Taiwanese corporations have been accustomed to the pattern of procuring technology, machinery, and material from Japan and after assembly, export to the US market.[225] After the US decides to take a tough measure to demand its trade partners enjoying large surplus with the US to appreciate their currency, Taiwan experiences an "economic bubble": NT appreciates dramatically, the land price surges, the labor cost increases, and the labor movement booms. Taiwanese businessmen decide to cope with these hardships by moving their production overseas, and the KMT government introduces IT industry into Taiwan to fill in the gap which is caused by the relocation of the traditional industry. Therefore, the structure of Taiwan's industry experiences a parallel shift from the former champion industries such as footwear, umbrella and textile to IT and service industries. However, the outflow of traditional indus-

[225] Even Taiwan's well known IT sector falls into this pattern. Take TFT-LCD as an example, all Taiwanese TFT-LCD makers pay royalty to Japanese companies to acquire technology, buy most of the machinery equipments and key components from Japan. As for the manufacturers of CD-ROM, they also buy their key components like pick up head from Japan.

tries signals the first wave of westbound investment but not the last. As the current worldwide IT industry encounters the difficulty of "micro-profit", or even "nano-profit[226]", in order to lower the cost, Taiwanese IT manufacturers are following the westward footstep of their traditional counterparts to cope with the difficulty of diminishing profit by moving their production to China.

Figure 3-2 Taiwan's Exports in Selected Industries

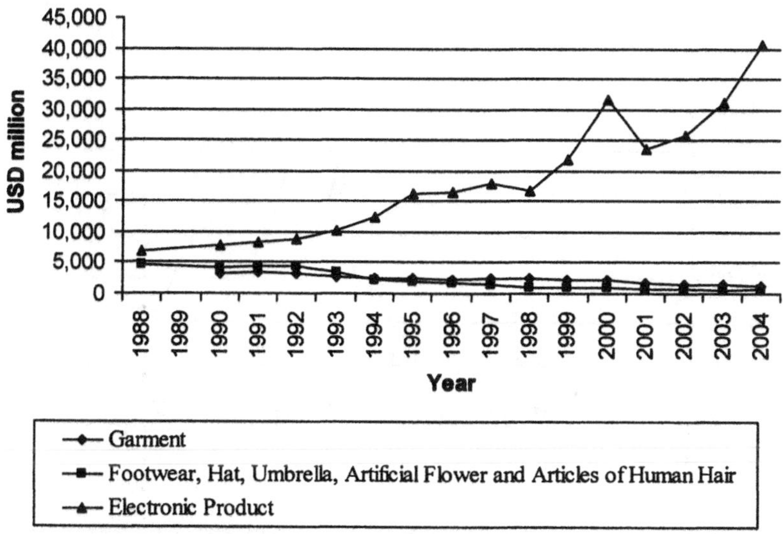

Source: Ministry of Finance, Executive Yuan, ROC

The Figure 3-2 introduces the transition in Taiwan's export structure. The amount of the exports in Taiwan's former champion industries such as footwear, umbrella, and garment is on the decline but the amount of the exports in electronic products is on the rise. The amount of exports in garment almost follows downward trajectory from 1990's USD 3.19 billion to 2004's USD 1.3 billion and this indicates a 59% decline in a period of 15 years. Similarly, the amount of exports in footwear, hat, umbrellas, artificial flowers and articles of

226 "Micro-profit" and "nano-profit" are common terms to describe the dramatic shrinkage of profit in IT industry. When Kuen-Yao Lee, President of BenQ Inc. was interviewed, "he said the trend in margins is quickly going from 'microprofit to nanoprofit' and will result in a landscape in which Taiwanese ODMs make the same razor-thin margins of the EMS industry." http://www.eetimes.com/story/OEG20030708S0036

human hair goes almost all the way down from 1988's USD 4.5 billion to 2004's USD 615 million; this indicates a 86% of decrease in a period of 17 years. In contrast, Taiwan's exports in electronics products mounts almost all the way up from 1988's USD 6.69 billion to 2000's USD 31.67 billion, but the global economic downturn in 2001 causes a sharp decline of the exports in electronic products. In 2001 the exports in electronic products drops to USD 23.6 billion but in 2002 increases again to USD 25.84 billion and rises in 2003 to USD 31.16 billion and increases again in 2004 to USD 40.53 billion. The amount of exports in electronic products increases almost five-fold in 17 years.

Figure 3-3 The Approved Outward Investment of Traditional Industry

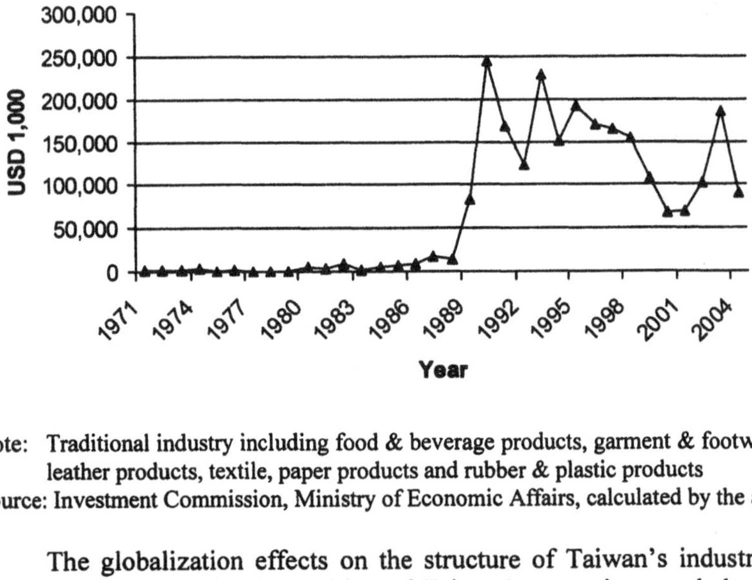

Note: Traditional industry including food & beverage products, garment & footwear, fur & leather products, textile, paper products and rubber & plastic products
Source: Investment Commission, Ministry of Economic Affairs, calculated by the author.

The globalization effects on the structure of Taiwan's industry reflect not only on the structural transition of Taiwan's exporting goods but also on the trend of Taiwan's outward investment. Figure 3-3 illustrates that the capital outflow of traditional industry commences in the early 1980s, gathers momentum in the late 1980s and peaks in the early 1990s. In 1980, the amount of the approved outward investment of traditional industry for the first time reaches USD 5.76 million, but in 1981, the amount declines to USD 2.7 million. In 1982, it increases to USD 8.96 million and decreases to USD 1.76 million in 1983. From 1984 to 1986, the amount lingers between USD 6 million to USD 9 million. In 1987, the amount mounts to USD 17.94 million which almost double the previous year's USD 8.99 million. In 1988, it slides down to USD 13.34 million but surges to USD 82.9 million in the following year. In 1990, it reaches its peak by almost quadrupling 1989's USD 82.9 million to USD 245.35 million. However, it decreases to USD 167.47 million in 1991 and slides again in 1992 to USD 123.84 million. From 1995, the amount of outflow capital from traditional industry slides almost all the way down to 2000's USD 67.33 million. In 2001, the outflow amount increases to USD 70.14 million, it climbs up to USD 102.39 million in 2002, and increases again to USD 185.2 million, yet in 2004, it drops to USD 90.32 million. Therefore, Figure 3-3 indicates that the outward investments of Taiwan's traditional industry booms in the early 1990s, and gradually slows down in the following years.

Figure 3-4 Outward Investments of Electronic & Electric Appliances Industry

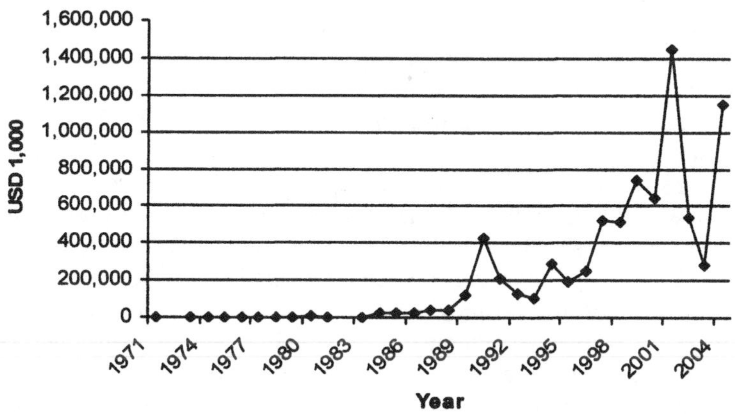

Source: Investment Commission, Ministry of Economic Affairs

Unlike traditional industry, Figure 3-4 illustrates that the capital outflow of Taiwan's electronic & electric appliances industry commences in the mid 1980s, gathers its momentum in the late 1990s and reaches its acme in the early 2000s. From 1980 to 1988, the amount of approved outward investment from the electronic & electric appliances industry has never exceeded USD 39.58 million, but in 1989, it almost triples the previous year's USD 39.49 million to USD 121.85 million. In 1990, it further increases to USD 423.92 million but decreases to USD 209.31 million in 1991. From 1991 to 2001, it follows a zigzag path up to the peak: it first slides down to 1993's USD 104.24 million, and then rebounds to USD 289.65 million in 1994; in 1995 it declines again to USD 195.1 million, and up again to 1996's USD 251.36 million and 1997's USD 525.79 million; in 1998, it slides slightly to USD 515.11 million and goes up to USD 737.91 million in 1999; in 2000, it decreases to 604.41 million and reaches the peak of USD 1,451.09 million in 2001. It decreases again in two consecutive years from 2001's USD 1,451.09 million to 2003's 279.89 million, but rebounds to USD 1,146.75 million.

Instead of cultivating the former champion industries like footwear, garments, umbrellas and so on, Taiwanese government take a parallel shifting policy to develop IT industry and to allow the production base of traditional industries to relocate overseas. However, the poor performance of traditional industries in Taiwan's export does not imply the lackluster future of Taiwanese companies in traditional industries. As an example, the relocation of footwear manufactures leads to the decline of the exports of Taiwan's footwear products, but Taiwanese footwear manufacturers such as Pou Chen Group and Feng Tay Enterprise Co. have shipped over two thirds of the world sports shoes and outpaced their Korean arch-rivals since they relocated most of their production line to China.[227] Therefore, the barrier of Taiwan's economic development does not lie in the relocation of Taiwanese firms but Taiwan's role in the global deployment of Taiwanese firms. In other words, it is not the outward investments hinders economic expansion; on the contrary, it is how the home country positions itself in the international deployment of its national companies induces the problem. If the national companies export their high-skilled jobs, the home country should be able to connect itself with the operation of the companies to provide labor and environment suitable for the development of low-skilled jobs to fill the vacancy in the value chain of the companies; correspondingly, if the companies export their low-skilled employment overseas, the home country must offer talents and infrastructures fitting for high-skilled jobs to complete the requirements of the firms. In order to maintain their prosperity, countries have to fit into the international division of labor of firms.

Table 3-6 indicates that for Taiwanese firms, China-bound investment is a movement covered multifarious industries. Over 50 percent (54 percent of April 30, 2004) of the companies whose stocks are listed in Taiwan Stock Exchange (TSE) & Gre Tai Securities Market (OTC) have invested in China. In rubber industry and auto industry, all stock-listed companies invest westward. In glass-ceramic, paper-making, plastic & chemical and electric & mechanical industries, over 70% of listed companies invest in China. In food, shipping, electronic, and cement industries, more than 50% of listed companies invest in China. In trade & department store industries, steel, textile and biochemical industries, more than 40% of listed companies invest in China. However, only 18.18% of the listed Taiwanese companies in building material & construction invest in China. As for the companies which are difficult to be categorized,

[227] Lin, 2001, P. 98

30.77% of them invest in China. Table 3-6 also illustrates another trait of Taiwan's economic development. Electronic industry has been the backbone of Taiwan economy. Electronic companies account for one half of total listed companies and 60.59% of the listed electronic firms have invested in China.

Table 3-6 Taiwan's TSE & OTC Listed Companies Investing in China (as of April 30, 2004)

Industry	Total	Investing in China	%
Glass-Ceramic	7	6	85.71
Food	23	16	69.57
Paper-Making	7	5	71.43
Building Material & Construction	55	10	18.18
Trade & Department Store	17	7	41.18
Rubber	10	10	100.00
Steel	33	15	45.45
Shipping	22	12	54.55
Plastic & Chemical	25	18	72.00
Electric & Mechanical	66	49	74.24
Electronic	576	349	60.59
Cement	8	5	62.50
Textile	67	30	44.78
Biochemical	61	30	49.18
Auto	4	4	100.00
Others	156	48	30.77
Total	1137	614	54.00

Source: Taiwan Economic Journal (Taiwan Jing Ji Xin Bao), calculated by the author.

Instead of cooperating with the "host country" which Taiwanese companies choose, Taiwan has tried to alienate itself from further economic integration with China. On the one hand, most of the Taiwanese firms have chosen China as their destination of investments, but on the other hand, Taiwanese government so far deems China as an enemy state. The conflict nature concerning cross-Strait relationships between public and private organizations has aroused the unsettlement within Taiwan's society and will eventually impair Taiwan economy. Since Chinese mainland has become the FDI destination of most Taiwanese enterprises, even though Taiwanese government may temporarily delay the capital outflow by political interference, China will eventually possess more clout over Taiwanese businesses. The political irreconcilability and uncooperativeness between China and Taiwan will deprive Taiwan's right on governing its businesses. Moreover, even though Taiwanese government has the right to impose laws and regulations on private actors to demand their sacrifice for Taiwan's national security, in the globalization era, private actors can implement thousand tactics to eschew the governmental interference and the most radical method which a private actor can adopt is to transform itself into a foreign firm and to completely eradicate its local operations.

The unique political complexes between Taiwan and China have already compounded the simple economic decision of Taiwanese enterprises. As China has emerged as a world economic power, Taiwanese government has little chance to win in the wrestle over the support of private actors.[228] As a result, Taiwan economy will hinge on how Chinese authority deals with Taiwanese enterprises. When China garners enough bargaining power against Taiwanese businessmen, if they were forced to choose between their host country and home country, which side will they select? So far the answer seems to Taiwan's disadvantage.[229] As investments in China become an indispensable arrangement of their global deployment for Taiwanese corporations, if Taiwanese government insists on placing its political requests prior to their economic demands and intends to reverse the process of the cross-Strait economic integration, it will be surprised to discover that most of its local firms disappear from its governance.

3.3.1 The Barrier to the Implementation of Taiwan's Economic Policy

The domestic politics of Taiwan has been the dominant force to construct and to impede the development of Taiwanese economy. The political decision to introduce high-tech industry into Taiwan and to allow the relocation of traditional industry sustains the economic growth in the 1990s. However, in order to alienate Taiwan from China, any economic plan regarding promoting the interdependence between China and Taiwan will be twisted, shelved or abolished, regardless of the effectiveness of the plan to enhance the development of Taiwan economy.

Since Taiwanese manufacturers relocate their manufacture base and the domestic output in the manufacturing sector is on the decline, in order to sustain Taiwan's high economic growth rate, Taiwanese government have considered shifting the future development of domestic economy from manufacture

---

[228] Hsu Wen Long, a pro-independence Taiwan business tycoon, was singled out by Chinese authority as an unwelcome investor but Hsu insisted on his investment in China. Moreover, in order to invest in China, Hsu issued an open statement to support one China principle and China's Anti-Secession Law. "Hsu Wen Long Said, 'Chi-Mei Has to Invest in China,'" Jul 9, 2004, Economic Daily; "Gov't Blasts Beijing as Tycoon Drops Independence Stance" Mar 28, 2005, China Post.

[229] After President Chen Shui-bian's inauguration speech in 2004, China publicly declared those pro-independence Taiwanese businessmen were not welcome in China. Even so, Taiwanese investors were adamant at their mainland deployment plan. The mainland-bound investment of the first half year of 2004 increased 68.18 percent comparing with the same period of 2003, and the investment amount was USD 3.39 billion. "Tai Shang Capital Flight to Mainland, the First Half Year Increase 68%," July 21, 2004, *Economic Daily*

industry to service industry. Therefore, Executive Yuan brings up the *Asia-Pacific Regional Operations Center Program* in the hope of coping with the economic transformation caused by globalization.[230] However, as Taiwanese political leaders deem China as a major threat to Taiwan's national security and sovereignty, the plan of building Taiwan as an Asia-Pacific regional operations center will inevitably invite China's economic force into Taiwan and therefore is aborted. In order to lessen the economic dependence on China and at the same time maintain its high grow rate, Taiwan determines to strive for its economic expansion by strengthening its capacity in technology and science.

Asia-Pacific Regional Operations Center was designed for the purpose that both local and foreign companies could have taken advantage of Taiwan as a base to perform their Asia-Pacific business operation. In fact, the economic officials realize the importance of cross-Strait relations, and also propose to exploit the special relations to Taiwan's benefit.[231] According to the original design of Asia-Pacific Regional Operations Center Program, the China market is one of its major targets. Taiwan inclines to serve as a gateway for corporations to exploit business opportunities in the whole Asia-Pacific region including mainland China.[232]

The economic officials have a vision on developing Taiwan into an operation center by focusing on six major sectors—manufacturing center, sea transportation center, air transportation center, financial center, telecommunications center and media center. Four out of the mentioned six sectors are highly interdependent on the cross-Strait relations. Especially the goal of media center is to create "an optimal environment for Chinese-language media production[233]". With the 1.3 billion people who speak Chinese, China should be and would be the target market for Taiwan's Chinese-language media production. Without

---

[230] See "*The Plan for Developing Taiwan into an Asia-Pacific Regional Operations Center*", Council for Economic Planning and Development, Executive Yuan, Republic of China, July 24, 1997 Part 1, P.1. "The Republic of China on Taiwan is at the threshold of a new era in the development of its economy. Its domestic economic structure has been transformed by a series of speedy adjustments, with profound implications for its industrial development. It has had to face the challenge of dramatic changes in the world economy, especially the rapid economic growth and integration of the Asia-Pacific region. And it has had to respond to the tremendous impact of swiftly developing trade and economic relations across the Taiwan Strait."

[231] See Ibid, Part 1, P. 7. In which, it states, "Cross-Strait economic relations are an important factor that cannot be disregarded in developing Taiwan as a regional operations center. In the mid to long term, the stable development of cross-Strait economic relations will be an essential pre-condition for Taiwan completely achieving its aim of becoming a full-scale operations center."

[232] See Ibid, Part 1, P. 3.

[233] See Ibid, Part 2, P. 7.

the China market, Taiwan's media center would not bring forward any concrete achievement.

China market is required for Taiwan to serve as a Chinese-language media production center. Taiwan also needs China market to operate as a transportation center. In 2004, China's total trade volume excluding Hong Kong's reached USD 1,154.6 billion (Table 2-3) and China ranked as the world's third largest trading country and is largest in Asian area. Thus no matter Taiwan intends to develop a sea transportation center or an air transportation center, without direct transportation connection with Chinese mainland, Taiwan's goal to function as a transportation center can best only be half-realized.

In its Plan for Developing Taiwan into an Asia-Pacific Regional Operations Center", Taiwan also plans to establish a financial center aiming at constructing a financial structure fully conforming to international standards, and relaxing all confinements on capital movements.[234] Since over one half of Taiwanese investments flow into China (according to the official record of Taiwan, Table 2-22), without a benign relationship with China, the establishment of the financial center will cause more pain than gain to Taiwan's society because the government will maintain a suspicious attitude on those Taiwanese corporations and wonder whether they are conducting the notorious tactic of "taking their money to mainland China while leaving their debts in Taiwan (Qian Jin Da Lu, Zhai Liu Tai Wan)".

Since in Taiwan's framework, its telecommunications center and manufacturing center are more internally oriented and less susceptible to the influence of external environment. The former focuses on increasing "the mobile phone subscribership", decreasing "the average traffic congestion rate for mobile phone stations" and building "digitalization of telecommunication lines"[235], so the improvement of the domestic infrastructure is the major concern; the latter intends to construct Taiwan as an island of "science and technology"[236], so the internal technological strength will be the main focus. Therefore, Taiwan can work on these two targets without the concern of external environment.

This plan with grand vision to transform Taiwan industry from manufacture-led to service-oriented vanishes due to the political concerns of Taiwanese politicians. As President Lee Teng-hui dismisses the plan of treating China as Taiwan's "economic hinterland", and expresses his disapproval by saying it is "a dog in the manger" (Jou Zhan Que Cao) by twisting the strive for establishing the Asia-Pacific Regional Operations Center to serve as an excuse for the westward activities of Taiwanese companies.[237] Furthermore, Lee brings forth

---

[234] See Ibid, Part 2, P. 5.
[235] See Ibid, Part 2, P. 6.
[236] See Ibid, Part 2, P. 3.
[237] Quoted from News 7 Weekly, No. 494, (in Chinese)

the "no haste, be patient" policy to restrain the cross-Strait exchanges. In view of the superior's intention, the economic experts thus promote no further the Plan for Developing Taiwan into an Asia-Pacific Regional Operations Center.

As the structural transformation of global economy is still on its way, the subsidence of the Plan for Developing Taiwan into an Asia-Pacific Regional Operations Center does not facilitate Taiwan's role in the global economy. In order to alleviate China's influence, Taiwan decides to devote its energy on promoting Taiwan as an island of science and technology. The newly-elected DPP government promulgates a "Two Trillion, Twin Star" program to improve the competitive edge of Taiwan in the global economic system. The "Two Trillion" indicates "the semiconductor and display industries which are forecast to each reach an annual production value of above NT$1 trillion within a few years"; the "Twin Star" means "the digital content and the biotechnology industries, which count among the future star industries".[238]

As the "Twin Star" industries—digital content and biotechnology industries are still in their embryo-stage, up to now, there is no astonishing discovery to well equip Taiwan economy against depending on China economy. And the "Two Trillion" industries are basically the subdivision of IT industry. The development trajectories of "Two Trillion" industries can be fully depicted through the introduction of how IT industry of Taiwan is developed in the following sections. However, since most of the IT manufacturers have relocated their production base to China,[239] it will be highly questionable that the development of "Two Trillion" industries can safeguard Taiwan economy from depending on China.

3.3.2 IT Industry of Taiwan in the Global Supply Chain

To understand the hardship of Taiwan economy, it is a prerequisite to understand the structure of Taiwan's information technology manufacturing industry (IT). Since Taiwan maintains as an island of "Made in Taiwan" but not "Designed by Taiwan" or "Brand of Taiwan", when the traditional industries like footwear, umbrellas, hats are no longer competitive in the international arena, instead of encouraging the promotion of the upstream or downstream integration in the traditional industries, the government leads a parallel shift from the traditional industries to the ones which are capital intensive and technology intensive with a more complicated manufacturing procedure, like petroleum-chemical, electronics and information technology (IT) sectors. Of them, Tai-

---

http://www.new7.com.tw/weekly/old/494/article074.html

[238] Refer from the official website of Industrial Development & Investment Center, Ministry of Economic Affairs.
http://investintaiwan.nat.gov.tw/moea-web/InvestOpps/Type/2-2/#2

[239] From Table 3-5, 60.59% of stock-listed electronic firms have invested in China.

wan is especially famous for its IT sector. As a research report of Council for Economic Planning and Development[240] illustrates that the IT products not only enhance Taiwan's exports and domestic investments but also reduce the domestic unemployment rate.[241] IT industry is the backbone of Taiwan's economic development and the center of Taiwan's "Two Trillion, Twin Star" plan.

The establishment of Taiwan's IT industry should be contributed to some government officials like Li Kwoh-ting (K. T. Li) and Sun Yun-suan.[242] They construct the foundation of the research institutes such as The Industrial Technology Research Institute and Institute for Information Industry, and endeavor to recruit science and technology talents from the US. The overseas returnees have been the talent pool for Hsin Chu Science Park, which has been addressed as a Silicon Valley of the East.[243] The close relations between Taiwan and the US contribute to Taiwan's booming IT industry. Taiwanese students studying in the US come back to Taiwan during the 80's, and with their US experience and intimate relationships with the US firms, Taiwan is able to position itself in the IT product value chain. The IT industry successfully fills into the blank caused by the relocation of those traditional industries beginning in the 1980s and takes over the responsibility of bringing the continuous prosperity to this island.

The Economist points out that the Original Equipment Manufacturing (OEM) model of doing business is the most significant feature of Taiwanese high-tech firms. Taiwanese OEM manufacturers produce the goods to their buyers' specifications and do all the labor to complete the products. However, although OEM buyers may never touch the goods, those goods are sold under their brand names and the names of Taiwanese OEM manufacturers are no where to be found on the finished goods.[244] Taiwan is well known for its Original Equipment Manufacturing (OEM) model of doing business, and recently moves a minor step towards Original Design Manufacturing (ODM) but still lags behind the goal of Original Brand Manufacturing (OBM).

Most of the Taiwanese businesses focus on improving the efficiency of manufacturing processes, because they either are constrained by eagerness to

---

240 A governmental apparatus which is listed under Executive Yuan takes in charge of Taiwan's economic analysis and planning.

241 The statistics is referred from a report in the official website of Council for Economic Planning and Development, Executive Yuan, ROC. "Tai Wan Jing Ji Yu Zi Xun Ke Ji Gong Ye Jing Qi Bo Dong Zhi Yan Jiu"
http://www.cepd.gov.tw/eco-plan/research/twn-eco-info.pdf

242 K. T. Li has been recognized as Taiwan's Technology Godfather (Tai Wan Ke Ji Jiao Fu).

243 Mathews, 1997

244 See "Survey: Taiwan: Silicon Valley (east)" by Christopher Anderson, *The Economist*. London: Nov 7, 1998. Vol. 349, Issue 8093; pg. S14, 3 pgs

make a quick profit thus with no intention to increase the extra expense (either on R&D or on marketing) or by the lack of the ambition to explore the possibility of self-branding or product-innovating. Therefore, in the product value chain, Taiwan occupies primarily the middle of the chain—processing and assembling. On the upstream of the chain, there are the US, European and Japanese firms which either focus on R&D and product innovation, or concentrate on the production of complex machinery or key components. On the downstream of the chain, because the major consumption markets are concentrated on the North America, Japan and Western Europe, the brand names are generally owned by their MNCs and the distribution channels are mostly under the control of their local firms. Taiwanese companies lack the resources to conduct market research in these major consumption markets to create their brand names and do not have the competence or confidence to compete with them locally. As a result, the lack of the brand names and distribution channels trap Taiwanese enterprises in the middle of the global value chain.

The OEM business model permeates multifarious IT segments in Taiwan, from Notebook (NB), Desktop PC (DT), to Digital Still Camera (DSC) and even more and more Motherboards (MB) are produced under the business model of OEM. Table 3-7 indicates that in 2000, Taiwanese manufacturers produce 27.66 million desktop PCs, 82% of which are labeled under the brand names of their buyers. In 2001, although the total number of desktop PCs made by Taiwanese firms decreases to 25.41 million, the percentage of OEM desktop PCs rises to 83%. In 2002, 87.02% of desktop PCs made by Taiwanese firms are under the business model of OEM. In 2003, the total number of Taiwanese desktop PCs reaches 29.86 million and 93.8% of them are manufactured under the OEM model. In 2004, Taiwanese producers manufacture 34.65 desktop PCs, and 96.2% of them are sold under the brand names of their contract buyers.

Although the volume of Taiwanese NBs accounts for 72.4% of the total world production in 2004 and the market share of Taiwanese NB is expected to rise to 82.4% in 2005,[245] less than 10% of NBs made by Taiwanese manufacturers are labeled under their own brand names. In 2000, 90.01% of 12.71 million NBs made by Taiwanese firms are sold under OEM. In 2001, the percentage of OEM NBs increases to 92.02%; in 2002, it nudges down a little to 92%. In 2003, the percentage of Taiwanese NBs manufactured under the OEM model rises to 95.8%, but in 2004, it declines to 93.6%.

Regarding DSC the business model of OEM also prevails in Taiwanese manufacturers. In 1999, 89.51% of 1.62 million DSCs made by Taiwanese firms are sold under the brand name of their buyers. In 2000, the percentage of

[245] Data come from Institute for Information Industry, Market Intelligence Center.

OEM DSCs increases to 92.15% but in 2001 slides to 90.05%. In 2002, it drops again to 83.66%. However, in 2003, 85.3% of 14.28 million DSCs manufactured by Taiwanese firms are sold under the OEM business model. In 2004, the number of Taiwanese made DSCs for the first time breaks 20 million pieces and reaches 22.58 million, and 20.41 million DSCs accounting for 90.4% of the total Taiwanese DSCs are manufactured for the contract buyers.

At the start-up stage of business, most of the motherboards made by Taiwanese firms are sold under their own brand names. However, as the fierce competition among the world's first tier IT firms, they have to look for low-cost supplies and because Taiwanese firms are competitive in design, manufacture and cost-efficiency, they have to outsource their production needs to Taiwanese manufactures. In 2004, Taiwanese manufactures produce 96.5% of the world's motherboards and it is expected that the market share of Taiwanese firms will rise to 98.3% in 2005.[246] In 1999, 29% of 64.38 million motherboards made by Taiwanese firms are sold under the business model of OEM. In 2000, the percentage of OEM motherboards increases to 35.79% and the amount also increase from 1999's 18.67 million to 30.2 million. Although in 2001, the percentage decreases to 33.9%, in 2002, it picks up the momentum and reached 38.69%. In 2003, 49.44% of 103.86 million motherboards made by Taiwanese firms are sold to their contract buyers and in 2004, the percentage of OEM motherboards made by Taiwanese manufacturers increases to 53.96%.

Playing the role as contract manufacturers of the world first tier IT brand names, such as new HP (HP merged with Compaq), IBM and Dell, Taiwanese firms have concentrated on assembly phase in the supply chain of the global IT production.[247] Stan Shih, the founder of the Taiwan-based Acer Inc, coins the term "smiling curve" to depict a U-shaped value curve regarding the profitability of each phase in the value chain. While Acer first comes up with the idea of spinning off the OEM business and concentrating on the management of brand name, its employees are against it. Shih successfully persuades them by applying this smiling curve to gaining their understanding. As processing and assembling phase creates the lowest profit margin in the smiling curve, Acer has to move to the upstream or downstream of the value chain to gain ascendancy.

---

[246] Data come from Institute for Information Industry, Market Intelligence Center.

[247] See "Survey: Taiwan: Silicon Valley (east)" by Christopher Anderson, *The Economist*. London: Nov 7, 1998. Vol. 349, Issue 8093; pg. S14, 3 pgs

Table 3-7 The Statistics of Business Type of Selected Taiwanese IT Hardware

Unit: Million

Type	Year	1999	2000	2001	2002	2003	2004
Desktop PC	Total Amount	-	27.66	25.41	24.96	29.86	34.65
	OEM	**-**	**22.68**	**21.09**	**21.72**	**28.01**	**33.33**
	%	**-**	**82.00**	**83.00**	**87.02**	**93.8**	**96.2**
	Own Brand	-	4.98	4.32	3.24	1.85	1.32
	%	-	18.00	17.00	12.98	6.2	3.8
Notebook	Total Amount	-	12.71	14.16	18.38	25.24	33.41
	OEM	**-**	**11.44**	**13.03**	**16.91**	**24.18**	**31.27**
	%	**-**	**90.01**	**92.02**	**92.00**	**95.8**	**93.6**
	Own Brand	-	1.27	1.13	1.47	1.06	2.14
	%	-	9.99	7.98	8.00	4.2	6.4
Digital Still Camera	Total Amount	1.62	5.73	7.94	8.75	16.74	22.58
	OEM	**1.45**	**5.28**	**7.15**	**7.32**	**14.28**	**20.41**
	%	**89.51**	**92.15**	**90.05**	**83.66**	**85.3**	**90.4**
	Own Brand	0.17	0.45	0.79	1.43	2.46	2.17
	%	10.49	7.85	9.95	16.34	14.7	9.6
Motherboard	Total Amount	64.38	84.37	80.57	86.55	103.86	114.56
	OEM	**18.67**	**30.2**	**27.31**	**33.49**	**49.44**	**53.96**
	%	**29.00**	**35.79**	**33.90**	**38.69**	**47.6**	**47.1**
	Own Brand	45.71	54.17	53.26	53.06	54.42	60.6
	%	71.00	64.21	66.10	61.31	52.4	52.9

Source: Institute for Information Industry (III), MIC, calculated by the author.

Figure 3-5 illustrates in 1960s and 1970s, the early development stage of PC industry, the assembly phase is profitable. However, after IBM opened its architecture to outside hardware and software developers, more and more manufacturers competed in this assembly phase because of its low entry barrier. As a result, the midstream of PC production chain is transformed into a low-value added phase. He points out the most profitable phases of PC are shifted to the upstream and the downstream as the entry barriers are higher. The up-stream includes the development of technologies and the production of key components; the downstream contains brand-name, marketing channel and logistics. The lowest value-added phase of PC production is the midstream which involves labor-intensive processes such as assembly. [248]

---

[248] Shih, 2002, P. 298-300

Figure 3-5 The Position of Taiwan's PC Industry in Stan Shih's Smiling Curve

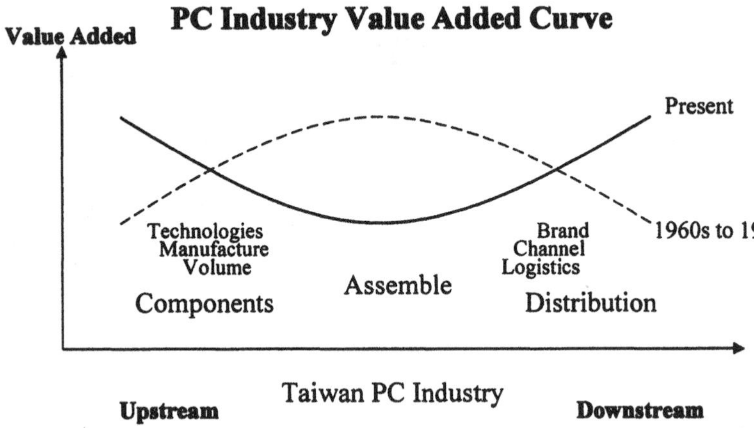

Source: Shih, 2002, modified by the author.

Moreover, because of the fierce competition among those world-class firms, as these world-class IT firms tend to distribute their orders to several OEM manufacturers, they take over the procurement right of some key components from their OEM manufacturers to gain the advantage of production scale. Even though the number of NBs made by Taiwanese firms accounts for 72.4% of the world production in 2004, they still have to render the purchase right of the major components to their contract buyers. The major components of NB include Central Processing Unit (CPU), Dynamic Random Access Memory (DRAM), Hard Drive (HD), Panel, and Slim CD-ROM; now only Slim CD-ROM is left to the procurement of the contract manufacturers; others will be determined by those world-class big firms.[249] Table 3-8 illustrated that Taiwanese companies lack the ability to produce CPU and HD, whose cost has accounted for around half of total material cost (47%-55%). Moreover, as brand name companies control the purchase right of over 80% of material cost, they can exert their influence not only on the finished-good suppliers but also the component suppliers. Therefore, when brand name companies demand their Taiwanese suppliers to move westward, Taiwanese NB makers have to bend over to their request. As a result, although Taiwanese government do not lift the ban on NB manufacturing investments in China until late 2001, in 2004 Taiwanese NB makers produce 82% of their NBs in China and in Sep 2005

[249] Information comes from the industry research report of Barits International Securities.

they move the last OEM production line to China—that is to say, Taiwanese firms will no longer produce mass productive NBs in Taiwan..[250]

Table 3-8 The Component Purchase Right of Taiwanese Notebook OEM Manufacturer

Component	CPU	DRAM	HD	Slim CD-ROM	Panel
The Cost Accounts for the Total Cost*	35%-40%	3%~5%	12%-15%	8-10%	30%-35%
Controllable by Contract Firms	×	×	×	˅	×
Local supply	×	˅	×	˅	˅

Note: *The total cost means the cost of all raw materials and components.
The Cost is estimated according to a NB which is worth of USD 750-800.
Source: Barits International Securities

Taiwanese manufacturers can produce the components of DRAM, Slim CD-ROM and Panel but even though they can produce those components, the technologies of those major components are controlled by their foreign counterparts. As a result, Taiwanese companies have to pay technology transfer fee and royalties. Even though Taiwanese DRAM manufacturers produce 18% of the total world volume of DRAM, without autonomous technology, they are under the threat of technological disruption. Once their technology-suppliers decide to withdraw from the DRAM market or to disconnect the cooperative relationships, Taiwanese DRAM manufacturers will be forced out of the market.[251]

Taiwan's Panel industry is also developed on the basis of acquiring foreign technologies. In order to control key component of NB—panel (the Notebook panel is generally made from Thin Film Transistor-Liquid Crystal Display (TFT-LCD)) which was primarily controlled by South Korean and Japanese companies, especially the Japanese companies,[252] Taiwanese manufac-

---

[250] "Notebook, Lights-out on Taiwan (Bi Ji Dian Nao , Tai Wan Chui Xi Deng Hao)," Sep. 18, 2005 *United Daily News* (in Chinese)

[251] Steve Appleton, the CEO of Micron—the world's second largest DRAM manufacturer—claimed Taiwan DRAM manufacturers were not "complete" DRAM manufacturers and posed no threat to Micron because they did not have their technologies. He pointed out further that the famous Taiwan DRAM manufacturer Winbond was forced out of the market when its technology-supplier—Toshiba decided to withdraw from the DRAM market. That is the result of not possessing technological autonomy. "Micron Predicted the Decline of Taiwan DRAM (Mei Kuang Chang Shuai Tai Wan DRAM)," May 15, 2004, *China Times*, (in Chinese)

[252] Liu, 1999, P. 264. (Liu, Shang-Jyh)

turers sought for any possibility of technology transfer but before the Asian financial crisis happened, Taiwanese firms were not able to access the technology. However, after the Asian financial crisis emerged, because of the aggressive expansion of Korean companies, the competition pressure from Korea and the financial difficulty, Japanese firms decided to transfer the technology to Taiwanese firms and to team up with them to compete against the Korean TFT-LCD makers.

Taiwanese LCD manufacturers—AUO[253] and CPT—forerun all other LCD manufacturers to establish their LCM plants in China, but LG Phillips LCD and Samsung soon match up their Taiwanese competitors' move.[254] At the same time, Japanese manufactures, in short of capital, plan to cooperate with Chinese companies on the production of TFT-LCD.[255]

Table 3-9 The Source of TFT-LCD Technology

Taiwan TFT-LCD Manufacturer	Technology Transfer Source
Prime View International	In-house Technology
Unipac Optoelectronics*	Panasonic
Chi-Mei Optoelectronics	Industrial Technology Research Institute (Partially from Fujitsu)
Acer Display*	IBM Japan
Chunghwa Picture Tubes (CPT)	Mitsubishi/ADI (Advanced Display)
HanStar Display	Toshiba, Hitachi
Quanta Display	Sharp

Note: * Unipac Optoelectronics and Acer Display have merged into AUO.
Source: Liu (Liu, Shang-Jyh), 1999, Modified by the Author

Table 3-9 illustrates that all Taiwanese TFT-LCD manufacturers acquire their technology from Japanese firms except Prime View International (concentrates mostly on small-size TFT-LCD) and Chi-Mei Optoelectronics as they obtain their technology locally. Unipac Optoelectronics purchases from Panasonic, Acer Display from IBM Japan, Chunghwa Picture Tubes from Mitsubishi and Advanced Display, HanStar Display from Toshiba, and Quanta Display from Sharp. Moreover, it takes USD 500-650 million to build a new TFT-LCD fabrication plant (fab), and thereamong technology transfer fee takes USD 100-130 million and equipment expenditure costs USD 400-520

253 AUO is merged from Acer Display and Unipac Optoelectronics.
254 See "TFT-LCD Manufacturers Look to China" July.2,2002
255 "The Expanding Nexus of the TFT-LCD Triumvirate" This article is based on a report by James W. Murphy and Sean Wu of the Market Intelligence Center (MIC), Taiwan, May 07, 2003.

million.[256] To maintain its competitiveness, a TFT-LCD manufacturer has to manage continuous capital spending because the rapid progression in substrate size and technology, thus the capital must be put in to construct new fabs. Therefore, once a manufacturer joins the competition; the sunk cost will make it difficult to exit the market.

Table 3-10 The Deployment of Large-size TFT-LCD Manufacturers in Yangtze River Delta

Location	Company	Product Type
Shanghai	NEC (Joint venture with Shang Hai General Electronic Digital Technology Co., Ltd.)	Panel
Shanghai	Chi Mei[a], Quanta Display[b]	LCM
Su Zhou	AUO, Samsung, Hitachi	LCM
Wu Jiang	CPT	LCM
Nan Jing	HanStar, LG Phillips LCD	LCM

Note: [a] Although Chi Mei has expressed its will to set up an advanced liquid crystal display module (LCM) plant in Shanghai area (Ningbo)[257], because its former chairman, Hsu Wen-lung, is an active pro-Taiwan-independent businessman, Chinese authority has claimed to boycott all investments from pro-Taiwan-independent businessmen. However, after Hsu publicly supports China's Anti-Secession Law, Chi Mei should be able to fulfill its plan.[258]

[b] DigiTimes: "*Quanta Display to invest US$12 million in Shanghai LCM plant*"

Source: DigiTimes Research 2002/10, Modified by the Author

Moreover, because of the political interference, to mitigate the influence from China, Taiwan discards the "Plan for Developing Taiwan into an Asia-Pacific Regional Operations Center" and diverts to "Two Trillion, Twin Star" program, yet in order to further develop the TFT-LCD industry (one of the "Two Trillion" industries in the grand economic plan of Taiwanese government), Taiwanese manufacturers move their liquid crystal display module (LCM, the back-end stage to manufacture LCD panel) to China. Because the LCM is the most labor-intensive phase in the production of LCD panel and most of the TFT-LCD buyers such as NB manufacturers and LCD Monitor makers have already relocated their manufacturing base to China, Taiwanese TFT-LCD makers have to export the production of LCM to China to lower the

[256] See Ibid.

[257] See Business Briefs, Taipei Times, Apr. 01, 2003, P. 11.

[258] "China said it 'doesn't welcome' investments from Chi Mei Optoelectronics Corp. Chairman Hsu Wen-long and other Taiwan business people who 'use money made on the mainland to support independence' for the island." Quoted from "China 'Doesn't Welcome' Pro-Independence Taiwan Businessmen," Bloomberg, May 31, 2004.

production cost, to get close to their customers and to compete with their gigantic South Korean competitors— Samsung and LG Phillips LCD.[259]

Table 3-10 offered the location of TFT-LCD manufacturers' mainland deployment in the Yangtze River Delta. All the major large-size TFT-LCD Taiwanese and Korean manufacturers have already moved the manufacturing process of LCM or plan to move their LCM to China. NEC has a joint venture with Shang Hai General Electronic Digital Technology Co., Ltd. in producing TFT-LCD panel in Shanghai area. Quanta also invests a LCM factory in Shanghai and Chi Mei plans to invest a LCM factory in Shanghai. AUO, Samsung and Hitachi build LCM factories in Su Zhou, CPT in Wu Jiang. HanStar and LG Phillips LCD have LCM factories in Nan Jing. Now the only question left here is when the upstream manufacture of TFT-LCD will be propelled to move to China by forward linkages.

Therefore, on the downstream of NB industry, OEM buyers are squeezing the profit margin of Taiwanese OEM manufacturers; on the upstream, Taiwanese manufacturers do not control the technologies of many key components and cannot control the price either. Taiwanese NB manufacturers are positioned in the middle of the value added chain, and assembly is exactly the lowest value-added-part of Stan Shih's smiling curve. The NB industry is a representative microcosm of Taiwan's IT industries. As OEM manufacturers, Taiwanese corporations serve as production providers in the international supply-chain and face the challenge of replacement by cheaper and more efficient manufacturers. If Taiwanese manufacturers want to survive, they have to follow the order of "the people who make the key decisions on what is produced, where and how, and who designs, directs and manages to sell successfully on the world market,"[260] because aside from production, Taiwanese firms lack the capacity to promote their products worldwide. Although Taiwan had been the main production base of many products like shoes, umbrellas, DTs, NBs and so on, Taiwan still remains as an island without its worldwide brand name. Although Taiwanese manufacturers supply more than half of the world demand in items like NB, LCD Monitor, CDT Monitor and Motherboard (MB), they still play a role as an anonymous hero. This structure weakness of Taiwan industry severely compresses the profitability of Taiwanese firms, confines their autonomy of production and worst of all caps their capacity of upward and downward integration.

However, it is easier for Taiwanese manufacturers to resolve their own difficulty of survival. When they face the request of their customers, they can

[259] Samsung enjoys the 19.7 percent of market share and ranks the first place in the global market; LG Phillips LCD follows behind with 18.2 percent of market share. See Xin Hua Net News Center, Dec. 22, 2002 (in Chinese)

[260] Lawton and Michaels, 2000, P. 57

take the advice of their customers to migrate their production lines to backward areas to seek for cheap labor, land and resources. As private actors, Taiwanese firms can survive without investing in uncertainty. For upstream integration, Taiwanese manufacturers must invest heavy capital in R&D to control the key technology, key components or even the machinery; for SMEs, it takes courage, vision and ambition to spend money on unforeseeable R&D. For downstream integration, they have to invest in channel construction, market research and brand-name-creation; since all the major consumption markets[261] are too far away from Taiwan, Taiwanese firms do not have enough resources to construct supranational logistic and it takes higher risk and gets no immediate benefits to build a brand-name.[262]

Thus, if Taiwanese government wants to promote IT industry to win economic autonomy from China, it first has to reform the structure of Taiwan's IT industry. Furthermore, it has to curb the intuitive investment urge of Taiwanese firms, because in order to benefit from the emerging China market, many Taiwanese IT manufacturers have started to deploy their resources into China. On one hand, they move to China under the pressure of their contract buyers; on the other hand, the common language and shared culture offer Taiwanese businesses a hope to tap better profit from the China market and to take advantage of the China market as its hinterland. As China has become the primal choice of Taiwanese IT firms, instead of being independent from China, Taiwan's IT industry has deeply involved into China. The divergence between Taiwanese government and its IT companies will certainly impair its grand plan of striving for Taiwan's economic autonomy by promoting IT industry.

3.3.3 Chinese Cultural Effects on the Development of Taiwanese Enterprises

Taiwan's industrial structure basically is the product of Chinese cultural and politics. The concept of "rather than be a cow-tail, be a chicken-head"[263] contributes to the boom of small and medium enterprises (SMEs) in Taiwan. Many

---

[261] So far the major consumption markets indicate the US market and the European market. The emerging Chinese market will constitute a good chance for Taiwan companies to create their own brand name, but will post a challenge to the security concern of Taiwanese government.

[262] "In fact, brethren usually try to persuade OEM customers not to place order to Acer, because Acer has its own brand name...Recently, some of the brand-name companies went through crises in Taiwan, and many people contributed the crises to their ambition of brand-name-creation." Shih Stan (2002, P. 115)

[263] This is an equivalent to the American saying: "I'd rather be a big fish in a small pond than a small fish in a big pond."

Taiwanese SMEs are established by "black hand" (Hei Shou)[264] masters who are former "black hand" apprentices. When economic prosperity commences, many "black hand" masters will leave their original working places and start up their own businesses to be "black hand" bosses. As most of these "black hand" bosses are competing with one another in cost reduction, not only in reducing production cost but also in minimizing management cost,[265] their wives have to play a multifunctional role in their family businesses to cut down the cost. The wives have to be human resources managers, financial managers, managerial managers, sales managers, purchase managers and even sometimes the production managers. As Chinese prefer to work for themselves and to manage and finance the company by their own family,[266] the scale of Taiwanese family businesses is usually confined, unless the owner is willing to change his mode of doing business when the business expands.

Moreover, after retreating to Taiwan, in fear that the surge of the private power would cultivate another political force, the KMT government had been cautious in avoiding capital concentration in private sector.[267] In afraid of an emerging political force from economic gains,[268] the KMT government discouraged the formation of large private corporations to ensure its imperative rule. Therefore, it promoted the virtue of small enterprises and the importance of capital diversification.[269] As a result, during the early period of KMT rule, almost all large corporations were state-run or party-owned so they were easily placed under the control of the KMT party-government. Because the KMT put most of its effort on managing the large corporations, therefore, it left the section of small and middle enterprises (SMEs) wide open, and the SMEs thrived

---

[264] Those who do not accept formal education or are less educated and are trained as apprentices to be machinists are addressed as "black hand" or "Hei Shou" in Chinese. See Wu and Huang, 2003, P. 4.
[265] Ibid.
[266] See "Survey: Taiwan: An army of ants" by Christopher Anderson, *The Economist*. London: Nov 7, 1998. Vol. 349, Issue 8093; pg. S8, 2 pgs
[267] KMT government was primarily constituted by so called "mainlanders", the late immigrants, in contrast to those early immigrants, Taiwanese. Thus Lauridsen commented that "the growing interest for SMEs had partly to do with the ethnic division on the island." Quoted from "Policies and Institutions of Industrial Deepening and Upgrading in Taiwan II – the Small-scale Industry Policy with Particular Emphasis on Downstream Plastic Parts and Mould Industries, Vol. 5. (Working Paper No. 12)" by Laurids S Lauridsen, A Comparative Study of Policies and Institutions of Industrial Upgrading in Thailand and Taiwan
[268] Gold (1986, P. 58) mentioned the KMT government was "a defeated force in a hostile and disarray and devoid of confidence."
[269] Ibid

on Taiwan. As a result, Taiwan had the highest density of companies in the world with one company for every 18 people in Taiwan.[270]

Table 3-11 demonstrates that Taiwanese SMEs permeate into all industrial sectors, and through the change of time, SMEs maintains as an important player in Taiwan's economic development. From 1991 to 2002, the number of Taiwanese enterprises increases from 850,679 to 1,130,525 and that of Taiwanese SMEs also proportionally rises from 825,556 to 1,104,706. In 1991, the ratio of Taiwanese SMEs accounting for total Taiwanese enterprises is 97.05; in 1992, the ratio decreases 0.28% to 96.77%; in 1993, it slides to 96.49%; in 1994, it decreases again to 96.26%; however, in 1995, the ratio bounces back to 97.97%; from 1996 to 2002, the ratios linger in a range narrower than 1%, between 97.72% to 98.18%. Furthermore, the ratio of SMEs in manufacture sector has declined from 1991's 98.12% to 2002's 97.36%; the ratio of SMEs in service sector increases from 1991's 96.63% to 2002's 98.15%; the ratio of SMES in the remaining sectors goes a zigzag path but ends up the same of 91.31% from 1991 to 2002; therefore, Table 3-11 further indicates that Taiwanese SMEs show a strong establishment in all sectors.

SMEs not only dominate Taiwan economy in terms of the number of firms but also contribute to a large share in employment. Table 3-12 illustrates that Taiwanese SMEs constantly recruit 68.28% to 70.83% of total Taiwanese workers from 1991 to 2004; on the other hand, the percentage of employees in governmental organizations gradually declines from 1991's 17.05% to 2004's 13.94% and the percentage of employees in large enterprises climbs up from 1991's 14.67% to 2004's 17,3%. Moreover, as the gigantic number of the employers in Taiwanese SMEs, SMEs accommodates overwhelmingly more personnel than government and large firms. From 1991 to 2004, SMEs take up 77.18% to 79.75% of total Taiwanese workforce. Therefore, even through the change of time, Taiwanese SMEs are still the major force to lower down Taiwan's unemployment rate.

The most significant aspect for the development of SMEs on Taiwan is that its stable growth of number is almost proportional to the increase of the total number of corporations on Taiwan. This implies even though the political restraints have been removed, Taiwanese people still maintain their entrepreneurship of "being a boss". The Chinese cultural ethics provide a base for institutionalizing Taiwanese businesses. The SMEs which account for the majority of Taiwanese businesses reflect the achievement of Chinese culture emphasizing on the family value and personal relationship (Guang Xi). The family-centered ideology makes "family" instead of individual the basis of the social

---

[270] See "Survey: Taiwan: An army of ants" by Christopher Anderson, *The Economist*. London: Nov 7, 1998. Vol. 349, Issue 8093; pg. S8, 2 pgs

unit and even the basis of business unit. Person-to-person relations weave an inter-business complex. As a result, the numerous Chinese family SMEs further devise the mechanism of Taiwanese businesses which contribute to the shape of Taiwan economy.

Kang points out, in the US, the analysis of relational exchanges focuses on the exchanges between "business organizations"; on the contrary, in Taiwan, the exchanges between "business owners" become the center of analysis. The difference comes from the concept toward corporate organizations. For Taiwanese businessmen, the interaction between SMEs is equivalent to personal interchange between the owners of SMEs. Therefore, in the arguments of Western scholars, relational exchanges imply the long term relationship based on legal contract, and corporations need to spend more time, money and energy on legal processes to ensure each transaction being completed according to the contract. However, relational exchanges in Taiwan indicate the long term relationship based on personal relations. Mutual trust and commitment becomes the base of each transaction for Taiwanese entrepreneurs.[271]

The Western Protestant beholds the idealism which each individual is an independent entity and a force to reshape the society. Therefore, it facilitates the awareness of each individual on rights-conscious, thus each individual has learned his obligation and responsibility within a clearly defined legal frame work, and each individual is encouraged to strive for his self interests under the social norm. On the contrary, the Eastern Confucianism regards individual as a center of relationships. The Confucian ethics introduce the five cardinal relationships to position each individual into an intertwined social network: between ruler and subject, father and son, husband and wife, between brothers and between friends. In Chinese societies, each individual's behaviors are therefore strictly defined by his social relation web, thus he should play as a team man and maintain harmonious human relations. In Confucian ethics, to fully comply with the social norm and to bear the social responsibilities enable an individual to be qualified as a gentleman. On the contrary, those who deviate from the social norm are deemed to induce vicious effects on the whole society, and the social force has the obligation to rectify the devious behavior. Since each individual is viewed as an element to the society, the sacrifice of an individual to accomplish the social harmony is deemed righteous. The Chinese traditional ethics, the Confucianism, dictate the rigidity of the pecking order in Chinese societies. The unchallengeable authority therefore is embedded in Chinese norm.[272]

---

[271] Kang, 1998
[272] Chen,1997

Table 3-11 The Ratio (%) of SMEs on Taiwan

		Total Industries	Manufacture	Commerce	Others
1991	Total No. of Enterprises	850,679	157,035	514,337	179,307
	The No. of SMEs	825,556	154,077	496,992	174,487
	Ratio (%)	**97.05**	**98.12**	**96.63**	**97.31**
1992	Total No. of Enterprises	900,801	159,163	542,211	199,427
	The No. of SMEs	871,726	156,013	522,653	193,060
	Ratio (%)	**96.77**	**98.02**	**96.39**	**96.81**
1993	Total No. of Enterprises	934,588	158,093	558,857	217,638
	The No. of SMEs	901,768	154,755	537,179	209,834
	Ratio (%)	**96.49**	**97.89**	**96.12**	**96.41**
1994	Total No. of Enterprises	969,094	157,005	571,987	240,102
	The No. of SMEs	932,852	153,473	548,150	231,229
	Ratio (%)	**96.26**	**97.75**	**95.83**	**96.30**
1995	Total No. of Enterprises	1,012,212	157,187	598,171	256,854
	The No. of SMEs	991,615	154,367	585,445	251,803
	Ratio (%)	**97.97**	**98.21**	**97.87**	**98.03**
1996	Total No. of Enterprises	1,024,360	153,845	611,251	259,264
	The No. of SMEs	1,003,325	150,806	598,266	254,253
	Ratio (%)	**97.95**	**98.02**	**97.87**	**98.07**
1997	Total No. of Enterprises	1,043,286	150,855	629,617	262,814
	The No. of SMEs	1,020,435	147,507	615,506	257,422
	Ratio (%)	**97.81**	**97.78**	**97.76**	**97.95**
1998	Total No. of Enterprises	1,069,116	148,990	646,842	273,284
	The No. of SMEs	1,045,117	145,281	632,444	267,392
	Ratio (%)	**97.76**	**97.51**	**97.77**	**97.84**
1999	Total No. of Enterprises	1,085,430	146,719	656,882	281,829
	The No. of SMEs	1,060,738	142,686	642,196	275,856
	Ratio (%)	**97.73**	**97.25**	**97.76**	**97.88**
2000	Total No. of Enterprises	1,091,245	144,912	658,501	287,832
	The No. of SMEs	1,070,310	141,340	646,312	282,658
	Ratio (%)	**98.08**	**97.54**	**98.15**	**98.20**
2001	Total No. of Enterprises	1,098,185	141,287	662,936	293,962
	The No. of SMEs	1,078,162	137,551	651,841	288,770
	Ratio (%)	**98.18**	**97.36**	**98.33**	**98.23**
2002	Total No. of Enterprises	1,130,525	138,288	687,372	304,865
	The No. of SMEs	1,104,706	133,684	674,364	296,658
	Ratio (%)	**97.72**	**96.67**	**98.11**	**97.31**

Note: As ROC redefined its industry category in 2003, the related data of 2003 & 2004 was not in accordance with that of the previous years. See 2004 Small & Medium Enterprise White Paper, P. 424.

Source: From the Combination of 2000 & 2003 Small & Medium Enterprise White Paper

Table 3-12 The Workforce, Employees of Different Organizations

Unit: thousand

Year	Organization	Number of Employees	%	Total Work-force	%
1991	Government	966	17.05	966	11.45
	Large Enterprises	831	14.67	836	9.91
	SMEs	**3,869**	**68.28**	**6,637**	**78.65**
1992	Government	1,002	17.11	1,002	11.61
	Large Enterprises	835	14.26	838	9.71
	SMEs	**4,019**	**68.63**	**6,792**	**78.68**
1994	Government	1,001	16.25	1,001	11.20
	Large Enterprises	854	13.86	860	9.62
	SMEs	**4,305**	**69.89**	**7,078**	**79.18**
1995	Government	1,003	16.02	1,003	11.09
	Large Enterprises	823	13.15	829	9.17
	SMEs	**4,434**	**70.83**	**7,213**	**79.75**
1997	Government	1,024	15.94	1,023	11.15
	Large Enterprises	950	14.79	956	10.42
	SMEs	**4,449**	**69.27**	**7,197**	**78.43**
1998	Government	975	14.87	975	10.50
	Large Enterprises	1,044	15.93	1,049	11.29
	SMEs	**4,536**	**69.20**	**7,265**	**78.21**
2000	Government	956	14.18	956	10.08
	Large Enterprises	1,121	16.63	1,125	11.86
	SMEs	**4,664**	**69.19**	**7,405**	**78.06**
2001	Government	961	14.29	961	10.24
	Large Enterprises	1,129	16.78	1,134	12.09
	SMEs	**4,636**	**68.92**	**7,288**	**77.67**
2003	Government	988	14.33	988	10.32
	Large Enterprises	1,155	16.75	1,159	12.11
	SMEs	**4,754**	**68.93**	**7,425**	**77.57**
2004	Government	994	13.94	995	10.17
	Large Enterprises	1,234	17.30	1,238	12.65
	SMEs	**4,903**	**68.76**	**7,553**	**77.18**

Source: Small & Medium Enterprise White Paper, 1999 to 2004
Small and Medium Enterprise Administration, Ministry of Economic Affairs

Three out of the five cardinal relations which the Confucian accentuates discuss about the family relationships (father and son, husband and wife, brothers), which provides evidence to prove that the family is the most fundamental unit in Chinese societies. For Westerners, the society is constructed by each individual; for Chinese, the society is constituted by each family. This concept brings in the materialization of Chinese family business (CFB)[273]. The CFB further strengthens the managerial structures of Taiwan industries and constitutes the base for the establishment of SMEs. Therefore, the SMEs permeate the whole sectors of Taiwan industries but a few which are forbidden by the government or require a gigantic amount of capital, like energy, wafer foundry, and so on.

However, although few conglomerates have been formed in Taiwan, because of the emphasis on the relationships, Taiwanese SMEs are informally organized into an effective and efficient production network. The network style production has the advantage of flexibility, but the flexibility will turn into the managerial black hole of Taiwanese government, because this production network will be extremely susceptible to the alteration of environment. When the downstream manufacturers have to relocate their production, they usually do not move by themselves but with all their upstream suppliers. Table 2-23 illustrates that in 2002 33.36% of Taiwanese manufacturers are motivated to invest outward by their foreign buyers and 27.19% by their Taiwanese buyers. As a result, almost one out of two Taiwanese manufacturers which deploy overseas is due to the pressure from its customers. Since each Taiwanese manufacturer accounts only a small portion of the network, the outflow will be expeditious, efficient and systematic.

Moreover, according to the research report of China Credit Information Service, Ltd. (CCIS), it points out most of Taiwanese enterprises are developed into a conglomerate based on the strict family organization. Almost all of Taiwanese conglomerates are full of "family tincture". Thus, CCIS straightforwardly labels those conglomerates as family conglomerate rather than discusses whether the certain family can exert its clout on the conglomerate.[274] Since most of the Taiwanese enterprises regardless of their scales are family-centered, this indicates where the family is, sooner or later where the center of the business will be located. As many Taiwanese entrepreneurs have sent their second generation to Chinese mainland[275] and some even bring their ancestor's spirit tablet with them to China, sooner or later the outflow of Taiwanese enterprises will put pressure on the development of Taiwan economy.[276] According to Wu's research, many Taiwanese businessmen (Tai Shang) in Shanghai have

[273] Whitley, 1990 and Chen, 1997

[274] Quote from Huang ,1996, P. 251

[275] "Under the Yang-ming Mountain, the 'China Fever' of Taiwanese Entrepreneurs' Second Generation," Feb 2, 2002, *Da Kung Pao* (in Chinese)
"Strive Hard to Win, Taiwanese Entrepreneurs' Second Generation March to Mainland," July, 1998, No. 53, *Fortune China Monthly*, (in Chinese)

[276] "The Disappearance of Tai Shang (II): Taiwan Self-Reserved, Tai Shang Going Westwards Have a Hard Time to Go Back," June 27, 2004, *Economic Daily*, (in Chinese)

become the new immigrants. They bring up their family in Shanghai, settle down, and identify the city as their hometown.[277] If the situation continues, eventually Taiwan will be transformed into a residual nostalgia for Taiwanese businessmen in China. As a result, it will be extremely difficult for them to discard their mainland operations to support its home state if some misfortune happens and they have to choose between Taiwan and China.

3.3.4 The Shortage of Resources for SMEs on R&D

Although SMEs are booming in terms of numbers in Taiwan, because of government's laissez-faire[278] attitude toward them, they face a serious challenge—fund-raising. The lack of capital has been the major drawback of SMEs. Without sufficient fund to devote on R&D and advertisement, they have encountered the difficulty of technology upgrading and brand name creating. This shortcoming further influences the structure of Taiwan industries, and made Taiwan industries "headless"[279], "rootless"[280] and susceptible to the influence of outside force.

Table 3-13 illustrates that most of the large corporations can tap financial institutions or even money market for funding, but the SMEs have to borrow money from private channel like relatives or friends. In 1986, for the large companies, 68.2% of their borrowings come from financial institutions, 15% from money market and 16.8% from personal channel. In contrast, the personal loans account for 41.9% of SMEs' total borrowings, loans from financial institutions 55.9% and loans from money and bond markets merely 2.2%. Although in 1989 and 1992, the percentage of SMEs' borrowings from financial institutions increases to 63.1% and 64.7% respectively, large firms comparatively are still the favor of financial institutions as the percentage of their loans from financial institutions is 79.3% in 1989 and 76.5% in 1992. Moreover, it is difficult for SMEs to finance from money and bonds market. In regard to the

---

277 Wu, 2004

278 Basically, during the early period of KMT's rule, the government devoted all its energy on large corporations, but Terry Gou thinks the attitude of the government towards SMEs is worse than careless. According to Terry Gou, the value of Taiwan SMEs stems from their fortitude and resilience. Because the government was too lousy, the SMEs had to be tough to survive. He further emphasized the inefficiency of Taiwanese government contributes to the adroitness of Taiwanese SMEs in face of adversities.
Chang, Chang and Lu (2003, P. 65)

279 Headless indicates the insufficiency of technological autonomy, especially the dearth of patents, self-made equipments and key components. "Headless Industry, the Crisis of the Two Trillion Industry (Wu Tou Gong Ye, Liang Zhao Chan Ye Wei Ji)" April 20, 2005, Commercial Times

280 Rootless indicates Taiwanese companies do not have their own world-wide brand name and marketing channel. Su, 2005

capability of raising fund, the large corporations are always far superior to the SMEs in Taiwan as Table 3-14 will reconfirm the disadvantage of being a SME in financing.

Table 3-13 Sources of Borrowing by Private Firms: Large Firms vs. SMEs*

Year	Type	Financial institutions (%)	Money and bond markets (%)	Households, other enterprises and government agencies** (%)
1986	Large	68.2	15	16.8
	SMEs	55.9	2.2	41.9
1989	Large	79.3	9.6	11.1
	SMEs	63.1	1.4	35.5
1992	Large	76.5	12.6	10.9
	SMEs	64.7	1.5	33.8
1987-91 (average)	Large	76.9	10.9	12.2
	SMEs	62.6	1.7	35.7

Note: * Firms with a paid in capital of less than NT $400 million are classified as SMEs
** Borrowing from government agencies is always less than 5 percent of the total borrowing from households and other enterprises in the data period for the whole sector of private enterprises.

Source: Dessus, Shea and Shi, 1995, Table 5.4

Table 3-14 reinforces the impression of SMEs' weakness in fund raising and points out that even the first rotation of Taiwan's ruling party in 2000 do not SMEs in tapping the bank loans. The structural disadvantage of SMEs places them into an inferior condition in competing for bank loans with their large counterparts. In 1995, bank loans to SMEs account for 35.53% of total Taiwanese bank loans; in 1996, the ratio of bank loans to SMEs declines to 33.79%; in 1997, it decreases further to 31.16%. The ratio of bank loans to SMEs went all the way down to 2004's 18.57%. From the comparison of the growth rate of total loans to the loans to SMEs, it is obvious that the growth rate of total loans is faster than the growth rate of loans to SMEs. In 1995, Taiwan's total bank loans grew at 10%, but the loans to SMEs grew only 5.07%. In 1996, the former grows at 5.57%, but the latter grows at 3.37%. In 1998, when the former grows at 6.48%, the latter even contracts at a rate of 0.02%. In 2002, when the total bank loans suffer a contraction of 2.95%, the loans to SMEs suffer an even more serious contraction at 14.97%. In 2003 and 2004, when the total bank loans pose positive growth at 2.96% and 6.26% respectively, the bank loans to SMEs suffer 0.28% and 1.45 contractions respectively. Table 3-14 reconfirms the message displayed in Table 3-13 that SMEs have never been the preference of Taiwanese banks.

Table 3-14 The Indicators of Taiwanese Bank Loans to SMEs

Unit: %

Year	The Ratio of Bank Loans to SMEs	The Growth Rate of Bank Loans to SMEs	The Growth Rate of Total Loans
1995	35.53	5.07	10.00
1996	33.79	3.38	5.57
1997	31.16	7.91	16.87
1998	29.24	-0.02	6.48
1999	26.32	-0.26	6.90
2000	25.94	0.99	1.59
2001	23.59	-3.80	5.79
2002	20.67	-14.97	-2.95
2003	20.02	-0.28	2.96
2004	18.57	-1.45	6.26

Source: 2005 Small and Medium Enterprises White Paper, Ministry of Economic Affairs

The booming SMEs and their difficulty in raising fund contribute to the formation of headless and rootless Taiwan industries. Without sufficient financial support, SMEs encounter the challenge of survival or evanescence in their daily operations. As a result, those activities which do not produce immediate profits will be deliberately circumvented. Moreover, during the take-off stage of Taiwan economy[281], the labor-intensive product-processing sector is very profitable. The profitability of processing and assembly has trapped Taiwanese businessmen into the habitual model of business operation. Even though the profit of processing and assembly decreases while the newly industrializing countries (NICs) like Thailand, Indonesia, and Malaysia joining the competition and the US demanding Taiwanese government to balance the trade imbalance between Taiwan and the US by opening domestic market and appreciating NT dollars, Taiwanese firms simply move their production base and resume their processing and assembly overseas. As the processing and assembly in the traditional industry is no longer profitable in Taiwan, Taiwanese government restructures Taiwan industry by shifting the development from the labor-intensive industry to technology-intensive or capital-intensive industry. As a result, instead of assembling low-value added products such as footwear, garment, and umbrella, Taiwan starts to assemble high-value added products such as motherboard, notebook and desktop PC.

Taiwan could have devoted more resources on upgrading the traditional industries. By increasing technical and designing sophistication and strengthening the ability of the brand-name-creation and global-logistics, Taiwan still

---

[281] 1960s is seen as the take-off stage of Taiwan economy. "Economic Take-off", Chinese Academy of Social Sciences, http://www.cass.net.cn/zhuanti/taiwan_1/yueqyy/histysts/045.htm

has a chance to maintain its title as "umbrella kingdom" and "footwear kingdom". However, Taiwan chooses another path to transformation—Taiwan devotes its resources on the newly emerging IT industry and repeats its past successful model in which Taiwan focuses on the assembly and production portion of the IT product value chain. Moreover, as many Taiwanese SMEs are operated by "black hand" masters, when the business is booming, their apprentices will leave to start their own business. Therefore the high turnover rate of employee and the limited scale of the firms hinder the accumulation of capital and technology.[282]

Some scholars argue that the size of firm is not the threshold of corporate research activities and small firms can be as progressive as large firms in pursuing technology innovation.[283] However, Cohen, Levin and Mowery allege business unit size determines the probability of conducting R&D.[284] Moreover, by empirically examining the commercialization of emerging biotechnology, Shan proves firm size determines a company's technological dependence. Instead of making any cooperative arrangement, larger firms tend to acquire technology internally. Although a firm's technological capabilities also determine a company's R&D activities, the size can decide how bountiful the resources a company have to allocate to R&D activities.[285] Gonzalez and Canto point out, since the activities of R&D require the congregate of massive resources, small firms face the difficulty in competing with large firms, and their empirical research also confirms that a company's resources and capabilities in R&D are highly relevant[286]. Cohen and Klepper also construct a model based on the concept of R&D cost spreading to prove the advantage of large size in R&D by concluding that the larger the firm is, the greater the costs of R&D over the output can be averaged.[287]

According to Wang's empirical research, among his 51 sampling high-tech SMEs in Taiwan, over half of them spend under 5% of their total expenditures on R&D. Table 3-15 indicates most of Taiwan's high-tech SMEs, up to 45.1 percent, spend only 3 to 5 percent of their total expenditure on R&D; 9.8 percent of them spend less than 3 percent. The high-tech SMEs which devoted over 15 percent of the total expenditure on R&D accounted for 31.4 percent of the total sampling firms.[288]

---

[282] Chang, Chang and Lu, 2003, P. 103
[283] Adams, 1970 and Sherer, 1991
[284] Cohen, Levin and Mowery, 1987
[285] Shan, 1990
[286] Canto and Gonzalez, 1999, P. 896
[287] Cohen and Klepper, 1996, P.926
[288] Wang, 2001

Table 3-15 R&D Expenditure Accounting for Total Expenditure of High-Tech SMEs

R&D Expenditure /Total Expenditure	Under 3%	3-5%	5-10%	10-15%	Over 15%	Total
Number of Firms	5	23	5	2	16	51
Ratio	9.8%	45.1%	9.8%	3.9%	31.4%	100%
Accumulated Ratio	9.8%	54.9%	64.7%	68.6%	100%	

Source: Wang, 2001

Aside from the insufficient R&D expenditure of Taiwanese high-tech SMEs, they are also short of man power in conducting R&D. Table 3-16 illustrates that according to Wang's research, among 51 sampling Taiwanese high-tech SMEs, for over half of them, their R&D staffs account for less than 10% of their total employees. For 33.3% of them, R&D staffs account for less than 5% of their total employees. Only 17.7% of the sampling high-tech SMEs recruit over 20% of their total employees as their R&D staff.[289] The shortage of fund becomes the primary weakness of SMEs, which impedes them from not only investing on R&D but also competing with their large counterparts for high quality and usually well paid R&D talents.

Table 3-16 R&D Staff of Total Employees

R&D Staff /Total Employees	Under 5%	5-10%	10-15%	15-20%	Over 20%	Total
Number of Firms	17	13	5	7	9	51
Ratio	33.3%	25.5%	9.8%	13.7%	17.7%	100%
Accumulated Ratio	33.3%	58.8%	68.6%	82.3%	100%	

Source: Wang, 2001, P. 69

Nevertheless, Taiwanese firms may not allocate their resources on R&D, but they are eager to pay technology transfer fee and royalties to buy the ready-to-use technology. Since the acquisition of technology is not confined on in-house R&D, companies can also obtain the technology-know-how from external resource. As the result of investing in R&D is uncertain, many Taiwanese high-tech firms would rather wait for the overseas new technology than devote on R&D.[290] As a result, while Taiwanese firms face a buy-or-make decision for R&D projects, they would buy first and make follow up research later. Since R&D requires long-term commitments, most Taiwanese SMEs do not have the ambition and energy to devote themselves on huge amount of R&D activities

---

289 Ibid.

290 Quote from Zeng, 2001, P. 217

which do not guarantee the success of the outcome. For them, to pay technological transfer fee and royalty for a ready-to-use technology is comparatively expedient and economical.

Table 3-17 Technology Balance of Payments

Unit: thousand N.T.

Year	Export(A)	Import(B)	Total(A+B)	Net(A-B)	Ratio(A/B)
1987	390,085	4,555,118	4,945,203	-4,165,033	0.09
1988	353,200	7,771,979	8,125,179	-7,418,779	0.05
1989	344,289	12,474,784	12,819,073	-12,130,495	0.03
1990	785,499	12,297,722	13,083,221	-11,512,223	0.06
1992	2,117,911	13,733,175	15,851,086	-11,615,264	0.15
1993	1,269,753	13,684,814	14,954,567	-12,415,061	0.09
1994	821,331	14,513,099	15,334,430	-13,691,768	0.06
1995	728,079	18,240,483	18,968,562	-17,512,404	0.04
1997	1,593,283	32,417,343	34,010,626	-30,824,060	0.05
1998	922,434	38,910,038	39,832,472	-37,987,604	0.02
1999	1,223,723	39,003,452	40,227,175	-37,779,729	0.03
2000	3,949,130	40,727,452	44,676,582	-36,778,322	0.10
2002	11,260,745	45,245,838	55,506,583	-33,985,093	0.25

Note: The data of 2003 is not released in Indicators of Science and Technology Republic of China 2004.

Source: Indicators of Science and Technology Republic of China 2000 to 2004.

Table 3-17 suggests that Taiwan enterprises maintain a business operation model of acquiring foreign technology to commercialize their product, because the amount of technology imports constantly far surpasses of technology exports. In 1987, Taiwan imports NTD 4.56 billion (around USD 14.30 million at the exchange rate of 31.78 NTD/USD) but exports only NTD 0.39 billion, and the technology deficit reaches NTD 4.17 billion. As the amount of technology imports grows larger, the differences between technology import and export enlarge from 1988's NTD 4.17 million to the peak of 1998's NTD 37.99 billion in 1998. In 1999, 2000 and 2002, the increase of technology exports enable the divergence between the technology imports and technology exports to shrink, but the differences still maintain at a high level of NTD 37.78 billion, NTD 36.78 billion and NTD 33.99 billion respectively. Although the technology deficit shrinks from the peak of 1998's NTD 37.99 billion to 2002's NTD 33.99 billion, the situation that Taiwan imports more technologies than exports remains unchanged. Table 3-17 implies the attitude of Taiwanese enterprises toward in house R&D; they would buy the ready-to-use technology and work on the follow-up research rather than devote their scarce resources on the result-unknown R&D.

Table 3-18 Coverage Ratio of Technology Balance of Payments*

Country \ Year	1997	1998	1999	2000	2001	2002
ROC	**0.05**	**0.02**	**0.03**	**0.10**	-	**0.25**
Australia	-	0.46	-	-	-	-
Austria	0.78	0.79	0.87	1.00	-	-
Belgium	1.30	1.23	1.27	1.33	-	-
Canada	1.20	1.58	1.43	1.99	-	-
Czech Republic	0.73	0.56	0.50	-	-	0.58
Denmark	-	-	1.57	-	-	-
Finland	0.19	0.26	2.04	1.48	1.23	1.19
France	0.71	0.83	0.87	1.04	1.19	-
Germany	0.83	0.83	0.75	0.75	0.67	0.74
Hungary	0.63	0.44	0.43	-	-	-
Italy	0.94	0.84	0.79	0.80	0.78	0.99
Japan	1.90	2.13	2.34	2.39	-	-
Mexico	0.26	0.31	0.08	0.11	0.10	0.07
New Zealand	0.59	-	2.14	-	-	-
Norway	0.66	0.68	0.74	0.82	-	1.16
Poland	0.48	0.35	0.19	0.17	-	-
Portugal	0.39	0.34	0.38	0.43	0.47	0.56
Spain	0.15	0.19	-	-	-	-
Switzerland	2.45	2.23	1.30	1.49	0.99	1.02
United Kingdom	1.72	1.81	2.00	2.07	2.22	-
United States	3.63	3.17	2.93	2.46	2.36	2.29

Note: * Coverage Ratio of Technology Balance of Payments = Receipts/ Payments
The data of 2003 is not released in Indicators of Science and Technology Republic of China 2004.

Source: Indicators of Science and Technology Republic of China 2003, 2004.

Table 3-18 provides further evidence to prove that Taiwan's technological development depends heavily on the procured technology. Taiwan's ratio of technology balance of payments (Receipts/Payments) is far lower than that of those major developed countries. Taiwan spends one dollar on technology procurement but only receives 5 cents back in 1997; at the same time, the US earns 3.63 dollars while paying one dollar to buy technology. Taiwan's ratio of technology balance of payments lags behind not only those developed countries' like the US, Japan, the UK, Switzerland, but also most of the former communist countries' like Czech Republic, Poland and Hungary. In 1998, 1999 and 2000, Taiwan's ratio of technology balance of payments remains as the lowest among all the listed nations. In 2002, although Taiwan's ratio of technology balance of payments improve from 2000's 10% to 25%, however,

Taiwan's ratio of technology balance of payments is lower than all the listed nations' but Mexico's.

Table 3-19 R&D Expenditures as a Percentage of GDP

Unit: %

Year / Country	1998	1999	2000	2001	2002	2003
ROC (Taiwan)	**1.97**[d]	**2.06**[d]	**2.06**[d]	**2.17**[d]	**2.31**	**2.45**
Australia	1.51	-	1.53	-	-	-
Austria	1.78	1.86[e]	1.86[e]	1.92[p]	1.93[p]	1.94[p]
Belgium	1.90	2.04	2.17	-	-	-
Canada	1.79	1.82	1.92	2.03	1.91[p]	1.87[b,p]
Czech Republic	1.24	1.24	1.33	1.30	1.30	-
Denmark	2.06[e]	2.19	-	2.40	2.52	-
Finland	2.88	3.23	3.40	3.41	3.46	-
France	2.17	2.18	2.18[a]	2.23	2.20[p]	-
Germany	2.3[e]	2.44	2.49[e]	2.51	2.52[e]	2.50[e]
Hungary[d]	0.68	0.69	0.80	0.95	1.02	-
Israel[d]	3.35	3.83	4.72	5.04[p]	4.72[p]	-
Japan	2.94	2.96	2.99	3.07	3.12	-
Korea[g]	2.65	2.47	2.65	2.92	2.91	-
Mexico	0.38	0.43	0.37	0.39	-	-
Netherlands	1.94	2.02	1.90	1.89	-	-
New Zealand	-	1.02	-	1.18[a]	-	-
Norway	-	1.65	-	1.60	1.67	-
Poland	0.72	0.70	0.66	0.64	0.59[b]	-
Portugal	0.69[e]	0.75	0.80[e]	0.85	0.93[e]	-
PRC	0.70[m,v]	0.83[m]	1.00[a]	1.07	1.23	-
Russia	0.92	1.00	1.05	1.16	1.24	-
Singapore	1.82	1.90	1.88	2.10	2.15	-
Spain[m]	0.89[e]	0.88	0.94	0.96	-	-
Sweden	-	3.65	-	4.27	-	-
Switzerland	-	-	2.57	-	-	-
United Kingdom	1.80	1.87	1.84	1.86	1.86	-
United States[j]	2.60	2.65	2.72	2.74	2.67[p]	2.62[b,p]

Note: [a]: Break in series with previous year for which data is available.
[b]: Secretariat estimate or projection based on national sources.
[d]: Defense excluded (all or mostly).
[e]: Estimate.
[g]: Excluding R&D in the social sciences and humanities.
[j]: Excludes most or all capital expenditure.
[m]: Underestimated or based on underestimated data.
[p]: Provisional.
[v]: The sum of the breakdown does not add to the total.

Source: Countries except ROC: Main Science and Technology Indicator, 2003/1, OECD.

Table 3-19 illustrates that Taiwan's R&D expenditures have accounted for 1.97 percent to 2.30 percent of GDP from 1998 to 2002, and Taiwan's ratio of R&D expenditures against GDP is on an upward trajectory. In 1998, it is 1.97%; in 1999, it rises to 2.05%; in 2000, it maintains at 2.05%; in 2001, it increases to 2.16%; in 2002, it increases again to 2.3%. In terms of the R&D expenditures as a percentage of GDP, Taiwan still lags behind the US, Japan, Finland, Sweden, Israel, Germany and South Korea, but surpasses the UK, Belgium, Canada and Australia.

Table 3-20 signifies that compared with the R&D expenditures of developed countries like the US, Japan, Germany, Belgium, Denmark, etc., Taiwan's R&D expenditures still rely heavily on the spending of government sector. For Austria, Belgium, Ireland, Israel, Sweden, Switzerland, the UK and the US, their government R&D spending accounts for less than 10 percent of their national R&D expense, and for Canada, Denmark, Finland, France, Germany, Italy, Korea, Netherlands, Norway, Portugal, Singapore and Spain, their government R&D spending accounts for 10% to 20% of their national R&D expense. Taiwanese government contributes more than 20% of domestic R&D expense. Moreover, the expenditure of Taiwan business enterprise accounts for around 63% of total R&D spending which is less than Germany's 70%, Belgium's 71.6%, Sweden's 77.6%, Switzerland's 73.9%, the UK's 67.4%, and the US' 72.9%. This suggests in the field of technological development, due to scale problem, Taiwanese private actors are not as devoted as their counterparts in the developed countries.

Although Taiwan depends on purchased technologies, Taiwan has performed well in getting patents granted by the US. From Table 3-21, the number of patents (excluding new design) which Taiwan obtains from the US lags only behind the US, Japan and Germany in all the listed years. In 2000, Taiwan obtains 4,667 patents; in 2001, Taiwan earns 5,371 patents; in 2002, Taiwan receives 5,431 patents; in 2003, Taiwan gets 5,298 patents from the US.

Table 3-20 R&D Expenditures by Sector of Performance, Selected Economies

Unit: %

Country & Year \ Sector of Performance		Business Enterprise	Government	Higher Education	Private Non-Profit
ROC	**2002**	**62.2[a]**	**24.8[a]**	**12.3**	**0.7**
(Taiwan)	**2003**	**62.5**	**24.9**	**12.0**	**0.6**
Australia	2000	47.1	23.1	27.1	2.8
Austria	1998	63.6	6.4	29.7	0.3
Belgium	2001	73.7	6.0	19.2	1.1
Canada	2003[p]	53.7	11.2	34.9	0.2
Czech Republic	2001	60.2	23.7	15.7	0.5
Denmark	2002	69.3	7.0[a]	23.1[a]	0.6
Finland	2002	69.9	10.4	19.2	0.6
France	2002[p]	62.2	16.9	19.5	1.4
Germany	2003[e]	69.9	13.8[o]	17.1	..
Greece	1999	28.5	21.7	49.5	0.3
Hungary	2001	40.1	25.9	25.7	..
Ireland	2001[e]	69.7	7.9	22.4	..
Israel	2002[a,p]	72.9	5.8	17.5[g]	3.8
Italy	2001	49.1	18.4	31.0	..
Japan	2002	74.4	9.5	13.9	2.1
Korea	2002	74.9[g]	13.4	10.4[g]	1.3[g]
Mexico	1999	25.5	45.0	26.3	3.1
Netherlands	2001	58.2	14.2	27.0	0.5
New Zealand	2001[a]	36.5	33.2	30.3	..
Norway	2002	57.4	15.8	26.8	..
Poland	2001	35.8	31.3	32.7	0.2
Portugal	2002	40.5	18.9	32.1	8.5
PRC	2002	61.2	28.7	10.1	..
Russian Federation	2002	69.9	24.5	5.4	0.2
Singapore	2002	61.4	13.2	25.4	..
Spain	2002	54.6[a]	15.4	29.8	0.2
Sweden	2001	77.6	2.8	19.4	0.1
Switzerland	2000	73.9	1.3	22.9	1.9
United Kingdom	2002	67.0	8.9	22.6	1.5
United States	2003[p]	68.9[j]	9.0[n]	16.8[j]	5.3[j]

Note: [a]: Break in series with previous year for which data is available.
[e]: Estimate.
[g]: Excluding R&D in the social sciences and humanities.
[j]: Excludes most or all capital expenditure.
[n]: Includes elsewhere.
[o]: Includes other classes.
[p]: Provisional.

Source : Indicators of Science and Technology Republic of China, 2003 and 2004

However, the patents acquired by Taiwan do not improve the technological autonomy, Taiwan IT industry still spend heavily on technology transfer fees and royalties, because Taiwan enterprises favor the operation model of buying ready-to-use technology and then making the follow-up researches. As a result, Taiwan's R&D expenditures and competitive quantity of patents do not transform into technology innovation, not to mention technological autonomy. The R&D embedded in the SME-structural industry becomes what Zeng describes. Taiwan does not own any central research laboratory. Taiwan SMEs primarily manufacture low-cost and mature technology products, so they almost do not have the capital to invest in the R&D of the high risk and high profit products. They are also short of the capability to predict the trend of technology products, to establish the specifications and to market the products globally.[291]

Table 3-21 Number of U.S. Patents (Excluding New Design) Granted and Rank by Nationality

Unit: Cases

	2000		2001		2002		2003	
Country	Number	Rank	Number	Rank	Number	Rank	Number	Rank
The US	85,072	1	87,607	1	86,977	1	87,901	1
Japan	31,296	2	33,223	2	34,859	2	35,517	2
Germany	10,234	3	11,260	3	11,277	3	11,444	3
ROC	**4,667**	**4**	**5,371**	**4**	**5,431**	**4**	**5,298**	**4**
Korea	3,314	8	3,538	8	3,786	7	3,944	5
France	3,819	5	4,041	5	4,035	5	3,869	6
UK	3,667	6	3,965	6	3,838	6	3,627	7
Canada	3,419	7	3,606	7	3,431	8	3,426	8
Italy	1,714	9	1,709	10	1,750	9	1,722	9
Sweden	1,577	10	1,743	9	1,675	10	1,521	10

Source: Indicators of Science and Technology Republic of China, 2004.

Table 3-22 provides information relating to the R&D expenditures of Taiwanese private enterprises. As a result, Taiwanese firms focused heavily on experimental development and applied research, but the basic research is almost disregarded in Taiwan. In 1998, Taiwanese firms allocate NTD 797 million on basic research which accounted for 0.78% of the total R&D expenditures of Taiwanese firms. In fact, Table 3-22 illustrates from 1998 to 2003, Taiwanese firms have never devoted more than 1% of their total R&D expenditures on basic research. In contrast to the insufficient funding in basic research, experimental development garners the largest share of the R&D expenditures of Taiwanese firms, and applied research has the second largest.

[291] Ibid, P. 85-84

The amount of R&D expenditures of Taiwanese firms on experimental development follows an upward trajectory from 1994's NTD 44.18 billion to 2003's NTD 117.51 billion, and the percentage of R&D expenditures on experimental development ranged from 73.28% to 82.75%. At the same period of time, the amount of the expenditures of R&D on applied research fluctuated between the lowest NTD 13.93 billion and 28.06 billion, and the expenditures of R&D on applied research accounted for 17.01% to 26.72% of total R&D expenditures.

Table 3-22 R&D Expenditures of Taiwanese Private Enterprises by R&D Type

Unit: NTD million

R&D type / Year	Total		**Basic Research**		Applied Research		Experimental Development	
	Amount	%	Amount	%	Amount	%	Amount	%
1994	59,450	100	-	-	15,269	25.68	44,181	74.32
1995	65,970	100	-	-	13,933	21.12	51,974	78.78
1996	73,459	100	-	-	19,576	26.65	53,883	73.35
1997	87,441	100	-	-	23,363	26.72	64,078	73.28
1998	102,087	100	**797**	**0.78**	24,916	24.41	76,374	74.81
1999	111,866	100	**678**	**0.61**	28,062	25.09	83,126	74.31
2000	116,047	100	**584**	**0.50**	25,211	21.72	90,251	77.77
2001	120,967	100	**301**	**0.25**	23,225	19.20	97,441	80.55
2002	130,843	100	**312**	**0.24**	23,037	17.61	107,493	82.15
2003	142,005	100	**334**	**0.24**	24,158	17.01	117,514	82.75

Source: Indicators of Science and Technology, Republic of China, 2004

Table 3-23 can further illustrate that Taiwan is a big technology buyer. Taiwan's expenditure on technology procurement overseas maintains at a relatively stable ratio to the capital which private organizations spend on R&D. When Taiwanese enterprises spend one dollar on R&D, at the same time, they also spend at least 24 cents or at most 36 cents on buying technology. In 1992, the ratio of technology imports against private funds on R&D is 0.30, which implies that when Taiwanese enterprises spend NT one dollar on R&D, they will pay NT 30 cents to buy foreign technology. In 1993, the ratio decreases to 0.26; in 1994, it decreases further to 0.24; however, in 1995, it bounces back to 0.26. In 1997, it rises to 0.35. In 1998, it increases slightly to 0.36. In 1999, 2000, 2002, it maintained at the level of 0.33. Taiwanese enterprises tend to buy technology first and then reallocate resources on the follow-up research to improve the efficiency of production. This operation model explains that although Taiwan's R&D expenditure as a percentage of GDP ranked in the middle of the nations listed on Table 3-19, Taiwan's ratio of technology balance of payments maintains at a relatively low level in comparison with most of the nations' listed on Table 3-18.

Table 3-23 Comparison between Private R&D Expenditure and the Amount of Technology Import

Unit: Million NT

Year	Amount of Technology Import(A)	Private Funds on R&D(B)	Ratio(A/B)
1992	13,733	45,319	0.30
1993	13,685	52,885	0.26
1994	14,513	60,296	0.24
1995	18,240	70,337	0.26
1997	32,417	93,491	0.35
1998	38,910	108,874	0.36
1999	39,003	118,394	0.33
2000	40,727	123,464	0.33
2002	45,246	138,964	0.33

Note: The data of 2003 is not released in Indicators of Science and Technology Republic of China 2004.

Source: Indicators of Science and Technology Republic of China 2003 and 2004.

In view of the fact that Taiwan has been a worldwide well-known IT manufacture base,[292] it is a reasonable conjecture that Taiwan buys technology to produce. This assumption coincides with Zeng's conclusion.[293] He divides R&D activities according to the content of research into three types: "prospective innovation", "catch-up" and "follow-up". He argues that Taiwan's IT industry, including the Industrial Technology Research Institute (ITRI), a non-profit R&D organization, is not able to engage in high-level R&D, but is only capable of adjusting parameters and improving technique. Therefore, Taiwan's IT industry focuses on "replication and duplication" instead of "research and development". Taiwanese enterprises import expensive machinery equipments and technology-know-how, stock factories with more machinery equipments to save space and take three shifts to increase efficiency. Since those enterprises have spent heavily on buying ready-to-use technology and price-competition is their major concern, they will not waste more money on innovative and creative in-house R&D. Thus he concludes that Taiwan technological industry is a kind of "technique production" industry which emphasizes on manufacture and production without the substance of technological innovation.[294]

---

[292] Taiwan produced USD 47.8 billion of information hardware in 2002 and raked 4th place only after the USA, PRC, and Japan.
http://www.taipeitradeshows.com.tw/computex/industrybg.htm

[293] Zeng, 2001

[294] Zeng, 2001, P. 49, 164

Since most of the Taiwanese enterprises are SMEs, most of them enjoy the advantage of flexibility but suffer from the insufficiency of fund. This structural disadvantage has caught Taiwanese businesses in the middle of global value chain. In the upstream of the international supply chain, they do not have the technological base to push forward their own industry specification and to control the resources of key components. In the downstream of supply chain, they do not have their own brand name and cannot control the distribution channel. As a result, they do not devote too much of their energy and resources on unforeseeable R&D and marketing research. The goal of Taiwanese government, to construct Taiwan as a science and technology island, will be difficult to attain when the private organizations do not have the ambition to engage on the development of creative and innovative technologies.

3.4 The Growing Influence of China over Business Sector

During the initiate stage of economic integration between China and Taiwan, Taiwan has managed to restructure its manufacturing sector by maintaining the capital-intensive and technology-sophisticated sector at home and moving the low-technology and labor-intensive production into China.[295] However, as China emerges as a major consumption market and a world's factory, by offering incentives and restraints, it can reshape the mainland operation plans of "foreign investors[296]". As an unrivalled arbiter in the domain of national laws and regulations, the government has a final say in determining its domestic economic format, and whichever organization is interested in joining the local market will be confined by national laws and regulations and susceptible to the influence of the national government. China is not content with what "foreign firms" has offered, but tries to develop its own technology and even sets up its own technological standards to rewrite the rule of global technological competition.[297] Therefore, accompanying with its buoyant economic strength, China grows out of the complete dependence on foreign investors in terms of capital and new technology, and regains its dominance over business sector.

China is currently the largest mobile phone market by users in the world. The number of China's mobile phone users has already surpassed the number of its fixed lines in 2004. Table 3-24 illustrates the speedy expansion in the use of the mobile phone and fixed lines. In 1999, the number of mobile phone user is 43.34 million and in 2000, it increases to 85.26 million and the yearly growth rate is 97.19%. In 2001, it increases again to 144.81 million and the yearly growth rate declines to 69.85%. In 2002, it rises to 206.62 million but the yearly growth rate decreases to 42.68%. In 2003, it increases to 268.69 mil-

---

295 See Naughton, 1997, P. 13. He complimented that Taiwan had accomplished an impressive job at "restructuring within the manufacturing sector itself .... Total manufacturing value-added has continued to grow even as manufacturing employment has dropped.

296 Foreign investors here indicate all those investors who do not have Chinese citizenship.

297 China intended to implement its Wireless Authentication and Privacy Infrastructure (WAPI) technology standard. As WAPI is not compatible with chips based on the existing global standard—Wi-Fi, the adoption of new standard will enable Chinese wireless technology firms to compete under the Chinese standard. Although Beijing argued that the implementation of WAPI standard is to ensure the wireless connection in China is secure, however US technological firms thought Beijing's motive was to boost its nascent chip industry. WAPI does not work well with chips based on the existing global standard known as Wi-Fi. American technological firms are afraid that if China set its own rule, Chinese companies will be able to build their expertise in grabbing the large share of growing Chinese market, and later after they reach economic scale, they are going to grow strong enough to compete with their American counterparts worldwide. See "Why China Is Making the Valley Fret; U.S. Chipmakers Worry That a New Wi-Fi Standard Puts Their Businesses at Risk," by Edwards, Cliff, *BusinessWeek*, 29 March 2004, No. 3876

lion yet the yearly growth rate dwindles to 30.04%. In 2004, it increases to 334.82 million but the yearly growth rate fell to 24.61.

On the other hand, although the expansion of the fixed lines grows at a comparatively moderate pace while comparing to the growth of the mobile phone users, the growth rate of fixed lines maintains at a two-digit annual rate. In 1999, there are 108.81 million fixed lines in China, and in 2000, the number of fixed lines increases to 144.41 million and the yearly growth rate is 32.72%. In 2001, it rises to 179.03 million but the growth rate decelerates to 23.98%. In 2002, it increases again to 214.42 million yet the yearly growth rate declines to 19.76%; in 2003, it increases to 263.31 million and the growth rate rises to 22.8%. In 2004, it increases to 312.44 million yet the growth rate decreases to 18.66%.

Table 3-24 The Statistics of China's Mobile Phone User and Fixed Lines (Cumulative)

Unit: 1,000

Item / Period End	Mobile Phone Users		Fixed Lines	
	Number	Growth Rate	Number	Growth Rate
12/31/2004	334,824	24.61%	312,443	18.66%
12/31/2003	268,693	30.04%	263,305	22.80%
12/31/2002	206,616	42.68%	214,419	19.76%
12/31/2001	144,812	69.85%	179,034	23.98%
12/31/2000	85,260	97.19%	144,407	32.72%
12/31/1999	43,238	-	108,807	-
Average	-	52.87%	-	23.58%

Source: Ministry of Information Industry, PRC, calculated by the author.

Even though China has become the world's largest mobile phone market, however as the world's most populous country, its mobile phone penetration still has much room for improvement. Figure 3-6 illustrates that in 2002, China's mobile phone density is 16.19% which is far lower than that of all the developed countries. Taiwan's mobile phone density is as high as 106.45% singling out the phenomenon of multiple phone usage. Iceland's mobile phone density is 90.28%, Sweden's 88.5%, Finland's 84.5%, the UK's 84.49%, Norway's 84.33%, Austria's 82.85%, South Korea's 67.95%, Japan's 62.11%, and the US' 48.81%. With China's low mobile phone density and its two-digit annual growth rate of mobile phone users, Chinese users will eventually dictate what global telecom industry standards should be.[298] As a result, whether Taiwanese mobile phone makers are interested in developing their own brand name or striving for the OEM orders from well-known brand-names, China market has become the indispensable factor for their expansion.

Figure 3-6 Mobile Phone Subscribers per 100 Inhabitants by Selected Nations (Data of 2002)

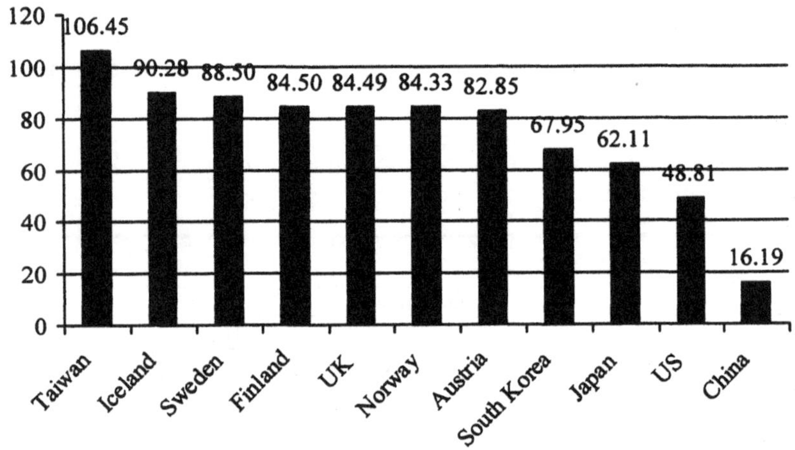

Source: International Telecommunication Union & Ministry of Information Industry of PRC

Aside from the telecommunication products, China also becomes a major IT consumption market. According to Gartner Dataquest's report (Table 3-25), China market accounts for over 40 percent of the PC consumption in Asia Pacific region excluding Japan in 2001, and it also predicts that China's PC market will have an annual growth rate of 8.7 percent in 2002, and it will consume 9,291,950 units of PC which are more than the sum of the PC consumption in South Korea, Australia, Taiwan, India and Malaysia. China now acts as not only the world factory but also one of the largest consumer markets. China

[298] Edward S. Tian is President and Chief Executive Officer of China Netcom Corporation. Quoted from "Envisioning China in 2006", Apr.19, 2001, *Envisioning China in 2006*, World Economic Forum

is not only the largest PC market in Asia Pacific excluding Japan, but also the world second largest PC market, second only to the US. [299]

Table 3-25 Asia/Pacific PC Unit Shipment Estimates by Country, 2002

Country	2002 Shipments	2002 Market Share (%)	2001 Shipments	2001 Market Share (%)	Growth (%)
China	**9,291,950**	**42.9**	**8,551,509**	**42.9**	**8.7**
South Korea	2,983,149	13.8	2,964,324	14.9	0.6
Australia	2,106,588	9.7	1,924,259	9.6	9.5
India	2,055,010	9.5	1,838,063	9.2	11.8
Taiwan	1,250,852	5.8	1,112,943	5.6	12.4
Malaysia	775,200	3.6	669,509	3.4	15.8
Thailand	717,627	3.3	513,505	2.6	39.8
Hong Kong	567,274	2.6	591,105	3.0	-4.0
Indonesia	495,200	2.3	445,091	2.2	11.3
Singapore	482,085	2.2	483,668	2.4	-0.3
New Zealand	349,405	1.6	305,102	1.5	14.5
Philippines	264,686	1.2	248,467	1.2	6.5
Vietnam	177,266	0.8	147,991	0.7	19.8
Others	148,462	0.7	145,992	0.7	1.7
Total	**21,664,754**	**100.0**	**19,941,528**	**100.0**	**8.6**

Note: Japan is excluded.
Source: Gartner Dataquest (February 2003)

Table 3-26 indicates that the Chinese PC makers, Lenovo and Founder ranks as the largest PC vendor and the fifth respectively in Asia Pacific region excluding Japan market. With China market as its home market, Lenovo sell 3.08 million PCs in 2002 and 3.59 million PCs in 2003, and its market share is 12.4% and 12.7% respectively. Founder also enjoys China market as its market base; it sells 1.03 million PCs in 2002 and 1.42 million PCs in 2003 and its market share is 4.1% and 5% respectively. At the same time, the top three PC vendors of the world, Dell, HP and IBM rank fourth, second and third respectively in Asia Pacific excluding Japan. It is astonishing that Lenovo has been a China-bound[300] company, and a dominant position in China market has enabled Lenovo to top its world's first-tier competitors in Asia Pacific. Founder serves

[299] "Gartner Dataquest Says Asia/Pacific PC Shipments Experience a 9 Percent Increase in 2002," Feb. 5, 2003, *Gartner Dataquest 2003 Press Release.*

[300] Although Legend has thought of expanding globally by aiming to expand its out-of-China sales from the current 7 percent to 25 percent to 30 percent by 2006, so far China market contributes to most of its PC sales. According to research from IDC, Legend accounted for 27.7 percent of Chinese PC market as of 2002. See "Can China's Legend go global?" April 5, 2003, *CNET News.com*

as the second largest PC vendor in China. Therefore, China market is large enough to cultivate 2 top five PC vendors in Asia Pacific region at the same time.

Playing a role as the world's factory, China not only has the capability to consume gigantic quantity of IT finished goods but also serves as an expanding integrated circuit (IC) market. In terms of IC consumption, the former champions, Americas[301], Europe and Japan, gradually lose the ground to the emerging ROW region[302], and in the ROW region, China is the rapidest growing IC market. According to the estimation of IC Insights, China will be the world's largest IC market in 2005.

Table 3-26 Asia/Pacific (Exclude Japan) PC Vendor Unit Shipment

Unit: 1000

Company	2002 Shipments	2002 Market Share (%)	2001 Shipments	2001 Market Share (%)	Year-on-Year Growth (%)
Lenovo	**3,593.3**	**12.7**	**3,085.9**	**12.4**	**16.4**
Hewlett-Packard	2,761.9	9.7	1,944.6	7.8	42.0
IBM	1976.8	7.0	1,574.6	6.3	25.5
Dell	1,801.5	6.3	1,254.9	5.0	43.6
Founder	**1,422.8**	**5.0**	**1,026.6**	**4.1**	**38.6**
Others	16,824.9	59.8	16,090.8	64.4	4.6
Total	**28,381.3**	**100.0**	**24,977.4**	**100.0**	**13.5**

Note: Hewlett-Packard and Compaq are reported as one company.
Source: IDC

Figure 3-7 illustrates that in 1999 the IC market of Americas accounts for 33% of world's IC market, Japan's 20%, Europe's 22% and ROW's 25%. In 2003, with 39% of the market share, ROW replaces Americas, whose market share declines to 21%, to become the world's leading IC market. In 2004, the market share of ROW expands further to 42%; Americas' IC market share drops 1% to 20%, and both Europe's and Japan's decline to 19%. In 2005, according to the forecast, the market share of ROW will continue its expansion to 44% and will reach 54% in 2009. At the same time period, Americas' market share will contract to 19% and then further to 15%; Europe's will decrease to 18% and then 14%; Japan's will maintain at 19% in 2005 but decline to 17% in 2009.

---

[301] Americas segment includes the U.S., Canada, Mexico, Central America, and South America.

[302] ROW IC market includes Asia-Pacific countries such as China, Taiwan, Singapore, Korea, etc.

Among this fast growing IC market, ROW, China/Hong Kong area is the fastest growing region. In 1999, the amount of the IC market of that region is USD 6.6 billion and accounts for 20.4 % of the total IC market of ROW region following Taiwan's USD 7.5 billion and South Korea's USD 6.8 billion. However, in 2000, the IC demand of China/Hong Kong increases to USD 9.8 billion surpassing that of South Korea and second only to that of Taiwan. In 2001, the IC market of China/Hong Kong region expands to USD 9.9 billion and ranks as the largest IC market in ROW. From then on, the IC market of China/Hong Kong grows to 2002's USD 14.3 billion, 2003's USD 20 billion and 2004's USD 31 billion. The market share of China/Hong Kong IC also increases from 2001's 29% to 2002's 32.4%, 2003's 37.1% and 2004's 41.2%. Even though the amount of Taiwan's IC demand increases from 2002's USD 8.7 billion to 2004's USD 13.6 billion, Taiwan's market share drops from 19.7% to 18.1%. South Korea and Singapore also suffer from the loss of market share. The market share of South Korea shrinks from 2002's 17.9% to 2004's 17.1%, and that of Singapore also shrinks from 12.9% to 10.4%. Moreover, the IC market of China/Hong Kong region is estimated to expand further to USD 34.3 billion in 2005, USD 41.4 billion in 2006, USD 52.6 billion in 2007, USD 74.1 billion in 2008, and USD 82.9 billion in 2009. The estimated market share of China/Hong Kong region will account for over half of total ROW IC market in 2008.

China's population has reached 1.3 billion people. Although not all of them are IT consumers at current stage, the statistics illustrates that the number of Chinese IT consumers is fast growing. Since China has successfully transformed itself from a market with potential to a market with profitability, its magnetism to attract private firms is increasing. Although the trend of globalization has diminished the function of the traditional national border in transnational economic activities and granted private actors such as firms and non-government organizations (NGOs) more power in shaping up international economy, the existence of national border offers sovereign states power to balance the influence of private actors. Since China can determine which company is allowed to operate in China, whichever company is interested in operating in China will have to abide by China's regulations or even the will of Chinese authorities, and this will grant Chinese government supremacy to reward those companies which fit in their political demands and to discriminate those who are politically incorrect.

Figure 3-7 World Wide IC Market by Region (1999-2009)

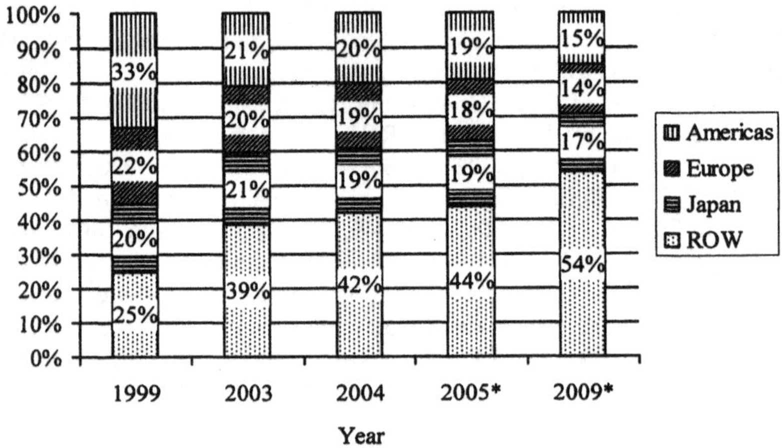

Note: * Forecast
Source: IC Insights

Table 3-27 ROW IC Market by Country

Unit: USD Billion

Year	China/H.K.		Taiwan		S. Korea		Singapore		Other	
	Amount	%	Amount	%	Amount	%	Amount	%	Amount	%
1999	6.6	20.4	7.5	23.2	6.8	21.1	4.9	15.2	6.5	20.1
2000	9.8	22.1	10.6	23.9	9.0	20.3	6.4	14.4	8.5	19.2
2001	9.9	29.0	7.1	20.8	6.1	17.9	4.8	14.1	6.2	18.2
2002	14.3	32.4	8.7	19.7	7.9	17.9	5.7	12.9	7.5	17.0
2003	20.0	37.1	10.0	18.6	9.2	17.1	6.3	11.7	8.4	15.6
2004	31.0	41.2	13.6	18.1	12.4	16.5	7.8	10.4	10.5	13.9
2005*	34.3	44.3	13.5	17.4	11.9	15.4	7.5	9.7	10.3	13.3
2006*	41.4	47.2	14.7	16.7	12.7	14.5	8.0	9.1	11.0	12.5
2007*	52.6	49.5	17.2	16.2	14.6	13.7	9.1	8.6	12.7	12.0
2008*	74.1	53.2	21.2	15.2	17.7	12.7	10.9	7.8	15.4	11.1
2009*	82.9	55.8	21.7	14.6	17.8	12.0	10.8	7.3	15.3	10.3

Note: * Forecast
Source: IC Insights

Moreover, the huge domestic market also grants Chinese government another privilege: China can establish its domestic technological standards to restructure the market order. According to OECD report, up to 80 percent of trade (equivalent to around USD 4 trillion annually) is affected by standards or associated technical regulations.[303] Figure 3-8 clearly depicts that, after early 1990s, the standard-setting enters a new era in which the number of international and regional standards grows rapidly but on the contrary that of the national technical standards declines. As the national specifications wane and the regional and international standards wax, the standard-setting plays an even more important role in international trade. While different technical standards competing, those who have the right to determine technical standards will influence the outcome of competition—which standard can stay in the market and which one will be obsolete. As a result, the standard-setting will result in a reward of all-or-nothing for private actors' R&D efforts.

Most of the firms have recognized the importance of standard-setting and realized the danger of losing control over the standard-setting to their competitors. As the late-comers in the IT industry, Chinese firms have to follow the rules which have been established by foreign firms or institutions. However, with China's prosperous domestic market, China stands a relatively good chance to reverse the trend of growing transnational standards by constructing its own national standards to support its domestic enterprises. As a result, the Chinese firms can dominate their domestic market, and instead of paying the patent fees to those technological frontiers, they can swap the right of patents to their foreign counterparts which are interested in the huge China market.

According to Mattli and Buethe's survey, 68% of US firms disagree or strongly disagree with the assumption that "standards have little or no effect on our opportunities to export our products", and 64% of their European counterparts disagree with that. Moreover, 88% of US firms and 95% of European firms agree or strongly agree with "standards will increasingly be developed at the international level." Therefore, the non-trade barriers, especially the standard-setting emerges as a new battlefield for MNEs.[304] As China market alone has reached economic scale, any single company which grabs the largest share of China market can be a leading company in Asia Pacific and China has been the world's third largest IT hardware producer following the US and Japan.

China has an insatiable appetite for not only IT products but also basic food, energy and industrial commodities. China's 2004 intake of 382 million tons of grain was 104 million tons more than the US'. With meat, China consumed 63 million tons in 2004 and the US 37 million tons. China also surpassed the US in the consumption of coal and steel. In 2003, comparing with the 574 million tons of coal of the US, China burned 800 million tons of coal. At the same year, China used up 258 million tons of steel which was more than

---

[303] Regulatory Reform and International Standardization, Organization for Economic Cooperation and Development (OECD), Paris, OECD Working Party of the Trade Committee, 1999, P. 4.

[304] Mattli and Buethe, 2003, P. 32

twice of the 104 million tons of the US. In use of oil, the US still played a leading role in the world and China ranked the second. In 2004, the US used 20 million barrels per day and China 7 million barrels. However, as the world's largest populous nation and fastest expanding economy, China has the potential to replace the US as the world's leading oil consumer.[305]

Figure 3-8 New International (ISO and IEC), European, and National (German, I.E., DIN) Standards per Year (1986-99)

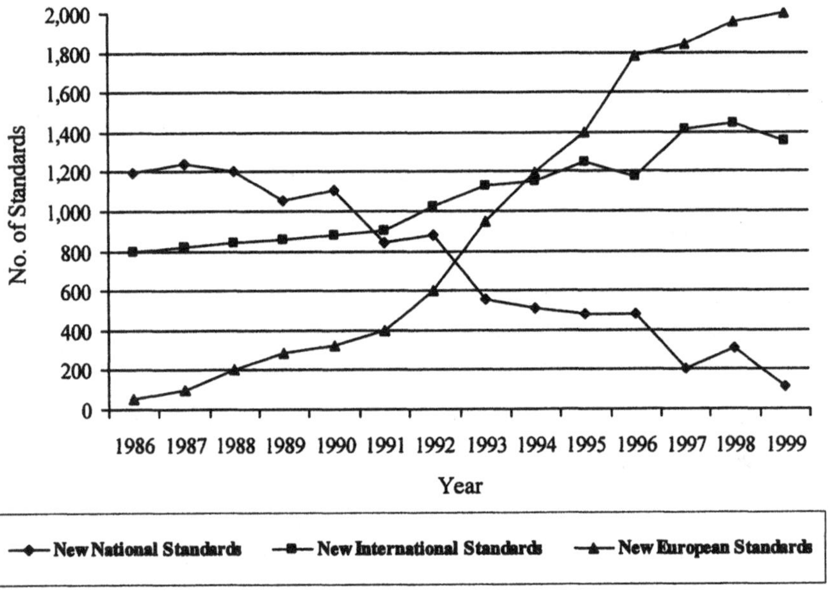

Note: DIN: the German Institute for Standardization
ISO: International Organization for Standardization
IEC: International Electro-technical Commission
Source: Mattli and Buethe, 2003, P. 3

[305] "China Replacing the United States as World's Leading Consumer," By Lester R. Brown, Feb 16, 2005, Earth Policy Institute

3.4.1 The Chinese Deployment of MNCs in IT Industry

China market attracts not only Taiwanese IT companies but also the world's first-tier IT firms. In order to access China market, many IT firms have set up operation centers or R&D centers in China. Table 3-28 illustrates that Applied Material and Tokyo Electron Ltd., the world's largest and second largest supplier of products and services in semiconductor industry establish their mainland operation centers in Shanghai. Intel, the world's largest chip maker constructed its Shanghai base as its largest operation center in North Asia, and its competitor, AMD, builds its Greater China operation center in Beijing. Not to mention KLA-Tencor, Analogue Devices, Phillips Semiconductor, Agilent Technologies, Advanced Micro Devices, ON Semiconductor, and MIPS Technologies, almost all leading semiconductor firms more or less devote themselves on China market by constructing operation or R&D centers. Siemens has an Asia operation center in Shanghai; Alcatel also had an Asia-Pacific operation center in Shanghai. Sony Ericsson establishes an R&D center in Beijing; Nokia also establishes one in Beijing. However, Motorola is the most aggressive handy-maker in China market that owned one Greater China R&D center in Beijing, an advanced technology center in Tianjin and an IC design center in Suzhou. Aside from those semiconductor firms and handy makers, the software giant, Microsoft is also eager to tap China's human resources and huge market. Microsoft owns an Asia research center and an R&D company in Beijing and Shanghai respectively. Dell even sets up its first overseas R&D center in Shanghai, and its major competitor, HP also establishes a software-resolving center there. Aside from those major US, Japanese and European IT firms, two leading South Korean companies, Samsung and LG Electronics also set up research centers in China. Almost all major IT firms have been attracted to China.

China's economic potential draws not only foreign firms from the US, Japan and Europe but also Taiwanese firms. Taiwanese firms devote themselves in cultivating China into one of the world's major IT base. Most of Taiwanese IT firms while considering outward investments choose China as their destination. As a result, Taiwanese IT firms relocate most of their production line westwards.

Table 3-28 The Investments of Foreign Investors (IT Industry) in China

Industry	Enterprise	City	Function
Semiconductor	Applied Materials	Shanghai	Mainland Operation Center
	Tokyo Electron Ltd.	Shanghai	Mainland Operation Center
	Intel	Shanghai	North Asia Operation Center
	AMD	Beijing	Greater China Operation Center
	KLA-Tencor	Shanghai	Mainland Operation Center
	Advanced Micro Devices	Shanghai	South Asia-Pacific Operation Center
	National Semiconductor	Shanghai	Asia-Pacific Operation Center
	Analog Devices Inc. (ADI)	Shanghai	Asia Operation Center
	Phillips Semiconductor	Shanghai	Greater China Operation Center
	Agilent Technologies Inc.	Beijing	Mainland Operation Center
	ON Semiconductor	Shanghai	IC Design Center
	MIPS Technologies	Shanghai	Mainland Operation Center
Tele-communication	Siemens	Shanghai	Asia Operation Center
	Alcatel	Shanghai	Asia-Pacific Operation Center
	Sony Ericsson	Beijing	R&D Center
	Nokia	Hangzhou	R&D Center
	Motorola	Beijing	Greater China R&D Center
		Tianjin	Advanced Technology Center
		Suzhou	IC Design Center
Software	Microsoft	Beijing	Asia Research Center
		Shanghai	Software R&D Company
IT Hardware & Electronic Appliance	Hewlett-Packard (HP)	Shanghai	Software-resolving Center
	Dell	Shanghai	The First Overseas R&D Center
	Toshiba	Hangzhou	NB R&D
	Ricoh	Shanghai	Copy Machine Software R&D Center
	Pioneer	Shanghai	DVD Product Design & Technology
	Philips	Shanghai	Telecommunication Technology R&D
	SANYO	Shanghai	Technology Center
	Samsung	Su Zhou	House Electric Appliance R&D Center
	LG Electronics	Beijing	Research Center

Source: DigiTimes Research, News and the Websites of the Companies

Table 3-29 indicates that most of the outflow of Taiwanese IT hardware production base is destined to China, and less and less Taiwanese IT hardware is manufactured domestically. In 1992, 89.6% of Taiwanese IT hardware production is domestic, 10.4% from other regions and none from China. In 1993, the value of Taiwanese IT hardware produced in Taiwan increases from 1992's USD 8.4 billion to USD 9.7 billion, but the percentage of Taiwanese IT hardware manufactured in Taiwan decreases to 85.1% and the IT hardware production in other regions accounts for 14.9% of total Taiwanese IT production. Although the value of Taiwanese IT hardware produced domestically goes all the way up from 1992 to 2000 but the percentage of Taiwanese IT hardware manufactured in Taiwan goes all the way down to 2003. When Taiwanese IT manufacturers starts to relocate their production lines to China in 1995, both the volume and percentage of Taiwanese IT hardware production in China follow an upward trajectory: the volume goes up from 1995's USD 2.8 billion to 2004's USD 49.6 billion and is expected to reach USD 61.22 billion in 2005; except 2000, the percentage goes almost all the way up from 1995's 14% to 2004's 71.2% and is expected to reach 79.5%. Since the IT hardware manufacturers discover the business opportunity in China, China has allured most of their attention. In 1994, the percentage of Taiwanese IT hardware manufactured in other regions reached its peak to 20.6%. Since China joined the competition for the relocation of Taiwanese IT hardware firms, the other regions have lost their attraction to Taiwanese IT hardware manufacturers. As a result, from 1995 to 2004, the percentage of IT hardware produced by Taiwanese firms in the other regions ranges between 13.2% and 19.6%.

Table 3-29 The Production Locations of Taiwanese IT Hardware Industry

USD: Billion

Location / Year	Total	Domestic		China		Other	
	Value	Value	%	Value	%	Value	%
1992	9.4	8.4	89.6	-	-	1.0	10.4
1993	11.4	9.7	85.1	-	-	1.7	14.9
1994	14.6	11.6	79.4	-	-	3.0	20.6
1995	19.7	14.2	72.0	2.8	14.0	2.8	14.0
1996	24.2	16.4	67.9	4.1	16.8	3.7	15.3
1997	30.2	18.9	62.6	6.9	22.8	4.4	14.6
1998	33.8	19.3	57.0	9.8	29.0	4.7	14.0
1999	39.9	21.0	52.7	13.2	33.2	5.6	14.1
2000	47.0	23.1	49.1	14.7	31.3	9.2	19.6
2001	42.8	20.2	47.2	15.8	36.9	6.9	16.1
2002	48.4	17.3	35.7	23.0	47.5	8.1	16.8
2003	57.2	10.8	18.8	37.2	65.0	9.3	16.2
2004	69.7	10.9	15.6	49.6	71.2	9.2	13.2
2005*	77.0	5.2	6.8	61.2	79.5	10.6	13.7

Note: * Data of 2005 was estimated by MIC
Source: Institute for Information Industry (III) MIC

The outflow of Taiwanese IT hardware production covers almost all Taiwan's major products. From Desktop PC (DT), Motherboard (MB), notebook (NB), Monitor and so on, as long as Taiwanese government does not impose prohibitions on the investment to China, the production lines will be moved to China in no time. Table 3-30 points out that the number of LCD Monitor is on the rise and the traditional CDT Monitors is gradually replaced by CDT Monitor and that within 5 year Taiwanese firms have already constructed China as a major LCD Monitor manufacturing base. For CDT monitor, Taiwanese firms have almost exported all its production lines overseas. In 1999, the domestic production accounts for 19% of total CDT monitor production of Taiwanese firms, yet in 2000, the percentage of domestic production drops to 8%. The percentage of CDT production in China rises from 1999's 43% to 2000's 58%. In 2001, the percentage of domestic production decreases further to 2% and yet that of production in China increased to 66%. In 2002, the percentage of domestic production remains at 2%, but that of production in China expands further to 74%. In 2003, the percentage of domestic production drops to 1% and in 2004 Taiwanese manufacturers no longer produce CDT monitors in Taiwan, but the percentage of mainland production increases 90% in 2003 and rises again to 96% in 2004. In 1999, 100% of 1.92 million LCD monitors manufactured by Taiwanese firms are made in Taiwan. In 2000, 97% of 2.92 million LCD monitors are domestically made, and only 1% of them are produced in China. In 2001, the percentage of domestic production drops to 67% and that of production in China increases to 29%. In 2002, 69% of 19.44 million LCD monitors made by Taiwanese firms are manufactured in China, and the domestic production account for only 23%. In 2003, the percentage of mainland production rises to 80% but that of domestic production drops to 14%; in 2004, the percentage of mainland production rises again to 86% but that of domestic production drops again to 10%. Within five years, Taiwanese LCD monitor manufacturers shifted 85% of their production to China.

Table 3-31 illustrates that the overseas production of Taiwanese desktop PC makers gradually tilt towards China and after Taiwanese government lifts the ban on NB production in China, Taiwanese NB makers swiftly shift their production lines to China. For desktop PC makers, in 1997, the domestic production accounts for 7% of their total production; in 1998, the percentage of domestic production increases to 10%; in 1999, the percentage rises to 15%; in 2000, it increases to 16%; however, it decreases to 14% in 2001; in 2002, it drops to the level lower than 1998's 10% to 9%. On the contrary, the percentage of desktop PC production in China follows an upward trajectory aside from a setback in 1998 and 2003 and it increases almost all the way from 1997's 34% to 2004's 55.9%. For NB, after Taiwanese government lift the ban on the investment of NB in China in 2001, Taiwanese manufacturers swarm into

China. In 2001, 5.7% of 14.16 million NBs made by Taiwanese firms are produced in China and the percentage of domestic production declines from 2000's 93.3% to 88.5%. As Taiwanese government does not officially terminate its NB prohibition until Nov. 30, 2001[306], it is an astonishing achievement that Taiwanese manufacturers can produce 807,160 NBs in China within one month. In 2002, the percentage of NBs made in China increased seven-fold to 38.2%, and that of domestic production dropped to 56.7%. In 2003, the percentage of NBs made in China increases to 72% and that of domestic production drops to 26%; the percentage of NBs made in China increases to 82% in 2004 but that of domestic production decreases to 16%. Within less than 4 years, Taiwanese NB manufacturers have already produced 82% of NBs in China.

Table 3-30 The Production Locations of Taiwanese Monitor Manufacturers

Unit: Million

	1999	2000	2001	2002	2003	2004
Total Number of Monitors	55.88	62.25	55.18	63.28	71.38	83.3
The Number of CDT Monitor	53.96	59.33	46.17	43.84	38.14	33.94
Domestic (%)	19	8	2	2	1	0
China (%)	**43**	**58**	**66**	**74**	**90**	**96**
Other (%)	38	34	32	24	9	4
The Number of LCD Monitor	1.92	2.92	9.01	19.44	33.24	49.36
Domestic (%)	100	97	67	23	14	10
China (%)	-	**1**	**29**	**69**	**80**	**85**
Other (%)	-	2	4	8	6	5

Source: Institute for Information Industry (III) MIC

PC and monitor are surely not the only two items relocated most of their production to China. In 2002, 62% of motherboards manufactured by Taiwanese firms are produced in China and 69% of DSCs also. As for the production of CD-ROM, DVD-ROM, CD-RW, Combo and DVD-ReW, the production in China accounted for as high as 94% of total production of Taiwanese manufacturers in 2002.[307] As a result, Taiwanese IT hardware manufacturers contribute

[306] "Taiwan Announces a List of Newly-Increased Mainland Investments (Tai Wan Gong Bu Xin Zen Da Lu Tou Ze Qing Dan)" Nov. 30, 2001, *BBC News*

[307] The statistics also came from III, MIC.

70% of China's IT hardware production in 2003,[308] and at the same time, China becomes the profit-generator of many Taiwanese manufacturers.

Table 3-31 The Production Locations of Taiwanese PC Manufacturers

Unit: Million

	1997	1998	1999	2000	2001	2002	2003	2004
The Number of PC	13.61	20.42	28.83	40.37	39.57	43.34	54.91	68.06
The Number of DT	9.14	14.33	19.12	27.66	25.41	24.96	29.67	34.65
Domestic (%)	7	10	15	16	14	9	2.4	1
China (%)	**34**	**25**	**30**	**45**	**48**	**55**	**49.7**	**55.9**
Other (%)	59	65	55	39	38	36	47.9	43.1
The Number of NB	4.47	6.09	9.71	12.71	14.16	18.38	25.24	33.41
Domestic (%)	100	100	96.7	93.3	88.5	56.7	26	16
China (%)	**0**	**0**	**0**	**0**	**5.7**	**38.2**	**72**	**82**
Other (%)	0	0	3.3	6.7	5.8	5.1	3	2

Institute for Information Industry (III) MIC

Table 3-32 pointes out that although the profitability of the China-bound investments of Taiwanese firms fluctuates from year to year, the percentage of gaining a profit from Chinese investments is constantly higher than the percentage of suffering a loss. As a result, it will be difficult for Taiwanese firms to give up China in concerns of political uncertainty. In 1998, the companies gaining large profit from their China investment account for 3.2% of total Taiwanese firms investing in China; the percentage of gaining small profit is 43.1%; the companies suffering minor loss account for 24.9%; the percentage of suffering serious loss is 2.1%. In 1999, the percentage of gaining large profit increases to 3.5%; the percentage of gaining small profit also increases to 50.7%; the percentage of suffering minor loss decreases to 17.4% but the percentage of suffering serious loss maintains at 2.1%. In 2000, the percentage of gaining large profit rises again to 5% and the percentage of gaining small profit simultaneously rises to 52.2%; the percentage of suffering minor loss decreases to 12.9% but the percentage of suffering serious loss increases to 4.3%. In 2001, the companies profiting from China-bound investments account for 56% and 20.4% of Taiwanese firms suffer a loss. In 2002, the percentage of gaining profit declines 0.9% to 55.1% and that of suffering loss simultaneously decreases 2% to 18.4%. In 2003, companies benefiting from China investment decreases to 44.5% and the percentage of posing losses increases to 26.7%. In 2004, the percentage of gaining profit increases to 52.9% and the percentage of

[308] "The Current Condition and Prospect of Cross-Strait Economic and Trade Relations (Liang An Jin Mau Guan Xi Xian Kuang Yu Qian Jing)", by Kao, Charng, Aug 10, 2004, E-Paper issued by Industrial Development & Investment Center, Ministry of Economic Affairs.

posing losses also increases to 30.4%. As a result, for Taiwanese firms, over 50% of their Chinese operations constantly contribute to their profit. Moreover, 11.5% of Taiwanese companies are optimistic about their Chinese operations and believe they will make a huge profit in 2005 and 58.1% of them believed they will make some profit and 9.9% of them predict they will suffer a minor loss and only 0.5% of them thought they will suffer a serious loss. As most of Taiwanese firms still expect to gain profit from their China investments, China will be able to exert its influence on them to gain political interests from Taiwan by using a common practice called "to use commerce to contain politics" (Yi Shang Wei Zheng).

Table 3-32 The Profitability of the Chinese Operations of Taiwanese Firms

Unit: %

Year	Huge Profit	Small Profit	Break Even	Minor Loss	Serious Loss
1998*	3.2	43.1	26.7	24.9	2.1
1999*	3.5	50.7	26.4	17.4	2.1
2000*	5	52.2	25.2	12.9	4.3
2001*	3.5	52.5	23.6	18.9	1.5
2002*	3.4	51.7	26.6	15	3.4
2003*	3.1	41.4	28.8	25	1.7
2004*	8.4	44.5	16.8	28.8	1.6
2005[e]	11.5	58.1	19.9	9.9	0.5

Note: *Year survey was conducted
[e] The estimates of Taiwanese companies
Source: Chinese National Federation of Industries

For Taiwanese firms, Chinese operations have become a resource of their income, and more and more Taiwanese firms target at China market. Before 1988, 52.72% of the Taiwanese firms whose Chinese operations are aimed at a third place outside of Taiwan and China, 10.71% at Taiwan market, and 36.57% at China market. During 1989-1992, the percentage of Taiwanese firms which aiming at China market declined to 35.63%, but then experiences a surge to 46.01% during 1993-1998. In 2001, 47.8% of Taiwanese firms aiming their Chinese operations at China market, 8.8% at Taiwan market and 43.3% at other market. Although the percentage of Taiwanese firms whose Chinese operations aiming at China market declines to 44.54% in 2002, it rebounds to 48.15% in 2003 and goes higher to 54.39% in 2004. As a result, more and more Taiwanese firms make China market as their target market and this will bestow more power on China to influence their political preference as now Chinese government controls not only their production bases but also their major market.

Table 3-33 The Target Market of the Chinese Operations of Taiwanese Firms

Unit: %

Target / Period	China Market	Taiwan Market	Other Market
Before 1988	36.57	10.71	52.72
1989-1992	35.63	14.51	49.26
1993-1998	46.01	16.29	37.35
2001*	47.80	8.80	43.30
2002*	44.54	17.57	37.89
2003*	48.15	16.30	35.56
2004*	54.39	7.68	37.93

Note: * Year survey was conducted.
The data before 1998 came from Kao, 2001, Table 13, and the rest from the survey conducted by Chinese National Federation of Industries.

Source: Kao, 2001 & Chinese National Federation of Industries

China's magnetism over business community can even subjugate the new infectious disease, SARS[309], which has never been identified before 2003. However, in 2003, China still poses a gain in its FDI with a contractual foreign investment of USD 115,070 billion and an actual utilized foreign investment of USD 53,505 billion, an increase of 39.03% and 1.44% over 2002 respectively.[310] Neither do Taiwanese investors withdraw from China market. According to the official statistics, in the same year, Taiwan pours USD 4.59 billion into China, an increase of 19.08% over 2002.[311]

SARS could not expel Taiwanese investors from injecting capital into China; neither could the political threat from Chinese government ward off Taiwanese investors. Even after China's Taiwan Affairs Office announced on May 24, 2004 that Beijing "does not welcome people who make money on the mainland and return to Taiwan to support independence,"[312] Table 3-34 proved that the pronouncement of China's tough stance against "pro-Green"[313] Taiwanese entrepreneurs influences only slightly or not at all to the mainland deployment of Taiwanese businessmen. In 2004, Taiwanese investors pour USD 6,940.66 million into China, a 33.8% increase over 2003's USD 4,594.99 million. During the last half-year of 2004, Taiwanese entrepreneurs invest USD

309 SARS indicates Severe Acute Respiratory Syndrome.

310 An Overview of Chinese Absorption of Foreign Direct Investment in 2003

311 The result is calculated from the data of Investment Commission, Ministry of Economic Affairs, ROC and the retroactive registration is excluded.

312 "Pro-independence Investors Not Welcome" June 22, 2004, China Daily

313 Pro-green indicates the support of current ruling party, DPP, which supports Taiwan independence.

3,550.65 million in China, an increase of 4.74% over the first half-year 2004 and a 27.36% increase over the last half-year 2003.

Table 3-34 Taiwan Investments in Mainland China before and after China Repudiated Pro-Independence Taiwanese Businessmen

Unit: USD million

Period	Amount	Period	Amount	Period	Amount
Jan.-June 2004	3,390.02	July-Dec. 2003	2,579.30	2003	4,594.99
July-Dec. 2004	3,550.65	July-Dec. 2004	3,550.65	2004	6,940.66
Grow Rate	4.74%	Grow Rate	27.36%	Grow Rate	33.80%

Source: Investment Commission, Ministry of Economic Affairs, ROC, Calculated.

3.4.2 The Imbalance of Economic Clout between China & Taiwan

Taiwanese businesspersons march westwards boldly in no fear of the outbreak of SARS; even the political tension between two sides across the Strait can not impede their deployment in China. As most of the MNCs around the world throng in China, Chinese government can discriminate in favor of its political desire. So far, without exception, all Taiwanese businessmen who have been targeted by Chinese government yield to China's request. From Chang Yung-Fa[314], Stan Shih[315], Nita Ing[316] to Hsu Wen-lung[317], they all are dissuaded by Chinese government to get involved in cross-Strait politics and determine to alienate Taiwan's ruling party.

By adopting the strategy of discrimination, China successfully subjugates Hsu Wen-lung, the most notorious long-term Taiwan independence advocate in China's mind. When China proclaimed that it did not welcome the investment form "pro-Green" Taiwanese businessmen, it singled out Hsu Wen-lung as an example of "pro-Green" entrepreneur and China did not welcome

[314] Chang is the founder and chairman of Evergreen Group, which is the world's largest containership owner.

[315] Shih is the founder of Acer Group, which contains Acer, BenQ and Wistron. Acer ranks among the top five branded PC vendors in the world; BenQ is the former Acer Communication and Multimedia; Wistron is one of the largest ODM/OEM suppliers for the PC industry in the world.

[316] Ing is the president of Continental Engineering Corp and chairwoman of Taiwan High Speed Rail Corp. Taiwan High Speed Rail is one of the most important infrastructure projects in Taiwan.

[317] Hsu is the founder of Chi Mei Group, which includes Chi Mei Optoelectronics, Chi Mei Co, Chi Mei Museum, and Chi Mei Hospital. Thereamong, Chi Mei Co. is the the largest ABS/SAN manufacturer in the world and Chi Mei Optoelectronics is one of the world's top 5 TFT-LCD manufacturers.

his investment,[318] but Hsu still insisted "to invest in China is a must."[319] However, although Hsu Wen-lung retired from the chairmanship of Chi-Mei Group, China still blocked all further investments from Chi Mei Group to China until Hsu issued a statement to renounce his long-term political stance and to support One-China Principle right before the eve of a mass rally holding by Taiwan's ruling party to protest China's Anti-Secession Law.[320]

Hsu Wen-lung is not the first and apparently will not be the last Taiwanese entrepreneur who shifts his political stance to protect his mainland investment, but he definitely is the last one down in the top four "pro-Green" entrepreneurs listed by China's media (Cai Jing Shi Bao): Hsu Wen-lung, Stan Shih, Chang Yung-Fa and Nita Ing. When Chen Shui-bian wins the presidency in 2000, China's media for the first time ever publicly identifies these four Taiwanese businesspersons as "pro-Green" and pro-independence, and appeals for strong action against these four who make money in China and at the same time advocate Taiwan independence.[321]

After Stan Shih is named as a "pro-Green" businessman because he is a member of Chen Shui-bian's coterie of tycoon-advisers, on April 2000, he travels to Beijing to emphasize his neutral stance in Taiwan's politics[322] and when interviewed by New York Times he claims that he does not favor an independent Taiwan.[323] Chang Yung-fa is not only one of Chen's tycoon-advisers but also Chen's most important patron.[324] After Chen wins the presidential election on March 18, 2000, two days later Chen personally visits Chang at the headquarter of Evergreen and Chang is the first entrepreneur Chen visits after his victory. However, not to offend China, on April of the same year, Chang Yung-fa sends the video tape relating to the conversation between him and the newly elected president to China to clarify Beijing's misunderstanding of his supporting Taiwan independence.[325] Although Nita Ing does not invest as heav-

---

318 "Pro-independence Investors Not Welcome" June 22, 2004, China Daily

319 "Hsu Wen-lung Said, 'Chi-Mei Has to Invest in China,' (Hsu Wen Lung: Tou Ze Da Lu, Chi Mei Yi Din Yao Qu)" Jul 9, 2004, *Economic Daily* (in Chinese)

320 "Non-peaceful Means in Play: MAC", Mar. 29, 2005, Taipei Times

321 "China's Media for the First Time Identified and Criticized Four Pro-Bian Taiwanese Businesspersons, (Da Lu Mei Ti Shou Du Dian Min Si Tin Bian Tai Shang)" April 12, 2000, *China Times* (in Chinese)

322 "China Plays Hard-Ball, Who Is in the Black List, (Da Lu Yin Biao Tai, Shui Shi Hei Ming Dan)" May 25, 2004, Zhong Hua Zi Xun Wang, in Chinese

323 "Taiwan's Politics Are Straining Trade with China," Landler, Mark, June 20, 2000, New York Times

324 After graduating from law school, Evergreen served as Chen Shui-bian's first major client. Moreover, Chang Yung-fa was also Chen's major campaign sponsor.

325 "China Plays Hard-Ball, Who Is in the Black List, (Da Lu Yin Biao Tai, Shui Shi Hei Ming Dan)" May 25, 2004, Zhong Hua Zi Xun Wang, in Chinese

ily as the other tycoon-advisors, and on the contrary, she places a heavy stake on Taiwan High Speed Rail Corp, however she keeps a low-profile during the 2004 presidential election to avoid drawing any unwanted trouble.

Hsu Wen-lung is the only one stubborn Taiwan independence advocate left in China's eye after the 2004 presidential election. Especially when Chen Shui-bian encounters mysterious gunshots at the last day of the 2004 presidential campaign, he is rushed into Chi Mei hospital, which is not on the list of hospitals designated to treat the President in case of emergencies. As Hsu is the owner of Chi Mei hospital, China therefore blames Hsu as an accomplice of Chen's conspiracy to win the presidency.[326] As a result, China blocks all Chi Mei's further investments in China and grants the major competitor of Chi Mei to tap China's resources and China market.[327] The implementation of the Anti-Secession Law thaws the stalemate between China and Hsu Wen-lung. China's Anti-Secession arouses the antagonism of Taiwanese people against China, and the hatred toward China will cultivate the social base for the pro-independence force. Therefore, Taiwan's pro-independence ruling party manage to manipulate the Anti-Secession Law to its favor by holding a protest demonstration on March 26, 2005. However, to counter the plan of Taiwan's ruling party, China capitalizes on Hsu, a staunch Taiwan independence supporter as a leverage to reverse the sentiment of Taiwanese people and to dismantle the morale of pro-independence force. Hsu issues an open letter to support China's Anti-Secession Law and One-China Principle. His action effectuates the discordance within the "pan-Green"[328] camp: some feel sympathetic for the motive behind his action but some condemn his apostasy. However, after Hsu publicly alters his "pro-Green" stance, Chi Mei wins its ticket to China investments and China successfully dissolves the unity of "pro-Green" camp.

When all the "pro-Green" Taiwanese tycoons abstain from the free expression of their political belief under China's pressure, Taiwanese government faces a dilemma of how to balance the economic and political gains across the Strait. Taiwan's ruling party can insist on its old path at the price of Taiwan's economic prosperity by rallying the masses to rival against China and its fellow travelers yet the group of China's fellow travelers is expanding to include Taiwan's business elites, willingly or unwillingly. On the other hand, it can compromise with China and face its internal political chaos as it is difficult for the ruling party to disavow its pro-independence stance.

---

326 "'Green' Taiwan Businessmen Not Welcomed: Official", Consulate General of the People's Republic China in Houston

327 "Korea Manufacturer Pushes Forward, Hsu Wen-lung Pledges His Support of One China, (Han Chang Jin Bi, Hsu Wen Lung Biao Tai Zhi Chi Yi Zhong)", Mar. 27, 2005, China Times, in Chinese

328 "Pan-Green" camp indicates pro-independence parties such as the DPP and TSU.

With respect to the international competition, the criterion to distinguish a winner from a loser lies with the aggregate strength instead of the political system, the human rights record or the national will. As China emerges as a regional power and a possible world power, Taiwan has already lost its political influence in the international community and is losing its economic influence over private actors. As a result, no matter how Taiwanese government tailors its China policy on the perspective of economy, it does not have any chance to regain its economic autonomy from China. When Taiwan tightens its control over the economic exchanges across the Strait, it simply jeopardizes the survival of Taiwanese firms or forces them to turn their mainland operations underground. If Taiwan relaxes its constraints on cross-Strait exchanges without political compromise, China can exert its influence on Taiwanese businessmen to pursue its political goal.

When the globalization is in process, in order to raise its standard of living, a country must successfully position itself in the world division of labor. However, owing to the political power struggle across the Strait, Taiwanese government has the difficulty to position itself in this era of an emerging China. As the phenomena such as dispersing production worldwide and financial deregulation prevails in all major economies, when more and more MNCs are pursuing a promising land to do business, Taiwanese firms are also forced to roam all around the world in search for a place with cheaper resources and the least governmental restraints. In late 1980s, the traditional industries like garment, footwear, and umbrella commenced the era of Taiwan's industrial migration. From 1991 to 1997, IT hardware industries such as desktop PC, keyboard, and mouse followed the footstep of traditional industries to look for cheaper production base. From 1998 up to recently, TFT-LCD Monitor, NB and IT upstream products like IC design, semiconductor and foundry started to feel the pull of China market.[329] As China plays not only a cheap-resource provider but also a giant market, to survive in the global competition, Taiwanese firms feel the urge to establish themselves in China.

By sharing the same culture, language, and ancestry with China, Taiwan can best position itself in the "Chinese Economic Sphere (CES)". However, due to the political factor, Taiwanese government is hesitant to facilitate the further economic integration across the Strait, but Taiwanese businessmen have already acted on their own to fuse themselves into CES. As the process of globalization starts, each actor strives for a better position to thrive and not to be marginalized. When regional integration takes effect, Switzerland has to bend over to the Schengen Visa in order to compete with Schengen Countries

---

[329] "Corporation Marching Westwards, Cultivated in China and Profit-Shared by Taiwan," April 24, 2004, Economic Daily (in Chinese)

for tourists; otherwise it is sacrificing its tourism.[330] Switzerland may not have to join EU but it has to position itself in EU to maximize its national interest. Taiwan may not want to unite with China but Taiwan as a small trading island requires a home market to sustain its economic development and China is the best candidate. China may not be the only solution to Taiwan's economic hardship but in the eyes of Taiwanese entrepreneurs China is the best choice so far. Therefore, Taiwanese government has to face not only the challenge from China but also the pressure to repeal the prohibition on China investments from Taiwanese firms.

Taiwanese companies have to act on their own to explore China market, yet their competitors from the US, Europe and Korea have the support from their governments. In China's territory, Taiwanese firms are spared under the mercy of Chinese government. In fact, Taiwanese government is placed in a better position in assisting its businessmen than all the other governments in dealing with China because Taiwan can trade its political difference with China for economic benefits. The political disagreement between China and Taiwan does not prevent Taiwanese firms from joining the regional economic activities of East Asia but prohibits Taiwan from participating in the integration of East Asia. As a result, without China's cooperation, Taiwan is destined to be marginalized in the trend of globalization.

[330] The 15 Schengen countries are: Austria, Belgium, Denmark, Finland, France, Germany, Iceland, Italy, Greece, Luxembourg, Netherlands, Norway, Portugal, Spain and Sweden. As Switzerland is surrounded by Schengen countries, if it refused to accept Schengen Visa, the inconvenience might have forced the tourists to circumvent Switzerland. Therefore it allows those tourists with Schengen Visa to make a short stop over Switzerland.

4. Cross-Strait Dilemma: Independence vs. Unification

There is no compromise in an ideological confrontation. When Chinese Communist Party (CCP) waged an ideological war against Kuomintang (KMT), consequently, between Communism and Three People's Principles[331] only one ideology would prevail in China, and the other must be perished. When this phenomenon is introduced to the international competition, it rules out the possibility of de jure coexistence for communist China and three-people-principle Taiwan in any international organization. Thus, when China took over Taiwan's seat in the United Nations (UN) to represent all Chinese, Taiwan was driven out of the UN; when China joined the Asian Development Bank, Taiwan was forced to have an official-title change to "Taipei, China".

Dutta states that in a two-player zero-sum game the payoffs of one player are just the negative of the payoffs of the other player. One player wins if and only if the other player loses. Therefore, the cooperation between players will be out of the question.[332] Owen points out that the essence of most parlor games is of the zero-sum nature.[333] In a political context where the resource is indivisible, not a single party can afford to yield as there is no middle ground in a zero-sum game. Actors in a zero-sum game can not afford to trust each other. Therefore, the conflicts between two sides are expected, and the chance for both sides to cooperate will be dim.

When cross-Strait relationships are examined in a broader perspective, the competition between Taiwan and China could not be categorized as a zero-sum game. Although there are zones of conflicts between Taiwan and China, both parties share the same interests especially in the aspects such as economy, social order and cultural exchange as well. However, when both parties focus on politics, especially the issue of independence versus unification, the extreme contradictory nature of the ideologies regarding independence versus unification has enabled the competition between China and Taiwan to be qualified as a zero-sum game. The gain of independence will be at the expense of unification and vice versa.

Since the Democratic Progressive Party (DPP) is renowned for its pro-independence ideology and it even engraves "Taiwan Independence Clause" on its party platform, therefore, the DPP can be labeled as the representative force of Taiwan independence. On the other hand, China has a One-China Principle which preserves the idea that both sides across the Strait belong to one country,

---

[331] "Three People's Principles" (Three Principles of the People, San Min Chu Yi) is a political philosophy developed by Sun Yat-sen, the nation-founder of ROC.

[332] Dutta, 2001, p.139

[333] Owen, 1982,

so China can be branded as the major force to push for the unification between two sides across the Strait. As a result, the compromise between China and the DPP government is near impossible.

However, President Chen Shui-bian is optimistic about China's concession on its One-China Principle. After taking over the presidency of ROC on May 20, 2000, and then swearing in as the chairman of the DPP on July 21, 2002, President Chen declared in his address to the National Day Rally in 2003 that after his reelection in 2004, the cross-Strait stalemate would be resolved and China would realize the unreality of its One-China Principle and "one country, two systems"; only by putting aside the One China Principle and "one country, two systems" formula, the "door to cooperation" could be open.[334] In an interview with USA Today on Oct 31, 2003, he again expressed his confidence that after 2004 presidential election, with the new vox populi of Taiwanese people, China would have no other choice but to dialogue with him without setting any precondition.[335]

Contradictory to President Chen's optimistic assumption, my hypothesis is that the Communist China will never officially negotiate with the pro-independent DPP government, unless it forsakes the ideology of Taiwan independence or publicly come back to the "one-China roof" (Yi Zhong Wu Ding). However, with the reality that the pro-independence voters constitute the social base of the DPP, it will be near impossible for the DPP to accept China's One-China Principle. Thus, as long as the DPP still holds the reign over Taiwan, the political stalemates between two sides across the Strait will continue until either side moves the situation to its favorite ends, and the tilt toward either extreme will compound the cross-Strait confrontation which may prompt a violent showdown. Therefore, the current coexistence of unification force and independence force should attribute to the success of the US strategic ambiguity policy; as the current Bush administration shifts its cross-Strait policy to a clear and status-quo-maintained policy, the US will face the challenges from China's emergence and the unpredictable Taiwan's domestic politics.

---

[334] President Chen said, "I have no doubt that after the presidential election next year, the development of cross-Strait trade will enter a new phase. Over the past three years, our government has not veered from the fundamental position of 'firmly maintaining our stance and moving forward pragmatically.' We believe that the 'door to cooperation' and the 'door to peace' will always exist between the two sides of the Taiwan Strait. The 'door to cooperation' can open only if the 'one China' and 'one country, two systems' formulas are put aside. The 'door to peace' can open only when China renounces its threat to resort to the use of force and halts its strategic attempts to isolate Taiwan internationally." The content of the speech can be checked out from http://www.taipei.org/even/chen1010.html

[335] The news released by ROC government (in Chinese) http://www.gov.tw/news/cna/politics/news/200310/200310310243.html

4.1 One-China Principle

Although the confrontation between unification and independence is a zero-sum game, the relationships between China and Taiwan can vary according to the transition of the international environment and the essence of the issues involved. In dealing with Taiwan issue, China adopts strategies such as "to use links[336] to encourage reunification" (Yi Tong Cu Tong), "to use commerce to contain politics" (Yi Shang Wei Zheng), "to use civilians to coerce officials" (Yi Min Bi Guan) and "to use military to threat independence" (Yi Wu Xia Du). All those strategies follow the context of separating economy from politics and isolating the independence force from the massive Taiwanese civilians. On the contrary, Taiwanese government is afraid that the "peaceful evolution" (He Ping Yan Bian) caused by economic integration will erode its sovereignty and dwarf Taiwanese government into the position of a local government. Thus Taiwan adopts a strategy of taking economic issues as bargaining chips to allure Chinese government to forsake its One-China Principle in exchange for economic favors. However, when China's economic power is advancing at a high speed and China is capable of attracting worldwide investments, Taiwan's strategy of easing the cross-Strait economic exchanges for political benefits is no longer attractive to China. Moreover, China will never trade its political ideology of unifying Taiwan for its economic advantages.

When two parties have an equal claim to a good; according to the laboratory experiments, the object is usually divided on a fifty-fifty base. But in real world bargaining, the divisions differ according to the needs, contributions, abilities, and other characteristics of each participant.[337] However, when the object in dispute contains an indivisible trait, participants face a situation of all or nothing, thus the compromise between two parties is infeasible. In light of the fact that China suspends any official dialogue between two sides across Strait right after President Lee Teng-hui brings up "Two-State Theory" which interprets the relationship between Taiwan and China as a "state-to-state relationship", China has proved its adamant stance on the eventual unification with Taiwan, and any framework based on "Two Chinas" or "One China, One Taiwan" will provoke China's radical response.

"Taiwan's return to the embrace of the motherland" has been China's ultimate goal in dealing with Taiwan issue. Ever since China broke any official, quasi-official dialogue with Taiwan, China has repeated its request that if Taiwan wants to resume cross-Strait dialogue, Taiwan has to accept first One-

[336] Links mean "Three Links" indicating direct post, direct trade, and direct transport.
[337] Young, 1998, P. 113

China Principle.[338] On the contrary, Taiwan authority insists that both sides can discuss the One-China Principle as an issue, but refuses to accept it as a precondition for negotiations.[339] As a result, because China will never forsake its One-China Principle, when President Chen declares that unless China puts aside its "one China" and "one country, two systems" formulas, "the door to cooperation" will not be open.[340] He officially shuts down "the door to cooperation" between China and Taiwan.

The question why One-China Principle is so important to China and its leaders will be answered from the following aspects: historical complex, domestic power struggle, and domino effect.

4.1.1 Historical Complex

"Being patriots, we do not tolerate any encroachment on China's national dignity or interests.... Having suffered aggression and oppression for over a century, the Chinese people will never again allow themselves to be humiliated as they were before." – Hu Yaobang to the Twelfth Congress of the Chinese Communist Party, September 1, 1982.[341] For Chinese people on mainland, Taiwan's separation from China symbolizes its colonial humiliation of the last century. As Taiwan independence is an emotional and sensitive issue for Chinese, if a war is an unavoidable price in the process of unification, even the high cost of a war will not intimidate China from regaining Taiwan.[342]

China has deemed itself as a civilized center and celestial court (Tian Chao). However, during the late Qing Empire and the early Republic, China suffers the humiliation of foreign invasions and domestic turmoil. After defeated by the foreign hegemonic powers, Chinese government witnesses its sovereignty sabotaged by them, and several leased areas are under the foreign authorities. The existence of those colonies doubtlessly accounts for China's incompetence. After China wining the Second World War, most leased areas, including Taiwan, are recovered by Chinese government. Hong Kong[343] and

---

[338] "China tells Taiwan 'One China' principle is indisputable," March 30, 2000 Agence France Presse

[339] "The National Committee on American Foreign Policy's Visit to Taiwan and China" in http://www.ncafp.org/record/2000/june00ftr.htm

[340] "President Chen's Address to the National Day Rally" in Taiwanese official website: http://www.taipei.org/even/chen1010.html

[341] Whiting, 1983, P. 913

[342] Diamond, 2002, P7

[343] After the First Opium War, Qing Empire in China was defeated and signed the Treaty of Nanking in 1842 to cede Hong Kong to the United Kingdom.

Macau[344] are the remaining stigma of China's vulnerable past, and this colonial disgrace does not put a stop till the end of the twenty century. However, after Communist China successfully defeats Chiang's Nationalist (KMT) government, Chiang Kai-shek relocates the government of Republic of China to Taiwan. As a result, Taiwan's colonial past[345] and "renegade-province" present represent an unfinished mission of preserving the completeness of national territory to current Chinese government.

None of the Chinese leaders has ever forgotten his mission of regaining Taiwan. The control of Chinese governing apparatus has been transferred from Mao Ze-Dong, Deng Xiao-ping, Jiang Zemin, to Hu Jintao, and the tactics to accomplish unification vary from appealing to the use of force, rhetorically threatening to use the military force, to proposing a peaceful unification but reserving the use of force as the last resort, but one thing remains unchanged: China insists upon its One-China Principle. During Mao's era, China would rather exist without membership in the United Nation than effectuate the two-China formula in the international community. In 1971, Chinese Premier Chou En-lai tells Henry Kissinger that Beijing will not accept dual representation in any form. For Chinese government, Taiwan's status is more important than China's membership in the United Nation, and China will never take the seat under the dual-representation formula[346].

Many China's official documents also reflect how the historical complex compels Chinese leaders to shoulder the historical responsibility of unifying Taiwan.

In January 1, 1979, China issues **Message to Compatriots in Taiwan**, in which:

> Throughout its (Chinese) history, foreign invasions and internal strife have failed to split our nation permanently. Taiwan's separation from the motherland for nearly 30 years has been artificial and against our national interests and aspirations, and this state of affairs must not be allowed to continue.[347]

In August 1993, China issues **White Paper—the Taiwan Question and Reunification of China.** It emphasizes that Taiwan has been part of China's territory since ancient time. Taiwan is an inalienable part of China, and it is the

344 The Portuguese had long settled on Macau since 1557. In 1845, the Portuguese used force to occupy Macau, and since then, Macau no longer paid rent to Chinese government.
345 China lost Taiwan to Japan after its defeat in Sino-Japanese War (1894-95).
346 Dual-representation formula indicated the U.N. accepted PRC and ROC both as U.N.'s formal members. Kissinger, P. 784
347 http://www.china.org.cn/english/taiwan/7943.htm

sacred right of every sovereign state to preserve national unity and territorial integrity.[348]

In February 4, 2000, Chinese Premier Zhu Rongji says in a Lunar New Year's message, "After Hong Kong and Macau returned to the motherland, the sacred mission to resolve the Taiwan issue and completely reunite the motherland has become even more prominent for all the Chinese people."[349]

In February 21, 2000 China issues another **White Paper—the One-China Principle and the Taiwan Issue** to emphasize that "Taiwan is an inalienable part of China." It attributes the cause of "Taiwan issue" to a series of historical events, like the Sino-Japanese War, the civil war between Chinese Communist Party (CCP) and Chinese Nationalist Party (KMT) and the Korean War. However, the Chinese government insists that "there is only one China in the world, Taiwan is a part of China and the government of the PRC is the sole legal government representing the whole of China."[350]

China has iterated and reiterated that from historical point of view, Taiwan is a part of China. The current status quo across the Taiwan Strait is a temporary phase of the unfinished civil war between CCP and KMT. For Chinese politicians, Taiwan's unification with China indicates not only the end of the one-century long Chinese historical humiliation but also the glory of those politicians who unify the nation. On the contrary, if Taiwan successfully separates itself from China, the historical humiliation will be hinged on the Chinese leaders who are incompetent at maintaining the integrity of Chinese territory. The historical burden has imposed heavy pressure on all Chinese leaders. AS being addressed as a "historical sinner" is a personal humiliation to Chinese leaders, therefore to eschew the humiliation, no Chinese leader dare and will deviate from the One-China Principle.

4.1.2 Domestic Power Struggle

The cross-Strait relations can never been viewed as exchanges between Taiwanese and Chinese governments, but in fact involve the domestic politics on each side. When Putnam's[351] "two-table" metaphor is applied to the cross-Strait relations, not only the cross-Strait game board is laid in front of the political leaders across Taiwan Strait but also the domestic game board. This two-level game complicates the calculation of gain and loss behind every move of the players. As a rational move at one game board may appear reckless at the other and a gain at one game board may turn out to be a loss at the other,

---

[348] http://www.china-embassy.org/eng/zt/twwt/White%20Papers/t36704.htm
[349] http://www.cnn.com/2000/ASIANOW/east/02/04/china.new.year/
[350] http://www.china-embassy.org/eng/zt/twwt/White%20Papers/t36705.htm
[351] Putnam, 1988, P. 434

the political leaders usually have a difficult time in striking a balance between these two. As a result, they tend to weigh more at the domestic gain than the cross-Strait interest based on the concern of personal political power.

For Chinese leaders, Taiwan issue concerns not only China's future development, but also their personal career. When interviewed with Far Eastern Economic Review (FEER), Singapore Senior Minister Lee Kuan Yew said, "A word of caution: There is a point beyond which no Chinese leader can survive if Taiwan is seen to be drifting away under his watch."[352] As a result, China is willing to suffer huge trade deficit against Taiwan and put up with Taiwan's unilateral restraints on the import of Chinese products, but it can not tolerate the rhetoric advocacy of Taiwan independence.

Lee Kuan Yew is certainly not the only person who recognizes the sensitivity of Taiwan issue, Li Ruihuan, the former Chairman of the National Committee of the Chinese People's Political Consultative Conference (CPPCC) also reaffirms that to maintain the integrity of motherland is the responsibility of Chinese politicians. During his visit in Japan, when asked why Beijing declines to renounce the use of force in solving Taiwan issue, he responds, "No Chinese leader nor any generation of the Chinese leadership has the right to discard Taiwan from its motherland." [353]

In fact, to maintain completeness of Chinese territory is far beyond the subjective judgments of any single Chinese politician. It is the will of almost all Chinese people on mainland. Lilley observes that Chinese people may launch hunger strike on Tiananmen Square and block the train to transport soldiers in Beijing suburb to demonstrate their dissatisfaction with Chinese government, but they all deem themselves as patriots. They identify themselves passionately with their homeland. They will protect their national interests and oppose any foreign invasion. [354] Emmott further points out that in China, the unification with Taiwan is a patriotic issue; all Chinese people including the political dissidents will hold no objection about it.[355] Taiwan issue is very sensitive and is easily manipulated to the favor of a political faction. No Chinese leader can be soft on Taiwan issue without paying political price. As bringing back Taiwan is the major vox populi of 1.3 billion Chinese, any Chinese leader who dares to take the initiative to adjust one-China Principle will also face his own demise of being victimized in an internal power struggle.

---

[352] "Transcript of FEER's Interview with Senior Minister Lee Kuan Yew on 26 MAY 2000," Singapore Government Media Release, Media Division, Ministry of Information and The Arts http://www.gov.sg/interviews/260500lky.htm

[353] "Chinese Leader Reiterates China's Stance on Taiwan," Dec. 14, 1999, *People's Daily*

[354] Lilley, 2003, P. 304

[355] Emmott, 2003, P. 90

It becomes common knowledge that no Chinese leader can accept Taiwan independence and at the same time remain in power. The military superiority of the US will not be able to coerce Beijing to accept dual recognition; the economic integration between China and Taiwan can not dissuade China from using force as its last resort to bring back Taiwan. For Chinese politicians, the integrity of Chinese territory reflects not only the historical value, but also the political righteousness. Whoever violates the rule is equivalent to commit political suicide. Moreover, as the transfer of political power in China inevitably arouses factional infighting among politicians and the losers usually ends up miserably, in terms of rational calculation, no Chinese leader will be willing to commit an error in Taiwan issue.

Throughout the history of People's Republic of China, the fierce infighting is almost the only way for Chinese politicians to maintain or to strive for the leadership and a new leader's coming to power is almost inevitably followed by a massive purge. As a result, the fear of losing everything drives Chinese politicians to crave for the consolidation of personal power. As a single-party state, Chinese Communist Party (CCP) in fact reigns over governmental apparatus. The existence of governmental organs is to fulfill the policies and ideologies of the party. Therefore, any political power struggle within China is tantamount to the factional infighting of CCP.

CCP's intraparty power struggle started right after Chang Kai-shek was defeated and retreated to Taiwan in 1949. According to Hollingworth's analysis, Chairman Mao sent Chinese troops to join the Korean War to consolidate the control of the central government. Mao Zedong sometimes feared his generals might establish themselves as warlords, and Korean War offered him a chance to mobilize military forces to disrupt the potential threat that those generals would have garnered political force through the control of military force. The Korean War offered Mao a chance to reshuffle his generals and the reallocation of the generals successfully suppress the possible establishment of the "Red Warlordism".[356] Mao assumes that the political power is based on the control of the force. He has a famous saying, "Political power grows out of the barrel of a gun." In this phrase, the gun is a metaphor for the military power. Therefore, it is not a groundless conjecture that Mao has the intention to deprive the military power of his generals by the Korean War, and this is the prelude of China's domestic power struggle.

Aside from using foreign threat to garner domestic power, Mao also used a different economic strategy as an excuse to purge his political counterparts to control party apparatus. Mao purged Gao Gang, who was also one of those who had been awarded the accolade which was reserved for Chairman

[356] Hollingworth, 1985

Mao's close comrades in arms.[357] After the catastrophes of the Great Leap Forward, Liu Shaoqi and Deng Xiaoping intended to force Mao to stand down as the Head of State, and by 1960 Mao could no longer access the media as it was under the control of Liu. However, with the support of Lin Biao[358], Defense Minister, Mao launched the Cultural Revolution to purge Liu and Deng, and successfully deprives their political power.

In the late 1960s the Chinese press described Lin Biao as 'Mao's close comrade-in-arms' and in the 1969 Lin was designated the eventual successor to Mao by Mao himself. However, in 1971 Lin encountered a mysteriously death in an airplane crash in Mongolia. Lin's mysterious death remains unsolved. The official version is that Lin was afraid Mao had turned against him and plotted to have Mao assassinated, and his own daughter was reported to have ratted on her father. After Lin's plot was disclosed, Lin tried to flee to Soviet Union, but was killed in an unexplained plane crash.

After Mao's death, Hua Guofeng succeeded Mao as China's leader. However, Deng Xiaoping by trotting out the reform thoughts effectively wrested power from Hua. As a result, Hua, the successor of Mao, was cast out of the power circle by Deng's silent revolution. When Deng conducted a power struggle against Hua, Hu Yao-bang and Zhao Zi-yang were Deng's protégés. However, when student demonstrations and anti-government protests erupted, Hu, the then General Secretary of the CCP, was accused of being "soft" towards the protesters and removed from his position by Deng as Hu had conducted negotiations with the students and wanted to offer more space to political forces outside of the party. His position was taken over by Zhao Zi-yang. When the Tiananmen massacre happened, Zhao was discredited for his "soft" attitude towards the pro-democracy demonstrators and forced to step down by Deng. Deng therefore appointed Jiang Zemin to succeed as the General Secretary of the CCP. To safeguard the CCP regime is all Chinese leaders' objective. Whoever fails to fulfill the goal will be discarded ruthlessly.

In retrospect, though China is a single-party state, the intraparty confrontation within CCP is no less fierce than the power struggle in biparty or multiparty states, sometimes even worse. The fierce intraparty power struggle within CCP explains the tension when the whole world is holding their breath to see whether Hu can smoothly take over the governing apparatus from Jang Zeming, because it is highly possible that the transfer of power may cause a new round of internal political struggle within China.

The line a politician chooses will determine whether he have the capacity to maintain his political edge. A former champion may turn into a loser

[357] Ibid, P. 78-79

[358] Lin Biao was the then Defense Minister.

when he stands on the wrong side, just like Hua Guo-feng, the successor of Chairman Mao, suffers from the erosion of power by Deng's reformist ideology. When corporations compete for the market share, they have to differentiate themselves to attract the potential customers. Politicians are also required to differentiate themselves from others and hope to possess a greater share in the power market. As Downs argues, ignorance removes voters' perfect competence to relate every party policy to ideologies, unless they are willing to devote their resources to find out what the policies are. As the resources can be money and time, and it will be rational for voters to apply money and time for the use of private purposes instead of public fields. Therefore, instead of comparing government policies with opposition proposals, voters tend to vote on ideological competence.[359]

Though ideologies per se are only statements, however by conducting an ideological inter- or intra-party fight against each other, politicians can easily position themselves in the power market. Therefore, there exist power struggles over different ideologies such as conservatism vs. libertarianism, reformist vs. traditionalist, reactionary vs. progressive, or Right vs. Left. Like Downs mentioned the mobilization of ideologies may effect only in a short period of time with respect to the rational behavior, because it effectively serves as one major criterion for people to judge their chosen party before they can fully acknowledge how its planned policies will take effect and whether the outcomes of the policies will coincide with their expectation[360]. However, when rational behavior reemerges, most of time, people have already suffered from the consequence of the ideology which they previously endorsed.

Ross once mentioned that the strategic location of Taiwan could pose a threat to China if Taiwan were allied with China's enemy but if it were controlled by China; China's political position will be enhanced. Thus, Chinese leaders could never agree to let Taiwan go independent.[361] As a result, Taiwan issue can be ultimately analogous to a national security issue. Under the concern of patriotism and nationalism, any Chinese leader who shows soft on national security will not have a chance to stand against attacks from his rivals. Segal mentioned as the communist ideologies phased out, Chinese nationalism acts as the obvious organizing guideline for China's domestic and foreign policies[362]. In fact, Taiwan issue is often used by CCP to promote Chinese solidarity and consensus. Payne and Veney also points out that CCP has taken advantage of nationalism to strengthen its uncertain legitimacy. Nationalism is a

---

[359] Downs, 1957a, P. 98-99

[360] Ibid, P, 99

[361] Taiwan was at one time addressed by American statesmen an "unsinkable aircraft carrier". Ross, 1986, P. 256

[362] Segal, 1994

cohesive power to unify the nation under the rule of CCP[363]. Therefore, unifying with Taiwan is the political righteousness[364] for Chinese leaders. So far, none of Chinese leaders ever has the courage to renounce the claim over Taiwan because to maintain the territorial integrity and national security is an unchallengeable ideology.

No matter which side politicians choose, they have to take a position which is deemed as politically righteous to cover their basis of political interests. As Taiwan experienced its economic downturn in late 2000 and the entire 2001, the concept of "striving for the economic development" (Ping Jing Ji) became the political righteousness which not a single politician has the courage to defy the idea, but only another politically righteous concept "national security" can rival it. Therefore, when President Chen Shui-bian declared that he would hold an "Economic Development Consulting Committee" (EDCA), which he would personally chair in hopes of swiftly reviving Taiwan economy,[365] although the opposition parties questioned the essence and nature of the EDCA, they still appointed party delegates to join it.[366]

While turning pages of Chinese history, the politicians recognize the essence of "losers are always in the wrong, (Cheng Wang Bai Kou)". As there is no easy way to exit in the political power contest, the power struggle is fierce. In order to acquire the political power, a politician must consolidate his power and influence by providing a distinct prospect and an exclusive ideology[367] to entice followers and to remove his opponents from their power bases. When maintaining the territorial integrity is beyond any debate in China, those Chi-

---

[363] Payne and Veney, 1998, P. 869

[364] Political righteousness here indicates major value judgment of subjects that constitute the power sources, and power sources differ according to political systems. When a democratic political system is referred, the direct power source comes from the votes of state citizens, and voters' value judgment counts. However, sometimes the press and media and ruling parties' executive bodies can exert clouts over the decisions of voters; thus their value judgment will prevail as political righteousness. When a totalitarian political system is discussed, the power may derive from armed forces, dictators' personal charismata or even religions; therefore, their philosophy will dictate the political right and wrong.

[365] See news on May 29, 2001 *Taiwan News*

[366] The Executive Yuan (Cabinet) had held "National Knowledge Economy Committee", "National Economy Committee", "National Technology Committee", "National Industrial Development Committee" and "National Executive Committee" within a short period of time, and the major function of all the committees was served for economic development. The public opinion criticized the DPP government did not appeal to actions to revive economy but tried to raise false hopes by holding more and more committees. See Lee, 2004, P. 167.

[367] An ideology here is defined "as a verbal image of the good society and of the chief means of constructing such a society." This definition is borrowed from Downs,1957a, P. 96

nese leaders who don't insist on the One-China Principle will certainly fall an easy prey to their ambitious rivals. As a result, One-China Principle becomes a political dogma which so far no Chinese politician has the nerve to question its essence.

4.1.3 Domino Effect

The domino theory was first applied to Southeast Asia by President Dwight Eisenhower in 1954, and brought up to justify the righteous of the US to join the Vietnam War in the 1960s. The US proposed the "domino theory" which argued that if the first domino was knocked over then the rest toppled in turn. Therefore, if South Vietnam was taken by communists, then the neighboring countries would fall one by one like dominos.

Baldwin applied the essence of domino theory to explain the cause of regionalization. He emphasized that forming a trade bloc or enlarging an existed regional trade area will induce the "pressure for inclusion" on non-participating countries. Moreover, the magnetism to nonmembers will grow stronger as a trading bloc expands[368]. However, Rasul Shams criticized that Baldwin's domino theory failed to explain the origin of the regional integration by solely elaborating on the phenomenon of domino effect on non-participants.[369] The domino effect may be derived from historical incidents, competition from other groupings, or political necessity. It is proven by a real-life experience that the fall of a single domino does not always induce a chain reaction. The fall of a small domino does not necessarily topple the one adjacent to it. On the contrary, when one large domino falls, the chance for it to bring down its entire neighboring dominos is higher. Therefore, my presumption is it is the scale which dominates the standing or falling of the dominos.

The domino theory failed to confirm the fact that the fall of Vietnam did not bring down the entire Southeast Asia into the hand of communists because when the domino theory was applied to the case of Vietnam War, it failed to consider the factor the importance of Vietnam in the whole Southeast Asian area and it did not make any argument on identifying Vietnam as the linchpin of the Southeast Asian domino. Baldwin concluded that the larger the trading bloc grows the more fatal attraction the trading bloc will exude to its non-member neighbors,[370] which suggested the scale should be taken into consideration when domino theory is applied.

The build-up of the one-China domino started from the civil war between CCP and KMT. Though both parties fought a decades-long civil war,

[368] Baldwin, 1993
[369] Shams, 2002
[370] Baldwin, 1993

they both shared a common ground that they belonged to one nation, but had the disagreement on which party should hold the reign over the whole China. Now the situation has been altered. Ever since President Lee Teng-hui put forward the "two-state" theory which depicted the relation between China and Taiwan as a state-to-state relation or at least a special state-to-state one[371], Taiwan has gradually drifted away from the One-China Principle, and moved toward the framework of "two Chinas" or " one China, one Taiwan". President Lee's successor, Chen Shui-bian, who has been a pro-Taiwan-independent activist, even advocated publicly that there was in fact "one country on each side" of the Taiwan Strait[372]. Though under China's military threat, Taiwan dares not formally declare Taiwan independence, President Chen's attitude reconfirmed that Taiwan authority no longer wants to abide by the One-China Principle. Consequently, the foundation of the One-China Principle has been eroded by Taiwan's obscure attitude.

For several decades, Taiwan and China bolstered the world-wide recognition of the One-China Principle. Now Taiwan has rhetorically withdrawn its recognition to the One-China Principle, and China becomes the single force to sustain the worldwide One-China Principle. Once the One-China Principle is unsettled by Chinese government, it will be difficult for China to restore the One-China Principle again, because Taiwan will push down the domino by lobbying the US to give up its support for the One-China Principle, and promote the domino effect all over the world. When Chinese don't want to uphold the One-China Principle, the rest of the world does not have any reason or obligation to support the principle. In fact, China acts as the sole linchpin in the one-China domino. As long as China does not insist on the One-China Principle, then Taiwan can work on the worldwide dual recognition to substantiate Taiwan independence. Taiwan will lobby the US to give up its support on the One-China Principle, and it is highly likely that the entire international community will follow the suit.

In addition, the collapse of One-China Principle will make China more difficult to manage its internal independent movement. When Taiwan acts as the first domino to separate from China, China will face more pressure from the separatist movement in Tibet and Xingjian. Beijing is in fear that Taiwan independence will trigger a domino effect which will upset the entire China[373].

---

371 http://www.taiwanheadlines.gov.tw/19991214/19991214p3.html

372 http://www.gio.gov.tw/taiwan-website/4-oa/20020812/2002081201.html

373 Payne and Veney (1998, P.868-869) pointed out "Having experienced long periods of internal warfare and faced with ongoing threats of internal disintegration, the PRC regards territorial unification as a national priority. Taiwan's independence, from China's perspective, would exacerbate internal problems with separatist movements and weaken China's international status. National unity is believed to be threatened by traditionally non-Han

This fear may not be realized in the real world scenario, because Taiwan is too small and indecisive for the future of Tibet and Xingjian just like the independence of Estonia, Latvia and Lithuania from the former Soviet Union does not guarantee the success of Chechnya independence from Russia. Russia can play a major role in the breakup of the former Soviet Union but it does not imply that it will let Chechnya go free.[374] It is arguable that Chinese government will crack a leak on its One-China Principle for Taiwan without worrying about its domestic turbulence. Therefore, China's insistence on its One-China Principle is expected and so far there is no cause to dissuade it from taking this position.

regions such as Tibet, Xinjiang, and Inner Mongolia. Muslim ethnic minorities, who chafe under Chinese rule in Xinjiang, have begun to reassert demands for greater autonomy."

[374] When the Republic of Estonia, the Republic of Latvia, and the Republic of Lithuania intended to restore their independent statehood, they also faced the economic sanction from the USSR. Chechnya sought for independence from Russia after the breakup of the USSR in 1991, but three years later Russia used military force to regain control.

4.2 Sino-Taiwan-US Relations: An Entangled Triangle

Taiwan has no other choice but to get involved with China, neither does the US have any other alternative but to get entangled in the complicated cross-Strait relations.[375] Since China reopened its door to the world, Taiwanese businessmen have made their profit-driven pilgrimages to China because of China's cheap resources, geographical proximity, shared culture and common language. The deeply interwoven economic relations have imposed pressure on Taiwan's China policy. As too much political emotion is involved in cross-Strait relations, Taiwan cannot deal with China purely in the concern of economy. On the political front, Taiwan intends to determine its own fate on the independence issue; on the economic front, Taiwan has already lost its autonomy. For the US, it can not sit idly by to let China coerce Taiwan's compliance because its reputation of guarding democracy as a universal value will be ruined and Taiwan remains as an important pawn in its geopolitical strategy, but it has no intention to engage a war with China at this moment as it is waging a war on terrorism and sinking itself in the Iraq quagmire. Furthermore, China owns the world's third largest nuclear arsenal. The consequence of blasts in the world's largest and third largest nuclear arsenals will be unpredictable to the whole world.

The Sino-Taiwan-US triangle is delicately balanced: China abstains itself from using force to bring Taiwan back because it is in fear of the US military involvement in Taiwan affair; Taiwan restrains itself from publicly announcing independence because it is afraid the US will refrain its military assistance to Taiwan when cross-Strait war erupts because of Taiwan independence; the US is reluctant to publicly support Taiwan independence because it does not want to engage a war against China at current stage. As a result, this trilateral relationship is trapped in a deadlock. No one can move the situation to its favor without arousing the opposition of the others. The status quo which the US supports is opposed by both Taiwan and China because China wants unification and Taiwan wants independence. China and the US collaborate to confine Taiwan's free choice to Taiwan independence because they have no intention to get involved in a war against each other for Taiwan independence at current stage; the US cooperates with Taiwan to contain the military threat

---

375 Without Korean War, the US would not have interfered into the infighting between Chiang's KMT government and Mao's Communist China; Taiwanese government would not have existed. Without the cold war between the US-led free world and the Soviet Union-led communist camp, Taiwan would have lost its chance to nurture on America's open trade policy towards its allies and to achieve its economic "miracle" under the shelter of the US. Furthermore, without the economic "miracle", Taiwan would not have been able to sustain itself form the military threat and the diplomatic containment from the Communist China. Thus, the US plays a key role in the existence of Taiwan.

from China because the US does not want to lose its strategic pawn on Pacific for China's containment. Therefore, the US support is the cause for stabilizing this dynamic status quo across the Strait which is the result of compromise among these three parties.

As the US plays a crucial role on Taiwan issue, a cautious demarche is required on the US side to avoid a premature collision.[376] To maintain the status quo, the US reiterates its support for three communiqués and one-China policy, and at the same time it also stresses on its "Taiwan Relations Act". On the other hand, American officials maintain a cautious attitude when dealing with "Taiwan independence", and mostly they will make a statement such as "do not support Taiwan independence" instead of "oppose Taiwan independence".[377] However, the terminology of "do not support" offers the space for the advocates of Taiwan independence to maneuver. At least it will be easier for them to interpret the terminology of "do not support" as: Taiwan independence will be a viable option for Taiwanese people and the US will respect the will of Taiwanese people without opposing it. Although the US has sensed the threat from the issue of Taiwan independence and try to take preventive actions[378], however as Taiwan has walked on the trajectory towards independence, the US may have to choose between severing any ambiguous connection with Taiwan independence force or confronting with China militarily.
House of Commons, Second Report from the Foreign Affairs Committee: Grenada, HMSO, March 1984:

---

[376] Before 911, the US targeted China as its chief enemy. Although at the current stage the common threat from terrorism draw China and the US together, the US does not treat China as a friend but a foe. On the other hand, China realizes it must be well prepared to balance the US force for the unification with Taiwan. Both parties have their own security consideration. As a result, the Sino-US conflict is delayed but not defused.

[377] See "Bush spokesman, reporters hold war of words on Taiwan democracy", *Taiwan News*, Dec 12, 2003, White House Spokesman Scott McClellan said, "...the President, in the meeting, made it very clear that we support the one China policy and the Taiwan Relations Act, which is part of the three joint communiqués, and that we do not support Taiwan independence..."
See "Washington's message", *Taiwan News*, Nov 11, 2003, Deputy Assistant Secretary of State Randall Schriver confirmed that "the policy position determined by U.S. President George W. Bush is; 'we (the US) do not support Taiwan independence.'"
See "Officials reaffirm US' Taiwan policy" in *Taipei Times*, Jun 28, 2003, Christopher LeFleur, State Department special envoy for northeast Asia security consultations, said, "We, of course, maintain fully our obligations under the Taiwan Relations Act. We also, of course, do not support Taiwan independence."

[378] See "The status quo's true foe is China" in *Taipei Times*, Jan 07, 2004. "We oppose any unilateral decision, by either China or Taiwan, to change the status quo," cautioned President Bush, "And the comments and actions made by the leader of Taiwan indicate that he may be willing to make decisions unilaterally that change the status quo, which we oppose."

As the world has so often learned in the past, and at such great cost, wars break out and alliances fall apart, no so often as the result of deliberate decisions by the major powers, but as the result of inability of the great power system, and the alliances which support it, to cope with the problems of small countries in faraway parts of the globe.[379]

The US has been led to the trajectory of an inevitable collision with China by the small state—Taiwan. The status discrepancy model suggests that it is easier to arouse a state's conflict when its status on one dimension (size) is incompatible to the status on another dimension (development). The empirical evidence suggested that the large developing states and the small developed states tend to take a more confrontation gesture than the large developed states and small developing states in international affairs.[380] The large developing states in their evolving process to attain the status as a regional power or a world power tend to adopt a non conciliatory attitude and the small developed states in fear of losing their current edge in the global competition are inclined to take aggressive measures. China acts as a large state which is struggling upward from its backwardness; on the other hand, Taiwan is small but accumulates enough wealth to seek for self-identification. The status-disequilibrium of China and Taiwan raises the possibility of future military confrontation which may embroil the US in.

Aggression caused by rank disequilibrium is not inevitable. Under the following preconditions, aggression might be avoided: an authoritative mechanism exists to re-establish the equilibrium; the culture habituates a non-violent nature; there exist other means such as negotiation to rectify the situation. The aggression may take the form of crime in a structure of individuals, the form of revolution in a structure of groups and the form of war in a structure of nations. The rank disequilibrium requires adjustments; otherwise the one who is caught in the social position not matching his capacity will deviate from the predetermined order.[381] It is highly likely that China will appeal to aggressive measures in clearing its way, if it faces obstacles on its way to its self-assertion, Therefore, in the cross-Strait disagreement, the US acts as a safe valve which prevents China and Taiwan from collision.

At current stage, though China clings to its One-China Principle, on the contrary, Taiwan authority has tried to careen through the world-wide one-China obstacle and reach the goal of an equal-footing with China, which implies if "two Chinas" or "one China, one Taiwan" can assist Taiwan gain an equal status with mainland China, under the premise that China abandons the

---

379 Quoted from Harden, 1985, P. 2-3

380 East, 1973

381 Galtung, 1964, P. 98-99

use of force against Taiwan, Taiwan will not hesitate to officially announce its independency[382]. The ideological conflict between China and Taiwan emerges with the rise of Taiwan independence force[383]. As no sign shows that China is going to forsake its stance on One-China Principle, Taiwan President Chen Shui-bian's statement, "we must walk our own way, walk the right way"[384] indicates that Taiwan will be the only variable in the sustainability of the One-China Principle. No matter which way Taiwan walks on, as long as it is not a way towards unification, Taiwan will risk a direct collision with China. Under the military threat from mainland China, Taiwan does not have any choice but to abide by the One-China Principle, unless Taiwan is willing to engage warfare against China to win its independency. Most import of all, in light of China's enormity, Taiwan can never win an independence war without the US assistance.

According to Tang's research, after examining six historical cases in China, he concluded that a small[385] state cannot resist a hostile great power's aggressive ambition (annexation or restraint) unless it has a strong and faithful ally[386]. Taiwan acts as a small state in the unification-demand from China, and the US serves as a strong but questionable ally. After examining the relations between the US and South Korea, Chen concluded that to maintain the national security, small states must enhance its national defense, increase the economic strength and maintain a flexible foreign diplomacy to maneuver in the conflicts of the great powers. Small states can depend on its volatility and fragility, its contribution to its great power ally, and the important position in geopolitics to be an indispensable partner to its great power ally. Aside from strengthening its comprehensive national power, the small state has to entice assistance from large states or even tie its destiny with large states to extort the assistance to survive through the ambition of a hostile great power[387].

---

[382] Ever since President Lee Teng-hui brought up "two-state" theory on 9 July 1999, and followed by President Chen Shui-bian's "one country on each side" on 3 August 2002,

[383] Ever since President Lee Teng-hui decided to launch pragmatic diplomacy under which Taiwan was willing to accept dual recognition, Taiwan started to promote the concept which Taiwan and China are indeed two separate political entities and should coexist in the international society.

[384] See President Chen's comment in an interview with Time magazine. Feb. 16 http://www.time.com/time/nation/article/0,8599,591348,00.html

[385] "Small" here is referred as a relative term. When Vietnam is compared with China, then Vietnam is a small state, but when compared with Cambodia, Vietnam is a large state. When Iraq is confronted against the US, Iraq is a small state, but when it faces Kuwait, it should be termed as a large state (Tang, 2000, P. 14)

[386] Tang, 2000

[387] Bian, 1991

As referring to an ally, when cross-Strait relations are under scrutiny, Taiwan relies on the support of the US to survive through China's challenge. America is not only the major weapon-supplier of Taiwan, but also the only hegemon of the world. Moreover, in order to maintain its hegemonic status, the US has been in deep concern of China's rising and intends to contain China's expansion. Nevertheless, the US can serve as a strong ally to Taiwan, but a questionably faithful one. The US attitude will determine how far Taiwan authority can reach towards the ends of Taiwan independence, and the outcome of One-China Principle will depend on its power struggle with China instead of Taiwanese's free will, because it is clear that China will use military force to enforce its One-China Principle when the One-China Principle is officially[388] violated and the chance for Taiwan to survive through the military invasion from China without the support of the US is slim. Worst of all, even with the military aid from the US, Taiwan may no longer survive through the hardship of a prolonged war against China. Vietnam War and the current Iraqi War serve as the best illustrations of the American military interference. Figure 4-1 shows that only with the wholehearted support from the US will Taiwan stand a chance to go on its own way to independence, which indicates that the US has to use military force to interfere into the cross-Taiwan-Strait confrontation. Consequently, a war between two great powers will pose an unpredictable risk to the whole world[389]. Without the military assistance from the US Taiwan won't be able to sustain a protracted warfare against China. Therefore, the US attitude is going to decide whether China can maintain its One-China Principle without arousing any disturbance in the world security[390].

---

[388] So far, Taiwan authority rhetorically brought up "two-state" theory and the concept of "one country on each side, but without any constitution-adjustment to fit the rhetoric declaration. On the contrary, President Chen Shui-bian offers his assurance that he will maintain the status quo and he will not declare Taiwan independence in any form on several occasions.

[389] Though the US is the dominant military power in the world, China has been a member of nuclear club since 1964. The potential threat of a nuclear warfare between China and the US will drag the whole world into the nuclear catastrophe.

[390] All Taiwanese leaders recognize the potential disturbance in "Taiwan independence issue" and the importance of the US in the cross-Strait relations. When interviewed by Jonathan Mirsky, President Lee Teng-hui told the reporter that he would never proclaim "an independent Republic of Taiwan," and Lee gave Mirsky the impression that it looked like Lee realized that the name in particular could trigger a violent reaction from across the Taiwan Straits. Though Lee Teng-hui believed that under the US-Taiwan Relations Act, Washington was obliged to supply weapons, he was not certain that the US would send troops to secure Taiwan. Lee said "Supplying troops would depend on the situation and would of course be a decision for Washington."
http://www.democracy.org.hk/pastweek/97_nov/mirsky971110.htm

However, the US should bear in mind that Taiwan is the medicine which China is willing to take. China resents any form of foreign interference, but it cannot deny the benign suggestions from its kinship—Taiwan, which it claims to be part of it, especially when those suggestions potentially enhance the political power of those politicians and improve the welfare of Chinese people at the same time. Unification vs. independence is a zero-sum game, but the cooperation on social, economic, cultural issues can easily create a win-win situation. However, all those cooperation should be conducted through governmental or quasi-governmental organizations because China can easily assimilate those nongovernmental organizations into China's system. Take the incident of "Green Taiwanese businessmen" as an example. Although China authorities reiterate harsh threats against pro-independence Taiwanese businessmen and demand them not invest in China, even those who are labeled as "Green Taiwanese businessmen" are not willing to withdraw from China market. Therefore, Taiwan can officially engage with China to contain any irresponsible move by China. Through the engagement, Taiwan can channel China's military budget into the purposes of improving educational system, enhancing cultural cultivation, facilitate social welfare, and enriching environmental consciousness, especially under the premise that Taiwan will conduct "coopetition" with China in social, political, economic system, not politics per se. Because if Taiwan renounces its right to declare Taiwan independence, Taiwan will lose not only its most powerful bargaining chip over China but also the most important "stick" to discipline China for its misbehavior .

When President Chen Shui-bian deliberately delivered the "five-no" statement to the world community, especially to China and the US, in his inauguration speech to assure as long as China has no intention to use force against Taiwan, he will not officially declare Taiwan independence in any form. Moreover, Chiu Yi-jen, General Secretary at the Presidential Office, had a famous saying "Will it work that we don't hug American's thigh (Wo Men Bu Bao Mei Guo De Da Tui Xing Ma)?" to imply that Taiwan has to bend itself to please the US in exchange for the support from the US The related remarks can be checked out from the following websites: http://www.npf.org.tw/PUBLICATION/NS/092/NS-B-092-008.htm http://www.rocusabc.org.tw/chinese/index.html (both in Chinese).

Figure 4-1 The Consequence of Taiwan's Choice on the Unification Issue

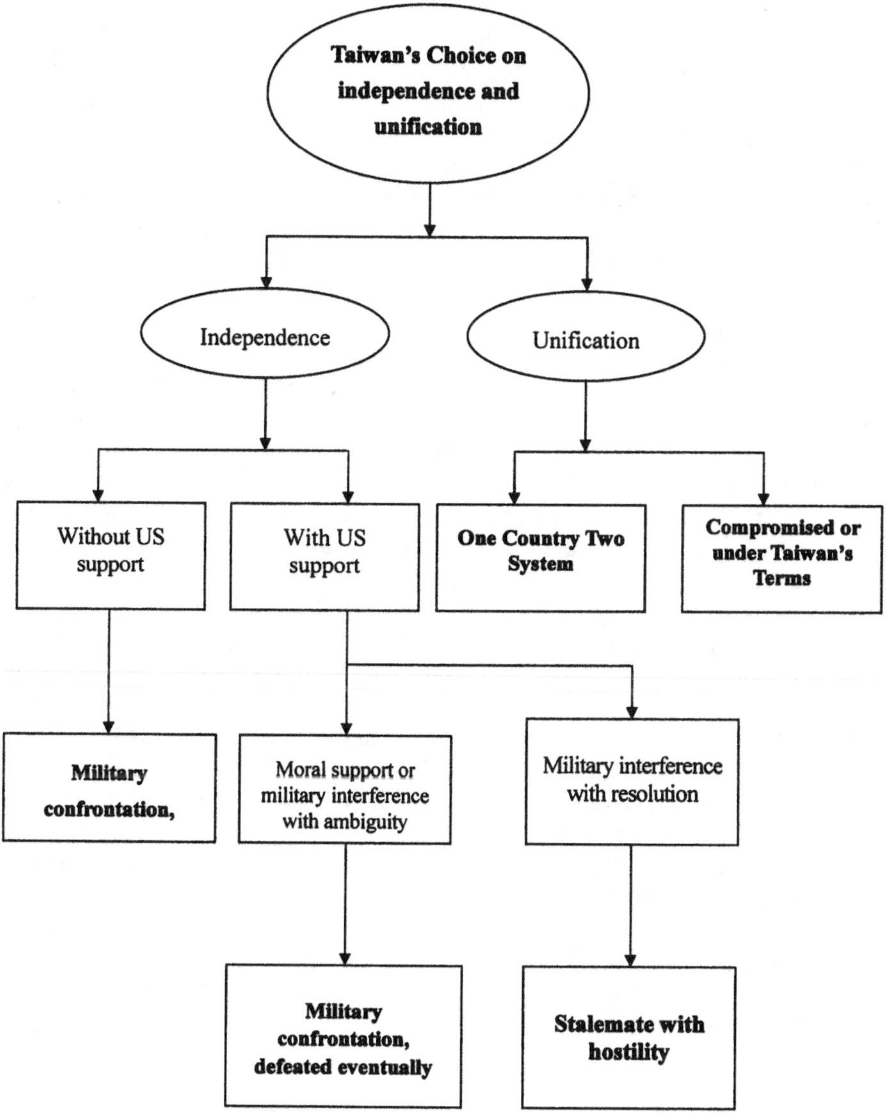

Complied by the author

4.3 China vs. Taiwan in the International Arena

McDevitt pointed out the cruelty of geostrategic reality: whether Taiwan enjoys being neighbored by China, China is always only 90 odd miles from Taiwan and the unalterable geographic proximity places Taiwan under the influence of China's growing power.[391] Since Taiwan can never eschew the influence from Chinese mainland, when Taiwan engages a confrontation against China, the reality of the geographical proximity limits Taiwan's alternatives on the most sensitive independence issue. The geographical proximity destines Taiwan and China the intertwined competition. At first, they fought for the legitimacy of reigning over the whole China; now they fought over Taiwan independence. That is a fight between two sides across the Strait but the whole world is engulfed in inevitably.

Ever since the civil war between Chiang-led[392] KMT and Mao-led[393] CCP came to a halt after Chiang was defeated on mainland and fled to Taiwan, the Chinese civil war has gradually faded into a phase of pro forma existence. Though there were sprinkling battles between two sides across-Taiwan-Strait at the beginning of KMT's reestablishing its ROC government in Taiwan, as the US was determined to neutralize the Taiwan Strait, China and Taiwan have not launched a full-scale war against each other. As a result, China keeps reiterating One-China Principle with the premise that Taiwan is only one of China's provinces, positioning cross-Strait relations as Chinese internal affairs, and waging a diplomatic war against Taiwan. Taiwan took a similar strategy during the "two-Chiang's" era. Taiwan also consented with the concept of One-China Principle but instead of recognizing Communist China's sovereignty, Taiwan insisted on its orthodox Chinese inheritance and advocated that KMT government would recover Chinese mainland eventually. However, the intensive argument between Taiwan and mainland China gradually shifts from which party is the legitimate and sole ruler of China to whether Taiwan could openly embrace its statehood and independency and even eventually pursue its de jure independence in international arena.

During the cold war, the bi-polarizing world offered the then-defeated KMT government a "breathing space" to rehabilitate itself in Taiwan. The US at first had its expectation on the newly establishing Communist China's regime and intended to give up Chiang's regime,[394] but China's apparently tilting

---

[391] McDevitt, 2003

[392] Chiang Kai-shek

[393] Mao Ze-Dong

[394] The US determined to abandon the defeated KMT government was obvious. The US issued its white paper (United States Relations with China, 1944-1949) on Aug. 5 1949 to declare the defeat of KMT government was due to the corruption of Chiang's regime and the

toward Soviet Union in its foreign policy by signing Treaty of Friendship, Alliance, and Mutual Assistance with the Soviets in February 1950 disappointed the US. In June 1950, the Korean War erupted, and in fear of the expansion of communism in Asia, as well as the US domestic booming anti-communism,[395] the Truman administration decided to support Chiang' regime in Taiwan. In 1951, Dean Rusk, Assistant Secretary of State for Far Eastern Affairs, set the tone for U.S.-China policy for the next two decades by saying, "The regime in Peiping [Beijing] . . . is not the government of China. . . . We recognize the national government of the Republic of China, [which will] . . . continue to receive important aid and assistance from the United States."[396] During the period of 1951-1971, the US supported all kinds of anti-communism forces surrounding Communist China to carry out harassment against China, but aside from the Korean War, the US avoided any direct military confrontation against Beijing regime, and in the UN, the US supported ROC government (Taiwan) as the legitimate representative of China.[397]

The US and the Taiwanese government signed a mutual defense treaty to place Taiwan under U.S. protection in December 1954. However, both sides had their disagreements in the essence of the treaty. Taiwanese government was hoping to consolidate its regime, overthrow Communist China and regain Chinese mainland through the cooperation with the US. On the contrary, the US had no intention to directly confront Beijing government. Although the US kept its China policy by denying the Communist China's regime, America was aimed at protecting the security and legitimacy of Taipei government and at the same time maintained a containment strategy against Communist China in the hope for China would depart from the Soviet Union and improve its relations with the US[398]

Though after the eruption of Korean War, Taiwan enjoyed the support from the US to stabilize its membership in UN, however, China gradually exerted its clout on the Third World nations[399] and eroded Taiwan's diplomatic

---

US had done all it could to mediate the Chinese civil war. Moreover, when Chiang's government moved its capital to Guang Zhou, John Leighton Stuart, the then U.S ambassador to China, did not follow. See Jia-Qi Mao, 1988, P. 7 Thomas J. Bellows, 1976, P. 594, Wei Wei Zhen, 2001, P. 5 and Public Papers of the Presidents, Harry S. Truman 1945-1953, The President's News Conference in January 5, 1950.
http://www.trumanlibrary.org/publicpapers/index.php?pid=574&st=China&st1=

[395] That was the beginning of Republican Senator Joseph McCarthy of Wisconsin started his witch hunt for communists within the US government.

[396] See http://www.pbs.org/wgbh/amex/china/timeline/timeline2nf.html

[397] Hu, 2001, P. 7-13

[398] Ibid, P. 18-20

[399] There are two ways to distinguish worlds among the world. China claimed that the US and Soviet Union, these two super powers constituted the First World; the remaining devel-

base. In the 1950s, in order to protect itself from U.S. pressure, China operated its Third World policy in the South and Southeast Asia to lure its Asian neighbors' support against the US but failed. However, in the 1960s, the decolonialization movement in Africa offered China another chance to revitalize its Third World Policy[400]. Though China failed to build an anti-American united front with the Third World nations to protect itself from the US political and military pressures, with the assistance from the Third World nations, China successfully expelled Taiwan from UN and replaced Taiwan as the permanent member in UN Security Council.

Taiwan authority realized diplomatic relations may impede or assist the survival of the regime, but under the cold-war atmosphere in a polarized world, Taiwan took the side with the US and lived under the US protection. In contrast, although Communist China teamed itself with Soviet Union at its founding stage by signing the Sino-Soviet Treaty of Friendship, Alliance and Mutual Assistance (February 14, 1950), later due to the clash of interests and the power struggle for supremacy, China took a road against the Soviet imperialism and criticized the Soviet leader and his followers were "revisionists". Moreover, after the Korean War, China had prepared itself to emerge as a great power and proved its ability to resist the forces of imperialism[401].

Chou En-lai made the following comment: "The Third World is the main force in combating colonialism, imperialism, and hegemonism. China is a developing socialist country belonging to the Third World[402]." As China defined itself as a Third World nation, after the dethronement of Stalin, it started to encourage intra-Communist-bloc freedom[403] to strengthen its influence in the bloc and to lift its position vis-à-vis the Soviet Union. Moreover, China even took advantage of racism to woo the friendship from African countries by

---

oped industrial countries , the countries of Western Europe and Japan, aside from these two super powers belonged to the Second World; the rest underdeveloped, developing countries the Third World. China categorized itself as a Third World nation and teamed itself with the Third World countries. See Wei Zhen Hu (2001, P. 59-60) George T. Yu (1977, P. 1039), Trong R. Chai (1979, P. 391) and Chuang Shi and Yu Lin (1999, P.86-87). However, Alfred Sauvy, a French demographer, classified the capitalist world (the US led free camp) as the first world, the communist world (the Soviet-led communist camp) as the second, and all the other countries aside from the first world and second world are the third world countries. See http://www.uwec.edu/geography/Ivogeler/w111/3world.htm

400 Yu, 1977, P. 1037

401 Crozier, 1964 and Gittings, 1964)

402 Yu, 1977, P. 1036

403 John Gittings said, (1964, P.66) "China gave full support to the Polish demands for independence and equality, adding a warning against Soviet 'big-nation chauvinism'."

arguing Chinese were colored people, like Africans[404]. Therefore, during this stage, China sought for the Third World assistance and to form a new international order not only to ward off the pressures from the US, but also to balance the potential threat from the Soviet Union[405].

Table 4-1 Countries Recognizing the PRC between October 1, 1970 and September 31, 1971

Country	Date
Canada*	10/13/70
Equatorial Guinea	10/15/70
Italy*	11/06/70
Ethiopia	11/24/70
Chile*	01/15/71
Nigeria	02/10/71
Cameroon*	03/26/71
Kuwait	03/27/71
San Marino	03/06/71
Austria	05/28/71
Libya*	06/11/71
Sierra Leone*	07/29/71
Turkey	08/05/71
Iran*	08/17/71

Note: *Countries previously recognizing Republic of China (Taiwan)
Source: Bellows, Thomas J. (1976, P. 596)

From Table 4-1, it clearly depicted the success of China's Third World Policy. Within less than one year, China build formal diplomatic ties with Canada, Equatorial Guinea, Italy, Ethiopia, Chile, Nigeria, Cameroon, Kuwait, San Marino, Austria, Libya, Sierra Leone, Turkey and Iran and among them, Canada, Italy, Chile, Cameroon, Libya, Sierra Leone, and Iran had severed ties

[404] In March 12, 1962, the Kenya paper, *Daily Nation* mentioned, "In private lobbying the Chinese are adopting an openly racist line. These Europeans, they say, are all the same whether they are French, Americans, Russians or Poles; we non-whites must get together. One Chinese delegate even went so far as to talk about the importance of us blacks sticking together.' (Brian Crozier, 1964, P. 443)

[405] Yu, George T. pointed out, (1977, P. 1036) "The twin foundations of this policy (China's Third World policy) of uniting the Third World against the United States and Soviet Union and organizing the peoples of Africa, Asia, and Latin America to form a new international order was largely Mao's creation, based upon his world view and other factors."

with Taiwan to switch their recognition to China. China's Third World Policy had achieved a great success and directly contributed to the expulsion of Taiwan from UN.

From Table 4-2, during the 1950s, Taiwan and its allies had successfully blocked the Communist China's admission to UN and Taiwan's supporters outnumbered China's at least 15 votes. However, in December 1955, the horse-trading deal between the Western Allies and the Soviet Union brought sixteen new members into United Nation and enhanced the difficulty for Taiwan to defend its seat in UN, and in 1960, Resolution 1514 (entitled "A Declaration on the Granting of Independence to Colonial Countries and Peoples") granted statehood to the former colonial areas by affirming "inadequacy of political, economic, social or educational preparedness should never serve as a pretext for delaying independence."[406] From then on, Third World countries thrived in the United Nations and Taiwan gradually lost its edge over China. Consequently, the support for PRC's entry began to mount and the margin narrowed down in China's favor in the 1960s. Although Taiwan strived hard to win friends in the Third World and offered technical assistance to the newly emerging nations, Taiwan did not gain any edge in the pure political-oriented diplomatic campaign. As a result, although those countries which supported China's bid for UN entry had outnumbered those against China's bid in 1970, Taiwan still maintained its UN seat by passing a resolution to treat China's representation as an "important question" that demanded a two third majority votes of the General Assembly. In 1971, Taiwan's technical blockade on China's entry failed. As 76 nations voted for China's entry into UN and 35 nations against, China was accepted as a member of UN.

As the Cold War alignment shifted[407], Taiwan's position in international organization was eroded further. Moreover, as the base of UN membership increased, China gradually gained the momentum in the UN entry bid from its increasing number of allies in the Third World. According to Qian Qi-chen, he attributed the success of China's entry into UN to the assistance from African nations. He pointed out that 26 out of 76 votes for China's entry came from its African allies and their adamant support also frustrated the attempt of the US and Western countries to impose pressure on China's human right issue.[408]

---

[406] See Harden, 1985, P. 17.

[407] As the US view Soviet Union as its major rival and the continuous border disputes between Soviet Union and China raised the hope for the US to woo China against the Soviet, as a result, U.S. support for Taiwan began to dwindle. See Hu, Wei Zhen (2001) and the border disputes between China and Soviet, see Allen S. Whiting (2001)

[408] Qian, 2003, P. 255

Table 4-2 the Result of Vote on China's Bid for UN Entry 1950-1971

Year	Number of Members	For China's Bid	Against China's Bid	Abstention	Absentee
1950	59	16	33	10	0
1951	60	11	37	4	8
1952	60	7	42	11	0
1953	60	10	44	2	4
1954	60	11	43	6	0
1955	60	12	42	6	0
1956	79	24	47	8	0
1957	82	27	48	6	1
1958	81	28	44	9	0
1959	82	29	44	9	0
1960	99	34	42	22	1
1961	104	37	48	19	0
1962	110	42	56	12	0
1963	111	41	57	12	1
1964	114	Extended			
1965	117	47	47	20	3
1966	121	46	57	17	1
1967	122	45	58	17	2
1968	126	44	58	23	1
1969	126	48	56	21	1
1970[a]	127	51	49	25	2
1971[b]	-	76	35	17	-

Note: [a] UN General Assembly formerly passed a resolution according to which China's representation was an "important question" that demanded a two third majority votes of the General Assembly to accept PRC's entry bid.

[b] General Assembly rejected the resolution to treat China's representation as an important question with 59 votes against, 55 votes for and 15 abstentions.

Source: Hu (2001), modified and the official website of PRC http://www.fmprc.gov.cn/eng/ziliao/3602/3604/t18013.htm

Although suffering a serious setback in the struggle for UN membership against Beijing, Taipei hanged on its One-China Principle in 1970s and 1980s. During an interview with Dennis V. Hickey in 1996, Fredrick Chien, Taiwan's foreign minister, pointed out Taipei government's position in the 1970s:

We took the same stand as mainland China. We both said there's only one China. We both said Taiwan is part of China. And we said only the Republic China is the legitimate government of China. They said only the People's Republic of China is the legitimate government of Chin. So, during this period we presented countries and international organizations of the world with a dilemma. They had to make a choice. They cannot do it "both" or "and." They have to do it "either/or".[409]

Ever since Beijing replaced Taipei as the sole Chinese representative in the UN, Taipei had suffered a serious setback in competing for more friends in the international arena. From Table 4-3, it indicated how seriously Taiwan's diplomatic base was eroded within a short period of less than 5 years, 1971-1975. After Taiwan was excluded from the UN, 29 countries decided to switch their formal recognition from Taiwan to China in this period of time. In contrast to Taiwan's eroding edge in international arena, China successfully branded its fate with the Third World. By wooing the assistance from the Third World countries, China emerged as a representative power for the Third World. Since China's entry into the UN, China had managed to play out the balancing act between value-orientation and power-orientation. At the beginning of its access to the UN, China maintained its pro-Third Word stance. According to Trong R. Chai, after analyzing China's voting behavior in the UN from 1971 to 1977, he concluded:

China was much more favorable to the Third World than to the Western nations and was more supportive of the developing nations than of the Communist camp on all except colonial issue. Even when these issues were included, the voting agreement between China and the Third World exceeded that between China and other Communist nations.... Our analysis suggests that China has for the most part succeeded in demonstrating its pro-Third World and anti-superpowers position, at least within the context of the United Nations and judging by available evidence will continue to do so in the foreseeable future.[410]

In order to offset China's victory, Taiwan strived even harder to seek new friends in the Third World[411]. Even so, the number of countries which maintained diplomatic relations with Taiwan kept dwindling. Till 1978, the number dropped to 21, the lowest on Taiwan's historical record. From then on, the number bottomed out and started to climb up, but it has seldom reached 30. In light of the fact that there were 192 nations in the world in 1997, Taiwan's backwardness in the international diplomatic competition against China is significant[412]. Although Taiwan joined the diplomatic competition against China in the Third World, and had offered financial aid, development assistance, long-term loans, and technical expertise, since China also rewarded its

---

409 Hickey, 1997, P. 1035

410 Chai,1979, P.403

411 See Thomas V. Biddick (1989, P. 803)

412 http://www.taiwannation.org.tw/republic/rep1-10/no02_02.htm (in Chinese)

friends with handsome packages, consequently, "money diplomacy" did not render Taiwan much edge over China.

Table 4-3 Countries Recognizing the People's Republic of China from October 24, 1971 to Nov. 13 1975 (listed chronologically)

Country	Date	Country	Date
Belgium*	10/25/71	Chad*	11/28/72
Bhutan	10/25/71	Australia*	12/22/72
Peru*	11/02/71	New Zealand*	12/22/72
Ecuador*	11/09/71	Spain*	03/07/73
Lebanon*	11/09/71	Upper Volta*	09/15/73
Rwanda	11/12/71	Guinea Bissau	09/30/73
Iceland	12/14/71	Botswana*	03/25/74
Cyprus*	12/14/71	Malaysia	05/31/74
Malta*	01/31/72	Trinidad and Tobago*	06/20/74
Mexico*	02/14/72	Venezuela*	06/28/74
Argentina*	02/19/72	Niger*	07/16/74
Bahrain	04/10/72	Brazil*	08/15/74
Greece*	06/05/72	Grenada	10/10/74
Guyana	06/27/72	Gambia*	12/17/74
Japan*	09/29/72	Portugal	01/06/75
West Germany	10/11/72	Philippines*	06/09/75
Maldives	10/14/72	Thailand*	07/01/75
Gabon*	10/16/72	Bangladesh	10/04/75
Malagasy Republic*	11/06/72	Fiji	11/05/75
Luxembourg*	11/16/72	Comoro Islands	11/13/75
Jamaica*	11/21/72	Western Samoa*	11/13/75
Zaire*	11/24/72		

Note: * Countries previously recognized Republic of China (Taiwan)
Source: Bellows, Thomas J., 1976, P. 597

Ever since the confrontation between China and Soviet Union subtly transformed the Sino-U.S. relations, the US had thought of aligning itself with China to contain its major competitor—Soviet Union. As the disruption between China and the Soviet Union offered the US to restructure the former Cold-War alliance system, the US decided to take the chance to play "China Card". Because China and the US intended to form an alliance to counter their mutual enemy, the relationship between Taiwan and the US suffered from a serious setback. In the early 1978, with the assistance form Cuba, Soviet Union started to expand its force in Middle East and Africa, which worried the US and pushed the US further towards China. The US was concerned about the international sentiment would tilt for Soviet's favor, and which pushed the US even more eager to play "China Card" to counter the strategic expansion of the Soviet Union. Henry Kissinger commented that the relationship between Communist China and the US was a marriage of convenience, and China was U.S. best anti-Soviet ally[413]. Even though each party had its own interests, under a perceived Soviet military threat, the security reason would lead to a growing cooperation[414].

Moreover, after Deng Xiaoping took over the reign in 1978, China gradually shifted its Third World Policy to a tri-lateralization-oriented policy which emphasized its economic, diplomatic, political and strategic ties with the US, Western Europe, and Japan—the members of the Trilateral Commission. At this stage, China reoriented its foreign policy to tilt to the Western nations in its developmental and geopolitical concerns. Instead of implementing its previous three-world theory to reformulate a new world order, at the post-Mao era, China strived to incorporate itself into the predetermined world order[415].

Hu commented the factors which determined the agreement between U.S. and China to establish diplomatic ties in the end 1978 were:

1. Deng Xiao-ping reemerged as China's leader;
2. China intended to develop its economy through the assistance from the US;
3. Because China was caught between two fires by the cooperation between Soviet Union and Vietnam, China needed the US to balance their containment.

Therefore, Deng Xiao-ping determined that the establishment of diplomatic ties should proceed and the dispute about U.S. arm-sale to Taiwan could be set aside. In January 1, 1979, the US formally severed its diplomatic tie but maintained unofficial relationships with Taiwan[416]. From then on, Taiwan depended on the US Taiwan Relation Act[417] to gain the assurance of security.

Bellows pointed out Taiwan's predicament that Taiwan would suffer from political isolation because of the diplomatic setbacks in the 1970s and the political isolation would lead to economic and cultural isolation and eventually

---

[413] Hu, 2001, P. 73

[414] Nass and Oldag, 1983, P. 108

[415] Kim, 1981, P.437

[416] Hu 2001, P. 87-88

[417] The Taiwan Relations Act which was initiated by the United States Congress was enacted into U.S. law on April 10, 1979, and it pledged to "help maintain peace, security, and stability in the Western Pacific and to promote the foreign policy of the United States by authorizing the continuation of commercial, cultural, and other relations between the people of the United States and the people on Taiwan, and for other purposes."

threat Taiwan's autonomy. However, he further pointed out that Taiwan had tactically expanded its diplomatic battlefields from pure political engagement to cultural, educational and economic exchanges. Although the trend of official diplomatic relations had been in the favor of China, through international trade and investment, Taiwan not only strengthened relations with countries which recognized it, but also facilitated interactions with countries which did not officially recognized it.[418]

Through the global trade, Taiwan has embedded itself in the supranational production network and made itself a dispensable agent in the international economy. Bellows commented that Taiwan's economic strength and the emphasis on international trade facilitated its position in the international community. Though Taiwan might not play an important role in the international political arena, it could play an indispensable role in the international production chain which would contribute to its survival. Since Taiwan's pure political competition in international arena against China was a given, its foreign diplomacy became more flexible. Although Taiwan may not have diplomatic ties with most of the nations in the world but has economic, cultural and educational ties with over 140 countries. Moreover, Taipei did not limit itself in engaging with those countries that do not recognize China but was willing to develop all kinds of relationships with those recognized China.[419]

As Taiwan continued its effort on economic development, at the same time, the "economic miracle" enabled Taiwan to transfer its economic performance into military defense to counter the threat from mainland China. Taiwan acted as a peculiar case which breached the cross-national norms that suggested trade-offs between defense burden and economic growth, as Davis and Chan noticed Taiwan bore a comparatively heavier burden in defense budget than most of developed and developing countries but at the same time Taiwan stood out as a fast-growing economy. Its average economic growth rate almost reached 9%.[420]

Although Taiwan's economic performance was impressive, however, Taiwan's economic success did not translate into political power to overcome its hardship in the diplomatic sphere. The US severed its diplomatic tie with Taiwan and switched its recognition to China on January 1, 1979, and Saudi Arabia and South Korea followed the suite on July 22, 1990 and Aug. 24, 1992 respectively. As South Africa President Nelson Mandela failed to use his personal prestige to create a "dual recognition" principle for Taiwan[421], on January

---

[418] Bellows, 1976

[419] Ibid

[420] Davis and Chan,1990

[421] Qichen Qian mentioned Nelson Mandela expressed his intention to establish diplomatic tie with China and maintained formal tie with Taiwan at the same time. Mandela intended to

1, 1998, South Africa cut its diplomatic tie with Taiwan for China. South Africa served as the last big nation to establish diplomatic relations with China in the world. From then on, countries which have diplomatic ties with Taiwan are from backward areas, and most of them eye on Taiwan's financial support.[422]

After losing its major ally—the US, Taiwan reoriented its attention to domestic economic development. Taiwan's economic expansion in the late 1980s and early 1990s had offered Taiwanese government enough financial resources to engage a diplomatic war against China. After President Lee Teng-hui took the presidency from late President Chiang Ching-kuo in 1988, because of internal and external pressures, Taiwan shifted its diplomatic context from insisting on "one-China" principle (indicating the policy of acting as the sole legitimate representative government of China) to "pragmatic diplomacy" (indicating Taiwan no longer claims as the sole legitimate representative government of China but practically acknowledges the co-existence of mainland China). From then on, Taiwan has derived its own identity and strived hard to win worldwide recognitions.

Su mentioned, before President Lee inaugurated as Taiwan president in 1988, Taiwan did not have a mainland policy. He pointed out before 1988 Taiwan was situated in a position with national stability, economic prosperity but

---

set a precedent for the "dual recognition" principle which the US, the U. K. and Japan all failed. However, the "dual recognition" would not be accepted by China. See Qian, 2003, P. 273

[422] Many reports have been concerned about Taiwan's "money diplomacy". In the report in *International Herald Tribune*, Mr. Lien Chan retorted to Beijing's accusation that Taipei has been using "money diplomacy" to buy friends by saying "our biggest bargaining chip in foreign relations is our economic strength." See "Taiwan: A Studied Exercise in Vacation Diplomacy [2 Edition]" by Michael Leifer, *International Herald Tribune*, Paris: Feb 11, 1994, P. 6.

BBC also reported an incident about Lee Teng-hui's announcement on US$ 300 million aid to Kosovo, which was assumed as an example of Taiwan's "money diplomacy". "Taiwan president's Kosovo aid pledge seen as 'money diplomacy'", *BBC Monitoring Asia Pacific – Political*, London: Jun 21, 1999, P. 1.

Hong Kong media also cautioned Taipei's "money diplomacy". As "money diplomacy" could not prevent Taipei's diplomatic allies from switching their diplomatic ties to Beijing. Since money can only buy friendship in a short period of time, such a tactic will eventually harm Taipei's image. "Secret Hurts" in *Hong Kong iMail*, Hong Kong: Mar 26, 2002. pg. 1

As Taiwan promised to offer economic and technical aid, Burkina Faso decided to reestablish diplomatic ties with Taiwan after a 20-year break. Beijing accused Taipei of "taking advantage of the temporary economic difficulties of some countries" to practice "money diplomacy". "Regional Briefing" in *Far Eastern Economic Review*, Hong Kong: Feb 17, 1994, Vol. 157, Issue 7, pg. 13

contracted international living space[423]. After Lee Teng-hui took over the presidency, Taiwan's sovereignty became his major concern, and he thought when more countries accepted communist China as the sole legitimate Chinese government, under the one-China framework, it would be to Taiwan's disadvantage. He expected the international community would take a pragmatic attitude toward the fact that China is divided into mainland China and Taiwan and adjust their China policy so Taiwan could be treated fairly. Moreover, he wanted communist China to face the reality and to forsake its activities of isolating Taiwan activities, thus both sides across Taiwan Strait could interact on the base of mutual-respect.[424]

However, Dittmer suspected the effectiveness of Lee's dogma, because after the Cold War, China took an even more conservative attitude in its Taiwan policy to strengthen its pressure on compressing Taiwan's international space. As a result, Taiwan's "pragmatic diplomacy" would gain no progress but be a nuisance to Beijing government.[425] Since Taiwan's "pragmatic diplomacy" was viewed as activities for Taiwan independence by China[426], instead of acquiescing to Taiwan's status as a de facto state, China adopted all measures to contain Taiwan's international living space as usual. Therefore, although Taiwan does not rule out the possibility of "dual recognition", so far the "dual recognition" has been limited as a concept without being realized.

Although the cross-Strait diplomatic contest is fierce and China predominate in this competition, from Table 4-4, Taiwan still maintain diplomatic ties with up to 30, down to 25 countries during the 1991 to 2005, and over two thirds of Taiwan's diplomatic allies are located in Central and South America and Africa. In North America, Taiwan has formal diplomatic ties with none. In Europe, Vatican is the only country that has formal tie with Taiwan. Because China does not accept Vatican involvement in China's religious system, the disagreements hinder their diplomatic normalization. As China rises as an economic power, it is getting more costly and less effective for Taiwan to implement "money diplomacy" against China. As a result, the number of Taiwan's diplomatic allies is going on a downward path. In 2005, Taiwan has only twenty five diplomatic allies.

---

423 Su, 2001a

424 Chu, 2003, P. 5-6

425 Lee, 2002, P. 8

426 So called "pragmatic diplomacy" is flagging the "international survival space" of Taiwan to create "two Chinas" or "one China, one Taiwan". Quoted from *A way gets nowhere: analyze "pragmatic diplomacy" promoted by Lee Teng Hui and Chen Shui-bian*, Guo Zheng-Yuan, a research fellow of China Institute of International Studies

Table 4-4 The Number of Diplomatic Allies of the ROC

Unit: Number of Countries

The End of the Year	**Total**	Asian Area	European Area	African Area	American Area
1991	**29**	5	1	7	16
1992	**29**	4	1	8	16
1993	**30**	4	1	9	16
1994	**29**	4	1	8	16
1995	**30**	4	1	9	16
1996	**30**	4	1	9	16
1997	**29**	4	1	10	14
1998	**27**	4	1	8	14
1999	**29**	5	2	8	14
2000	**29**	5	2	8	14
2001	**28**	5	1	8	14
2002	**27**	4	1	8	14
2003	**27**	5	1	7	14
2005*	**25**	6	1	6	12

Note: * As of the end of Nov. 2005
Source: Ministry of Foreign Affairs, ROC

After Chen Shui-bain's inauguration as Taiwan's president in 2000, China exerts all its influence to contract Taiwan's international space because of Chen's pro-independence background. In 2000, Taiwan still had diplomatic ties with 29 countries. In 2001, Republic of Macedonia broke off the formal diplomatic ties with Taiwan, and this commenced a new round of diplomatic battle between Taiwan and China. In 2002, while President Chen Shui-bian took over the chairmanship of the DPP, China deliberately announced its establishment of diplomatic relations with Nauru, one of Taiwan's allies. China's offensive gesture humiliated President Chen and he retaliated by suggesting a referendum on independence.[427] In 2003, Liberia cut diplomatic ties with Taiwan and resumed diplomatic ties with China. At the same year, Taiwan successfully lured China's former ally— Republic of Kiribati to swing recognition to Taiwan. In 2004, China won over the diplomatic ties of Commonwealth of Dominica. As the waging diplomatic war is an all-or-nothing competition, up to now neither side is willing to call for a truce.

Without China's consent on the "dual recognition", up to now it does not exist in the pragmatic international political system. One-China Principle still prevails even though Taiwan tries all kind of tactics—"pragmatic diplomacy", "money diplomacy", "transit diplomacy" or "vacation diplomacy". As China's

---

[427] The related news can be viewed in http://news.bbc.co.uk/2/hi/asia-pacific/2169788.stm and http://www.taipeitimes.com/News/edit/archives/2002/07/30/158310

comprehensive power is far superior to Taiwan's, Taiwan's direct confrontation against China in the diplomatic arena will backfire. When President Chen advocates that "we need to walk our own road"[428], even though he makes no clear definition about where the destination of "our own road" leads to, China has already marked his remark as a path toward Taiwan independence and adopted a stringent standard to examine Taiwan's international activities.[429] As Taiwan intends to reposition itself in the international community without China's approval, it is expected that China will exert all its clout to block Taiwan's road to anywhere but unification. The diplomatic war between China and Taiwan is going to wage on till the One-China Principle is taken care of.

---

[428] See "Interview With Taiwanese President Chen Shui-bian", *The Washington Post*, October 10, 2003

[429] China's comment about Chen can be viewed in several official Chinese websites http://english.peopledaily.com.cn/200208/06/eng20020806_100979.shtml

4.4 Taiwan's Domestic Politics

A nation-state is not a homogeneous entity. It is usually constituted by various political parties, civilian groups and official or semi-official institutions with complicated intra- and inter-relationships. Since Taiwan has entered a popular democratic phase and democracy is rule of the majority by means of election, therefore, in order to win the majority of votes, political parties offer the space for the civilian groups to influence the regulations of the government by means of lobbyism. The ruling party tries to manipulate all kinds of groups by compromising its policies and regulations to entice the support of the voters; on the contrary, the opposition parties must exert their clout to supervise the policies and regulations to ensure these will not hamper their way to being elected. Under this basic structure of democracy, to garner votes becomes the primary objective of politicians.

In order to win the election, Taiwanese politicians bipolarize Taiwan's society into pro-status quo[430] and pro-independence camps or "pan-blue" coalition and "pan-green"[431] coalition. Although pro-independence activists dominate the discourse on Taiwan's national identity which is intertwined with the emotion over the cross-Strait relations, the international environment assists pro-status quo camp to balance the booming pro-independence power. As a result, whenever mainland China launches verbal attacks against Taiwan or contains Taiwan's international activities, pro-independence camp will capitalize on China's hostile gestures to demand the recognition of Taiwanese voters for an independent Taiwan; at the same time, pro-status quo camp will exploit the possibility of a cross-Strait war to prevent Taiwanese voters from being drawn to independence camp.

In competing for votes, each party requires its trademark to differentiate itself from its opponent. The trademark represents its ideologies as well as its constituents. Once the trademark has been labeled, it will not be easy for a party to get off the impression which the trademark bestows on it. However, once the voters discover what they vote for is not what they expect for from the "trademark", they are going to withdraw their support. Thus, the voters, especially those trademark-loyal voters, hold the "stick" to demand the party abide by its ideology.

---

[430] Although the pro-independence camp always label its counterpart as a pro-unification camp, however its counterpart has never admitted that it supports unification, but stresses that Taiwan should peacefully coexist with China and leave the unification-independence for the future generation. Therefore, it will be more precise to term it "pro-status quo camp".

[431] "Pan-blue" is named according to the representative color of the KMT, "pan-green" the color of the DPP; "pan-blue" coalition supports pro-status quo, "pan-green" pro-independence.

The historical complex has determined the distinct identities for the KMT and the DPP. As a founder of Republic of China and an exile from Chinese mainland, the KMT government on Taiwan had kept a dream of regaining mainland for many years. With the historical background which strongly implies its root on China, KMT is still labeled as a pro-unification party especially by its opponent—the DPP, even though President Lee Teng-hui initiated a sequence of processes to modify its mainland policy and to deviate from the path to unification. On the contrary, the DPP walked through the era of suppression from the KMT regime. The "228 incident" which took place in 1947 marked a tragic massacre of the Taiwanese elites and later became the political asset of the DPP. During the autocratic rule of the KMT government, the major opposition was exiled overseas, and the KMT issued the "black list" to prohibit them from coming back to Taiwan. Consequently, they became firm advocates of the Formosan nationalism and sought for the founding of a new nation.

In order to win an election, Taiwanese politicians are willing to take advantage of cross-Strait relations, international affairs and economic issues for their personal gain. They will escalate the cross-Strait tension, upset the US—Taiwan's only patron state, and impose restrictions on the economic exchange between Taiwan and China. Whichever party controls the governmental apparatus will also dominate the discourse of Taiwanese culture and history. While the KMT was in power, Taiwanese people had to speak mandarin and study Chinese culture; when the DPP took over the reign, it intended to dilute the importance of mandarin by promoting "the language of mother tone" and to rewrite Taiwan's history to sever the umbilical between China and Taiwan. As a result, when the DPP is in power, unless the DPP is willing to disavow its ideology of Taiwan independence publicly, China will never conduct any official talk with Taiwan to avoid misunderstanding that China is soft on its One-China Principle.

4.4.1 The Investments in Ethnicity

The Han Chinese is the largest ethnic group in Taiwan, comprising roughly 98 percent of Taiwan's population. The indigenous people of Taiwan's eleven different aboriginal tribes and around 60 other non-Han minorities from Chinese mainland accounted for the remaining 2 percent. The Han Chinese on Taiwan is usually classified into two sub-groups: "Taiwanese" (Tai Wan Ren)[432] and mainlanders (Wai Sheng Ren). Mainlanders indicate those post World War II immigrants, most of who moved to Taiwan with KMT in 1949 after KMT was defeated by Chinese Communist Party (CCP), and those children whose fathers are mainlanders. Those who descend from the early Han Chinese immi-

[432] "Taiwanese" refers only to the descendants of the early immigrants.

grants are "Taiwanese", who can be subdivided even further into Hakka people, who are mostly from Guangdong Province, and Minnan people, who are mostly form Southern Fujianese. Minnan people account for roughly 64 percent of the total Han population in Taiwan, Hakka people roughly 21 percent, mainlanders slightly less than 15 percent.

Table 4-5 Composition of the KMT Central Committee, 1952-1993

Election Date		Congress	"Taiwanese"		Total
Year	Date		No.	%	No.
1952	Oct.19	7th	1	3.1	32
1957	Oct.23	8th	3	6.0	50
1963	Nov.22	9th	4	5.4	74
1969	Apr.8	10th	6	6.1	99
1976	Nov.17	11th	19	14.6	130
1981	Apr.3	12th	29	19.3	150
1988	Jul.12	13th	62	34.4	180
1993	Aug. 17	14th	112	53.3	210

Source: Kau, 1996, P. 291, Table 1, modified by the author.

Under the two Chiangs' regime, because of two Chiangs' mainlander background, the government was under the control of mainlanders. Therefore, though mainlanders were minority in Taiwan population, they dominated the political resources. Table 4-5 pointed out that in the seventh Party Congress, "Taiwanese" accounted for only 3.1 percent of KMT Central Committee[433]. In contrast, mainlanders accounted for less than 15% of Taiwanese population, but occupied as many as 96.9% of seats. In 1957, the number of "Taiwanese" elected in KMT Central committee increased to 3, and percentage increased to 6%; in 1963, the number increased to 4, but the percentage decreased to 5.4 percent; in 1969, the number increased again to 6, and the percentage rebounded to 6.1 percent. The percentage of "Taiwanese" in KMT Central Committee did not reflect the fact that "Taiwanese" were the majority. In 1988, the end of two Chiang's era, the percentage of "Taiwanese" elected to the KMT Central Committee reached 34.4 percent, but this percentage did not reflect the reality that "Taiwanese" was Taiwan's largest population. The power sharing with "Taiwanese" was apparently inadequate. Although as the time shifted, more and more "Taiwanese" were elected to the KMT Central Committee, during the two Chiangs' era (1949-88) "Taiwanese" were rela-

[433] Before Chiang Ching-kuo initiated the process of democratization, Taiwan was ruled by one-party government. KMT controlled not only the party machine, but also government and military.

tively deprived of their political participation. This phenomenon that minority ruled the majority was not improved until Lee Teng-hui took over the reign. Not until 1993, the fourteenth Party Congress, "Taiwanese" for the first time became the majority in KMT Central Committee.

Table 4-6 Ethnic Composition of Top Positions (1987)

Category	"Taiwanese"		Mainlander		Total
	No.	%	No.	%	No.
Party	33	13.6	210	86.4	243
Government	21	14.0	129	86	150
Parliament	220	16.9	1,080	83.1	1,300
Military	15	4.3	335	95.7	350
Police	11	7.3	139	92.7	150
Combined	300	13.7	1,893	86.3	2,193

Source: Kau, 1996, P. 291, Table 2.

Table 4-6 further verified the fact that mainlanders controlled not only the party machine, but also government, military, parliament and police. In 1987, mainlanders who accounted for less than 15% of Taiwanese population filled up 86.4% of high positions in party, 86% of high positions in government, 83.1% of high positions in parliament, 95.7% of high positions in military force, and 92.7% of high positions in police force. In contrast, "Taiwanese" composed around 85 percent of Taiwanese population on Taiwan but gained only a meager number of seats in all public sectors.

Table 4-7 Policy-level Officials of "Taiwanese" Origins (1983)

Cabinet Level		Provincial Level[a]		County-City Level[b]	
No.	%	No.	%	No.	%
7	40	18	75	21	100

Note: [a] Includes a provincial governor and members of the provincial council.
[b] Includes county executives, and mayors of the five cities under the jurisdiction of the Taiwan Province. (The mayors of Taipei and Kaohsiung are not included; they are both Taiwanese)

Source: Lu, 1985, P. 1088, Table 6

Table 4-7 indicated that mainlanders were the majority in central government, but they gradually released their political resources to "Taiwanese" in provincial level and county-city level. 100% of policy level officials in county-city level were "Taiwanese"; "Taiwanese" also filled up 75% of policy level positions in provincial level. However, in cabinet, mainlander accounted for 60% of policy level positions.

Though Chiang Ching-kuo intended to rectify the power imbalance between mainlanders and "Taiwanese" by implementing "Promote Young 'Taiwanese'[434] (Chui Tai Ching)", mainlanders still hold the major positions in central political organizations. Because of the historical background of the KMT, during the two Chiang's[435] era, mainlanders, the minority, controlled the political power in Taiwan regardless of the reality that "Taiwanese" constituted the major population of Taiwan. This imbalance of political power between mainlanders and "Taiwanese" intrigued the social unrest of the power struggle and moreover served as a base for the DPP to cultivate its "Taiwanese" racism. This imbalance of power between early and newly immigrants was invariably the driving force behind ethnic hostility, and the asset for the "Taiwanese" politicians to purge their dissidents. After all, the ill distribution of ethnics in governmental positions eventually backfired on the KMT government.

Aside from the imbalance of political power in "Taiwanese" and mainlanders, another major cause of the disturbance in Taiwanese ethnic disputes is the "228 incident", which also represents the "white terror" imposed on "Taiwanese" by the "alien regime"[436]—the KMT government. The "228 incident" happened in 1947 was attributed to the fault of KMT, and because early KMT was composed mostly by mainlanders, the mainlanders bear the guilt of political crackdown on civilians. The incident might pass long time ago, but some "Taiwanese" politicians successfully transformed the tragedy to their personal political assets, and the repeated emergence of the shadowy "228 incident" haunted both "Taiwanese" and mainlanders. The land-reform performed by KMT government constituted another cause for the resentment of "Taiwanese" to mainlanders. Since the land-reform redistributed the wealth of the "Taiwanese", some landlords who were forced to give up their lands resented the policy of the KMT government. As the officials of the KMT government were mostly mainlanders, the resentment from "Taiwanese" landlords to the KMT government also spilled over to the mainlanders. For that reason, the

---

[434] This movement intended to promote Taiwanese talents and to promote the localization of KMT and Lee Teng-hui was a major beneficiary from this movement.

[435] Two Chiangs indicate Chiang Kai-shek and Chiang Ching-kuo.

[436] The term "alien regime" was first coined by President Lee Teng-hui. When interviewed with Ryotaro Shiba in 1994, Lee Teng-hui described the KMT as an "alien regime", See "Taiwan Independence: Image and Reality," by Dennis Van Vanken Hickey, the paper for the annual meeting of the American Political Science Association, Atlanta, Georgia, September 2-5, 1999.

"mainlander" background becomes the original sin for Taiwanese politicians who were unfortunately born in a mainlander family.[437]

Breton pointed out that as long as nationalism exists in societies, the investments in nationality or ethnicity are profitable even though they are profitable only to specific and identifiable groups.[438] As winning an election becomes the provenience of political power and the political power struggle in Chinese history has been a winner-take-it-all type, many Taiwanese politicians are enticed to unscrupulously ruin the name of their competitors in order to win an election. For the then opposition party—DPP is constructed by "Taiwanese", especially Minnan people, ethnic mobilization becomes an expedient way for them to defeat the vested interest group, KMT, most of whose members are mainlanders. Because the DPP intends to dominate the discourse of "Taiwanese", the DPP clearly defines its political goals and platform as to build a free, democratic and independent nation on self-determination. In order to harvest the orthodox representative of indigenous "Taiwanese", the DPP claimed the KMT government as an "alien regime" from mainland China. By articulating the concept of the "sorrow of the Taiwanese people" which means from Qing Dynasty through the Japanese colonial rule till alien KMT regime, "Taiwanese" had never been the master of their fate. As the DPP connoted the KMT government as a Japanese-imperialism-like dictatorship, for "Taiwanese", the replacement of the alien KMT regime become the only way to redemption.[439]

However, the DPP's "Taiwanese" mobilization did not draw enough support from "Taiwanese" to rival against the KMT in Lee Teng-hui's era, because Lee i the first "Taiwanese" president. Lee successfully borrowed DPP's discourse to appeal for "Taiwanese" public to expel his political opponents within the KMT—most of them were mainlanders; at the same time, he weakened the strength of the DPP. Cheng Cheng-yu, a representative for the Southern Taiwan's society said Lee Teng-hui capitalized on the DPP to get ride of

[437] The most renowned example is in order to facilitate the winning chance of the DPP Taipei mayoral nominee—Lee Ying-yuan, President Chen openly smeared Ma Ying-jeou on his ethnicity. Ma was a mainlander born in Hong Kong, so Chen suggests Ma "has Hong Kong foot which will (itch to) take the Hong Kong Road". See "Born in Hong Kong" by Joe Hung, Sep 3, 2002, *National Policy Foundation Commentary*
James Soong, the former Taiwan Governor, is especially the scapegoat of ethnicity. His mainlander background and his broke-up with Lee Teng-hui—the father of Taiwan make him an easy target for the political smear game. He has been accused of "selling out" Taiwan to China.
See "'Traitor' Taut Goad PFP to Action," by Sandy Huang, Jul 13, 2003, *Taipei Times*
"Ultimate High-stakes Battle for Taiwan's Destiny," by Laurence Eyton, Mar 17, 2004, *Asia Times*
[438] Breton, 1964, P.376
[439] Quoted from Kau, 1996, P. 298

his mainlander opponents in the KMT and created the "Lee Teng-hui complex" which overwhelmed the DPP and guarded the KMT regime.[440]

After Lee took over the presidency from Chiang Ching-kuo, because he is a "Taiwanese", and "Taiwanese" are the majority of the Taiwanese population, to invest in ethnic dynamic offers him an edge over those mainlander-politicians. By appealing to the ethnic dynamic, Lee successfully drove off his mainlander-competitors within the KMT[441]. In order to dilute DPP's discourse of "Taiwanese", Lee adopted the tactics of Taiwanizing KMT and recruiting more "Taiwanese" into KMT's decision ranks. Putting on the aureole of the first "Taiwanese" president, Lee successfully manipulated the ethnic dispute to his personal benefit.

Lee successfully transformed KMT to a localized party by advocating Taiwan as a center rather than solely an appendage of China, and Lee even brought up the concept of "New Taiwanese" to facilitate the winning of Ma Ying-jeou[442] over Chen Shui-bian during the 1998 Taipei mayoral election, Lee himself garnered the support not only from the pro-unification supporters but

---

[440] Even the former DPP chairman Lin Yi-Hsiung admitted that the DPP has been beset by a so-called "Lee Teng-hui complex", because DPP was lazy and "placed its hopes on one leader." See "DPP Head Voices Moderate Stance on Referendum, Party Line," Mar 24, 1999, *China Times*

[441] After Chiang's death, Lee Teng-hui became the first "Taiwanese" president (in contrast to two Chiangs and Yen Chia-kan's mainlander background) in Taiwan's history. At the early era of Lee's presidency, the political power was dispersed among some powerful mainland-born figures. Lee Huan, the secretary-general of KMT, controlled the party machine; Yu Kuo-hwa, the prime minister, directed the cabinet, Chiang We-go, the secretary-general of National Security Council, served as a chief intelligence figure; Hau Pei-tsun, the Chief of the General Staff, took in charge of the armed force. The only role left for Lee Teng-hui to play was the figurehead of Taiwan.

From then on, he successfully garnered the support from the populace by waving the banner of reformist and his "Taiwanese" background. He purged his mainland-background political competitors one by one. The most renowned case should be the step-down of the former Premier Hau Pei-tsun. After the 1992 legislature election, the opposition party legislators demanded Hau to resign. If Lee did not encourage the legislators of then opposition party (DPP) to serve as his attackers, at least he acquiesced to their behaviors towards his cabinet head. Some KMT's pro-Lee legislators joined their counterparty's activities to assault Hau. Hau was deemed as an anti-Taiwan-independent leader with a mainland background. Those pro-independent DPP legislators had every reason to find fault with him, but those pro-Lee legislators who led by Huang Chu-wen also initiated attack on Hau, and asked him to step down. Democratization and Taiwanization became Lee's stratagems to purge their political rivals. With the purge of Hau Pei-tsun from the premiership, Lee Teng-hui successfully controlled the exclusive power in Taiwan. The transfer of executive power from the hands of mainland old-timers to the native elite was largely completed with the appointment of Lien Chan as the first native Taiwanese premier.

[442] Ma Ying-jeou is a mainlander born in Hong Kong.

also from the pro-independent ones. However, after KMT lost the regime in the 2000 presidential election, KMT's supporters deemed Lee as a sinner who sold out KMT and ROC to the pro-independent Chen Shui-bian, and Lee was forced to step down from the chairmanship of the KMT, and because he supported the foundation of Taiwan Solidarity Union (TSU) and campaigned for the TSU's candidates during the 2001 legislature election, he was formally expelled from the KMT. Ever since he resigned from the chairmanship of the KMT, he could only play the role of a pro-independent extremist to maintain his influence in Taiwan's politics. After Lee left the KMT, though the KMT positions itself as a guardian for status quo, the DPP labels the KMT a pro-unification party in Taiwan's political spectrum.

The ethnic mobilization has become the tool of power struggle for Taiwanese politicians. Worst of all, in order to take advantage of the "sub-ethnic" differences,[443] Taiwanese politicians further strengthen the "sub-ethnic" identity by involving the unification vs. independence issue into this "sub-ethnic" rivalry under the presumption that mainlanders are assumed to still hold the dream of reunification with China and "Taiwanese" are supposed to approve for Taiwan independence. The hardship of cross-Strait relationships gives "Taiwanese" politicians an opportunity to exploit for their personal gain. Since Taiwan's arch-rival, red Communist China can be easily portrayed as a vicious, wanton enemy, it surely will be an effective way for "Taiwanese" politicians to smear their political competitors—especially those mainlanders by labeling them as the "fellow-travelers of the Chinese Communist Party" or "the fifth column of China". After all, pro-independence "Taiwanese" politicians are advocating for "Chinese vote for Chinese" and "Taiwanese vote for Taiwanese". The insinuation is clear: mainlanders are pro-unification; they are not Taiwanese but Chinese, so they shouldn't get votes from Taiwanese, and Taiwanese should support "Taiwanese" politicians who advocate Taiwan independence.

During Lee Teng-hui's presidency, Lee had devoted to the creation of Taiwan identity in contrast to the two Chiang's China identity. By emphasizing "the sorrow of the Taiwanese people", he differentiated himself from the authoritative two-Chiangs' regime; by rivaling against the gigantic China, he established Taiwan identity on the destruction of China identity. Because the emergence of Taiwan identity comprising the Taiwanese nationalism and cultural pride has further distanced Taiwanese people from unifying with China, and the pro-independence politicians need Taiwan identity to demonize China and their political rivals to consolidate their political power, if the current situation continues, the emerging Taiwan identity will collide with China's nation-

[443] Since both "Taiwanese" and mainlanders are Han Chinese, instead of addressing "ethnic differences, I would prefer to call it "sub-ethnic" differences.

alism, and the result will be economically as well as politically destructive to Taiwan.

4.4.2 Pan-Blue vs. Pan-Green, a Bipolarizing Taiwan

Aldrich presented a one-dimensional spatial model to verify the distributions of activists in a two-party system and to confirm the existence of party cleavages in which there are stable distributions of activists in the two parties, and their activists are "relatively cohesive within each party and relatively divergent between parties." Because of the presence of activists, when a candidate is considering a winning strategy, he can not deviate from the party doctrine too far; otherwise his candidacy for the party might be challenged by the party's activists.[444]

Since the party activists (camp activists in Taiwan) have been the most active supporters of the party, by devoting their resources to the party, they dominate the right to interpret policies of the party's candidates and they are entitled to screen the policies because the phenomenon of bipolarization in Taiwan's society enables them to play a role as a significant minority. Because all candidates have recognized the fact that although to gain the votes of party activists does not guarantee a winning ticket, without the support of party activists, they are destined to lose. As a result, each camp has to provide most centripetal policies which emphasize on the central ideology of the camp to win the election. Moreover, in order to win the election, each camp has to intensify the political righteousness of its ideology and smear the opposite camp's thoughts to enlarge its social base.

Taiwan's society has been bipolarized by the wrestle between pro-unification and pro-independence ideologies in Taiwan's party politics. However, instead of a two-party system, on the spectrum of unification-independence, Taiwan has transformed into a multi-party but two-camp society, in which Pan-Blue coalition represents pro-unification force, Pan-Green pro-independence. The term of Pan-Blue is derived from the representative color of KMT; the term of Pan-Green indicates that of the DPP. Although the verbal propaganda of a party can influence the general perception regarding the stance of the party on the unification-independence issue, the behaviors of the party and the verbal attacks of its rival parties determine the popular recognition.

Figure 4-2 offers a clear structure relating to the positions of Taiwan's political parties on the issue of unification versus independence. The Pan-Green coalition locates on the right side of Status Quo and is composed by the DPP, TSU & TAIP (Taiwan Independence Party). Among them, TSU & TAIP are the extremist advocates of Taiwan independence, and the DPP shifts its

---

[444] Aldrich, 1983

stance between Taiwan independence and status quo according to the requirements of elections. The Pan-Blue coalition is constituted by the KMT, NP (New Party) and PFP (People First Party). Among them, the KMT has endeavored to contain both "Sinicization" and "Taiwanization" but its Chinese root suggests its pro-unification position; NP has been labeled as a mainlander party which marks it a loyal supporter for the unification; PFP has been labeled as a one-man party which implies that PFP will not exist without James Soong—the former Taiwan Governor and current PFP Chairman, and James Soong's mainlander background places the PFP in the middle between unification and status quo on this unification-independence spectrum.

Figure 4-2 Unification vs. Independence Spectrum of Taiwan's Political Parties

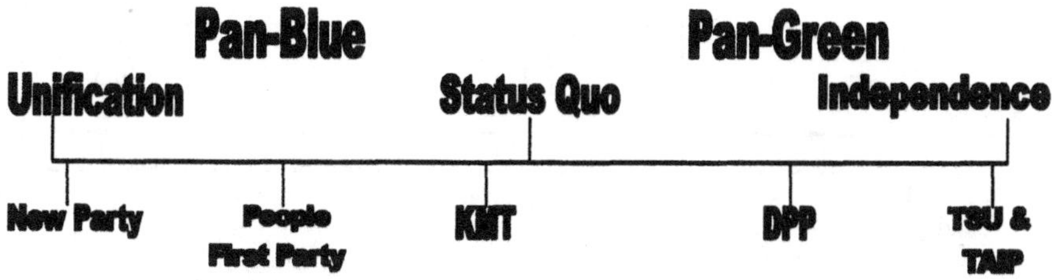

Compiled by the author

Table 4-8 clearly demonstrated that 36.1% of the KMT supporters tended to advocate the future unification; 22.1% had the tendency to support Taiwan independence; 36.7% held a neutral stance on the "unification-independence" issue and had not made any final decision; 5.2% had no idea at all about this issue. In contrast to the social base of the KMT, the DPP had overwhelmingly more pro-independent supporters; 53.1% of DPP supporters were pro-independence, 35.4% pro-status-quo, only 9.1% pro-unification. NP was on the opposite side of the DPP; 58.4% of NP supporters preferred unification; 26.3% wanted to maintain status quo; only 10.5% support Taiwan independence. Thus, Table 4-8 signifies the credibility about Figure 4-2 that the NP has a stronger tendency toward unification than the KMT; the KMT has a stronger tendency to maintain status quo than the DPP, the DPP is the most adamant advocate for Taiwan independence among these three parties. For the supporters of the DPP, one out of the two supported the permanent de facto Taiwan independence, but for the supporters of the KMT, the number dropped to one out of five. Since the KMT and its affiliation (NP) had covered most of the support from the pro-unification mass, the DPP was inevitably located on the other side of the unification vs. independence spectrum, and KMT was pushed toward pro-unification.

Table 4-8 Public Attitudes on the Unification Issue by Party Preference

Unit: %

Party Preference	KMT	DPP	NP[a]	IV[b]	NPP[c]
Immediate independence	3.6	21.0	0.6	4.4	5.4
Maintain status quo, seek independence later	6.9	24.1	5.3	8.5	11.6
Maintain status quo permanently	11.6	8.0	4.6	12.6	11.1
Sub-Total of Pro-independence[d]	*22.1*	*53.1*	*10.5*	*25.5*	*28.1*
Maintain status quo, wait for development	*36.7*	*35.4*	*26.3*	*37.9*	*27.9*
Maintain status quo, seek unification later	33.2	8.2	55.2	16.8	12.9
Immediate unification	2.9	0.9	3.2	3.0	3.6
Sub-Total of Pro-unification[e]	*36.1*	*9.1*	*58.4*	*19.8*	*16.5*
Don't know	5.2	2.3	4.8	16.8	27.4
Total	100	100	100	100	100

Note: [a]: New Party
[b]: Independent voters
[c]: No party preference
[d]: The sum of those who prefer "Immediate independence", "Maintain status quo, seek independence later" and "Maintain status quo permanently". As the status-quo is so-called de facto independence, I arbitrarily attributed "Maintain status quo permanently" to the category of "Pro-independence".
[e]: The sum of those who prefer "Maintain status quo, seek unification later" and "Immediate unification".

Source: Election Studies Center, National Chengchi University, island-wide, face-to-face interviews in summer 1995 and Liu (1999), modified by the author.

Table 4-9 points out that only 7% of Taiwanese people perceived the DPP was pro-unification; 52% thought the DPP was pro-independence; 25% recognized the DPP wanted to maintain status quo. For the stance of TSU on "unification vs. independence", 52% of Taiwanese people acknowledged the TSU as a pro-independence party, but only 17% thought the TSU intended to maintain status quo. As a result, the DPP had a stronger tendency to maintain status quo than the TSU. 39% of Taiwanese people perceived the PFP a pro-unification party; 34% thought the PFP wanted to preserve status quo, and 6% recognized the PFP as pro-independence. In contrast, 48% of Taiwanese people agreed that the KMT was pro-status-quo; 29% consented the KMT was a pro-unification party; only 5% thought the KMT was pro-independence. Therefore, Table 4-9 further verifies the credibility of Figure 4-2. The DPP tilts more to status quo than the TSU, and the KMT is positioned between the DPP and the PFP on the unification-independence spectrum.

Table 4-9 Public Perception on the Party Unification-Independence Position

Unit: %

Party / Status	DPP	KMT	PFP	TSU
Unification	7	29	39	8
Independence	52	5	6	52
Status Quo	25	48	34	17
No Answer/ Unknown	16	19	22	24

Source: TVBS Poll Center, July 30, 2002

The different perceptions regarding to the positions of the PFP and the NP on the independence-unification issue origin from that some former NP legislators openly embrace One-China Principle.[445] On the contrary, James Soong, the PFP leader, has tried to play down his support regarding One-China Principle. TAIP is an as extreme Taiwan-independence supporter as TSU. The foundation of TAIP is to construct a new nation on Taiwan. The founding purpose of the TSU is to rectify the official title of Taiwan from ROC (Republic of China) to ROT (Republic of Taiwan). As a result, both parties share the same goal at their establishments.

The creation of Taiwan identity commenced by Lee Teng-hui successfully alienates Taiwan form China. Table 4-10 clearly demonstrated the trend for Taiwanese people in seeking for "Taiwan identity". As a result, Taiwanese people who recognized themselves as exclusive Chinese are decreasing but at the same time those who perceive themselves as exclusive Taiwanese are dramatically increasing. Table 4-10 indicates that 23.2% of Taiwanese people think they are Chinese in 1992; thought the percentage increases to 26.2% in 1994, from then on, it slides all the way down to 6.3%. On the contrary, the percentage of people who recognize themselves as sole Taiwanese increases from 18.8% in 1992 to 40.6% in 2004. The percentage of Taiwanese people who perceive themselves as both Taiwanese and Chinese maintain its stability, ranging from the highest of 49.%1in 1992 to the lowest of 40.3% in 1998. This phenomenon of shifting self-perception is contributed by China's aggressiveness to Taiwan's international activities, the creation of Taiwan's national identity and the investments in ethnicity by Taiwanese politicians. If this trend of de-Sinicization continues, unless China is willing to disavow its One-China Principle, the collision between Taiwan and China will be inevitable.

---

[445] Such as Hsieh, Chi-ta and Feng, Elmer

Table 4-10 The Self-Perception of Taiwanese People

Year/Month	Exclusive Taiwanese	Both Taiwanese and Chinese	Exclusive Chinese	No Response
1992/12	18.8%	49.1%	23.2%	8.9%
1994/12	20.2%	44.6%	26.2%	8.9%
1996/12	26.2%	46.2%	21.4%	6.2%
1998/12	36.7%	40.3%	16.3%	6.7%
2000/12	37.3%	46.3%	9.1%	7.2%
2002/12	40.5%	45.4%	8.5%	5.6%
2004/06	40.6%	48.3%	6.3%	4.9%

Source: Election Study Center, National Chengchi University, Selected

The transition of self-recognition of Taiwanese people in "Taiwanese vis-à-vis Chinese" was coincided with Taiwan independence movement. Table 4-11 pointed out the transition of Taiwanese preference in the issue of "unification versus independence". For this period of almost one decade, from Dec 1994 to June 2004, the percentage of Taiwanese people who supported an immediate unification had never exceeded 5 percent: the highest was 4.4% and the lowest was 1.3%. Moreover, the percentage of those who requested for an immediate independence struggled around 5%: the highest was 6.7% and the lowest was 2.9%. This phenomenon indicated that the extremists on both ends were minority in Taiwan's society. However, the percentage of Taiwanese people who hold a position of pro-unification decreased from 20% of 1994 to 11.8% of 2004, but at the same period of time, the percentage of those who tilted towards independence increased from 20.9% to 40.4%. Unlike the percentage of Taiwanese people who supported unification or independence unveiled an unmistakable trend, the percentage of Taiwanese people who preferred status quo at the moment fluctuated from the highest 38.5% in the survey of 1994 December to the lowest 24.5% in 1995 December. However, after the 2000 presidential election, the percentage of Taiwanese people who supported status quo at the moment gradually gathered its momentum to bounded back to 34% to 37% from 30% of 2000.

Table 4-11 Public Attitudes on the Unification Issue in Taiwan, by Trend

Unit: %

YY.MM	I.U.[a]	T. U.[b]	**P.U.[c]**	**M.D.[d]**	M.P.[e]	T.I.[f]	I.I.[g]	**P.I.[h]**	N.R.[i]
94.12	4.4	15.6	**20**	**38.5**	9.8	8	3.1	**20.9**	20.5
95.06	2.8	15.8	**18.6**	**28.8**	16.2	7.4	2.9	**26.5**	26.1
95.12	2.3	19.7	**22**	**24.5**	15.5	8.1	3.5	**27.1**	26.3
96.06	2.2	18.1	**20.3**	**29.9**	16.2	9.3	3.6	**29.1**	20.9
96.12	3.3	22.3	**25.6**	**32.2**	13.6	9.9	5.1	**28.6**	13.6
97.06	3	17.7	**20.7**	**31.9**	16.3	11.7	5.5	**33.5**	14
98.06	2.4	15.9	**18.3**	**29.9**	15.9	11	5	**31.9**	19.9
98.12	1.7	15.8	**17.5**	**30.8**	15.9	12.2	6.7	**34.8**	16.8
99.06	2.4	14	**16.4**	**30.4**	19.3	13.4	4.4	**37.1**	16.1
99.12	1.7	18.7	**20.4**	**31.5**	17.3	14.2	5.6	**37.1**	10.9
00.06	1.8	17.2	**19**	**29.5**	19.6	12.5	3	**35.1**	16.3
00.12	2.8	18.2	**21**	**30.3**	16.8	6.5	3.8	**27.1**	21.7
01.06	2.8	17.2	**20**	**36.5**	16.5	10.6	2.9	**30**	13.5
01.12	2.8	18	**20.8**	**34.8**	16.2	10.4	5.1	**31.7**	12.7
02.06	2.3	15.7	**18**	**36.6**	15.2	14.1	3.8	**33.1**	12.1
02.12	2.9	15.7	**18.6**	**35.6**	14.7	13	5.2	**32.9**	13
03.06	2.1	14	**16.1**	**37.2**	16.6	13.7	5.1	**35.4**	11.3
03.12	1.8	11.4	**13.2**	**34.4**	18.2	14.8	6.5	**39.5**	12.9
04.06	1.3	10.5	**11.8**	**36.8**	21.0	15.1	4.3	**40.4**	11.0

Note: [a]: I.U. means Immediate Unification.
[b]: T.U. means Tilt towards Unification.
[c]: P.U.= I.U.+T.U., means Pro-Unification.
[d]: M.D. means Maintain Status Quo, Wait for Development.
[e]: M.P. means Maintain Status Quo Permanently.
[f]: T.I. means Tilt towards Independence.
[g]: I.I. means Immediate Independence.
[h]: P.I.=M.P.+T.I.+I.I., means Pro-Independence.
[i]: N.R. means No Response

Source: Election Study Center, National Chengchi University, calculated by the author

Aside from highlighting the increase of social base for Taiwan independence, Table 4-11 also signified another important feature: in Taiwan the potential independent supporters were outnumbering their counterparts. This also explained the behavior of President Chen Shui-bian, who brought forward "creating a new Constitution in 2006 and implementing it by 2008" to incite a pro-independence fervor, because without the support of "pro-immediate-independence" extremists, he would have lost the reelection in this tight competition. However, the social base of the pro-independence camp was not large enough for Chen to win a one-on-one election, his only chance to win was to bipolarize Taiwan's society and to transform those who want to maintain status quo at moment to maintain status quo permanently. Thus, by labeling his competitor a

Chinese with no love for Taiwan,[446] President Chen Shui-bian could dominate the discourse of Taiwan identity and Taiwan independence.

From the movement of diminishing Chinese-perception in the mindset of Taiwanese people and to that of enhancing Taiwan-independence consciousness, the Pan-Green is eroding the social base of Pan-Blue. Table 4-12 offered further evidence to prove that by promoting Taiwan independence movement and investing "Taiwanese" ethnicity, pro-Taiwan-independence politician was gaining ground in elections. From the election of Taiwan Legislative Yuan, Pan Green was gaining ground on the loss of Pan Blue. In 1995, the percentage of votes for Pan-Blue camp was 59.02%, the highest in the period of 1995 to 2004; it slid to 53.49% in 1998, dipped further to 49.74% in 2001 and dropped to its lowest point, 46.85% in 2004. At the same time, the percentage of votes for Pan Green increased from 1995's 33.17% to 2004's 43.58%. Less than a decade, Pan-Blue posed a 12.17% loss in its votes; on the contrary, Pan-Green gained 10.41% more of votes. The differences between the popularity of Pan-Blue and Pan-Green shrank from 1995's 25.85% to 2004's 2.27%.

Taiwan's multi-party, two-camp politics further complicates the issue of unification vs. independence because each party has to confront its rivals from other camp and at the same time to defy its allies from eroding its social base. On the level of inter-camp competition, each party has to hold the righteousness of "loving Taiwan". Pan-Blue insists on stabilizing the Sino-Taiwan relations by maintaining the status quo; Pan-Green on the other hand intends to unsettle the cross-Strait framework by seeking for Taiwan independence. Pan-Blue blames Plan-Green for dragging Taiwan into a war against China; Pan-Green ridicules Pan-Blue for trampling on Taiwan's national dignity. At the same time, on the level of intra-camp challenge, each party has to exalt its orthodoxy in its camp. The KMT and the PFP have to compete on the legiti-

---

[446] After 319 gunshot incident, in all over the southern and middle Taiwan the party members of the DPP distributed tons of green leaflets, in which written "Number one: Taiwanese. Number two: Chinese." One is Chen Shui-bian's candidate number; two is Lien Chan's. The insinuation is clear: Vote for number one because number one is Taiwanese.
"The Complete Text of Chairman Lien Chan's 520 Speech in Sun Yat-sen Memorial Hall," May 20, 2004, (in Chinese) http://www.npf.org.tw/Symposium/s93/930520.htm
"Lien Chan Interviewed by TV Asahi Questions Arrangements Planned Before the Gunshot Incident," Apr. 15, 2004, *Chinanews.com* (in Chinese)
Student delegates confronted Chen Shui-bian directly against his rhetoric dominancy on "loving Taiwan". One student delegate questioned Chen "Why do you often say other people don't love Taiwan (The question is in Taiwanese)?" He asked Chen not saying "voting for number 1 is 'loving Taiwan'; voting for number 2 is 'Chinese'." He concluded, "This is not identification; this is hatred."
See "Dialogues between Chen Shui-bian and Students, Students Said Chen Is Full of Nonsense," Apr. 12, 2004, *Chinanews.com* (in Chinese).

macy for the advocate of ROC; the DPP and the TSU have to strive for the proponent of ROT. As a result, the fear of being marginalized by the camp-activists keeps parties adherent to the pivot of the camp. Taiwan's politics is trapped in a vicious circle: Taiwanese politicians harvest on the polarization in Taiwan society; the polarization of Taiwan's society then circles back to condition the alternatives of Taiwanese politicians; and the limited alternatives, pro-Blue or pro-Green, further polarize Taiwan's society.

Table 4-12 The Percentage of Votes in Legislative Yuan Election

Unit: %

Camp / Year	Pan Blue	Pan Green	Nonpartisan	Total
2004	46.85	43.58	9.57	100
2001	49.74	41.14	9.12	100
1998	53.49	29.56	16.95	100
1995	59.02	33.17	7.81	100

Note: In 1995 and 1998, Pan Blue is composed by KMT and NP, Pan Green only DPP. In 2001 and 2004, Pan Blue adds one more member, PFT; Pan Green adds TSU.

Source: UDN News Center, and Election Study Center, National Chengchi University, calculated by the author.

As the fierce inter- and intra-camp competition polarizes Taiwan's society, Taiwanese people are driven towards the position of pro-independence and pro-status-quo, not pro-unification. Chinese compresses the international living space of Taiwan; at the same time, pro-independence politicians appeal to anti-unification and anti-China to win the approval of Taiwanese people. As the living space of pro-unification is compressed in Taiwan's society, based on the consideration of ballot, less and less Taiwanese politicians are willing to embrace unification. AS China believes in its One-China Principle and Taiwan strives for self-determination in which pro-unification is no longer a viable option, the parting political ideologies between Taiwan and China will escalate the danger of a cross-Strait confrontation.

Figure 4-3 clearly depicts that the Pan-Green coalition is on the extreme independence of the unification-independence spectrum, and China is on the opposite side, the unification, of the spectrum. There is no zone for China to compromise with Taiwan Pan-Green coalition. Although Pan-Blue locates in the center of the spectrum, in fear that its social base will be further eroded by Pan-Green if it consents on the unification, Pan-Blue will not openly embrace the unification with China until the anti-China sentiment subsides. Taiwan's domestic political competition scapegoats the cross-relations. As long as the bipolarization of Taiwan's society does not come to an end, the cross-Strait relations will be crucified, and the shadow of a cross-Strait war will loom over Taiwan.

Figure 4-3 The Political Positions of Major Actors on the Unification Issue

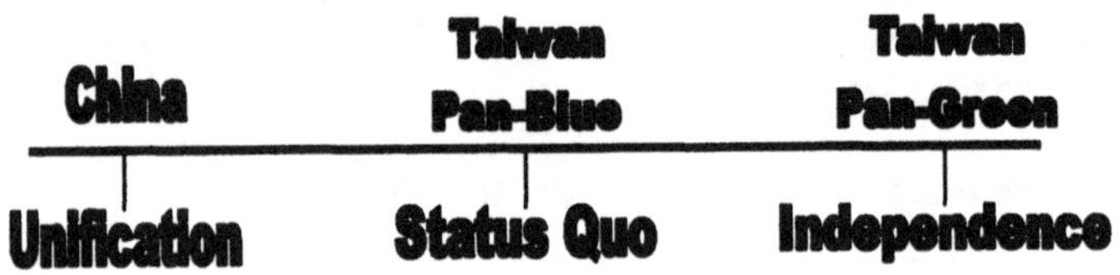

Compiled by the author

4.5 War vs. Peace

Taking off its old-shell of ideological advocate, China at current stage emphasizes on the economic development and international cooperation instead. With its economic ambition ahead, it is the last thing in the world for China to resort to any form of violence in solving Taiwan issue. In Long Yong-tu's rhetoric, China intended to construct a win-win mechanism in which China devoted on a "peaceful rising" and to transform itself to a large market.[447] Shambaugh also points out that based on economic reasons China prefers peaceful means on resolving Taiwan issue. He also argues China does not want to use force or coercion to bring back Taiwan because China realizes that once China appeals to violence to resolve the Taiwan issue, China will be ostracized by international community.[448]

Moreover, as the globalization has brought China wealth, the economic integration between China and Taiwan strengthens China's leverage over Taiwan. As a result, Chinese leaders believe that trends across the Taiwan Strait are moving in China's favor and time is on their side.[449] The use of force against Taiwan will arouse the public indignation which will impede China from becoming a great power. Even though Beijing realizes that the irreversible economic and social integration between China and Taiwan has placed it in a better strategic position in cross-Strait disagreement, however Taiwan's political dynamics has sent an alarming signal to Chinese leaders. As the price of allowing Taiwan to drift toward independence will be for them too high to pay, they have no other choice but to place Taiwan issue on priority.

In contrast to China's dominance in cross-Strait economic relations, the losing economic edge has driven pro-independence Taiwanese politician to seek for political means to shelter their advocacy of Taiwan independence. From "two-state theory", "one country on each side", "building a new nation in 2008", to "creating a new constitution in 2006 and implementing it in 2008", Lee Teng-hui plays the forerunner and Chen Shui-bian a follower.[450] As Lee Teng-hui and Chen Shui-bian in fact lead the TSU and the DPP respectively, the intra-camp power struggle forces these two Taiwanese political leaders to

[447] Quoted from "Peaceful Rising Addressed," news released through China's official website—China Economic Information Network.

[448] "Is China a Military Threat?" from Mark Sparrough's interview with David Shambaugh, American Defense Monitor, http://www.cdi.org/adm/1340/Shambaugh.html

[449] See Medeiros and Fravel (2003) and "Report on the National Committee on American Foreign Policy: Delegation Trip to the People's Republic of China and Taiwan, January 13-23, 2003," by George D. Schwab and Donald S. Zagoria.

[450] Lee introduced two-state theory in 1999; Chen brought up his "one country on each side" in 2002. In 2002, Lee advocated "building a new nation in 2008"; in 2003, Chen introduced "creating a new constitution in 2006 and implementing it in 2008."

tightly embrace the ideology of Taiwan independence. When Lee proposed the concept of "building a new nation in 2008", Chen supplemented with the idea of "creating a new constitution in 2006 and implementing it in 2008". They were racing towards Taiwan independence in order to be acknowledged as the leader of the Pan-Green alliance.[451]

Taiwan independence extremists intend to hold 2008 Olympics hostage for their Taiwan independent attempts.[452] Their move makes 2008 a very sensitive year for China. Former president Lee Teng-hui's remark on his advocacy for building a new nation in 2008 has revealed the intellectual worth. He said, "2008 will be the year when China's nationalism reaches its pinnacle. The dam in Sanxia (the Three Gorges Dam) will be completed, the highway connecting Nanjing and Chongqing will be finished, and Beijing will host the Olympic Games."[453] On the surface, Lee encouraged Taiwanese people to strengthen Taiwan nationalism to rival against China's booming nationalism accompanying with the accomplishment of major national infrastructure and the international fame of hosting Olympic Games. In fact, it was his another adventurism in a strategically calculating way to effectuate his "two-state" theory by taking advantage of China's hosting 2008 Olympic Game. Lee has tried this scheme once. In 1999, Lee brought up "two-state" theory to galvanize the fragile Sino-US relations and to woo the support from the US. At that time, the Sin-US relations were at their ebb because of the bombing of the Chinese Embassy in Belgrade. However, the Clinton administration responded to Lee's "two state" theory by its adamant support of One-China Principle and accused him a trouble maker. Lee's "two-state" theory backfired and constructed a base for the rapprochement between China and the US.

Because the purpose of Olympics is to establish a "peaceful and better world,"[454] Lee expects the peaceful purpose of Olympic Games will shackle China's use of force against Taiwan independence. Most of Taiwanese politicians share a common belief called "as long as the head passes through, the body will also follow through (Tou Guo Shen Jiu Guo)." If China does not respond right away to Taiwan's de jure independence, according to Taiwanese politicians' logic, it indicates the success of Taiwan independence, because China's nonresponse proves that the "head has successfully passed through," and all the rest is only a natural process of being. Moreover, in separatists'

---

[451] Quoted from "Chen's New Constitution Triggered all Kinds of Arguments," Sep 29, 2003, *BBC Chinese News*

[452] "Taiwanese separatists plan to turn the Beijing 2008 Olympics into a 'hostage' to their cause," quoted from "Taiwan separatists target Olympics", Nov. 21, 2003, China Daily.

[453] "Lee Cautions 2008 Carries China Threat," by Lin Mei-chun, Jul 25, 2002, *Taipei Times*

[454] See "House Resolution on Consideration of Beijing for 2008 Olympics," in the House of Representatives Sep. 28, 2000. http://japan.usembassy.gov/e/p/tp-r067.html

mindset, Taiwan still holds a trump card—an American card—to ward off the attack from China. President George W. Bush's "blank cheque" should be able to deter the military action from China[455]. Although Bush administration has stealthily readjusted its stance on cross-Strait issue from tilting toward Taiwan to tilting toward China, its subtle expression leaves enough room for Taiwanese politician to maneuver. After President George W. Bush personally delivered a message against Taiwan independence by claiming that the US oppose the comments and actions of Taiwan's leader intending to unilaterally change the status quo,[456] and James A. Kelly, Assistant Secretary of State for East Asian and Pacific Affairs reaffirmed the necessity of the US on its one China policy and its stance against Taiwan independence,[457] in the Survey on Taiwanese Public Perception of Cross-Strait Security conducted from June 25 to June 29 by the Election Study Center of National Chengchi University, up to 52% of Taiwanese interviewees thought the US would send military force to Taiwan's aid; 23.3% of interviewees thought the US would not help Taiwan.[458] The US attitude had lured most of Taiwanese people in believing that the US would come to Taiwan's rescue. Since Taiwan's independence timetable had been laid on the table, China's countermeasures would also be in place. The US verbal opposition would not deter the escalation form either side across the Strait.

4.5.1 The Failure of the US Cross-Strait Policy

As the US plays a pivot to deter an outbreak of war in the cross-Strait stalemate, a tilt toward Beijing will risk encouraging Beijing to harden its line as well as a

---

[455] When U.S. President George W. Bush openly declared that the United States would do "whatever it took to help Taiwan defend herself" in case of an attack from China," pro-independent extremists would grab the chance to interpret what he said was equivalent a "blank cheque" to Taiwan. Moreover, Chairwoman Therese Shaheen had told President Chen Shui-bian during his stopover in New York that Bush was his "secret guardian angel". Although George W. Bush also made a harsh rhetoric to Chen's intention to hold a referendum to unilaterally change the status quo, however the mixed signals from the Bush administration opened a door for Chen to select the messages he wanted to convey to Taiwanese people, and left the space for pro-independence extremist to maneuver in challenging China's One-China Principle.

See "Bush Pledges Whatever it Takes to Defend Taiwan," *CNN* White House Correspondent Kelly Wallace, Apr 25, 2001

"Illusions and Political Spin in Taipei," By David G Brown, Dec 11, 2003, *Asia Times*

"United States and Taiwan: Diplomatic But Triumphal Progress" By Susan V. Lawrence, Nov 13, 2003, *Far Eastern Economic Review*

[456] "President Warns Taiwan On Independence Efforts" Washington Post, Dec.10, 2003

[457] Testimony at a hearing on Taiwan, House International Relations Committee, Washington DC, April 21, 2004

[458] The survey is published by Business Weekly on July 22, 2004.

tilt toward Taipei will strengthen Taiwanese adventurism.[459] To preserve the cross-Strait stability, the US once had committed to strategic ambiguity by which the US maintained an ambiguous stance on how it would respond to China's attack on Taiwan. However, when George W. Bush took over the white house, he reflected the US desire for "moral clarity" on Taiwan issue by commenting the US would do "whatever it took to help Taiwan defend itself" and "the Chinese must understand that".[460] His remark undermined the US decades-long policy of strategic ambiguity. Moreover, in order to satisfy the need of American weaponry merchants, Bush administration escalated the etiquette for the reception of Taiwan President Chen Shui-bian, an obstinate Taiwan independence advocate in China's mind.[461] Although the US repeatedly emphasized the unofficial features of Chen's stopover in New York, Chen commenced several precedents as a Taiwan president on the US soil: he was the first Taiwan president to make comments to the media since the US severed the diplomatic ties with Taiwan in 1979; he was also the first Taiwan president allowed to make a public speech in a major American city since the break in diplomatic relations, and he was allowed to host a lunch for congressmen and a senator with media to cover his opening remarks[462].

In view of Chen's pro-independence background, undoubtedly it would trigger the fantasy of pro-independence extremists that Bush administration

---

[459] Nathan, 2000, P. 104

[460] In 1999, Paul Wolfowitz and Richard Armitage advocated for greater "moral clarity" on Taiwan's status by arguing that the US should unambiguously stand on the side of democratic Taiwan.
"The Lure of the Status Quo over Taiwan," by Janadas Devan, *Strait Times*, May 1, 2004.

[461] When Chen Shui-bian made his historical stopover trip in New York, he was arranged to share the same table with "merchants of death" in his award of Human Rights. Therese Shaheen, a more businesswoman than official, escorting President Chen all along his trip in the US, triggered serious disputes about her role as a broker in arms deal between Taiwan and the US or a true friend of Taiwan. Later, Bush administration posed a high profile to demand Taiwan to pass NT$610.8 billion (US$18.25 billion) budget for weapons purchases from the US. Taiwan's legislators wanted Washington to provide detailed quotes for the price of the equipment, but on the contrary, the US wanted Taiwan to pass the budget first, and then go out to bid for individual items. Moreover only two pages of vague cost summaries were provided by the US, and legislators complained it was impossible to make policy decision based on these.
See "The Letter from Taiwan: Chen Shui-bian's Breakthrough," Nov. 10, 2003, *BBC News*, (in Chinese), "Lawmakers defend and criticize Therese Shaheen," Jun 22, 2004, *Taipei Times*, "Weapons Budget Needed to Protect Nation, Says MAC," By Melody Chen, Jun 19, 2004, *Taipei Times*, and "Arms Talks Leave Wang Unsatisfied," By Charles Snyder, Jun 25, 2004, *Taipei Times.*

[462] See "United States and Taiwan: Diplomatic But Triumphal Progress," by Susan V. Lawrence, Nov 13, 2003, *Far Eastern Economic Review.*

had shifted its stance on its Taiwan policy from "not supporting" to "not opposing" Taiwan independence. As a result, the pro-independence politicians were encouraged to push the envelope by throwing out issues with significance of Taiwan independence such as adding "Issued in Taiwan" to the cover of ROC passports[463], rectifying the names of all relevant government agencies and state-owned firms to "Taiwan",[464] disintegrating Taiwan's history from China's history by claiming Taiwan's national history and geography should not cover China and Mongolia,[465] as well as campaigning for rectifying the name of Taiwan. Although all these gestures did not effectuate Taiwan independence, the animus of these actions was aimed at de-Sinicization to accomplish Taiwan independence and could not pass China's scrutiny without rousing strong protests from China.

Unlike China, which sternly inspected each movement of those Taiwan independence activists, the US overlooked their tactics of "salami slice" (or "creeping independence" as what China claimed) towards Taiwan independence until the campaign gathered its momentum and was difficult to control. The US deliberately or negligently tolerated the content behind the action of adding "Taiwan" on ROC passports by emphasized that Taiwan authorities' decision would not affect Washington's Taiwan policy.[466] Although the US could not interfere into how Taiwan defined its national history and geography, however, when the US realized that the Taiwan independence movement threatened the peaceful coexistence of the US and China and intended to implement crisis management by opposing Taiwan's intention to change the names of government agencies and state-owned enterprises as it was Taiwan's unilateral action to change the status quo,[467] the US could no longer contain the Taiwan independence movement. Although the US expressed its opposition through its daily press briefing, President Chen Shui-bian completely ignored it by vowing his determination to change the names and declaring that the US did not support Taiwan's moves to rectify the names because of China's opposition and the US simply conveyed China's attitude.[468]

---

463 See "Chang Gives His Approval to Passports," by Monique Chu and Ko Shu-ling, Jan 15, 2002, *Taipei Times.*

464 See "Chen Pledges to Change Names," by Huang Tai-ling, Dec 6, 2004, *Taipei Times.*

465 See "Test Must Be Related to Taiwan, Says Lin Yu-tee," Nov. 30, 2004, *Taipei Times.*

466 See "'Taiwan' Passport Doesn't Impact US," Jun 15, 2003, *Taipei Times.*

467 The US Department of State, Daily Press Briefing, Adam Ereli, Deputy Spokesman, Dec 6, 2004

468 "Bian Emotionally Rebuts the US, the President's Office: Mending after Election (Bian Gi Qin Din Mei, Fu Fang: Xuan Hou Zai Xiou Bu)," Dec 8, 2004, *China Times*, in Chinese "Say 'Taiwan' Aloud, Chen Urges People," by Jewel Huang, Dec 9, 2004, *Taipei Times*

If the US wished to deter a cross-Strait war by adopting one-way deterrence, the coming result would disappoint it. Moreover, the potential threat of a cross-Strait war was not clearly disclosed to Taiwanese people. Unless the US was willing to commit itself on a Taiwan independence war without second thought, the US should not send out confusing messages to be maneuvered by Taiwanese politicians. Taiwanese people have been too confused about the ambiguous messages from the US to make a clear judgment about the potential cross-Strait crisis. In order to serve their purpose of "building a new nation" (or controlling the political power), the pro-independence Taiwanese leaders often filtered the messages conveyed from the US to hold Taiwanese people hostage. As a result, the US will be dragged into a war against China or bear moral culpability of disavowing the free choice of a democracy. Lampton and Lieberthal noticed that the long lasting peace-maintaining mechanism across Taiwan Strait was eroded. Unless the peace framework across the Strait would be reconstructed, a cross-Strait war dragging in the US would be highly feasible.[469]

In dealing with the continuing and escalating tension between two sides across the Strait, if the US were not to be dragged into a cross-Strait war, it had to send out a clear message about its "strategic clarity"—the US did not want to be dragged into the war if Taiwan would pursue its way to independence, because the mixed signals from the US would not deter Taiwanese pro-independence politicians from the adventurism into the de jure Taiwan independence. However, based on its domestic interest and long-term strategic concern, the US traps itself in the dilemma of containing or engaging China. On the one hand, the US intends to woo economic interest from China; on the other hand, it suspects China's military enhancement accompanying by the emerging economic power will menace its hegemony. The US irresolute attitude towards China marks Taiwan an indispensable pawn in its grand strategy that the US is reluctant to extinguish Taiwan's hope for independence as Taiwan without the capability to pursue independence will lose its value in disrupting China's emergence.

China and the US have their fundamental differences. According to Friedberg, their positions in the international community and different domestic political systems caused them to distrust each other and to compete endlessly.[470] Thus, although the former US Secretary of State Colin Powell expressed his optimistic view by declaring "U.S. relations with China are the best they

---

[469] "Heading Off the Next War" by David M. Lampton and Kenneth Lieberthal, *The Washington Post*, April 12, 2004; Page A19

[470] Friedberg, 2002, P. 34

have been since President Nixon's first visit,"[471] in fact the recent improvement of atmosphere in Sino-US relations after 911 terrorist attacks reflected only a temporary assuagement between these two powers. After the **FY04 Report to Congress on PRC Military Power**[472] was released by the US Department of Defense, China accused the report to be full of cold war mentality. China pointed out "not long ago American people heard that the US-China witnessed the best of their relations in recent years,"[473] but all of a sudden, in the report of Pentagon, "China views the United States as the only country that poses a real military threat to China and the only country that can impose effective economic sanctions against the regime."[474]

Moreover, in the same report, although it was described as the suggestion from Taipei political and military leaders to acquire "weapon systems capable of standoff strikes against the Chinese mainland as a cost-effective means of deterrence", the hinted attack on "China's urban population or high-value targets, such as the Three Gorges Dam to deter Chinese military coercion" had aroused China's anger and suspicion towards the US.[475] Aside from the unpleasant report, Taiwan's Vice Minister of National Defense Tsai Ming-hsien believed that the US had sound intelligence on China and the US Department of Defense warned Taiwan that China might attack Taiwan in 2006 or 2008.[476] Moreover, although the US ruled out expanding the scope of the mutual security treaty with Japan, the fact that the US strengthened its military cooperation with Japan, China's arch-rival, surely set off alarm bells in Beijing.

Fearon brought up the concept that the higher the audience cost, the more difficult for a leader to retreat in a public confrontation.[477] The domestic politics of this trinity have already complicated the engagement among them and made political compromise difficult: for China, the Chinese people de-

---

[471] "Remarks by Secretary of State Colin L. Powell at the Elliot School of International Affairs," George Washington University, Washington, DC, September 5, 2003.

[472] http://www.defenselink.mil/pubs/d20040528PRC.pdf

[473] See "When Will Be the End of Cold War Mentality?" June 9, 2004, *People's Daily*.

[474] "FY04 Report to Congress on PRC Military Power," United States Department of Defense, Pursuant to the FY2000 National Defense Authorization Act,

[475] A Chinese general identified as Liu Yuan wrote in the official newspaper China Youth Daily to attack an unidentified American expert who said an attack on the Three Gorges Dam was a "very good idea." Liu said, "This allows us to see even more clearly that some people who wave high democracy and the flag of human rights . . . are actually a gang bent on stirring up hostility."
"China Warns Taiwan of Devastating Response If Three Gorges Dam Ever Attacked," Jun 16, 2004, *AP*
http://www.mytelus.com/news/article.do?articleID=1639512&pageID=world_archive

[476] See "MND Warns Attack Could Come Soon," by Debby Wu, Jun 10, 2004, *Taipei Times*.

[477] Fearon, 1994, P. 577

mand Chinese government stand against the US hegemony and protect the territorial integrity; for the US, the US people want its government to guard their business interests and to guarantee the national security; for Taiwan, Taiwanese people press for the dignity and political autonomy. The intention of the Bush administration to dominate the interpretation of evolving democratic trend will pose a more profound threat to the cross-Strait stability, as it is unpredictable when the US will shift its focus on "China's peaceful evolution" which Chinese government resents most.

If a war across the Strait erupts, it will be a war of no winners. Wang observed that "a people's war" had been the guideline of the Chinese PLA for its entire history. This doctrine aimed not only to motivate the trained military but also to mobilize the civilian power to defend the country, as it believed that human factors, not the weaponry system, determine the final result of a war.[478] China, the world's most populous country, might not be equipped with the most advanced weaponry, but its abundant human resources serve as its most effective weapon of deterrence. The US forces had encountered Chinese PLA in the Korean War. After experiencing China's "people's war" once, in Vietnam War, the US decided to withhold its ground troops from entering North Vietnam. China's "people's war" doctrine also succeeded in deterring Soviet from attacking China in the 1969 Sino-Soviet border dispute.[479]

China had maintained the world's largest armed force in order to compensate the weakness and deficiency in its weaponry technology.[480] Recently, China has engaged in military modernization and introduced the new doctrine of "people's war under modern conditions" by bringing in the new theories of "active defense" and "positive defense" which suggest China will replace the concept of letting invaders plunge into China by a mixed strategy of retreating in some circumstances but defending some selective high-value objects.[481] Even so, China still possesses the vast land and enormous population[482] which constitute the sine qua non for launching a people's war against any aggressor. Although the effectiveness of the "people's war" has not been tested under the innovated modern weaponry, one thing is certain that even the "people's war" does not guarantee a victory for Chinese PLA but certainly assures China's intruder a protracted, distressful, and troublesome path to victory.

---

478 Wang (1984, P. 1042)

479 Shulsky (2000, 73-77)

480 Romance (1980, 299)

481 Gerald Segal, 1988, 217-218

482 China is the world's most populous country. China's total population was 1.2591 billion in 1999, about 22% of total population in the world. China is the third largest country in the world, ranking after Canada and Russia. It has an area of 9.6 million square kilometers or one-fifteenth of the world's land mass. http://www.chinatoday.com/general/a.htm#POPU

4.5.2 Taiwan's Challenge to One-China Principle

Taiwan's status is not only a sensitive issue to China but also a valuable subject for "Taiwanese"[483] politicians to capitalize on. In a democracy, politicians compete for the votes to consolidate their personal power. As communist China can be easily depicted as a rogue state and the cross-Strait historical complex politically disintegrates China and Taiwan, "Taiwanese" politicians discover that China can be the best scapegoat. Provided that they can turn China into an external threat, they can cultivate hatred on the cross-Strait issue to mobilize the public. For "Taiwanese" politicians, it takes no effort to accomplish this task because as long as they challenge One-China Principle, Chinese politicians will make a knee-jerk response by using verbal threats or conducting military exercises and China's countermeasures surely hurt Taiwanese people's feelings.

To Beijing, the One-China Principle is unalterable. Even the slightest signal of lifting the official status of Taiwan by world powers will trigger its strongest retaliation. When Clinton administration decided to allow Lee's trip to his alma mater—Cornell University in 1995, Beijing adopted a series actions to express its anger. It suspended a series of high-level meetings, and postponed scheduled talks between the two governments relating to nuclear energy and the control of missile technology. Beijing escalated its pressure on the US by summoning back its ambassador and delayed the acceptance of President Clinton's appointee. China's pressure did not stop here. The Chinese army conducted military exercise in the East China Sea north of Taiwan. During the exercise, five Chinese missiles were fired into the waters off Taiwan's coastline. At last, Clinton administration secretly offered the promise of the "three noes" to patch the infringement with China.[484]

Clinton administration promised China that "the United States 1) would oppose or resist efforts by Taiwan to gain independence; 2) would not support the creation of "two China," or one China and a separate Taiwan; and 3) would not support Taiwan's admission to the United Nations."[485] Under this three-no framework, the volatile Sino-US-Taiwan relations were stabilized. When dealing with diplomatic issues, China has been extremely cautious about the "official status of Taiwan" to avoid the possibility of dual recognition. When China suspected Lee's trip to US might enhance the "official status of Taiwan" and set a precedent for others, it launched a missile test to express its umbrage over the potential erosion of its One-China Principle. It will be an inconceivable crisis if the US decides to reverse the course of its one China policy.

---

[483] See Section 4.4.1 for definition.
[484] Mann, 1999, P. 323-330
[485] Ibid, P. 330

This incident did not bring any concrete benefits to either party of the trinity: China validated the accusation of China threat; Taiwan suffered from capital flee and stock plunge; the US rendered "three noes" to China. However, China's missile tests united Taiwanese people under Lee Teng-hui's leadership and enable him to win the 1996 presidential election and he became the first-ever popularly elected president of the ROC. As a result, this missile test crisis accomplished only Lee's personal achievement. Taiwan was China's soft spot and would always be as long as Taiwan maintained its de facto independency. Chinese politicians had a difficult time in dealing with the provocative activities of Taiwanese leaders, because they always pushed the envelope on the one China issue. In view of the sensitivity of cross-Strait relations, Chinese authorities are trapped into a dilemma. On one hand, owing to the domestic politics, China can not tolerate any separatist remark from Taiwanese politicians, so it must release its discontent through one way or the other. On the other hand, China's verbal attacks on Taiwanese pro-independence political figures only inflame the resentment towards China and the pro-independence sentiment from Taiwanese people. Moreover, the credibility of China's verbal warning has been worn down by Taiwanese politician's remarks.[486]

The cross-Strait peace framework has been founded on two buttresses, "Taiwan does not declare its independency; China does not use its military force (Taiwan Bu Du, Zhong Kuo Bu Wu)." At first, both parties recognized the One-China Principle and engaged power struggle over the representation of orthodox China. The cross-Strait peaceful coexistence was hinged on the delicate equilibrium of one-China framework: there was only one China; officially, Taiwan regarded China as a rebel camp, and China considered Taiwan a renegade island. However, when President Lee brought up the two-state theory to cultivate "Taiwan conscious" in 1999, the cross-Strait equilibrium was agitated. Taiwan independence activists were hilarious over Lee's remark and argued what Lee did was to disclose "the king's new clothes". Nevertheless, China was provoked by Lee's remark and the stability of cross-Strait relations was seriously undermined.

Although after Clinton Administration repeatedly assured China that it would abide by the One-China Principle and blamed President Lee's intention to "rock the boat" and to "change the status quo", China did not appeal to violent means but use verbal attack on President Lee Teng-hui to assuage its internal pressure, however the breach between Taiwan and China was shaped and neither side intended to amend but to exploit it for domestic political gain.

---

486 Lee Teng-hui has likened China to a "barking dog that won't bite", and dismissed Chinese threats of war were no more than a war of words. See "China Gears Up for Showdown, Ball in Taiwan's Court," by Benjamin Kang Lim, Jul 5, 2004, *Reuters*

Therefore, when the pro-independence President Chen Shui-bian took over the reign in 2000, the buttress of "Taiwan does not declare its independency" was gradually eroded, because he took a tactic of transforming the name of Republic of China (ROC) into the entity of Republic of Taiwan (ROT). However, this tactic of "shell reactivation (Jie Ke Shang Shih)"[487] with which ROT borrowed the shell of ROC to appear on the market could no longer serve the domestic political aim of the pro-independence activists. Lee Teng-hui led a "Taiwan name rectification movement (Taiwan Zheng Min Yun Dong)" to seek for a formal name change.[488] As the pro-independence activists' appetence for an official name change was aroused, it would be Chen Shui-bian's dilemma about how far he would be pushed towards the name change without inciting a war.[489]

DPP defined Taiwan independence in three distinct ways: first, before Chen ran for the presidency in 2000, the DPP always assumed it had to go through a referendum to build a ROT and the DPP demanded a formal declaration of Taiwan independence; second, when Chen was running the 2000 presidential campaign, to attract the middle voters, the DPP promoted the concept that Taiwan had been a sovereign state and its official title was ROC, and the DPP wanted to maintain the status quo, the de facto independence and de jure conundrum; third, in Chen's 2000 inauguration speech, Chen bought up the idea that if China did not use force against Taiwan, there was no need for Taiwan to declare formal independence, to change its official title, to include two-state theory into its Constitution, and to initiate a referendum on independence and the DPP wanted to use Taiwan independence as a defensive weapon to deterred China's use of military force.[490]

Since the equilibrium between internal and external relations is in a dynamic mode, in order to play a balancing game to his personal advantage, when confronted by different pressure groups, a national leader may use different rhetoric to please different audience. However, as Putnam concluded about the two-level games of diplomacy and domestic politics, pressure groups will tolerate differences in rhetoric aimed at different audiences, but sooner or later, the real intentions of decision makers will be reflected on the implementation

[487] This concept of "shell reactivation" has been brought up by Guei Hong-Cheng, a research fellow in National Policy Foundation, in the article "What is the Status Quo of ROC?" NPF Commentary July 4, 2003

[488] "New Name Rests on Democracy," Sep. 8, 2003, *Taiwan News*

[489] An official name change will trigger a serious counteract from China; the temporization to pro-independence activists' demand will jeopardize the election of his party, because they are DPP's social base.

[490] "The DPP's New Definition on Taiwan Independence" Wu Yu-San, *BBC*, Aug. 14, 2002 (in Chinese)

of the policies.[491] Chen Shui-bian has been swinging back and forth between maintaining status quo and building a new nation out of ROC. It is very difficult to uncover the true intention of President Chen in dealing with cross-Strait issue as he always shifts his stance according to the audience.[492] Since what President Chen has done suggests that he will be more an opportunist than an ideologist, he will act more according to the strongest pressure group's will under the premise that his personal interest is covered.[493] However, whatever his decision will be, he surely cannot at the same time satisfy China and his pro-independence supporters.

President Chen Shui-bian was well-known for his philosophy of "conflict, compromise, and progress".[494] In order to create an opportunity, he would risk anything to arouse a conflict, and then no matter he had to compromise or his opponent had to, he gained progress from the conflict. By throwing out the issues like "issuing new passports with 'Taiwan' on the cover,[495]" "one country on each side," and "creating a new Constitution in 2006 and implementing it by 2008," Chen's purpose was not to declare Taiwan independence immediately, but to provoke an emotional response from China for his personal political gain. If China reacted to his provocation, the sentiment of Taiwanese people would tilt towards Taiwan independence and he would gain leverage over his domestic political opponents; on the other hand, if China did not respond, he could claim victory that his actions improved Taiwan's statehood.[496] By creating conflict against China, Chen galvanized the Taiwanese people's sense of Taiwan identity and as a pure-blood "Taiwanese",[497] he could benefit from

---

[491] Putnam, 1988, P.434

[492] When talking to business community, President Chen would express his goodwill at improving relations with China; when facing his pro-independence supporters, he would arouse the anti-China emotion to woo the votes. "Chen's Mixed Signals," by Willis Witter, Nov. 16, 2003, *The Washington Times*

[493] President Chen will surely defy any move against his interests even under gigantic pressure. For example, although President Chen from time to time claimed that he was the one most eager to discover the truth about the March 19 shooting incident, so far he refused to compose any independent committee to conduct a comprehensive and independent judicial inquiry into the incident. Since the further investigation into this incident may impair Chen's presidency, especially his reelection was largely contributed by the incident. Chen had lagged behind his competitor in poll almost during the campaign period, but the gunshot assisted him to woo sympathy vote.

[494] "A Bian (the Nickname of Chen Shui-bian) Claimed He Would Prudently Manage the Question of National Future," Jan 12, 2004, *BBC Chinese News*, in Chinese

[495] See "China Slams Taiwan for Issuing New 'Passport'," Jun 17, 2003, remarks by Chinese Foreign Ministry Spokesperson for China's response.
http://www.china-embassy.org/eng/sgxx/sggg/fyrth/t34973.htm

[496] "Chen's Mixed Signals," by Willis Witter, *The Washington Times*, Nov. 16, 2003.

[497] See Section 4.4.1 for definition.

the sentiment. After being reelected, Chen compromised with the reality and toned down his intention of creating a new constitution but amending the current one, but he already won his second-term of presidency.

After President Chen Shui-bian thrice challenged Beijing's "red-line", although the US made rhetoric reproaches to him by openly opposing his intention to unilaterally change the status quo, however the US did not exert all its might to condition Taiwan's choice for independence because the US did not want to lose the autonomy of capitalizing on Taiwan independence to contain China in case the Sino-US relations turned sour. The hostility of the Bush administration towards China is impossible to go unnoticed by Chinese authorities. As a result, to defuse the potential cross-Strait crisis, China adopted Anti-Secession Law not only to contain the behavior of Taiwan independence activists but also the cross-Strait strategy of the US.

For China, those Taiwan independence activists will never give up their activities until Taiwan wins its de jure independency which China will never allow. Therefore, China passed Anti-Secession Law in March 2005 to terminate Taiwan's challenge to One-China Principle and regained the dominance over cross-Strait political affairs. By providing the legal base for condoning military action against Taiwan independence force, China clearly drew a redline for Taiwan independence movements and limited the space for maneuvering not only to Taiwan independence activists but also to foreign forces. As the US is reluctant to send a clear message regarding to whether it will send troops to fight an independent war for Taiwan,[498] China determines to clarify the situation by defining Taiwan independence is a war against China whether Taiwan independence force has foreign aid or not.

China legalized its military threat, but at the same time extended olive branch to Taiwan's opposition party leaders. By inviting Messer Lien Chan, the then chairman of KMT and James Song, the chairman of the PPP to visit China and lavishing Taiwanese people with special gifts such as two giant pandas, golden monkeys and zero-tariff on Taiwan's fruit, China averted a possible downward spiral to a cross-Strait showdown and stabilized the cross-Strait relations. After China adopted its two-hand strategy combining both hard and soft tactics, China incited "China fever" among Taiwanese people to enhance the sentiment for unification and marginalized the independence-leaning ruling

[498] The US had a subtle way of handling Taiwan independence movement: it opposed any unilateral change to cross-Strait status quo. However, Bush administration claims it will come to Taiwan's rescue if China uses force to change the status quo, but it never mentions what it will do if Taiwan breaches the status quo.

party. As China has drawn the red-line and silenced the US[499], Chen Shui-bian can no longer slice the salami to apply his "conflict, compromise, progress" tactics on Taiwan independence issue. Chen is driven to a crossroad: peace or war; it will be Chen's final call.

4.5.3 The Deployment of the Game

China and Taiwan's current ruling party—DPP[500] are the major players in this zero-sum game, and the US represents a variable which will alter the environment of the game. In this game, China has three strategic options in dealing with unification issue: U_s1: China can threat to use the force if Taiwan declares formal independence; U_s2: China can appeal to the use of force; U_s3: China can denounce the use of force. Taiwan also has three strategic options: I_s1: Taiwan can threat to announce independence if China appeals to the force; I_s2: Taiwan can formally declare the de jure independence; I_s3: Taiwan can renounce the declaration of independence.

Since Chinese politicians have three major political objectives in their agenda, one is unification with Taiwan, another is to preserve the economic growth and domestic order, and the other is a hidden self-interest driven goal: maintain their political power; at the same time, Taiwanese politicians have two major political ambitions: one is to pursue their ends of independence; the other is the same as their Chinese counterparts: preserve their political power. As both sides want to maximize its payoff and simultaneously minimize its opponent's payoff, under the US strategic ambiguity policy, the status quo becomes the Nash equilibrium because both players want to play it safe. The two sides across the Strait choose to maintain the status quo with verbal threats: China chooses U_s1, at the same time, Taiwan I_s1. Given the uncertain level of US commitment in the cross-Strait conflict, Taiwan will not go for de jure independence at the risk of a war against China; neither China will use military force in fear of the US involvement. As the use of military force might provoke the US interference, since Chinese leaders are not certain about the victory of a unification war, a war involved with the US will certainly violate their goal of "economic development" and might jeopardize their domestic political positions. The US strategic ambiguity at the same time places Taiwanese leaders

---

499 Although the State Department publicly criticized China's Anti-Secession law as unhelpful to the cause of promoting cross-Strait and regional stability, the US government was extremely cautious not to utter the word "oppose".

500 Taiwan's society splits under this "unification versus independence" issue. Most of them are no willing to disturb the status quo until the further development of cross-Strait relations. On the other hand, if there is any pro-independence support in China, the number should be minute.

under the same anxiety of losing their power if they unilaterally announce independence without the military assurance from the US.

Thus, the strategic ambiguity policy successfully deters both sides from taking a reckless move to shift the situation towards their favor, and no one wants to deviate from the current equilibrium if the external conditions remain unchanged. As both sides across the Strait lack mutual trust, neither side is willing to make a concrete truce offer in case of backfire. Thus, China will not be willing to renounce its right to use the force; neither will Taiwan forsake its right to go de jure independence, so the cross-Strait stalemate persists.

However, after George W. Bush took over the reign, Bush administration started to shatter the triad relationships. First of all, after "Bush pledges whatever it takes to defend Taiwan,[501]" Pandora's Box is opened. Bush is considered as a "guardian angle" for Taiwan independence force. Bush's "blank cheque" has encouraged Taiwan to move towards independence. Although Bush administration has sent out signals to halt Taiwan from moving further toward independence, as the movement of Taiwan independence has garnered its momentum, under the belief that "in any case, the United Sates would not stand by idly,[502]" the movement towards independence is non-stoppable.

Worst of all, after Bush administration took a preemptive attack against Iraq to destroy the potential threat to the US national security, China now has an additional choice on its strategic policy list—U_s4: a preemptive strike on Taiwan independence force to safeguard its territorial integrity and national interest. Under the circumstance that Taiwan is shifting from its former strategy—threat to go independence, if the US cannot effectively assure China that it can effectively deter Taiwan from its independence, China may choose a preemptive strike to ensure its process of peaceful ascending since Taiwan independence has become a threat to Beijing's host for the 2008 Olympic Games.

In fact the international environment is to Taiwan's disadvantage as well as to the US'. China has emerged as the locomotive of Asian economic growth; the influence of its rapid economic expansion even ripples to the whole world. A war against China might wipe out the momentum of world economic growth. The economic interdependence among Sino-Taiwan-US triad will make a full-scale war devastating to all three parties. Moreover, as the US troops are currently trapped in the Iraq quagmire and the North Korean nuclear crisis is still pending, it will be highly questionable that how US is going to handle a war against China under current international environment. It is a common knowl-

[501] The news headline of CNN, "Bush Pledges Whatever it Takes to Defend Taiwan," Apr 25, 2001 http://www.cnn.com/2001/ALLPOLITICS/04/24/bush.taiwan.abc/

[502] Quoted from "Taiwan Hardliners Play with Fire in Push for Independence," by Lawrence Chung, Jul 3, 2004, *The Strait Times*

edge that the sheer size of China can translate China's turmoil into a world disaster in this globalized world.

5. Conclusion

The globalization has offered China a chance to emerge as an economic power. China's "open door" policy coincided with the trend of globalization successfully transformed the backward communist country into an expansionary economy which gradually restructures itself to "get on track (Jie Gui)" with the world. China is currently the world's third largest trading economy, lagging only behind the US and Germany, and the world's sixth largest economy in terms of GDP. If China's GDP is calculated on the base of PPP, China ranks the world's second largest economy, second only to the US. Moreover, China preserves the world's second largest foreign reserve, and China now serves as the most attractive FDI target nation. Aside from its past and current outstanding economic performance, China still has the potential to continue its current economic expansion—at a rate as high as 9 percent. The high speed growth rate facilitates China to transform itself into an attractive consumption market.

Although the globalization strengthens the economic interdependence among nations, however the international economic cooperation exists more in the form of bilateralism instead of multilateralism. As a result, instead of a free-trade world, more bilateral free trade agreements are signed and more trading blocs emerge. This phenomenon of regionalization grants large states more bargaining power over small ones. With its emerging economic power, China now plays as a cohesive role to integrate East Asian economy. China is willing to sacrifice its short term benefit in exchange for a long term economic integration between China and ASEAN. As China aggressively explores all the possibility in embedding itself in the regionalized Asian economy and expects its economic penetration in this region will have spillover effect on its political and diplomatic influence, Taiwan's role in Asia will be further marginalized.

Although Taiwanese government has viewed China as an arch-rival, Taiwanese businessmen have been attracted to the booming opportunities in China market. Taiwanese government successfully suffocates the inflow of capital, talents and goods from China to Taiwan; on the contrary, it fails in preventing Taiwanese businessmen from investing into China. The outflow of Taiwanese capital, talents and technologies places Taiwan in a dilemma. On one hand, without China, many Taiwanese SMEs cannot survive through the challenge of globalization; on the other hand, the further economic integration will render China more coercive power in the unification-versus-independence issue and jeopardize Taiwan's national security. Moreover, although governmental mechanism still control the power to establish and implement the national regulations to discipline private actors' activities, after the advancement of technology facilitated the expansion of global trade, the deregulation of international investment and the dispersion of worldwide production, in this globalized world, private organizations, especially MNEs are capable of bypassing the national regulations by conducting transnational activities. On the other hand, if nations want to prevent the private actors from circumventing their national regulations, they have to cooperate in constructing a supranational mechanism to bring those international organizations back to the domain of regulations.

As China poses as a fetal attraction to Taiwanese enterprises, the unilateral constraints by Taiwan authority can hardly impede Taiwanese enterprises from investing westwards. According to Taiwan's official statistics, the investments in China account for 56.51 percent of Taiwan's total outward investments as of the end of 2004. In fact, there is countless amount of Taiwanese capital flowing into China through underground channel. Even Taiwanese authorities understand their deficiency in restricting Taiwanese westbound investments; therefore from time to time they will offer a grace period for Taiwanese enterprises to retroactively register their unauthorized investments on mainland. The retroactively registered investments account for almost one fourth (27.22 percent) of the total westwards investments. This implies when Taiwanese businessmen legally invest three dollars in China, there will be one dollar more flowing into China through underground channel and waiting for the government's leniency. This phenomenon reflects the reality of globalization—without the cooperation of the host countries, the home countries can do little to control the overseas activities of their enterprises.

In order to eliminate the economic dependence on China, Taiwanese government even abolished the plan to promote Taiwan as an "Asia-Pacific Regional Operations Center", because an "Asia-Pacific Regional Operations Center" without "three links" with Asia's largest single market will be crippled. Because of the political concern, the "Asia-Pacific Regional Operations Center" Program remained as only paper work. Now Taiwan plans to transform itself into a technological island by promoting a "Two Trillion, Twin Star" program. However, the chance for Taiwan to successfully evolve into a technological island is barricaded by the structural weaknesses of Taiwan industry. Taiwanese enterprises are well-known for their manufacture and cost-efficiency instead of renovation and creativity. Because of the influence of Chinese culture and political constraints from the KMT government, Taiwanese enterprises are primarily constituted by SMEs and mostly are family-own businesses emphasizing the importance of relationships.

Because of the emphasis on relationships, Taiwanese SMEs are informally organized into effective and efficient production networks. This network style of production has the advantage of flexibility; the flexibility will also be reflected on the migration of production. Once the downstream manufacturers relocate their production, they will bring their suppliers along with since most of them are relatively small in scale. In terms of their scale and scarce resources, most of the Taiwanese SMEs would pay technology transfer fee and royalties to purchase ready-to-use technology rather than invest in R&D to acquire a result-unknown in-house technology. Not only are the major technology patents controlled by the foreign MNEs, but also the machinery and key components. As a result, Taiwan IT industry is established on the import of technology, machinery and key components. Under this industrial structure, it is very difficult to accomplish the goal of Taiwanese government—a technological island.

As Taiwanese enterprises emphasize primarily on OEM and slightly on ODM but scarcely on OBM, the lack of brand-name and logistic channel constitutes another structural weakness of Taiwan industry. Since the global competition has put pressure on the price of IT product, the profit-margin quickly slides from "micro-profit" to "nano-profit". Moreover, seeing that China emerges as one of the largest IT consumption market, in order to easily access to China market, all the major IT brand-name MNEs demand their contract manufacturers to relocate their production to China. Thus, with the cost-down pressure and under the buyers' request, Taiwanese manufacturers have no other choice but to move their manufacture base to China. Moreover, with the same cultural and language background, the emerging China market poses an opportunity for Taiwanese enterprises to develop their own brand name.

Therefore, owing to the political irreconcilable, Taiwanese government is deeply concerned about the economic integration between Taiwan and China; on the contrary, in pursuit of survival and expansion, Taiwanese enterprises devote themselves on China regardless of the concern of Taiwanese government. China's economic strength has rendered China more coercive power over Taiwan authority. Although economic boycott against Taiwan is still not an option for Chinese authorities, because to impose economic sanction on Taiwan will at the same time hamper the development of China's economy, China can perform a more effectively economic discipline by imposing extra restraints on those politically uncooperative Taiwanese enterprises. In other words, the "mass attack" will drive off most of Taiwanese investors; the "surgical strike" will have the effect of "killing the rooster to frighten the monkeys". After China publicly declared that the Chinese government does not welcome "pro-Green" Taiwanese businessmen and it even singled out Hsu Wen-lung, the founder of Chi-mei Group as a pro-Green Taiwanese businessman, so far none of the Taiwanese investors withdraw from China because of this political suppression; moreover, even Hsu Wen-lung personally expressed that his enterprise will continue its investment in China. Moreover, to sustain his investments in China, Hsu kowtowed to China's request to issue an open statement to defy Taiwan independence right before Taiwanese government launched an Anti Anti-Secession Law demonstration to protest against China's Anti-Secession Law.

Taiwanese businessmen inject capital, human resources, and technology into China; some of them even bring their ancestor's spirit tablet with them to China. As the Sinicization of Taiwanese westwards investors becomes an irreversible trend, the reluctance of Taiwanese government to position itself in the "Chinese Economic Sphere" will marginalize Taiwan but not those Taiwanese businessmen.

Since the unification versus independence is a zero-sum game, if both sides across the Strait emphasize on the political dispute, the collision between China and Taiwan will be inevitable. Because of the domestic politics, it is difficult for the pro-independence Taiwanese president Chen Shui-bian to waive his stance on the unification-independence issue. In light of the fact that President Chen, a "Taiwanese" has fully taken advantage of the sub-ethnic difference to mobilize his social base against politicians with mainland-background and cultivated the hatred toward China to garner political power, compounding with his versatile rhetoric, it is difficult for China to trust him. In fact, not only his opponents don't believe in him, but also his supporters. China's internal power struggle also prohibits any Chinese leader to be "soft" on the Taiwan issue. In the past, the cross-Strait status quo was maintained by the US strategic ambiguity. Without knowing the US reaction to the one who escalates, neither side is willing to take a reckless move to disturb the equilibrium.

However, after George W. Bush took over the presidency, the US has tilted towards Taiwan's favor. President Bush even publicly pledged that he would do "whatever it takes" to defend Taiwan from any Chinese attack, thus Bush is considered as a "guardian angle" to Taiwanese force. Bush administration's commitment to defend Taiwan has encouraged Taiwanese adventurism. Since the de jure Taiwan independence will surely provoke China's military action, Bush administration's one way deterrence is doomed to fail. Unless the US is willing to fight an independence war for Taiwanese people, it has to send out a clear message to Taiwan that Taiwan has to take the responsibility for the result of moving towards independence. The US should not send out any confused message to Taiwanese people, because any ambiguous message will be tailored by Taiwanese politicians to serve their domestic political purpose.

Although the US strategists have been worried about China's emerging economic strength will enhance its military power to unsettle the stability of East Asia and to endanger the US interest in this region, bouncing back and forth between "containment" and "engagement", the US does not propose a complete set of China policy to deal with China but some spontaneous schemes to cope with unexpected incidents. China now serves as the US third largest trading partner, and the US is China's second largest investor. As the globalization has deepened the economic interdependence between China and the US, the stakes are high and one reckless misstep will jeopardize not only China's continuing growth and development but also the US economic performance. Moreover, it is an absurd conjecture to predict that China will not go through another political reform to transform itself from totalitarianism to democracy. After Deng Xiao Ping took over the reign, he moderated the full-scale political control to selective and limited individual restraints, and the massive purges which were practiced under Mao Zedong have been diminished. As a result, the percentage of political prisoners in China dropped dramatically[503].

The US must realize to maneuver Taiwan as a pawn to contain China will provoke the resentment from Chinese; on the contrary, to use Taiwan as a catalyst to make China a better country will be appreciated. With the cross-Strait hostility diminishes, Taiwan can demand China to channel their national defense budget to education, culture and social welfare, and this will reduce the US anxiety on a military belligerent China. However, instead of focusing on China's political framework, the US should demand Taiwan to emphasize on the issues such as economic cooperation, social welfare, environmental protection and the judicial system. Any direct challenge to the political power of Chinese leaders will trigger their merciless counteraction—Tiananmen massacre has proved how merciless and powerful the counteraction will be; on the contrary, the cooperation to construct China as a fair society will assist Chinese leaders to consolidate their political power, as a result, this kind of interference from Taiwan will not be strongly opposed, especially Taiwan can use unification as a carrot to induce cooperation from Chinese leaders. While Taiwan independence will be Chinese leaders' stigma, the unification with Taiwan will be a historical accomplishment to any Chinese leader. Under the prerequisite that those Chinese leaders can preserve their political right, Taiwan's tactic of "carrot and stick" aimed at a better and fairer China will be acceptable.

---

503 The percentage of political prisoners dropped from 13 percent of the prison population in 1980 to one half of 1 percent a decade later. "U.S. Realism about China," by Mortimer B. Zuckerman, July 6, 1998, *U.S. News & World Report*

Bibliography

Acemoglu, Daron and Thierry Verdier (2000) "The Choice between Market Failures and Corruption," *The American Economic Review*, Vol. 90, No. 1, 194-211.

Adams, Karen Ruth (2003/04) "Attack and Conquer? International Anarchy and the Offense-Defense-Deterrence Balance," *International Security*, Vol. 28, No. 3, 45-83.

Adams, William James (1970) "Firm Size and Research Activity: France and the United States," *The Quarterly Journal of Economics*, Vol. 84, No. 3, 386-409.

Ahmed, Samina, David Cortright and Amitabh Mattoo (1998) "Public Opinion and Nuclear Options for South Asia," *Asian Survey*, Vol. 38, No. 8, 727-744.

Ahn, Choong Yong (2001) "A Search for Robust East Asian Development Models after the Financial Crisis: Mutual Learning from East Asian Experiences," *Journal of Asian Economics*, Vol. 12, No. 3, 419-443.

Ahrari, M. Ehsan (1997) "U.S. Military Strategic Perspectives on the PRC: New Frontiers of Information-Based War," *Asian Survey*, Vol. 37, No. 12, 1163-1180.

Aldrich, John H. (1983) "A Downsian Spatial Model with Party Activism," *The American Political Science Review*, Vol. 77, No. 4, 974-990.

Alesina, Alberto (1987) "Macroeconomic Policy in a Two-Party System as a Repeated Game," *The Quarterly Journal of Economics*, Vol. 102, No. 3, 651-678.

Alesina, Alberto (1988) "Credibility and Policy Convergence in a Two-Party System with Rational Voters," *The American Economic Review*, 78, 4, 796-805.

Alesina, Alberto, Enrico Spolaore and Romain Wacziarg (2000) "Economic Integration and Political Disintegration," *The American Economic Review*, Vol. 95, No. 5, 1276-1296.

André de Palma, Gordon M. Myers and Yorgos Y. Papageorgiou (1994) "Rational Choice under an Imperfect Ability to Choose," *The American Economic Review*, Vol. 84, No. 3, 419-440.

Ankie, Hooqvelt (1997) *Globalisation and the Postcolonial World*, Basingstoke, Hampeshire: Macmillan.

Arndt, Helmut (1976) "Power and Competition," in: Jacquemin, A.P. and H.W.de Jong (eds.) *Markets, Corporate Behaviour and the State: International Aspects of Industrial Organization.* The Hague: Nijhoff.

Arrow, Kenneth J. (1973) *Social Choice and Individual Values*, New Haven, Conn.: Yale Univ. Press.

Aslanbeigui, Nahid and Steven G. Medema (1998) "Beyond the Dark Clouds: Pigou and Coase on Social Cost," *History of Political Economy*, Vol. 30, Issue 4, 601-625.

Axford, Barrie (1995) *The Global System: Economics, Politics, and Culture*, New York: St. Martin's Press.

Ba Alice D. (2003) "China and Asean: Renavigating Relations for a 21st-century Asia," *Asian Survey*, Vol. 43, No. 4, P. 622-647.

Bagwell, Kyle and Robert W. Staiger (1998) "Will Preferential Agreements Undermine the Multilateral Trading System?" *The Economic Journal*, Vol. 108, No. 449, 1162-1182.

Baldwin, Richard E. (1993) *A Domino Theory of Regionalism*, Cambridge, Mass.: National Bureau of Economic Research.

Beck, Ulrich (2000) *What Is Globalization?* Oxford, UK: Polity Press.

Beck, Ulrich (1992) *Risk Society: towards a New Modernity*, London: Sage.

Bellows, Thomas J. (1976) "Taiwan's Foreign Policy in the 1970s: A Case Study of Adaptation and Viability," *Asian Survey*, Vol. 16, No. 7, 593-610.

Berry, Nicholas (2001) China Travels a New Road, Center for Defense Information, Asia Forum.

Bert, Wayne (1993) "Chinese Policies and U.S. Interests in Southeast Asia," *Asian Survey*, Vol. 33, No. 3, 317-332.

Bertin, Gilles Y. (1976) "Industrial Policy and the Structural Impact of Multinational Firms: an Analytical View," in: Jacquemin, A.P. and H.W.de Jong (eds.) *Markets, Corporate Behaviour and the State: International Aspects of Industrial Organization*. The Hague: Nijhoff.

Betts, Richard K. (1993-1994) "Wealth, Power and Instability: East Asia and the United States after the Cold War," *International Security*, Vol. 18, No. 3, 34-77.

Bhagwati, Jagdish (1990) "Departures from Multilateralism: Regionalism and Aggressive Unilateralism," *The Economic Journal*, Vol. 100, No. 403, 1304-1317.

Bhagwati, Jagdish (1991) *The World Trading System at Risk*, New York, NY: Harvester Wheatsheaf.

Bhagwati, Jagdish and Arvind Panagariya (1996) "The Theory of Preferential Trade Agreements: Historical Evolution and Current Trends," *The American Economic Review*, Papers and Proceedings of Hundredth and Eighth Annual Meeting of the American Economic Association San Francisco, CA, Vol. 86, No. 2, 82-87.

Bhagwati, Jagdish, David Greenaway and Arvind Panagariya (1998) "Trading Preferentially: Theory and Policy," *The Economic Journal*, Vol. 108, No. 449, 1128-1148.

Bian, Jin-Feng (1991) *The Research of the Relations between the U.S. and South Korea (1979-1990) – The Power Struggle between Large States and Small States,* Thesis for the Degree of Master of International Affairs and Strategic Studies, Tamkang University (in Chinese).

Biddick, Thomas V. (1989) "Diplomatic Rivalry in the South Pacific: The PRC and Taiwan," *Asian Survey*, Vol. 29, No. 8, 800-815.

Blomstrom, Magnus, Gunnar Fors and Robert E. Lipsey (1997) "Foreign Direct Investment and Employment: Home Country Experience in the United States and Sweden," *The Economic Journal,* Vol. 107, No. 445, 1787-1797.

Brams, Steven J. (1985) *Superpower Games: Applying Game Theory to Superpower Conflict,* New Haven: Yale Univ. Press.

Breton, Albert (1964) "The Economics of Nationalism," *The Journal of Political Economy*, Vol. 72, No. 4, 376-386.

Breton, Albert (1989) "The Growth of Competitive Governments," *The Canadian Journal of Economics*, Vol. 22, No. 4, 717-750.

Brooks, Risa A. (2003) "Making Military Might: Why Do States Fail and Succeed?" *International Security,* Vol. 28, No. 2, 149-191.

Brooks, Stephen G. and William C. Wohlforth (2000) "Power, Globalization, and the End of the Cold War: Reevaluating a Landmark Case for Ideas," *International Security*, Vol. 25 No. 3, 5-53.

Brown, Stephen P A and Jason L Saving (2002) "Government Organization and Power," *Economic Inquiry*, Vol. 40, Issue 3, 439-440.

Bruce, Jacobs J. (1979) "Taiwan 1978: Economic Successes, International Uncertainties," *Asian Survey*, Vol. 19, No. 1, 20-29.

Burles, Mark and Abram N. Shulsky (2000) *Patterns in China's Use of Force: Evidence from History and Doctrinal Writings,* Santa Monica, CA: Rand.

Byman, Daniel L. and Kenneth M. Pollack (2001) "Let Us Now Praise Great Men: Bringing the Statesman Back In," *International Security*, Vol. 25, No. 4, 107-146.

Cable, Vincent and Peter Ferdinand (1994) "China as an Economic Giant: Threat or Opportunity?" *International Affairs*, Vol. 70, No. 2, 243-261.

Campbell, Kurt (2002) Opening Remarks: Images and U.S. Strategic Thinking on China, China in the American Political Imagination Conference Report (Pre-publication Version), Center for Strategies & International Studies (CSIS).

Canto, J G and I S Gonzalez (1999) "A Resource-based Analysis of the Factors Determining a Firm's R&D Activities," *Research Policy*, Vol. 28, Issue 8, 891-905.

Cerny, Philip G. (1996) "Globalization and Other Stories: The Search for a New Paradigm for International Relations," *International Journal*, Vol. 51, No. 4, 617-637

Chai, Trong R. (1979) "Chinese Policy toward the Third World and the Superpowers in the UN General Assembly 1971-1977: A Voting Analysis," *International Organization*, Vol. 33, No. 3, 391-403.

Chai, Trong R. (1986) "The Future of Taiwan," *Asian Survey*, Vol. 26, No. 12, 1309-1323.

Chan, Steve (1984) "Mirror, Mirror on the Wall... Are the Freer Countries More Pacific?" *The Journal of Conflict Resolution*, Vol. 28, No. 4, 617-648.

Chan, Steve (1997) "In Search of Democratic Peace: Problems and Promise," *Mershon International Studies Review*, Vol. 41, No. 1, 59-91.

Chang, Ha-joon (1998) "Globalization, Transnational Corporations, and Economic Development: Can the Developing Countries Pursue Strategic Industrial Policy in a Globalizing World Economy?" In: Dean Baker, (eds.) *Globalization and progressive economic policy.* Cambridge: Cambridge Univ. Press.

Chang, Hsia Maria (1995) "Greater China and the Chinese 'Global Tribe'," *Asian Survey*, Vol. 35, No. 10, 955-967.

Chang, Hsu Yi, Dien Wen Chang and Chi Fang Lu (2003) *Three Hundred Billion Legend: Terry Gou's Hon Hai Empire,* Taipei: Commonwealth Publishing (in Chinese).

Chang, Hui-ling and Miao Chen (2003) "Zai Lun Dong Ya Qu Yu Jing Ji Zheng He," *Tai Wan Jing Ji Yan Jiu Yue Kan (Taiwan Economic Research Monthly)*, Vol. 26, No. 5, 39-43 (in Chinese).

Chao, Chien-Min (2003) "Will Economic Integration between Mainland China and Taiwan Lead to a Congenial Political Culture?" *Asian Survey*, Vol. 43, No. 2, P. 280-304.

Charney, Jonathan I. and J. R. V. Prescott (2000) "Resolving Cross-Strait Relations between China and Taiwan," *The American Journal of International Law*, Vol. 94, No. 3, 453-477.

Chen, Ezra N. H. (2003) The Economic Integration of Taiwan and China and Its Implications for Cross-strait Relations, Weatherhead Center For International Affairs, Fellows' Paper 2002-2003.

Chen, King C. (1977) "Peking's Attitude toward Taiwan," *Asian Survey*, Vol. 17, No. 10, 903-918.

Chen, Min (1997) *Asian Management Systems: Chinese, Japanese and Korean Styles of Business,* London: Reprinted by International Thomson Business Pr.

Chen, Qimao (1993) "New Approaches in China's Foreign Policy: The Post-Cold War Era," *Asian Survey*, Vol. 33, No. 3, 237-251.

Chen, Qimao (1996) "The Taiwan Strait Crisis: Its Crux and Solutions," *Asian Survey*, Vol. 36, No. 11, 1055-1066.

Chen, Tain-Jy and Ying-Hua Ku (2000) "The Effect of Foreign Direct Investment on Firm Growth: the Case of Taiwan's Manufacturers," *Japan and the World Economy,* No. 12, 153-172.

Chen, Wen-chun, Qingshan Tan and Peter Kien-hong Yu (2003) "Local Politics in Taiwan: Democratic Consolidation," *Asian Survey*, Vol. 36, No. 5, 483-494.

Chen Xiangming (1996) "Taiwan Investments in China and Southeast Asia: 'Go West, but Also Go South'," *Asian Survey*, Vol. 36, No. 5, 447-467.

Cheng, Chu-Yuan (1966) "The Power Struggle in Red China," *Asian Survey*, Vol. 6, No. 9, 469-483.

Cheng, Tun-jen Cheng and Yi-shing Liao (1998) "Taiwan in 1997: An Embattled Government in Search of New Opportunities," *Asian Survey*, Vol. 38, No. 1, pp. 53-63.

Cheng, Tun-jen and Tien, Hung-mao (1999) "Crafting Democratic Institutions," in: Tien, Hung-mao and Tsang, Steve (eds.) *Democratization in Taiwan: implications for China* Basingstoke, Hampshire: Macmillan.

Cheng, Tun-jen and Peggy Pei-chen Chang (2002) Limits of Statecraft: Taiwan's Political Economy under Lee Teng-hui, CGOTS (Conference Group on Taiwan Studies) Working Papers in Taiwan Studies # 52.

Chi, Wen-Shun (1969) "The Great Proletarian Cultural Revolution in Ideological Perspective," *Asian Survey*, Vol. 9, No. 8, 563-579.

Chiang, Han-Chi (2003) A Comparative Analysis for Manufacturing Development Strategy on Taiwan and Korea TFT-LCD Industry, Thesis for the Degree of Business Administration, National Chiao Tung University (in Chinese).

Chiou, C. L. (1986) "Dilemmas in China's Reunification Policy toward Taiwan," *Asian Survey*, Vol. 26, No. 4, 467-482.

Chou, Yu-Jen (1997) "The Analysis of Taiwan Government in the Role of Economic Regulation: the Direction for the Creation of an Incorruptible and competent Government," *Review of Taiwan Economics,* Vol. 2, No. 4 (in Chinese).

Christensen, Thomas J. (1992) "Threats, Assurances, and the Last Chance for Peace: The Lessons of Mao's Korean War Telegrams," *International Security*, Vol. 17, No. 1, 122-154.

Christensen, Thomas J (2001) "Posing Problems without Catching Up: China's Rise and Challenges for U.S. Security Policy," *International Security*, Vol. 25, No. 4, 5-40.

Christensen, Thomas J. (2002) "The Contemporary Security Dilemma: Deterring a Taiwan Conflict," *The Washington Quarterly*, Vol. 25, No. 4, 7-21.

Christoffersen, Gaye (1996) "China and the Asia-Pacific: Need for a Grand Strategy," *Asian Survey*, Vol. 36, No. 11, 1067-1085.

Chu, Chi-hua (2003) A Study on the ROC's Pragmatic Diplomacy, Thesis for the Degree of Master of Art, National Chengchi University (in Chinese).

Chu, Yun-han (1999) "The Challenges of Democratic Consolidation," in: Tien, Hung-mao and Tsang, Steve (eds.) *Democratization in Taiwan: implications for China* Basingstoke, Hampshire: Macmillan.

Chu, Yun-han and Larry Diamond, Larry (1999) "Taiwan's 1998 Elections: Implications for Democratic Consolidation," *Asian Survey*, Vol. 39, No. 5, 808-822.

Chu, Yun-han (2003) "Power Transition and the Making of Beijing's Policy towards Taiwan," *The China Quarterly*, Vol. 176, 960-980.

Clarete, Ramon, Christopher Edmonds and Jessica Seddon Wallack (2002) Asian Regionalism and its Effect on Trade in the 1980s and 1990s, Manila: Asian Development Bank.

Clark, Cal (1987) "The Taiwan Exception: Implications for Contending Political Economy Paradigms," *International Studies Quarterly*, Vol. 31, No. 3, 327-356.

CNP (Center for National Policy, 2003) China in the International Spotlight: Implications for the Cross-Strait Dynamic, Cross-Strait Forum.

Coase, R. H. (1960) "The Problem of Social Cost," *The Journal of Law and Economics*, Vol. 3, 1-44.

Coase, R. H. (1974) "The Lighthouse in Economics," *The Journal of Law and Economics*, Vol. 17, No. 2, 357-376.

Coase, R. H. (1994a) "The Nature of the Firm," *Economica*, New Series, Vol. 4, No. 16, 386-405.

Coase, R. H. (1994b) *Essays on Economics and Economists*, Chicago: Univ. of Chicago Press.

Cohen, Benjamin (2000) "Money in a Globalized World," in: Ngaire Woods (eds.) *The Political Economy of Globalization*, Basingstoke: Macmillan.

Cohen, Wesley M., Richard C. Levin and David C. Mowery (1987) "Firm Size and R&D Intensity: A Re-Examination," *The Journal of Industrial Economics*, Vol. 35, No. 4, The Empirical Renaissance in Industrial Economics, 543-565.

Cohen, Wesley M. and Steven Klepper (1996) "A Reprise of Size and R&D," *The Economic Journal*, Vol. 106, No. 437, 925-951

Copper, John F. (1987) "Taiwan in 1986: Back on Top again," *Asian Survey*, Vol. 27, No. 1, 81-91.

Cooley, Alexander and James Ron (2002) "The NGO Scramble: Organizational Insecurity and the Political Economy of Transnational Action," *International Security*, Vol. 27, No. 1, 5-39.

Cooper, Richard N. (1972) "Economic Interdependence and Foreign Policy in the Seventies," *World Politics*, Vol. 24, No. 2, 159-181.

Copper, John F. (1997) "New Taiwan, New China: Taiwan's Changing Role in the Asia-Pacific Region," *The China Journal*, No. 37, 185-186.

Cossa, Ralph A. (2003) "Taiwan Referendum: Waving a Red Flag," *PacNet*, No.48, Pacific Forum CSIS.

Crane, George T. (1993) "China and Taiwan: Not Yet 'Greater China'", *International Affairs*, Vol. 69, No. 4, 705-723.

Crawford, Timothy W. (2002) "Pivotal Deterrence and the Kosovo War: Why the Holbrooke Agreement Failed," *Political Science Quarterly*, Vol. 116, No. 4.

Cremer, Jacques and Thomas R. Palfrey (1999) "Political Confederation," *The American Political Science Review*, Vol. 93, No. 1, 69-83.

Crone, Donald (1993) "Does Hegemony Matter? The Reorganization of the Pacific Political Economy," *World Politics*, Vol. 45, No. 4, 501-525.

Crozier, Brian (1964) "The Struggle for the Third World," *International Affairs* (Royal Institute of International Affairs 1944-) Vol. 40, No. 3, 440-452.

Cuming, Maurice W. (1989) *The Theory and Practice of Personnel Management,* Oxford: Heinemann Professional.

Curry, Robert Lester and Lorry L. Wade (1968) *A Theory of Political Exchange: Economic Reasoning in Political Analysis,* Englewood Cliffs, NJ: Prentice-Hall.

Cutler, A. Clair, Virginia Haufler and Tony Porter (1999) "Private Authority and International Affairs," in: A. Clair Cutler, Virginia Haufler and Tony Porter (eds.) *Private Authority and International Affairs*, Albany, NY: State University of New York Press.

Dales, J.H. (1975) "Beyond the Marketplace," *The Canadian Journal of Economics*, Vol. 8, No. 4, 483-503.

Datta-Chaudhuri, Mrinal (1990) "Market Failure and Government Failure," *The Journal of Economic Perspectives*, Vol. 4, No. 3, 25-39.

Davis, David R. and Steve Chan (1990) "The Security-Welfare Relationship: Longitudinal Evidence from Taiwan," *Journal of Peace Research*, Vol. 27, No. 1, 87-100.

De Long, J. Bradford (1998) "What 'new' economy?" *The Wilson Quarterly*, Vol. 22, No. 4 14-26.

Dent, Christopher M. (2003) "Taiwan's Foreign Economic Policy: The 'Liberalization Plus' Approach of an Evolving Developmental State," *Modern Asian Studies*, Vol. 37, No. 2, 461-483.

Desch, Michael C. (2002) "Democracy and Victory: Why Regime Type Hardly Matters?" *International Security*, Vol. 27, No 2, 5-47.

Dessus, Sébastien, Jia-Dong Shea and Mau-Shan Shi (1995) Chinese Taipei: the Origins of the Economic "Miracle", Organization for Economic Co-operation and Development / Development Centre, Paris: Development Centre of the Organization for Economic Co-operation and Development.

Diamond, Larry (2002) Stabilizing the Cross-Strait Relationship: A Strategy for Taiwan's Dignity and Security, Remarks to the Formosan Association for Public Affairs-Northern California Chapter.

Dicken, Peter (1992) "International Production in a Volatile Regulatory Environment: the Influence of National Regulatory Policies on the Spatial Strategies of Transnational Corporations," *Geoforum* Volume 23, Issue 3, 303-316.

Dickson, Bruce J. (1998) "China's Democratization and the Taiwan Experience," *Asian Survey*, Vol. 38, No. 4, 349-364.

Dillon, Dana R., Balbina Y. Hwang and John J., Jr. Tkacik (2003) "ASEAN Regional Forum: Promoting U.S. Interests," *Backgrounder*, No. 1659, the Heritage Foundation.

Dixit, Avinash K. and Barry J. Nalebuff (1991) *Thinking Strategically: the Competitive Edge in Business, Politics and Everyday Life,* London: Norton.

Dixit, Avinash and Skeath Susan (1999) Games of strategy, New York: Norton.

Dixit, Avinash, Grossman, Gene M. and Gul, Faruk (2000) The Dynamics of Political Compromise, The Journal of Political Economy, 108, 3, 531-568

Domes, Juergen (1999) "Electoral and Party Politics in Democratization," in: Hung-mao Tien and Steve Tsang (eds.) *Democratization in Taiwan: implications for China* Basingstoke, Hampshire: Macmillan.

Downs, Anthony (1957a) *An Economic Theory of Democracy,* New York, NY: Harper & Row.

Downs, Anthony (1957b) "An Economic Theory of Political Action in a Democracy," *The Journal of Political Economy,* Vol. 65, No. 2, 132-150.

Downs, Erica Strecker and Phillip C. Sounders (1998-1999) "Legitimacy and Limits of Nationalism: China and the Diaoyu Islands," *International Security*, Vol. 23, No. 3, 114-146.

Dunning, John H. (1992) *Multinational Enterprises and the Global Economy, Wokingham,* England: Addison-Wesley.

Dunning, John H. (2000) "The New Geography of FDI," in: Ngaire Woods (eds.) *The Political Economy of Globalization*. Basingstoke: Macmillan.

Dutta, Prajit K. (2001) *Strategies and Games: Theory and Practice,* Cambridge, Mass: MIT Press.

East, Maurice A. (1973) "Size and Foreign Policy Behavior: A Test of Two Models," *World Politics*, Vol. 25, No. 4, 556-576.

Eichengreen, Barry (2001) "Capital Account Liberalization: What do Cross-Country Studies Tell Us?" *The World Bank Economic Review,* Vol. 15, No. 3, 341-365.

Emmott, Bill (2003) *20:21 Vision: the Lessons of the 20th Century for the 21st*, London: Allen Lane.

Ethier, Wilfred (1998) "Regionalism in a Multilateral World," *The Journal of Political Economy*, Vol. 106, No. 6, 1214-1245.

Ethier, Wilfred J. (1998) "The New Regionalism," *The Economic Journal*, Vol. 108, No. 449, 1149-1161.

Evans, Thammy (2003) "The PRC's Relationship with the ASEAN Regional Forum: Realpolitik, Regime Theory or a Continuation of the Sinic Zone of Influence System?" *Modern Asian Studies*, Vol. 37, No. 3, 737-763.

Evensky, Jerry (1993) "Adam Smith on the Human Foundation of a Successful Liberal Society," *History of Political Economy*, Vol. 25, No. 3, 395-412.

Ewing, Richard Daniel (2003) "Hu, Jintao: The Making of a Chinese General Secretary," *The China Quarterly*, Vol. 173, 17-34.

Fang, Kuan-Chung (2002) The Actions of Taiwan's Plastics SMEs under Economic Globalization, National Taiwan University, Thesis for Degree of Master of Arts (in Chinese).

Farmer, David John (1997) "Contemporary Conceptual Space: Reading Adam Smith," *Journal of Management History*, Vol. 3, Issue 3, 246-255.

Farmer, David John (2003) "Invisible Hand and Visible Management," *International Journal of Organization Theory and Behavior*, 2003, Vol. 6, Issue 2, P. 244.

Fearon, James D. (1994) "Domestic Political Audiences and the Escalation of International Disputes," *The American Political Science Review*, Vol. 88, No. 3, 577-592.

Feigenbaum, Evan A. (1995) *Change in Taiwan and Potential Adversity in the Strait,* Santa Monica, CA: Rand.

Field, G. Lowell, (1951) "Hypotheses for a Theory of Political Power," *The American Political Science Review,* Vol. 45, No. 3, 716-723.

Foldvary Fred E and Daniel B Klein (2001) "Technology and Market failure," *Regulation*, Vol. 24, Issue 2, 9-11.

Foot, Rosemary (2003) "Bush, China and Human Rights," *Survival*, Vol. 45, No. 2, 167-186.

Frankel, Jeffrey A. (1997) *Regional Trading Blocs in the World Economic System,* Washington, D.C.: Institute for International Economics.

Frankel, Jeffrey A. and David Romer (1999) "Does Trade Cause Growth?" *The American Economic Review*, Vol. 89, No. 3, 379-399.

Freedman, Lawrence (1998) "Military Power and Political Influence," *International Affairs*, Vol. 74, No. 4, 763-780.

Friedberg, Aaron L. (2002) "11 September and the Future of Sino-American Relations," *Survival*, Vol. 44, No. 1, 33-50.

Friedmann, Wolfgang (1968) "Interventionism, Liberalism, and Power-Politics: The Unfinished Revolution in International Thinking," *Political Science Quarterly*, Vol. 83, No. 2, 169-189.

Fujita, Masahisa, Paul Krugman and Anthony J. Venables (1999) *The Spatial Economy: Cities, Regions and International Trade,* Cambridge, Mass: MIT Press.

Funabashi, Yoichi, Michel Oksenberg and Heinrich Weiss (1994) An Emerging China in a World of Interdependence: a Report to the Trilateral Commission, New York, NY: Trilateral Commission.

Gaddis, John Lewis (1981) "Containment: Its Past and Future," *International Security*, Vol. 5, No. 4, 74-102.

Galtung, Johan (1964) "A Structural Theory of Aggression," *Journal of Peace Research*, Vol. 1, No. 2, 95-119.

Garver, John W. (1996) "War and Peace with China: First Hand Experiences in the Foreign Services of the United States," *China Quarterly*, No. 147, 971-973.

Gartner, Scott Sigmund and Gary M Segura (1998) "War, Casualties, and Public Opinion," *The Journal of Conflict Resolution*, Vol. 42, No. 3, 278-300

Gay, Peter (1993) *The Cultivation of Hatred,* New York: W. W. Norton

Gibb, Richard (1994) "Regionalism in the World Economy," in: Richard Gibb and Wieslaw Michalak (eds.) *Continental Trading Blocs: the Growth of Regionalism in the World Economy*. Chichester, England: John Wiley & Sons Ltd.

Gibney, Frank (1995) "Asia's Growth: Miracle or Myth?" *Foreign Affairs,* Vol. 74, No. 2, P. 170-176.

Gibson, James L. (1988) "Political Intolerance and Political Repression during the McCarthy Red Scare," *The American Political Science Review*, Vol. 82, No. 2, 511-529.

Gittings, John (1964) "Co-Operation and Conflict in Sino-Soviet Relations," *International Affairs*, Vol. 40, No. 1, 60-75.

Glaser, Bonnie S. (1993) "China's Security Perceptions: Interests and Ambitions," *Asian Survey*, Vol. 33, No. 3, 252-271.

Godwin, H.B. Paul (2004) "China as Regional Hegemon?" In: Jim Rolfe (eds.) *The Asia-Pacific: A Region in Transition*, Honolulu: Asia-Pacific Center for Security Studies.

Gold, Thomas B. (1986) *State and Society in the Taiwan Miracle,* Armonk: Sharpe

Gold, Thomas B. (1987) "The Status Quo is Not Static: Mainland-Taiwan Relations," *Asian Survey*, Vol. 27, No. 3, 300-315.

Goldstein, Avery (1997) "China in 1996: Achievement, Assertiveness, Anxiety," *Asian Survey*, Vol. 37, No. 1, 29-42.

Goldstein, Avery (1997-1998) "Great Expectations: Interpreting China's Arrival," *International Security*, Vol. 22, No. 3, 36-73.

Gowa, Joanne and Edward D. Mansfield, (1993) "Power Politics and International Trade," *The American Political Science Review*, Vol. 87, No. 2, 408-420.

Grampp, William D. (1948) "Adam Smith and the Economic Man," *The Journal of Political Economy*, Vol. 56, No. 4, 315-336.

Grampp, William D. (2000) "What did Smith Mean by the Invisible Hand?" *The Journal of Political Economy,* Vol. 108, Issue 3, 441-465.

Grieco, Joseph M. (1988) "Realist Theory and the Problem of International Cooperation: Analysis with an Amended Prisoner's Dilemma Model," *The Journal of Politics*, Vol. 50, No. 3, 600-624.

Grieco, Joseph M. (1988) "Anarchy and the Limits of Cooperation: A Realist Critique of the Newest Liberal Institutionalism," *International Organization,* Vol. 42, No. 3, 485-507.

Gries, Peter (1997) "China Can Say No; Studying in the USA; China Can Still Say No," *The China Journal*, No. 37, 180-185.

Hagan, Joe D. (1989) "Domestic Political Regime Changes and Third World Voting Realignments in the United Nations, 1946-84," *International Organization*, Vol. 43, No. 3, 505-541.

Hall, Chris and Charles Harvie (2003) A Comparison of the Performance of SMEs in Korea and Taiwan: Policy Implications for Turbulent Times, Economics Working Paper Series, University of Wollongong.

Halloran, Jack (1986) *Personnel and Human Resource Management,* Englewood Cliffs, NJ: Prentice-Hall.

Harden, Sheila (eds., 1985) *Small is Dangerous: Micro States in a Macro World,* London: Frances Pinter.

Harding, Harry (1992) *A Fragile Relationship: the United States and China since 1972,* Washington, DC: Brookings Inst.

Harris, Peter (1997) "Chinese Nationalism: The State of the Nation," *The Chinese Journal*, No. 38, 121-137.

Helleiner, Eric (1994) *States and the Reemergence of Global Finance: from Bretton Woods to the 1990s,* Ithaca, NY: Cornell University Press.
Herz, John H. (1950) "Idealist Internationalism and the Security Dilemma," *World Politics*, Vol. 2, No. 2, 157-180.
Hickey, Dennis Van Vranken (1988) "America's Two-Point Policy and the Future of Taiwan," *Asian Survey*, Vol. 28, No. 8, 881-896.
Hickey, Dennis V (1997) "U.S. Policy and Taiwan's Bid to Rejoin the United Nations," *Asian Survey*, Vol. 37, No. 11, 1031-1043.
Hollingworth, Clare (1985) *Mao and the Men against Him,* London: Cape.
Hood, Steve J. (1996) "Political Change in Taiwan: The Rise of Kuomintang Factions," *Asian Survey*, Vol. 36, No. 5, 468-482.
Hotelling, Harold (1929) "Stability in Competition," *The Economic Journal*, Vol. 39, No. 153, 41-57.
Howe, Christopher (1998) "The Taiwan Economy: The Transition to Maturity and the Political Economy of its Changing International Status," In: David Shambaugh (eds.) *Contemporary Taiwan*, Oxford: Clarendon Press.
Hsiao, Frank S. T. and Lawrence R. Sullivan (1980) "The Politics of Reunification: Beijing's Initiative on Taiwan," *Asian Survey*, Vol. 20, No. 8, 789-802.
Hsieh, John Fuh-sheng (1999) Taiwan's Domestic Politics and Its Mainland China Policy, Paper Prepared for Delivery at the Conference on War and Peace in the Taiwan Strait.
Hu, Ming-wen (2000), "The Evolution and Adaptability of SMEs: the Case of Taiwan", *Economic Papers*, Economic Society of Australia 19, 2, 57-73.
Hu, Ming-wen and Chi Schive (1998), "The Changing Competitiveness of Taiwan's Manufacturing SMEs", *Small Business Economics*, 11:4, 315-326.
Hu, Wei Zhen (2001) *The Evolution of U.S. "One-China" Policy: from Nixon to Clinton* (Mei Guo Dui Hwa "Yi Ge Zhong Guo" Zheng Ce Zhi Yan Bian: Cong Ni Ke Sen Dao Ke Lin Dun), Taipei: The Commercial Press (in Chinese).
Huang, Kuang-kuo (1996) "The Modernization of Chinese Style Family Business," in: Kuang-kuo Huang (eds.) *The Chinese Power Game*, Taipei: Chu-liu Books Co. (in Chinese).
Huang, The-fu and Ching-hsin Yu (1999) "Developing a Party System and Democratic Consolidation" in: Hung-mao Tien and Steve Tsang (eds.) *Democratization in Taiwan: implications for China* Basingstoke, Hampshire: Macmillan.
Hughes, Christopher R. (1999) "Democratization and Beijing's Taiwan Policy" in: Hung-mao Tien and Steve Tsang (eds.) *Democratization in Taiwan: implications for China* Basingstoke, Hampshire: Macmillan.

Imig, Douglas R. and Jeffrey M. Berry (1996) "Patrons and Entrepreneurs: A Response to 'Public Interest Group Entrepreneurship and Theories of Groups Mobilization'", *Political Research Quarterly*, Vol. 49, No. 1, 147-154.

Inayatullah, Naeem and David L Blaney (1999) "Towards an Ethnological IPE: Karl Polanyi's Double Critique of Capitalism," *Millennium*, Vol. 28, No. 2, 311-340.

Isogai, Takashi and Shunichi Shibanuma (2000) East Asia's Intra- and Inter-Regional Economic Relations; Data Analyses on Trade, Direct Investments and Currency Transactions, Bank of Japan Working Paper Series.

Jefferson, Gary H. (1999) Like Lips and Teeth: Economic Scenarios for Cross-Strait Relations. Paper was prepared for Seminar on Cross-Strait Relations and the United States at the Turn of the Century.

Jervis, Robert (1978) "Cooperation under the Security Dilemma," *World Politics*, Vol. 30, No. 2, 167-214.

Jia, Qingguo (1992) "Changing Relations across the Taiwan Strait: Beijing's Perceptions," *Asian Survey*, Vol. 32, No. 3, 277-289.

Jiang, Zhen-Yin (2003) "Yin Ying Jing Ji Quan Qiu Hua Zhi Liang An Jing Mao Guan Xi," *Tai Wan Jing Ji Yan Jiu Yue Kan (Taiwan Economic Research Monthly)*, Vol. 26, No. 1, 50-57 (in Chinese).

Johnson, D. Gale (2002) "Globalization: What It Is and Who Benefits," *Journal of Asian Economics,* Vol. 13, No. 4, 427-439.

Johnston, Alastair Iain (2003) "Is China a Status Quo Power?" *International Security*, Vol. 27, No. 4, 5-56.

Kang, Bi-Song (1998) A Reverse Relationship Process Model of Taiwan Industry, National Chung Shan University, Thesis for Doctor's Degree of Business Administration (in Chinese).

Kao, Charng (2001) "The Localization of Mainland-bound Investment by Taiwanese Manufacturers and Its Influence to Taiwan Economy," *Review of Taiwan Economics*, Vol. 7, No. 1 (in Chinese).

Kapp, Robert A. (2001) "NTR 2001: To Sing the Blues or Walk the Walk," *The China Business Revie*, Vol. 28, Issue 4, 6-7.

Kau, Michael Ying-mao (1996) "The Power Structure in Taiwan's Political Economy," *Asian Survey*, Vol. 36, No. 3, 287-305.

Kawai, Masahiro and Taizo Motonishi (2004) Is East Asia an Optimum Currency Area? Paper delivered at the conference on Financial Interdependence and Exchange Rate Regimes in East Asia sponsored by the Japan Ministry of Finance Policy Research Institute, December 2-3, 2004.

Kehoe, Patrick J. (1989) "Policy Cooperation among Benevolent Governments May Be Undesirable," *Review of Economic Studies* Vol. 56, No. 2, 289-296.

Kennan, George F. (1978) *The Cloud of Danger*, London: Hutchinson.

Keohane, Robert O. and Joseph S. Nye (1974) "Transgovernmental Relations and International Organizations," *World Politics,* Vol. 27, No. 1, 39-62.

Keohane, Robert O. and Joseph S. Nye (1977) *Power and Interdependence: World Politics in Transition,* Boston: Little, Brown.

Keohane, Robert O. and Joseph S. Nye (2000) "Globalization: What's New? What's Not? (And So What?)" *Foreign Policy*, Issue 118 (Spring), 104-119.

Khalilzad, Zalmay (1999a) *Congage China,* Issue Paper, Santa Monica, CA: Rand.

Khalilzad, Zalmay (1999b) *The United States and a Rising China: Strategic and Military Implications,* Santa Monica, CA: RAND.

Kim, Samuel S. (1981) "Whither Post-Mao Chinese Global Policy?" *International Organization*, Vol. 35, No. 3, 433-465.

Kissinger, Henry (1979) *White House Years*, Boston: Little, Brown.

Klein, Sherwin (2003) "The Natural Roots of Capitalism and Its Virtues and Values," *Journal of Business Ethics*, Vol. 45, Issue 4, 387-401.

Klintworth, Gary (2000) China and Taiwan-From Flashpoint to Redefining One China, Research Paper, Parliament of Australia, Parliament Library.

Kraig, Michael R. (1999) "Nuclear Deterrence in the Developing World: A Game-Theoretic Treatment," *Journal of Peace Research*, Vol. 36, No. 2, 141-167.

Krasner, Stephen D. (1976) "State Power and the Structure of International Trade," *World Politics,* Vol. 28, No. 3, 317-347.

Kreps, David M. (1997) *Game Theory and Economic Modeling,* Oxford: Clarendon Press.

Krishna, Pravin (1998) "Regionalism and Multilateralism: a Political Economy Approach," *The Quarterly Journal of Economics*, Vol. 113, No. 1, 227-251 .

Krueger, Anne O. (1990) "Government Failures in Development," *The Journal of Economic Perspectives*, Vol. 4, No. 3, 9-23.

Krueger, Anne O. (1999) "Are Preferential Trading Arrangements Trade-Liberalizing or Protectionist?" *Journal of Economic Perspectives*, Vol. 13, No. 4, 105-124.

Krugman, Paul (1994) "Is Bilateralism Bad?" In: Elhanan Helpman and Razin Assaf (eds.) *International Trade and Trade Policy* Cambridge, Mass: MIT Press.

Krugman Paul (1996) *Pop Internationalism,* Cambridge, Mass: MIT Press.

Krugman Paul (1998) "What's New about the New Economic Geography?" *Oxford Review of Economic Policy*, Vol. 14, No. 2, 7-17.

Krugman Paul (1999) "The Role of Geography in Development," *International Regional Science Review*, Vol. 22, No. 2, 142-161.

Kuhn, Philip A. (1997) "Chinese Nationalism," *The China Journal*, No. 37, 172-174.

Kuo, Wei-Chou (2003) The Analysis to Politics & Economy of the "No Haste, Be Patient" Policy, Thesis for the Degree of Master of Political Economy, National Cheng Kung University (in Chinese).

Kurlantzick, Joshua (2002) "China: Economic Power, Political Enigma," *The Washington Quarterly*, Vol. 23, Issue 3, 59-67.

Lai, David (2003) "A Referendum on Taiwan's Future: No Easy Exit," *Issues & Insights,* Vol. 3, No. 6.

Lal, Deepak (1985) *The Poverty of "Development Economics",* Cambridge, Mass.: Harvard Univ. Press.

Lampton, David M. (1997) "China and Clinton's America: Have They Learned Anything?" *Asian Survey*, Vol. 37, No. 12, 1099-1118.

Landecker, Werner S. (1963) "Class Crystallization and Class Consciousness," *American Sociological Review*, Vol. 28, No. 2, 219-229.

Lawrence, Robert Z. (1996) *Regionalism, Multilateralism, and Deeper Integration,* Washington, DC: Brookings Inst.

Lawton, Thomas C. and Kevin P. Michaels (2000) "The Evolving Global Production Structure: Implications for International political Economy," In: Thomas C. Lawton, James N. Rosenau and Amy C. Verdun, (eds.), *Strange Power: Shaping the parameters of international relations and international political economy,* Aldershot: Ashgate Publishing Ltd.

Lee, Jia-quan (2003) *The Complete Evaluation on Chen Shui-bian's Reign over Taiwan* (Chen Shui Bian Zhu Zheng Tai Wan Zong Ping Gu), Taipei: Hai Xia Xue Shu Chu Ban She (in Chinese).

Lee, Jian-rong (2004) *Blue Sky Reappear* (Lan Tian Zai Xian), Taipei: Commonwealth Publishing (in Chinese).

Lee, Kuan Yew (2004) "Current Events," *Forbes*, Vol. 173, Issue 8, 29.

Lee, Lai To (1997) "East Asian Assessments of China's Security Policy," *International Affairs*, Vol. 73, No. 2, 251-262.

Lee, Yue-Jing (2002) Taiwan's Pragmatic Diplomacy in APEC (1989-2001), National Taiwan University, Thesis for Degree of Master in Politics (in Chinese).

Leeds, Brett Ashley and David R. Davis (1997) "Domestic Political Vulnerability and International Disputes," *The Journal of Conflict Resolution*, Vol. 41, No. 6, 814-834.

Leng, Tse-Kang (1998) "Dynamics of Taiwan-Mainland China Economic Relations: The Role of Private Firms," *Asian Survey*, Vol. 38, No. 5, 494-509.

Leng, Tse-Kang (2002) "Economic Globalization and it Talent Flows Across the Taiwan Strait: The Taipei/Shanghai/Silicon Valley Triangle," *Asian Survey,* Vol. 42, No. 2, P. 230-250.

Lerman, Arthur J. (1977) "National Elite and Local Politician in Taiwan," *The American Political Science Review*, Vol. 71, No. 4, 1406-1422.

Levy, Philip I. (1997) "A Political-Economic Analysis of Free Trade Agreements," *The American Economic Review,* Vol. 87, No. 4, 506-519.

Lilley, James R. (2003) *James Lilley's Memoir,* Taipei, Taiwan: China Times Publishing Co. (In Chinese).

Lin, Cheng-yi (1997) "Taiwan's South China Sea Policy," *Asian Survey*, Vol. 37, No. 4, 323-339.

Lin, Ming-Ian (2003) An Integrated Supply Chain Study for the Notebook Industry in the Triangle Area of China's Yangtze River, Thesis for the Degree of Master of Business Administration, National Cheng Kung University (in Chinese).

Lin, Qin Ming (2002) "Dong Xie Qu Yu Jing Ji Zheng He," *Tai Wan Jing Ji Yan Jiu Yue Kan (Taiwan Economic Research Monthly)*, Vol. 25, No. 7, 61-68 (in Chinese).

Lin, Wei Jen (2001) "Pou Chen Shoe Maker: Learning from America," in: Yin Chun Wu (eds.) *Take Off from Taiwan*, Taipei, Commonwealth Publishing (in Chinese).

Lind, Jennifer M. and Thomas J. Christensen (2000) "Spirals, Security, and Stability in East Asia," *International Security*, Vol. 24, No. 4, 190-200.

Lindblom, Charles E. (1977) *Politics and Markets: The World's Political-Economic Systems,* New York: Basic Books, Inc.

Linder, Staffan B. (1986) *The Pacific Century: Economic and Political Consequences of Asian-Pacific Dynamism,* Stanford, CA: Stanford Uni. Press

Lipsey, Robert E. (1994) Outward Direct Investment and the US Economy, National Bureau of Economic Research, Working Paper 4691.

Liu, I-chou (1999) "The Development of the Opposition," in: Hung-mao Tien and Steve Tsang (eds.) *Democratization in Taiwan: implications for China* Basingstoke, Hampshire: Macmillan.

Liu, Shang-Jyh (1999) "The Competitiveness and Strategic Deployment of Our Emerging High-Tech Manufacturing Industry: Take the Development of TFT-LCD Industry as an Example," *The Report of Technological Development Policy*, No. SR8810, Science and Technology Information Center, NSC.

Lizza, Ryan (2000) "Red and the Blue," *The New Republic*, Vol. 222, Issue 13, 24-25.

Lowi, Theodore J. (2001) "Our Millennium: Political Science Confronts the Global Corporate Economy," *International Political Science Review*, Vol. 22, No. 2, 131-150.

Lu, Alexander Ya-li (1985) "Future Domestic Development in the Republic of China on Taiwan," *Asian Survey*, Vol. 25, No. 11, 1075-1095.

MacKuen, Michael B. (1983) "Political Drama, Economic Conditions, and the Dynamics of Presidential Popularity," *American Journal of Political Science*, Vol. 27, No. 2, 165-192.

Maggi, Giovanni (1999) "The Role of Multilateral Institutions in International Trade Cooperation," *The American Economic Review*, Vol. 98, No. 1, 190-214.

Mainland Affair Council (1998) Da Lu Zheng Ce Yu Liang An Guan Xi Da Ke Wen, (in Chinese).

Mann, James (1999) *About Face: a History of America's Curious Relationship with China, from Nixon to Clinton,* New York: Knopf.

Mao, Jia-Qi (1988, eds.) *Taiwan 30 Years: 1949-1979* (Tai Wan San Shi Nian: 1949-1979), He Nan Ren Ming Publishing, (in Chinese).

Mao, Meng-Chao (2003) Study on the Change of Taiwan's Mainland Trade and Economic Policy, National Chung-Hsing University, Thesis for Master's Degree of Arts, (in Chinese).

Maslow, Abraham H. (1970) *Motivation and Personality,* New York: Harper & Row

Mastanduno, Michael (1997) "Preserving the Unipolar Moment: Realist Theories and U.S. Grand Strategy after the Cold War," *International Security,* Vol. 21, No. 4, 49-88.

Mathews, John A. (1997) "A Silicon Valley of the East: Creating Taiwan's Semiconductor Industry," *California Management Review*, Vol. 39, No. 4, 26-54.

Mattli, Walter and Tim Buethe (2003) "Setting International Standards: Technological Rationality or Primacy of Power?" *World Politics*, Vol. 56, No. 1, 1–42.

Maxwell, Neville (1971) "The Threat from China," *International Affairs*, Vol. 47, No. 1, 31-44.

McDevitt, Michael (2003) Taiwan, China and the United States: The Security Situation—the Challenges are Clear, are Their Any Opportunities? The United States, China and Taiwan in Changing World: Opportunities and Challenges for the 21st Century, May 2003 Taiwan Conference Paper Abstracts, The Center for China-US Cooperation.

McGuire, Martin C. and Mancur, Jr. Olson (1996) "The Economics of Autocracy and Majority Rule: The Invisible Hand and the Use of Force," *Journal of Economic Literature*, Vol. 34, No. 1, 72-96.

McKinlay, Robert D. and Richard Little (1988) *Global Problems and World Order, Madison,* Wis.: Univ. of Wisconsin Pr.

McLaren, John (1997) "Size, Sunk Costs, and Judge Bowker's Objection to Free Trade," *The American Economic Review*, Vol. 87, No. 3, 400-420.

McMichael, Philip (1996) *Development and Social Change: a Global Perspective,* Thousand Oaks, Calif.: Pine Forge Press.

McVadon, Eric A. (2000) "A Purple China Policy for the U.S.," *Far Eastern Economic Review*, Vol. 163, Issue 51, 29.

Medeiros, Evan S. and Taylor M. Fravel (2003) "China's New Diplomacy," *Foreign Affairs*, November/December 2003.

Mengin, Françoise (1999) "State and Identity," in: Hung-mao Tien and Steve Tsang (eds.) *Democratization in Taiwan: implications for China* Basingstoke, Hampshire: Macmillan

Meyer, John W, John Boli, George M Thomas and Francisco O Ramirez (1997) "World Society and Nation-State," *The American Journal of Sociology*, Vol. 103, No. 1, 144-181.

Michalak, Wieslaw (1994) "The Political Economy of Trading Blocs," in: Richard Gibb and Wieslaw Michalak (eds.) *Continental Trading Blocs: the Growth of Regionalism in the World Economy*. Chichester, England: John Wiley & Sons Ltd.

Michie, Jonathan and Renee Prendergast (1998) "Government Intervention in a Dynamic Economy," *New Political Economy,* Vol. 3, Issue 3, 391-406.

Midlarsky, Manus I. (1988) "Rulers and the Ruled: Patterned Inequality and the Onset of Mass Political Violence," *The American Political Science Review*, Vol. 82, No. 2, 491-509.

Miller, Ross (1995) "Domestic Structure and the Diversionary Use of Force," *American Journal of Political Science*, Vol. 39, No. 3, 760-785.

Miller, Ross (1999) "Regime Type, Strategic Interaction, and the Diversionary Use of Force," *The Journal of Conflict Resolution*, Vol. 43, No. 3, 388-402.

Mills, Edwin S. (1986) *The Burden of Government,* Stanford, Calif.: Hoover Institution Press.

Rawnsley, Ming-Yeh T. (2003) "Communications of Identities," in Taiwan: From the 2–28 Incident to FTV, G. Rawnsley & M. Y. Rawnsley (eds.), Political Communications in Greater China: Construction and Reflection of Identity, London: Routledge Curzon.

Moerk, Ernst L. (1998) "From War-Hero to Villain: Reversal of the Symbolic Value of War and a Warrior King," *Journal of Peace Research*, Vol. 35, No. 4, 453-469.

Montaperto, Ronald, James Przystup and Gerald Faber (2000) "'One China' and Relations across the Taiwan Strait," *Strategic Forum* No.173, 1-4.

Moon, Eric P. (1997) "Single Non-Transferable Vote Methods in Taiwan in 1996: Effects of an Electoral System," *Asian Survey*, Vol. 37, No. 7, 652-668.

Morgan, T. Clifton and Kenneth N. Bickers (1992) "Domestic Discontent and the External Use of Force," *The Journal of Conflict Resolution*, Vol. 36, No. 1, 25-52.

Morse, Edward (1970) "The Transformation of Foreign Policies: Modernization, Interdependence and Externalization," *World Politics*, Vol. 22, No. 3, 371-192.

Mosher, Steven W. (2000) *Hegemon: China's Plan to Dominate Asia and the World,* San Francisco: Encounter Books

Mrozek, Janusz R (1999) "Market Failures and Efficiency in the Principles Course," *Journal of Economic Education*, Vol. 30, Issue 4, 411-419.

Mueller, John E. (1970) P"residential Popularity from Truman to Johnson," *The American Political Science Review*, Vol. 64, No. 1, 18-34.

Muller, Ronald E. (1976) "Systemic Instability and the Global Corporation at Home: the Role of Power in Economic Analysis," in: A. P. Jacquemin and H.W.de Jong (eds.) *Markets, Corporate Behaviour and the State: International Aspects of Industrial Organization.* The Hague: Nijhoff.

Myers, Ramon H. (1984) "The Economic Transformation of the Republic of China on Taiwan," *The China Quarterly*, No. 99, 500-528.

Myerson, Roger (1995) "Analysis of Democratic Institutions: Structure, Conduct and Performance," *The Journal of Economic Perspectives*, Vol. 9, No. 1, 77-89.

Nass, Matthias and Andreas Oldag (1983) "The Debate within NATO and the 'China Card'," *Journal of Peace Research*, Vol. 20, No. 2, 107-127.

Nathan, James A. and Charles Tien (2001) "The Polls--Trends: American Ambivalence toward China," *Public Opinion Quarterly*, Vol. 65, Issue 1, 124-138.

Nathan, Andrew J. (2000) "What's Wrong with American Taiwan Policy," *The Washington Quarterly*, Vol. 23, No. 2, 93-106.

Nathan, Andrew J. (2003) "China's Changing of the Guard: Authoritarian Resilience," *Journal of Democracy,* Vol. 14, No. 1, 6-17.

Naughton, Barry (1997) "The Emergence of the China Circle," in: Naughton, Barry (eds.) *The China Circle: Economics and Electronics in the PRC, Taiwan, and Hong Kong,* Washington, DC: Brookings Inst. Press.

Ness, Peter Van (1997) "The Impasse in US Policy toward China," *The China Journal*, No. 38, 139-150.

Neumann, Franz (1950) "Approaches to the Study of Political Power," *Political Science Quarterly*, Vol. 65, No. 2, 161-180.

Newman, Richard J. and Kevin Whitelaw (2001) "China: How Big a Threat? Inside the Bitter Fight over Assessing China's Intentions," *U.S. News & World Report,* Vol. 131, No. 3, 30.

Nincic, Miroslav (1982) "Understanding International conflict: Some Theoretical Gaps," *Journal of Peace Research,* Vol. 19, No. 1, 49-60.

Ninkovich, Frank (1994) *Modernity and Power: A History of the Domino Theory in the Twentieth Century,* Chicago: the University of Chicago Press

Niou, Emerson M. and Peter C. Ordeshook (1994) "'Less Filling, Tastes Great': The Realist-Neoliberal Debate," *World Politics*, Vol. 46, No. 2, 209-234.

Norrander, Barbara and Clyde Wilcox (1993) "Rallying around the Flag and Partisan Change: The Case of the Persian Gulf War," *Political Research Quarterly*, Vol. 46, No. 4, 759-770.

O'Hanlon, Michael (2000) "Why China Cannot Conquer Taiwan," *International Security,* Vol. 25, No. 2, 51-86.

Ohmae, Kenichi (1995) *The End of Nation State,* London: HarperCollins.

Olzak, Susan and Tsutsui Kiyoteru (1998) "Status in the World System and Ethnic Mobilization," *The Journal of Conflict Resolution*, Vol. 42, No. 6, 691-720.

Ostrom, Charles W. Jr. and Brian L Job (1986) "The President and the Political Use of Force," *The American Political Science Review*, Vol. 80, No. 2, 541-566.

Ostrom, Charles W. Jr. and Dennis M. Siom (1985) "Promise and Performance: A Dynamic Model of Presidential Popularity," *The American Political Science Review*, Vol. 79, No. 2, 334-358.

Overholt, William H. (2002) "Asia's Continuing Crisis," *Survival*, Vol. 44, No. 1, 97-114.

Owen, Guillermo (1982) *Game Theory,* San Diego: Acad. Press.

Panagariya, Arvind (2000) "Preferential Trade Liberalization: The Traditional Theory and New Developments," *Journal of Economic Literature*, Vol. 38, No. 2, 287-331.

Pang, Eul-Soo (2004) "Whither Free Trade Agreements? Proliferation, Evaluation and Multilateralism," *Contemporary Southeast Asia*, Vol. 26, Issue 1, 186-189.

Patrick, James and John R. Oneal (1991) "The Influence of Domestic and International Politics on the President's Use of Force," *The Journal of Conflict Resolution*, Vol. 35, No. 2, Democracy and Foreign Policy: Community and Constraint, 307-332.

Pauly, Louis (1995) "Capital Mobility, State Autonomy and Political Legitimacy", *Journal of International Affairs*, Vol. 48, 369-388.

Payne, Richard J. and Cassandra R. Veney (1998) "China's Post-Cold War African Policy,"*Asian Survey*, Vol. 38, No. 9, 867-879.

Peffley, Mark and Sigleman Lee (1990) "Intolerance of Communists during the McCarthy Era: A General Model," *The Western Political Quarterly*, Vol. 43, No. 1, 93-111.

Peltzman, Sam, Michael E. Levine and Roger G. Noll (1989) "The Economic Theory of Regulation after a Decade of Deregulation," *Brookings Papers on Economic Activity. Microeconomics*, Vol. 1989, (1989), 1-59.

Perroni, Carlo and John Whally (2000) "The New Regionalism: Trade Liberalization or Insurance?" *The Canadian Journal of Economics*, Vol. 33, No. 1, 1-24.

Petrov, Vladimir (1983) "China Goes it Alone," *Asian Survey*, Vol. 23, No. 5, 580-597.

Pillsbury, Michael (2001) China's Military Strategy toward the U.S.: A View from Open Sources, posted on the Project on Defense Alternative's Chinese Military Power web site. http://www.uscc.gov/strat.pdf

Pinkston, Dan A and Phillip C Saunders (2003) "Seeing North Korea Clearly," *Survival*, Vol. 45, No. 3, 79-102.

Pollack, Jonathan D. (1996) "China's Taiwan Strategy: A Point of No Return?" *The China Journal*, No. 36, 111-116.

Polanyi, Karl (1975) *The Great Transformation*, New York, NY: Octagon Books.

Powell, Ralph L. (1968) "Maoist Military Doctrines," *Asian Survey*, Vol. 8, No. 4, 239-262.

Preeg, Earnest H. (1989) "The GATT Trading System in Transition: An Analytic Survey of Recent Literature," *The Washington Quarterly*, Vol. 12, No. 4; Pg. 199.

Putnam, Robert D. (1988) "Diplomacy and Domestic Politics: The Logic of Two-Level Games," *International Organization*, Vol. 42, No. 3, 1988, 427-460.

Pye, Lucian W. (1997) "Money Politics and Transitions to Democracy in East Asia," *Asian Survey*, Vol. 37, No. 3, 213-228.

Qian, Qichen (2003) *Ten Stories of a Diplomat* (Waijiao Shi Ji), Beijing, Shi Jie Zhi Shi Chu Ban She, (in Chinese).

Rachman, Gideon (1996) "Containing China," *The Washington Quarterly*, Vol. 19, No. 1, 129-139.

Reed, William (2003) "Information, Power, and War," *American Political Science Review*, Vol. 97, No. 4, 633-641.

Riezman, Raymond (1999) "Can Bilateral Trade Agreements Help to Induce Free-Trade?" *The Canadian Journal of Economics*, Vol. 32, No. 3, 751-766.

Rodrik, Dani (1994) *Getting Interventions Right: How South Korea and Taiwan Grew Rich,* Cambridge, MA: National Bureau of Economic Research (NBER).

Rodrik, Dani (2000) "How Far Will International Economic Integration Go?" *The Journal of Economic Perspectives*, Vol.14, No.1, 177-186.

Romance, Francis J. (1980) "Modernization of China's Armed Forces," *Asian Survey*, Vol. 20, No. 3, 298-310.

Rose-Ackerman, Susan (1978) *Corruption: a Study in Political Economy,* New York, NY: Academic Press

Rosenau, James N. (1966) "Pre Theories and Theories of Foreign Policy," in: Farell R. Barry (eds.) *Approaches to Comparative and International Politics*, Evanston: Nortwestern Univ. Press.

Ross, Robert S. (1986) "International Bargaining and Domestic Politics: U.S.-China Relations since 1972," *World Politics*, Vol. 38, No. 2, 255-287.

Ross, Robert S. (2000) "The 1995-96 Taiwan Strait Confrontation: Coercion, Credibility, and the Use of Force," *International Security*, Vol. 25, No. 2, 87-123.

Ross, Robert S. (2002) "Navigating the Taiwan Strait: Deterrence, Escalation Dominance, and U.S.-China Relations," *International Security*, Vol. 27, No. 2, 48-85.

Roy, Denny (1994) "Hegemon on the Horizon? China's Threat to East Asian Security," *International Security*, Vol. 19, No. 1, 149-168.

Roy, Denny (1996) "The 'China Threat' Issue: Major Arguments," *Asian Survey*, Vol. 36, No. 8, 758-771.

Roy, Denny (2003) "China's Reaction to American Predominance," *Survival*, Vol. 45, No. 3, 57-78.

Ruffin, Roy J. and M D Anderson (1996) "Externalities, Markets, and Government Policy," *Economic Review-Federal Reserve Bank of Dallas*, Dallas: Third Quarter 1996, 24-29.

Rummel, R. J. (1969) "Some Empirical Findings on Nations and Their Behavior," *World Politics*, Vol. 21, No. 2, 226-241.

Russell, Bertrand (1965) *Power: a New Social Analysis,* London: Unwin.

Russett, Bruce M. (1963) "The Calculus of Deterrence," *The Journal of Conflict Resolution*, Vol. 7, No. 2, 97-109.

Sato, Kazumi (2003) "Dong Ya Jing Ji Zheng He Gou Xiang: Tai Wan De Si Kao Yu Tiao Zhan," *Tai Wan Jing Ji Yan Jiu Yue Kan (Taiwan Economic Research Monthly)*, Vol. 26, No. 5, 44-51 (in Chinese).

Sawyer, Jack (1967) "Dimensions of Nations: Size, Wealth, and Politics," *The American Journal of Sociology*, Vol. 73, No. 2, 145-172.

Saxonhouse, Gary R (1993) "Trading Blocs and East Asia," in: Jaime De Melo and Arvind Panagariya (eds.) *New Dimensions in Regional Integration,* Cambridge: Cambridge Univ. Press.

Scalapino, Robert A. (1999) "The United States and Asia in 1998: Summitry amid Crisis," *Asian Survey*, Vol. 39, No. 1, 1-11.

Schaar, John H. (1991) "Liberty/Authority/Community in the Political Thought of John Winthrop," *Political Theory*, Vol. 19, No. 4, 493-518.

Schaeffer, Robert K. (2003) *Understanding Globalization: the Social Consequences of Political, Economic, and Environmental Change,* Lanham, Md.: Rowman & Littlefield.

Schiff, Maurice and Alan Winters (1998) "Dynamics and Politics in Regional Arrangements: An Introduction," *The World Bank Economic Review*, Vol.12, No. 2, Pp. 177-195.

Schiff, Maurice and Alan Winters (2003) *Regional Integration and Development,* Washington, DC: World Bank.

Scholte, Jan Aart (2002) What Is Globalization? The Definitional Issue – Again, CSGR Working Paper No. 109/02.

Segal, Gerald (1988) "As China Grows Strong," *International Affairs*, Vol. 64, No. 2, 217-231.

Segal, Gerald (1994) "China's Changing Shape," *Foreign Affairs*, Vol. 73, Iss. 3, 43-58.

Sen, Amartya (1999) "The Possibility of Social Choice," *The American Economic Review*, Vol. 89, No. 3, 349-378.

Shambaugh, David (1996) "Containment or Engagement of China? Calculating Beijing's Responses," *International Security*, Vol. 21, No. 2, 180-209.

Shambaugh, David (2000) "A Matter of Time: Taiwan's Eroding Military Advantage," *The Washington Quarterly*, Vol. 23, No. 2, 119–133.

Shams, Rasul (2002) *Why Do Countries Form Regions? : The Political Economy of Regional Integration,* Hamburg: Hamburgisches Welt-Wirtschafts-Archiv (HWWA).

Shan, Weijian (1990) "An Empirical Analysis of Organizational Strategies by Entrepreneurial High-Technology Firms," *Strategic Management Journal*, Vol. 11, No. 2, 129-139.

Sheng, Lijun (1999) How China is Going to Respond to Lee Teng-Hui's "Two States" Theory, ISEAS Working Paper, No. 7.

Sherer, F.M. (1991) "Changing Perspectives on the Firm Size Problem," in Zoltán J. Ács and D. B. Audretsch (eds.) *Innovation and Technological Chang: An International Comparison*, New York: Harvester Wheatsheaf.

Shi, Chuang and Lin, Yu (1999, eds.) *99 Classics, Classic Speech 99,* (Jiu Jiu Jing Dian, Jing Dian Yan Jiang Jiu Jiu), San Dong Ren Ming Publishing (in Chinese).

Shiau, Chyuan-jenq (1999) "Civil Society and Democratization," in: Hung-mao Tien and Steve Tsang (eds.) *Democratization in Taiwan: implications for China* Basingstoke, Hampshire: Macmillan.

Shih, Stan (Shi Zhen-rong, 2002) *The Recreation of Acer,* Taipei: Commonwealth Publishing (in Chinese).

Shlapak, David A., David T. Orletsky, and Barry Wilson (2000) *Dire Strait? Military Aspects of the China-Taiwan Confrontation and Options for U.S. Policy,* Santa Monica, CA: Rand.

Shleifer, Vishny Andrei and Robert W. Vishny (1993) "Corruption," *The Quarterly Journal of Economics*, Vol. 108, No. 3, 599-617.

Shulsky, Abram N. (2000) *Deterrence Theory and Chinese Behavior,* Santa Monica, CA: Rand.

Sinclair, Timothy J. (1999) "Bond-Rating Agencies and Coordination in the Global Political Economy," in: Clair A. Cutler, Virginia Haufler and Tony Porter (eds.) *Private Authority and International Affairs*, Albany, NY: State University of New York Press.

Skaperdas, Stergios and Constantinos Syropoulos (2001) "Guns, Butter and Openness: On the Relationship between Security and Trade," *The American Economic Review, Paper and Proceedings*, Vol. 91, No. 2, pp. 353-357.

Sokolsky, Richard, Angel Rabasa and Richard Neu Carl (2000) *The Role of Southeast Asia in U.S. Strategy toward China,* Santa Monica, CA: Rand.

Smith, Adam (1977) *The Wealth of Nations,* London: Dent.

Snyder, Glenn H. (1984) "The Security Dilemma in Alliance Politics," *World Politics*, Vol. 36, No. 4, 461-495.

Stigler, George J (1971) "The Theory of Economic Regulation," *The Bell Journal of Economics and Management Science*, Vol. 2, No. 1, 3-21.

Stiglitz, Joseph E. (1989) "Perspectives on Economic Development Markets, Market Failures, and Development," *The American Economic Review*, Vol. 79, No. 2, 197-203.

Stiglitz, Joseph E. (2003) "Information and the Change in the Paradigm in Economics, Part 1," *The American Economist*, Vol. 47, No. 2, 6-26.

Strange, Susan (1992) "States, Firms and Diplomacy," *International Affairs*, Vol. 68, No. 1, 1-15.

Strange, Susan (1994) *States and Markets,* London: Pinter.

Strizzi, Nicolino (2001) An Overview of China's Inbound and Outbound Tourism, Markets Research Report, Canadian Tourism Commission.

Stuart, Douglas T. (1997) "Toward Concert in Asia," *Asian Survey*, Vol. 37, No. 3, 229-244.

Stuart-Fox, Martin (2004) "Southeast Asia and China: The Role of History and Culture in Shaping Future Relations," *Contemporary Southeast Asia*, Vol. 26, Issue 1, 116-138.

Su, Chi (2001a) "The Comparison of Mainland Policy between President Lee's Era and President Chen's," *National Policy Forum*, Vol. 1, Issue 1, 125-128 (in Chinese).

Su, Chi (2001b) "Comments on Bian Administration's China Policy," *National Policy Forum*, Vol. 1, Issue 2, 1-5 (in Chinese).

Su, Yuan-Liang (2005) *The Aggressive Reign of Electronic Taiwan* (Hao Hao Cang Lang: Kai Tuo Tai Wan Dian Zi Ye Xin Ban Tu), Taipei: Wealth Network Corp. (in Chinese).

Sullivan, John L., James Piereson and George E. Marcus (1979) "An Alternative Conceptualization of Political Tolerance: Illusory Increases 1950s-1970s," *The American Political Science Review*, Vo. 73, No. 3, 781-794.

Sung, Hsing-Chou (2002) "Demystifying the Delusion of Economic Globalization: Bringing the Politics Back in," *Review of Global Politics*, Vol. 1, 87-114 (in Chinese).

Sutter, Robert (2003-2004) "Why does China Matter?" *The Washington Quarterly*, Vol. 27, No. 1, 75-89.

Swaine, Michael D. and Ashley J. Jellis (2000) *Interpreting China's Grand Strategy: Past, Present, and Future,* Santa Monica, CA: Rand.

Swaine, Michael (2003) "Reverse Course? The Fragile Turnaround in U.S.–China Relations," *Carnegie Endowment Policy Brief*, No. 22.

Tang, Hsing-Wei (2000) Under the Threat of a Neighboring Strong Power, the Case Study of Modeling a Small State's Responding Strategy, Thesis for the Degree of Master of Political Science, National Taiwan University (in Chinese).

Tao, Wenzhao (2000) "U.S. Policy Ambiguities and Current Cross-strait Dilemmas," in Gerrit W. Gong (eds.) *Taiwan Strait Dilemmas: China-Taiwan-U.S. Policies in the New Century*, Washington, DC: The CSIS Press.

Tian, Zhi-li (1998) *Twenty First Century Chinese Economic Area*, (Er Shi Yi Shi Ji Zhong Hua Jing Ji Qu), Taiwan, Taipei: Li Xu Chu Ban She.

Tien, Charles and James A. Nathan (2001) "The Polls--Trends: American Ambivalence toward China," *Public Opinion Quarterly*, Vol. 65, Issue 1, 124-138.

Tien, Hung-mao (1995) "Taiwan in 1995: Electoral Politics and Cross-Strait Relations," *Asian Survey*, Vol. 36, No. 1, 33-40.

Tien, Hung-mao and Steve Tsang (1999) "Transferring a Party State into a Democracy," in: Hung-mao Tien and Steve Tsang (eds.) *Democratization in Taiwan: implications for China* Basingstoke, Hampshire: Macmillan.

Thompson, Kenneth W. (1973) "Moral Values and International Politics," *Political Science Quarterly*, Vol. 88, No. 3, 368-374.

Thompson, Thomas N. (1976) "Taiwan's Ambiguous Destiny," *Asian Survey*, Vol. 16, No. 7, 611-619.

Thun, Eric (2001) Growing Up and Moving Out: Globalization of "Traditional" Industries in Taiwan, MIT IPC Globalization Working Paper 00-004.

Thurow, Lester (1992) *Head to Head: the Coming Economic Battle among Japan, Europe and America*, New York, NY: Morrow.

Tkacik, John J. Jr. (2002) Strategic Risks for East Asia in Economic Integration with China, Heritage Research, Webmemo #171.

Tkacik, John J. Jr. (2003) "Time for Washington to Take a Realistic Look at China Policy," *Backgrounder*, The Heritage Foundation, No. 1717.

Tollison, Robert D. (2001) "The Interest-Group Theory of Government: Problems and Prospects," *Kyklos*, Vol. 54, No. 2/3, P. 465-472.

Tsang, Steve (eds.) *Democratization in Taiwan: Implications for China*, Basingstoke, Hampshire: Macmillan.

Tucker, Nancy Bernkopf (1991) "China and America: 1941-1991," *Foreign Affairs*, Vol. 70, No. 5, 75-92.

Tucker, Nancy Bernkopf (2002) "If Taiwan Chooses Unification, Should the United States Care?" *The Washington Quarterly*, Vol. 25, No. 3, 15–28.

Tung, Chen-Yuan (2004) Economic Relations between Taiwan and China, UNISCI Discussion Papers.

Uche, Chibuike Ugochukwu (2001) "The Theory of Regulation: A Review Article," *Journal of Financial Regulation and Compliance*, Vol. 9, Issue 1, 67-80.

Van Zandt, David E. (1993) "The Lessons of the Lighthouse: 'Government' or 'Private' Provision of Goods," *The Journal of Legal Studies*, Vol. 22, No. 1, 47-72

Waldron, Arthur (1997) "Eight Steps toward a New China Policy," *Orbis*, Vol. 41, Issue 1, 77-82.

Walt, Stephen M. (1989) "The Case for Finite Containment: Analyzing U.S. Grand Strategy," *International Security*, Vol. 14, No. 1, 5-49.

Wang, Chun Chieh (2001) The Research of Finance of High Tech Small and Medium Enterprises in Taiwan, Chang Jung Christian University, Thesis for Degree of Master of Business Administration (in Chinese).

Wang, Jianwei and Zhimin Lin (1992) "Chinese Perceptions in the Post-Cold War Era: Three Images of the United States," *Asian Survey*, Vol. 32, No. 10, 902-917.

Wang, Kao-Cheng (1997) "The Cross-Strait Diplomatic Struggle under Security Dilemma," *Wenti Yu Yanjiu* (Issues & Studies), Vol. 36, No. 12, 23-36, (In Chinese).

Wang, Kevin H. (1996). "Presidential Responses to Foreign Policy Crises: Rational Choice and Domestic Politics," *The Journal of Conflict Resolution*, Vol. 40, No. 1, 68-97.

Wang, Robert S. (1984) "China's Evolving Strategic Doctrine," *Asian Survey*, Vol. 24, No. 10, 1040-1055.

Ward, Adam (2003) "China and America: Trouble Ahead?" *Survival*, Vol. 45, No. 3, 35-56.

Warner, Geoffrey (1980) "The Korean War," *International Affairs*, Vol. 56, No. 1, 98-107.

Weng, Huang-Jie (2003) FDI Strategies and Domestic Economic Performance: Evidence from Taiwanese Firms, National Taiwan University, Thesis for Degree of Master of Economics (in Chinese).

Werner, Roy A. (1985) "Taiwan's Trade Flows: The Underpinning of Political Legitimacy?" *Asian Survey*, Vol. 25, No. 11, 1096-1114.

West, E. G. (1977) "Adam Smith's Public Economics: A Re-Evaluation," *The Canadian Journal of Economics,* Vol. 10, No. 1, 1-18.

Westad, Odd Arne (1992) "Rethinking Revolutions: The Cold War in the Third World," *Journal of Peace Research*, Vol. 29, No. 4, 455-464.

White, Lynn T. (1998) Taiwan's China Problem: After a Decade or Two, Can There Be a Solution? SAIS Policy Forum Series, Report Number Six.

Whitehead, Laurence (1999) "Democratization of Taiwan: A Comparative Perspective," in: Hung-mao Tien and Steve Tsang (eds.) *Democratization in Taiwan: implications for China,* Basingstoke, Hampshire: Macmillan.

Whiting, Allen S. (1983) "Assertive Nationalism in Chinese Foreign Policy," *Asian Survey*, Vol. 33, No. 8, 913-933.

Whiting, Allen S. (1996) "The PLA and China's Threat Perceptions," *China Quarterly*, No.146, 596-615.

Whiting, Allen S. (1997) "China as a Great Power: Myths, Realities and Challenges in the Asia-Pacific Region," *The China Journal*, No. 37, 178-180.

Whiting, Allen S. (2001) "China's Use of Force, 1950–96, and Taiwan," *International Security*, Vol. 26, No. 2, 103-131.

Whitley, Richard D. (1990) "Eastern Asian Enterprise Structures and the Comparative Analysis of Forms of Business Organization," *Organization Studies*, Vol. 11, No. 1, 47-74.

Winters, L. Alan (1996) Regionalism versus Multilateralism, Policy Research Working Paper 1687, The World Bank.

Wittman, Donald (1973) "Parties as Utility Maximizers," *The American Political Science Review*, Vol. 67, No. 2, 490-498.

Wittman, Donald (1983) "Candidate Motivation: A Synthesis of Alternative Theories," *The American Political Science Review*, Vol. 77, No. 2, 142-157.

Witztum, Amos (1998) "A Study into Smith's Conception of the Human Character: Adam Smith Problem Revisited," *History of Political Economy*, Vol. 30, Issue 3, 489-513.

Wong, John and Sarah Chan (2003) "China-ASEAN Free Trade Agreement: Shaping Future Economic Relations," *Asian Survey*, Vol. 43, No. 3, P. 507-526.

Woods, Ngaire (2000) "The Political Economy of Globalization," in: Ngaire Woods (eds.) *The Political Economy of Globalization*. Basingstoke: Macmillan.

Woon, Yuen-Fong (1999) "Labor Migration in the 1990s: Homeward Orientation of Migrants in the Pearl River Delta Region and Its Implications for Interior China," *Modern China*, Vol. 25, No. 4, 475-512.

Worden, Robert L. (1983) "China's Balancing Act: Cancun, the Third World, Latin America," *Asian Survey*, Vol. 23, No. 5, 619-636.

Woronoff, Jon (1986) *Asian's 'Miracle' Economies*, Armonk, NY: Sharpe.

Wright, Teresa (1999) "Student Mobilization in Taiwan: Civil Society and Its Discontents," *Asian Survey*, Vol. 39, No. 6, 986-1008.

Wu, Chih-Hsiang (2002) The Impact of Value Creation and Foreign Production on the Firm's Economic Performance: The Case of Taiwanese Electronics Hardware Producers in Mainland China, Thesis for the Master's Degree of Business Administration, National Taiwan University (in Chinese).

Wu, Rong-I (2002) Taiwan's Future Economic Place in the World, A paper presented at the "Taiwan: Economic Issues Ahead" Conference Hosted by the Center for Strategic & International Studies.

Wu, Rong-I and Chung-Che Huang (2003) Entrepreneurship in Taiwan: Turning Point to Restart, in: Entrepreneurship in Asia, 4th US-Japan Dialogue, cosponsored by the Maureen and Mansfield Foundation and the Global Forum of Japan.

Wu, Yu-Shan (1998) "Party vs. State in Post-1949 China: The Institutional Dilemma," *The American Political Science Review*, Vol. 92, No. 2, 495-496.

Wu, Yu-Shan (1999) Taiwanese Elections and Cross-Strait Relations: Mainland Policy in Flux, *Asian Survey*, Vol. 39, No. 4, 565-587.

Wu, Hsien-Ching (2004) Sweetheart, Old and New: Shifted Identity of the Taiwanese Businessmen in Greater Shanghai, Thesis for the Degree of Master of Art, Ming Chuan University, School of Social Science Executive Master of National Development & Cross-strait Relations (in Chinese).

Yahuda, Michael (1996) "The Chinese Way: China's Position in International Relations," *China Quarterly*, No. 147, 973-974.

Yang, Chyan and Shiu-Wan Hung (2003) "Taiwan's Dilemma across the Strait: Lifting the Ban on Semiconductor Investment in China," *Asian Survey*, Vol. 43, No. 4, P. 681- 695.

Yang, JieMian (1999) "U.S. China Policy and the 'Two-State' Theory," *Brown Journal of World Affairs,* Volume VI, Issue 2, P 23-34.

Yao, Dennis A. (1988) "Beyond the Reach of the Invisible Hand: Impediments to Economic Activity, Market Failures, and Profitability," *Strategic Management Journal*, Vol. 9, Special Issue: Strategy Content Research, 59-70.

Yin, Chi-ming (2004) *Taiwan Economy a Turning Point* (Tai Wan Jing Ji Zhuan Lei Shi Ke), Taipei: Business Weekly Publications, Inc. (Shang Zhou Chu Ban She), (in Chinese).

Young, H. Peyton (1998) *Individual Strategy and Social Structure: an Evolutionary Theory of Institutions,* Princeton, NJ: Princeton Univ. Press.

Yu, George T. (1977) "China and the Third World," *Asian Survey*, Vol. 17, No. 11, 1036-1048.

Zeng, Xiaoming (2001) *Taiwan De Zhi Shi Jing Ji: Kun Jin Yu Mi Si,* Taipei: Qun Xue Chu Ban She (in Chinese).

Zerbe, Richard O Jr. and Howard McCurdy (2000) "The End of Market Failure," *Regulation*, Vol. 23, Issue 2, 10-14.

Zhao, John Quansheng (1983) "An Analysis of Unification: The PRC Perspective," *Asian Survey*, Vol. 23, No. 10, 1095-1114.

Zweig, David (1995) "'Developmental Communities' on China's Coast: The Impact of Trade, Investment, and Transnational Alliances," *Comparative Politics*, Vol. 27, No. 3, 253-274.

Schriften zur Politischen Ökonomik
Evolutorische und ökologische Aspekte

Herausgegeben von Udo Müller, Oliver Budzinski, Yücel Calbay,
Jörg Jasper und Torsten Sundmacher

Band 1 Jörg Jasper / Torsten Sundmacher (Hrsg.): Ökologische Kompatibilität und technologischer Wandel. 2000.

Band 2 Torsten Sundmacher: Das Umweltinformationsinstrument Ökobilanz (LCA). Anwendungsbezug und instrumentelle Ausgestaltungsmöglichkeiten. 2002.

Band 3 Oliver Budzinski / Jörg Jasper (Hrsg.): Wettbewerb, Wirtschaftsordnung und Umwelt. Festschrift für Udo Müller. 2004.

Band 4 Robert König: Die Elementarschadenversicherung in der Bundesrepublik Deutschland als Element der finanziellen Risikovorsorge gegen Naturereignisse. Diskussion staatlicher Regulierungsoptionen am Fallbeispiel der Hochwasser 2002 unter Berücksichtigung versicherungswirtschaftlicher Präferenzen. 2006.

Band 5 Sven Twelemann: Stromwirtschaft im Spannungsfeld zwischen Wettbewerb und Klimapolitik. Eine Untersuchung am Beispiel des deutschen Strommarktes. 2006.

Band 6 Shin-Yuan Tsai: Globalization Effects on China's Influence on Taiwan Economy. 2007.

www.peterlang.de

Michael B. Hinner (ed.)

Chinese and Western Business Cultures

A Comparison and Contrast

Frankfurt am Main, Berlin, Bern, Bruxelles, New York, Oxford, Wien, 2005.
168 pp., num. tab. and graf.
Freiburger Beiträge zur interkulturellen und Wirtschaftskommunikation.
A Forum for General and Intercultural Business Communication.
Edited by Michael B. Hinner. Vol. 2
ISBN-10: 3-631-53680-1 / ISBN-13: 978-3-631-53680-3
US-ISBN: 978-0-8204-7699-5 · pb. € 34.–*

This series seeks to illuminate, highlight, and spotlight (intercultural) communication in the world of business. This second volume focuses on China in an intercultural business context. Due to China's growing importance in today's world, it is imperative to obtain some insights into Chinese culture in order to begin to understand Chinese business practices. By examining the issue from a Western and a Chinese perspective, a more comprehensive view becomes possible. What appears baffling to Western managers may become understandable after a comparison with and contrast to the Chinese perspective. This is what this volume accomplishes: Shed light on misperceived aspects of intercultural business encounters.

Contents: *M.B. Hinner*: General Introduction: Seeking to Harmonize the Conflicting Images of China · *D. Hohnberg*: Ethnical Stereotypes May Be Crucial for the Successful Preparation Process of Intercultural Business Situations · *G. Miroslawski*: Market Entrance in China within the Context of Intercultural Communication · *N. Möller*: Intercultural Differences in Management Processes of Sino-German Joint Ventures · *H. Xu*: Business Communication in China · *J. Zhu*: Cultural Differences between China and Other Countries · S. *Kistaubayeva*: Intercultural Business Communication as Demonstrated by a Joint Venture between Germany and China · Z. *Ma*: A Study of East-Asian Corporate Culture

Kolibri 360 GmbH
Ferdinand-Jühlke-Straße 7
99095 Erfurt, Deutschland
produktsicherheit@kolibri360.de

Druck:
CPI Druckdienstleistungen GmbH
im Auftrag der
Kolibri 360 GmbH
Ferdinand-Jühlke-Str. 7
99095 Erfurt